Volume 3

Written and Created by
Neil Gibson

Art by
Caspar Wijngaard, Jan Wijngaard, Atula Siriwardane, Jake Elphick, Seb Antoniou, Leonardo Gonzalez, Hugo Wijngaard

Cover art by
Leonardo Gonzalez

Lettering by
Jim Campbell

D1223753

ublished in English in 2012 By T Pub
opyright © T Pub. All rights reserved.
pub.co.uk

SBN (Print) 978-0-9569434-6-0
SBN (Digital) 978-0-9927523-1-6

Pub

EO / Creative Director: Neil Gibson
rt Director: Caspar Wijingaard
ead of Operations: Ryan O'Sullivan
arketing Manager: Will O'Mullane
istribution (Print): Rafael Mondragón
istribution (Digital): Dan Watters

To the readers for their support

Foreword

Somebody once told me that you can't please everyone and you shouldn't attempt to try. The lighter stories in Volume 2 pleased some people and resulted in an outcry in others. Here, we go back to our roots and I write the stories that I **want** to write, rather than trying to appeal to everyone. I get fan mail—which I love—and one person's favorite story is another person's least favorite. It truly amazes me how differently people react to stories. I want to stress that I still love feedback because I never want to stop getting better, but I accept that I cannot please everyone.

I never thought of myself as a horror writer. I still don't, but a lot of people who like horror seem to like TWISTED DARK. Above all, I aim to write stories that I find **interesting**. But, sometimes what is interesting is also horrifying. If TWISTED DARK is too dark for you, I can always suggest you try reading TWISTED LIGHT. It might be more your cup of tea.

I hope you enjoy this volume and actively **try** to see where the links between the stories are to be found. Some are very subtle which I only expect a few people to get, whilst others are telegraphed clearly—if you don't get the connections I think you should bang your head on a table until everything becomes clear.

Finally, I just want to remind you that not all of the stories have a twist to them. Some are just twisted in nature. Despite knowing this, my father was disappointed when one story had no twist. He was convinced he must have missed it, so he reread it three times to find it. I banged his head on the table until it became clear to him.

All the best and see you in Volume 4...

– Neil

Contents

Growth 9

Love of my Life 24

Drink Driving 40

Hitting Back 51

Silent Justice 62

Career Choice 81

Perfection 101

The Bid 125

Abandoned 145

Lifeboat 157

Peace and Quiet 161

Growth...

"People are like dirt. They can either nourish you and help you grow as a person or they can stunt your growth and make you wilt and die."

– Plato

Writer/Creator
Neil Gibson

Illustrator
Caspar Wijngaard

www.tpub.co.uk

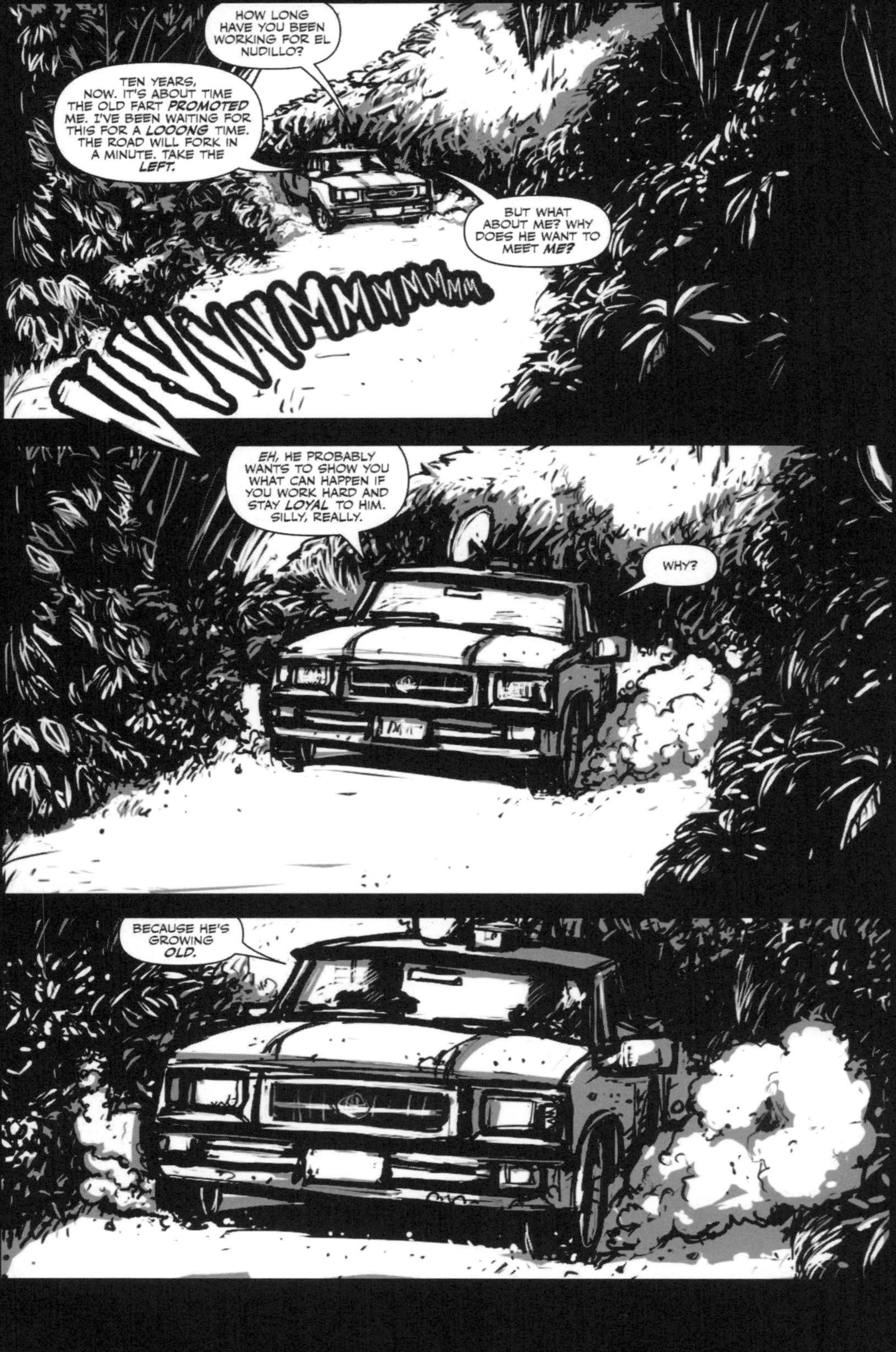
HOW LONG HAVE YOU BEEN WORKING FOR EL NUDILLO?
TEN YEARS, NOW. IT'S ABOUT TIME THE OLD FART *PROMOTED* ME. I'VE BEEN WAITING FOR THIS FOR A *LOOONG* TIME. THE ROAD WILL FORK IN A MINUTE. TAKE THE *LEFT.*
BUT WHAT ABOUT ME? WHY DOES HE WANT TO MEET *ME?*
VVVVMMMMMMMMmmm
EH, HE PROBABLY WANTS TO SHOW YOU WHAT CAN HAPPEN IF YOU WORK HARD AND STAY *LOYAL* TO HIM. SILLY, REALLY.
WHY?
BECAUSE HE'S GROWING *OLD.*

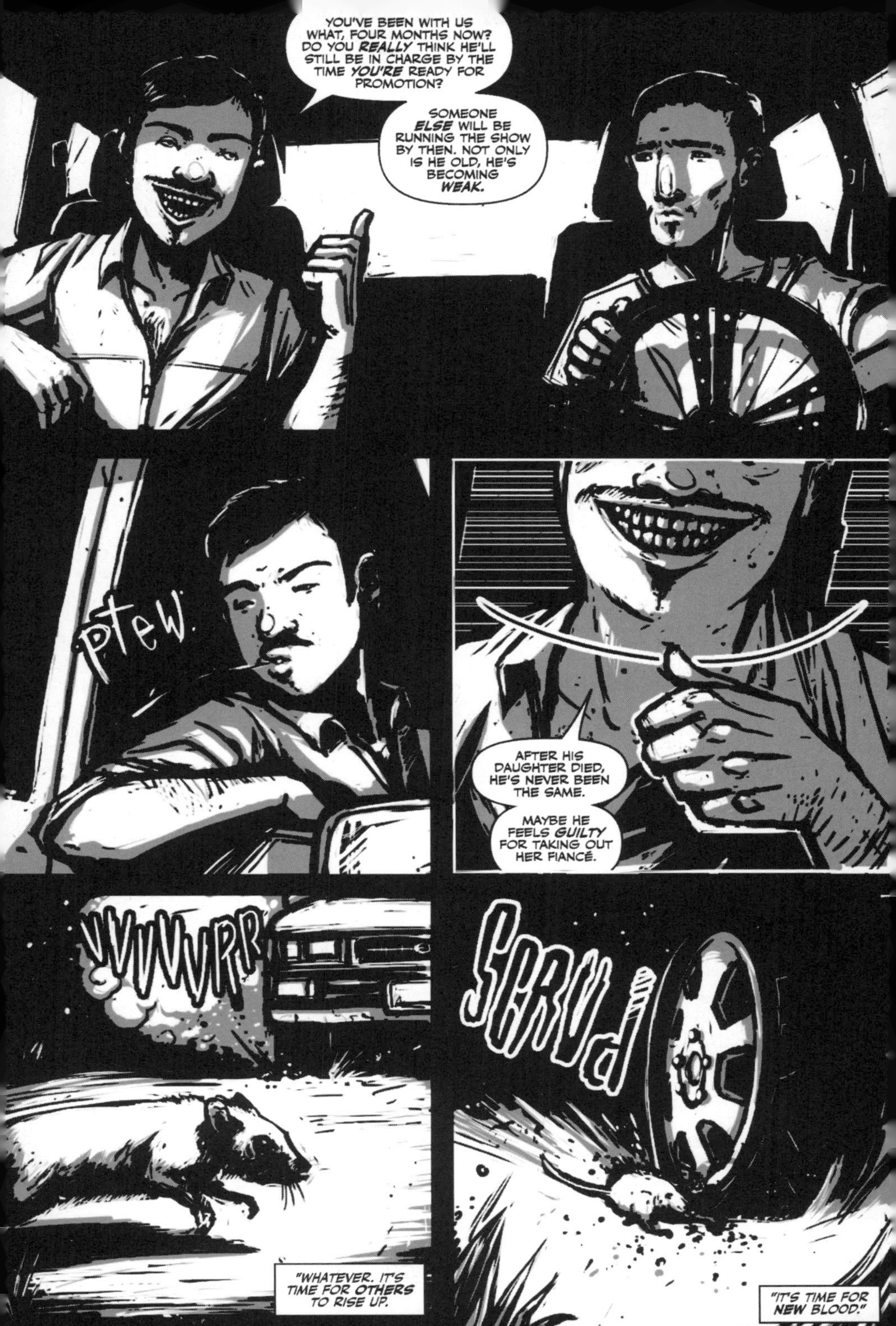
YOU'VE BEEN WITH US WHAT, FOUR MONTHS NOW? DO YOU REALLY THINK HE'LL STILL BE IN CHARGE BY THE TIME YOU'RE READY FOR PROMOTION?
SOMEONE ELSE WILL BE RUNNING THE SHOW BY THEN. NOT ONLY IS HE OLD, HE'S BECOMING WEAK.
ptew
AFTER HIS DAUGHTER DIED, HE'S NEVER BEEN THE SAME.
MAYBE HE FEELS GUILTY FOR TAKING OUT HER FIANCÉ.
VVVVVRR
"WHATEVER. IT'S TIME FOR OTHERS TO RISE UP.
"IT'S TIME FOR NEW BLOOD."

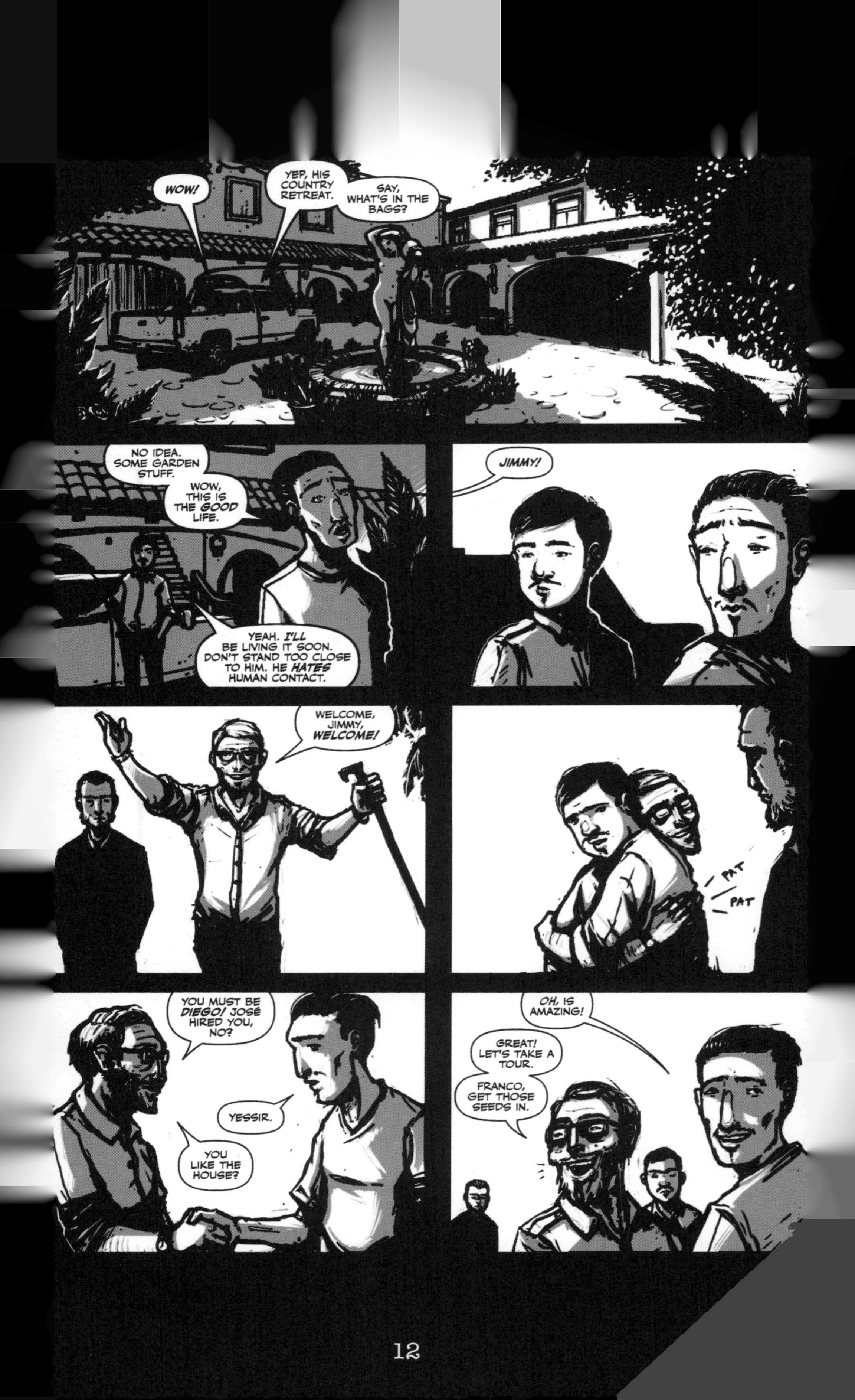
WOW!
YEP, HIS COUNTRY RETREAT.
SAY, WHAT'S IN THE BAGS?
NO IDEA. SOME GARDEN STUFF.
WOW, THIS IS THE GOOD LIFE.
YEAH. I'LL BE LIVING IT SOON. DON'T STAND TOO CLOSE TO HIM. HE HATES HUMAN CONTACT.
JIMMY!
WELCOME, JIMMY, WELCOME!
PAT
PAT
YOU MUST BE DIEGO! JOSÉ HIRED YOU, NO?
YESSIR.
YOU LIKE THE HOUSE?
OH, IS AMAZING!
GREAT! LET'S TAKE A TOUR.
FRANCO, GET THOSE SEEDS IN.

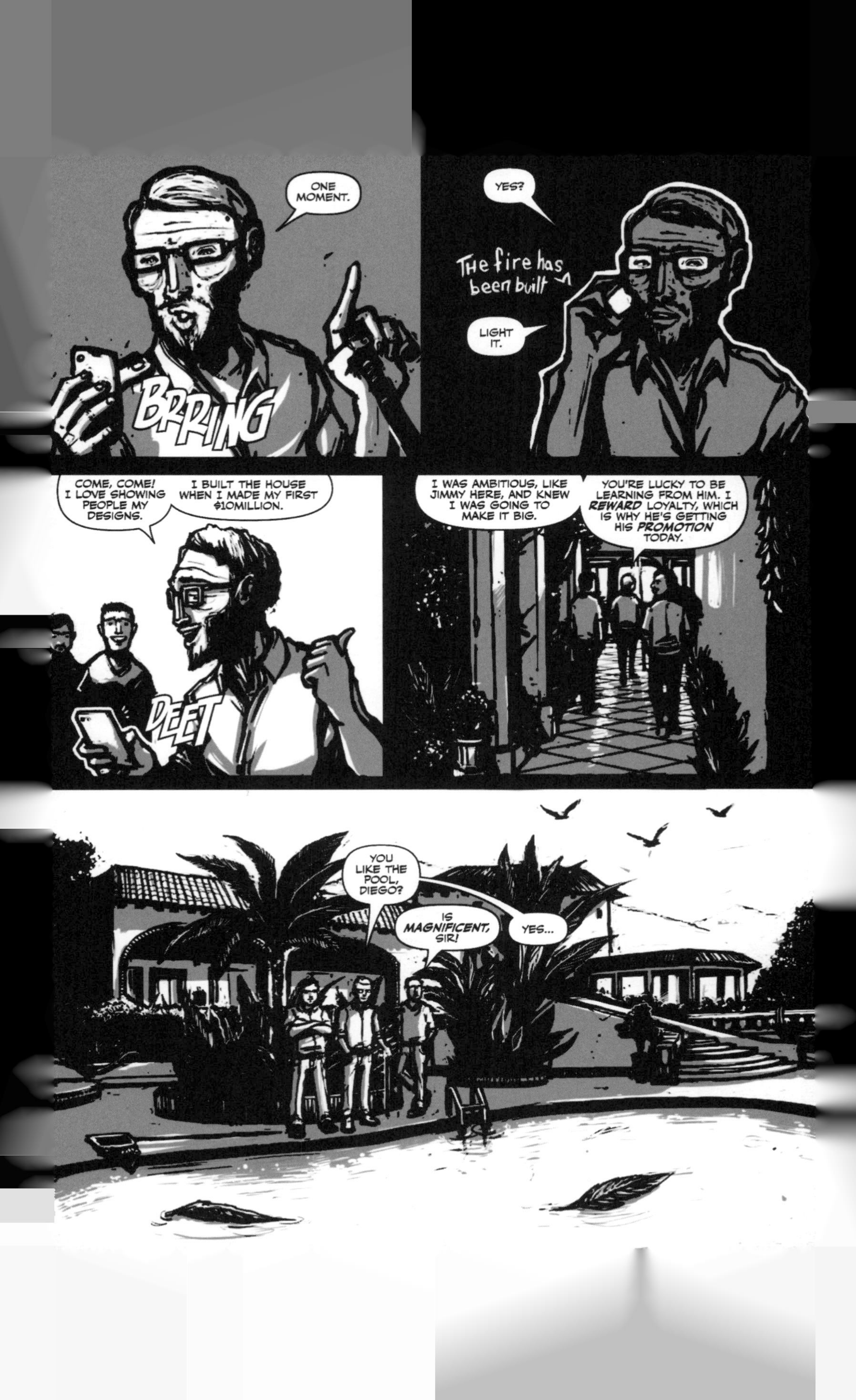
ONE MOMENT.
BRRING
YES?
The fire has been built
LIGHT IT.
COME, COME! I LOVE SHOWING PEOPLE MY DESIGNS.
I BUILT THE HOUSE WHEN I MADE MY FIRST $10MILLION.
DEET
I WAS AMBITIOUS, LIKE JIMMY HERE, AND KNEW I WAS GOING TO MAKE IT BIG.
YOU'RE LUCKY TO BE LEARNING FROM HIM. I REWARD LOYALTY, WHICH IS WHY HE'S GETTING HIS PROMOTION TODAY.
YOU LIKE THE POOL, DIEGO?
YES...
IS MAGNIFICENT, SIR!

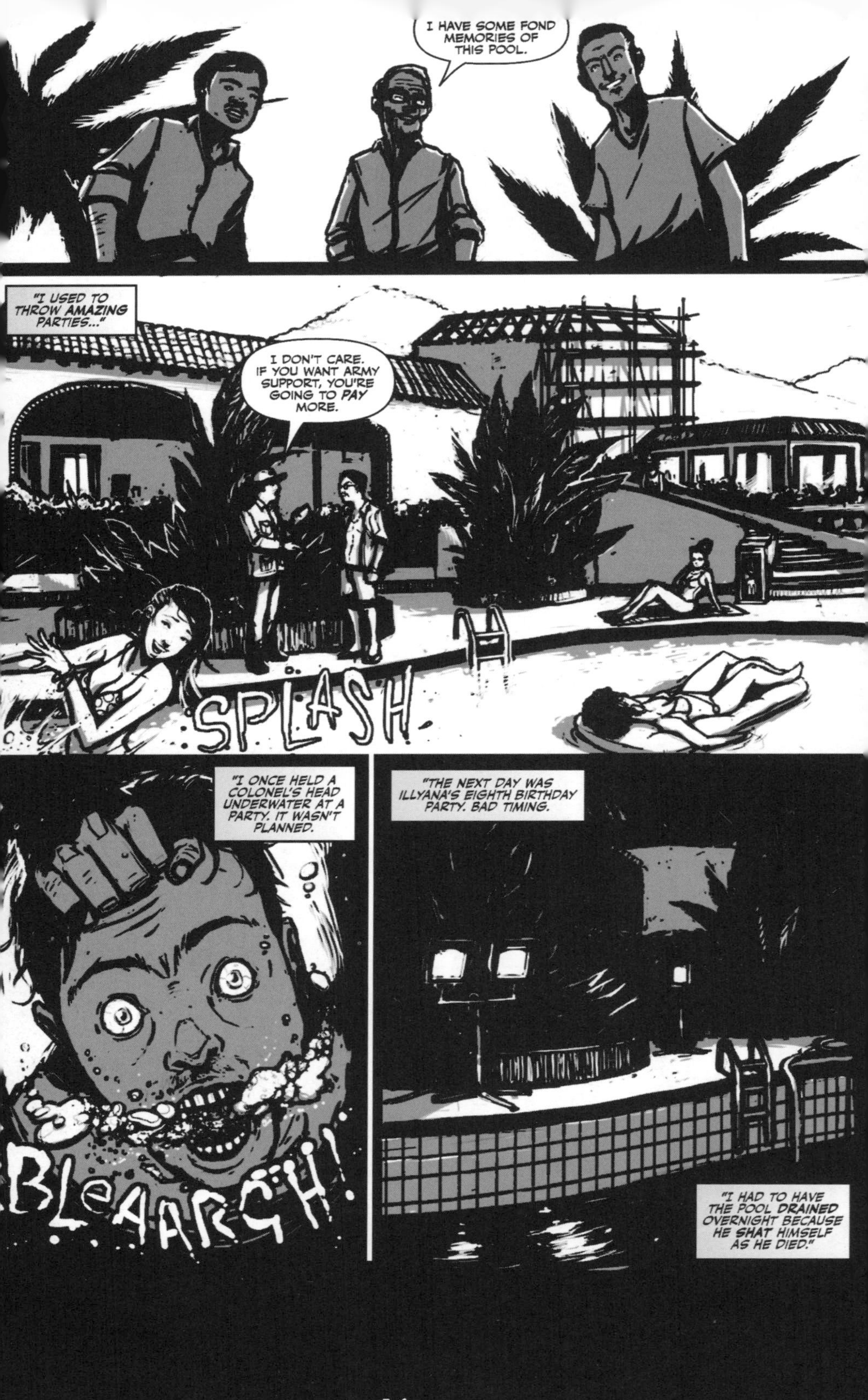
I HAVE SOME FOND MEMORIES OF THIS POOL.
"I USED TO THROW AMAZING PARTIES..."
I DON'T CARE. IF YOU WANT ARMY SUPPORT, YOU'RE GOING TO PAY MORE.
SPLASH
"I ONCE HELD A COLONEL'S HEAD UNDERWATER AT A PARTY. IT WASN'T PLANNED.
BLEAARGH!
"THE NEXT DAY WAS ILLYANA'S EIGHTH BIRTHDAY PARTY. BAD TIMING.
"I HAD TO HAVE THE POOL DRAINED OVERNIGHT BECAUSE HE SHAT HIMSELF AS HE DIED."

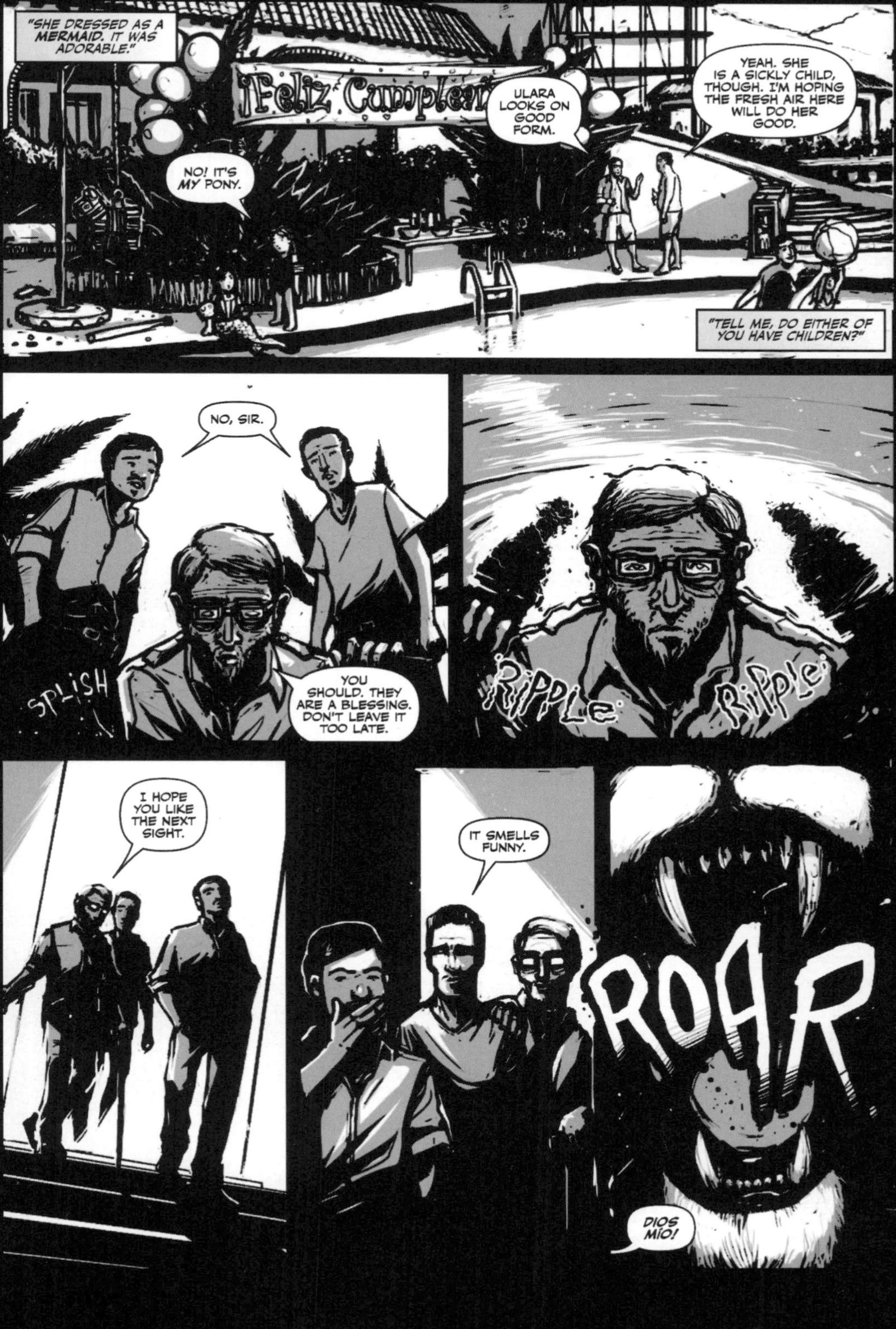
"SHE DRESSED AS A MERMAID. IT WAS ADORABLE."
¡Feliz Cumplea
NO! IT'S MY PONY.
ULARA LOOKS ON GOOD FORM.
YEAH. SHE IS A SICKLY CHILD, THOUGH. I'M HOPING THE FRESH AIR HERE WILL DO HER GOOD.
"TELL ME, DO EITHER OF YOU HAVE CHILDREN?"
NO, SIR.
SPLISH
YOU SHOULD. THEY ARE A BLESSING. DON'T LEAVE IT TOO LATE.
RIPPLE
RIPPLE
I HOPE YOU LIKE THE NEXT SIGHT.
IT SMELLS FUNNY.
ROAR
DIOS MÍO!

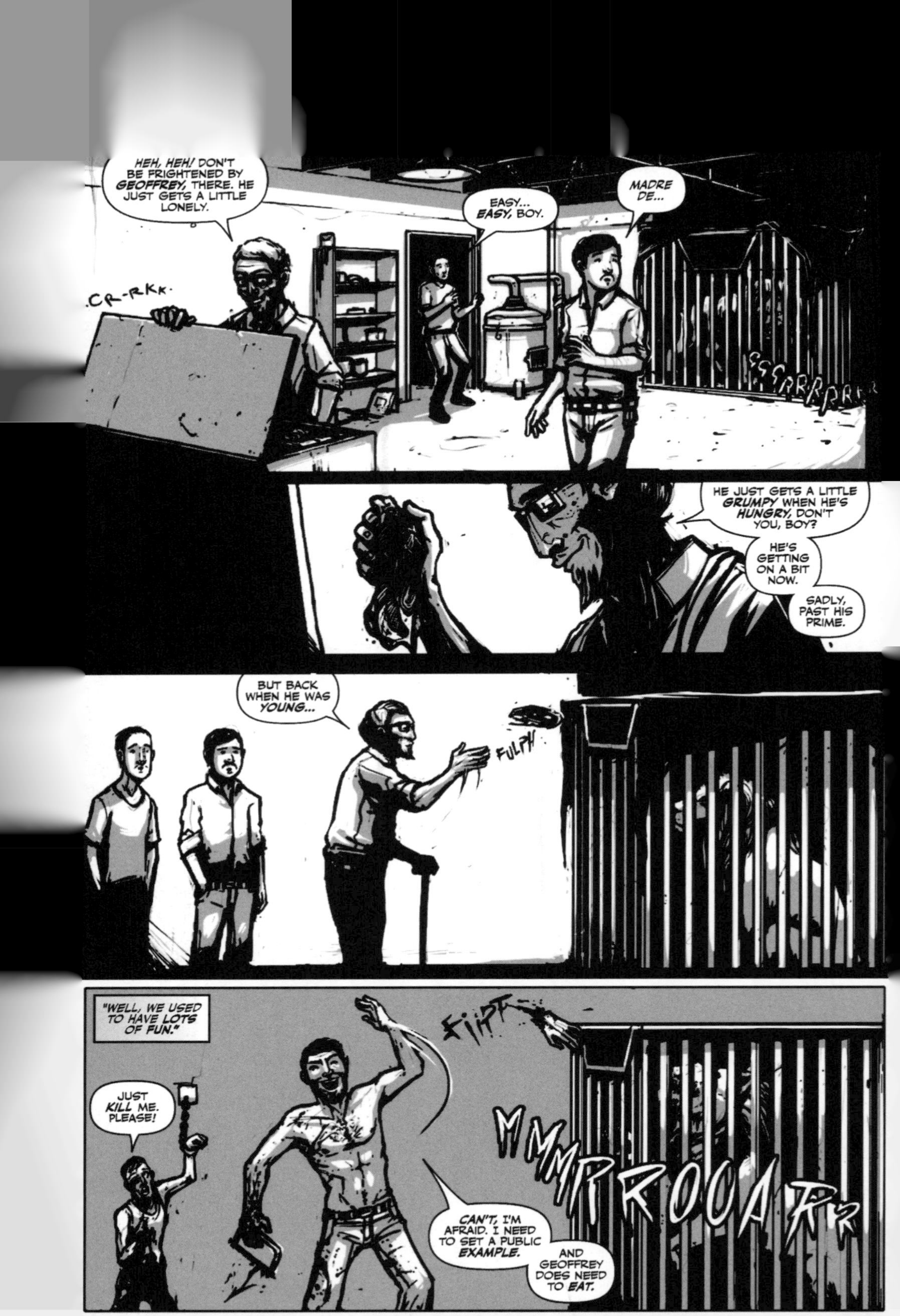

HEH, HEH! DON'T BE FRIGHTENED BY GEOFFREY, THERE. HE JUST GETS A LITTLE LONELY.
CR-RKK.
EASY... EASY, BOY.
MADRE DE...
GGGRRRRRRR
HE JUST GETS A LITTLE GRUMPY WHEN HE'S HUNGRY, DON'T YOU, BOY?
HE'S GETTING ON A BIT NOW.
SADLY, PAST HIS PRIME.
BUT BACK WHEN HE WAS YOUNG...
FULPH
"WELL, WE USED TO HAVE LOTS OF FUN."
FIIPT
JUST KILL ME. PLEASE!
MMMPROOARRR
CAN'T, I'M AFRAID. I NEED TO SET A PUBLIC EXAMPLE.
AND GEOFFREY DOES NEED TO EAT.

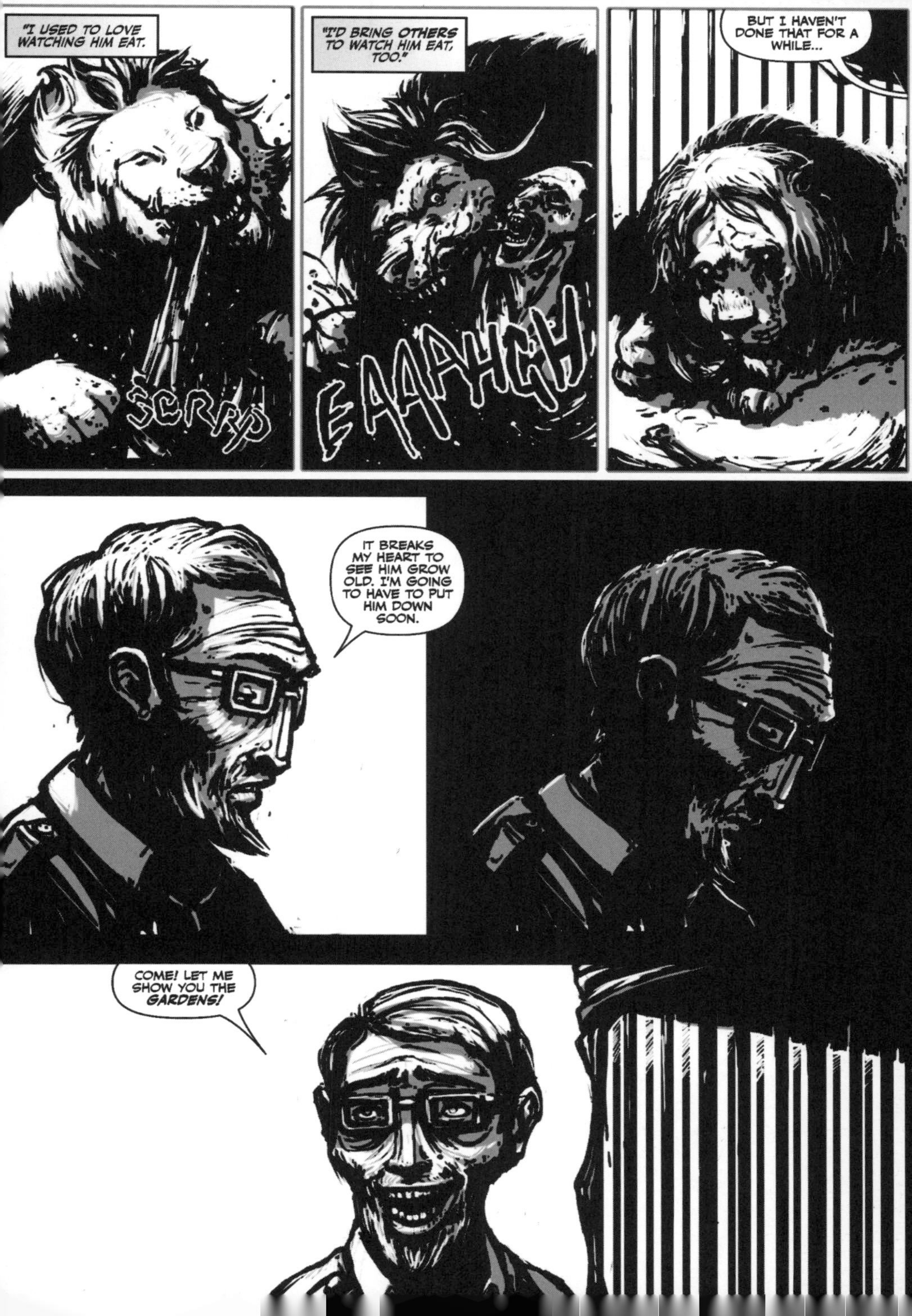
"I USED TO LOVE WATCHING HIM EAT.
SCRRP
"I'D BRING OTHERS TO WATCH HIM EAT, TOO."
EAAAHGH
BUT I HAVEN'T DONE THAT FOR A WHILE...
IT BREAKS MY HEART TO SEE HIM GROW OLD. I'M GOING TO HAVE TO PUT HIM DOWN SOON.
COME! LET ME SHOW YOU THE *GARDENS!*

I'VE ADDED A NEW *JAPANESE* SECTION IN THE FAR CORNER.

TIMES *CHANGE* AND WE ARE DOING FAR MORE BUSINESS WITH THE *YAKUZA* NOW.

I HEARD.

Heh

THE JAPANESE *INTRIGUE* ME. THEIR HONOR SYSTEM. THEIR *LOYALTY*.

IF A GANG MEMBER COMMITS A TRANSGRESSION, HE IS REQUIRED TO CUT OFF PART OF HIS LITTLE FINGER AND OFFER IT AS A SIGN OF HIS *APOLOGY*.

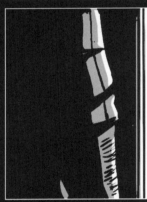

I'M THINKING OF *COPYING* IT FOR THOSE WHO CROSS ME.

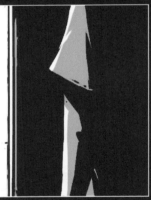

BUT WHAT *REALLY* INTRIGUES ME IS THEIR METHODS OF *TORTURE*.

THEY HAVE LOADS OF TECHNIQUES, BUT ONE IN *PARTICULAR* CAUGHT MY EYE.

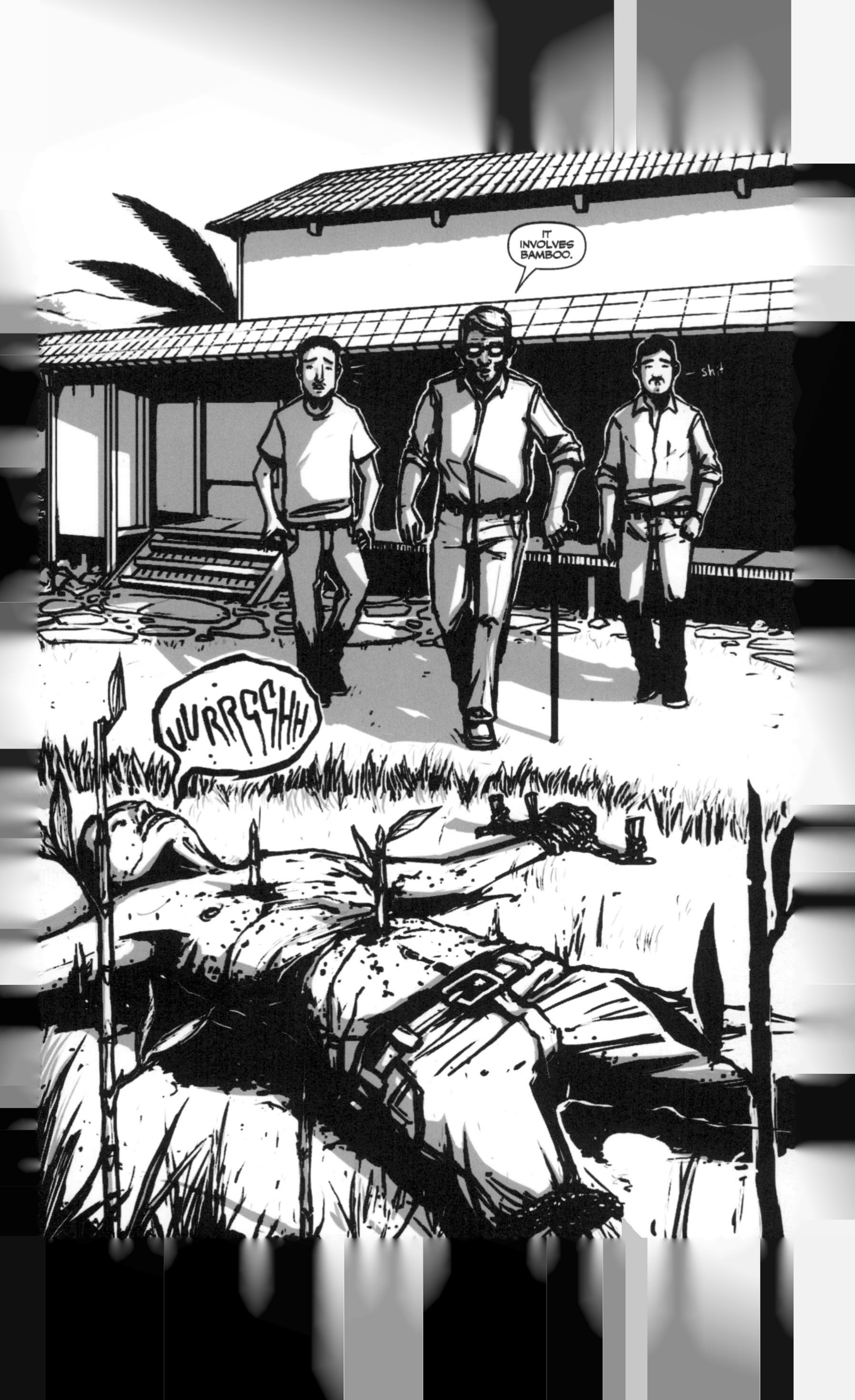
IT INVOLVES BAMBOO.
– shit
UURRGSHH

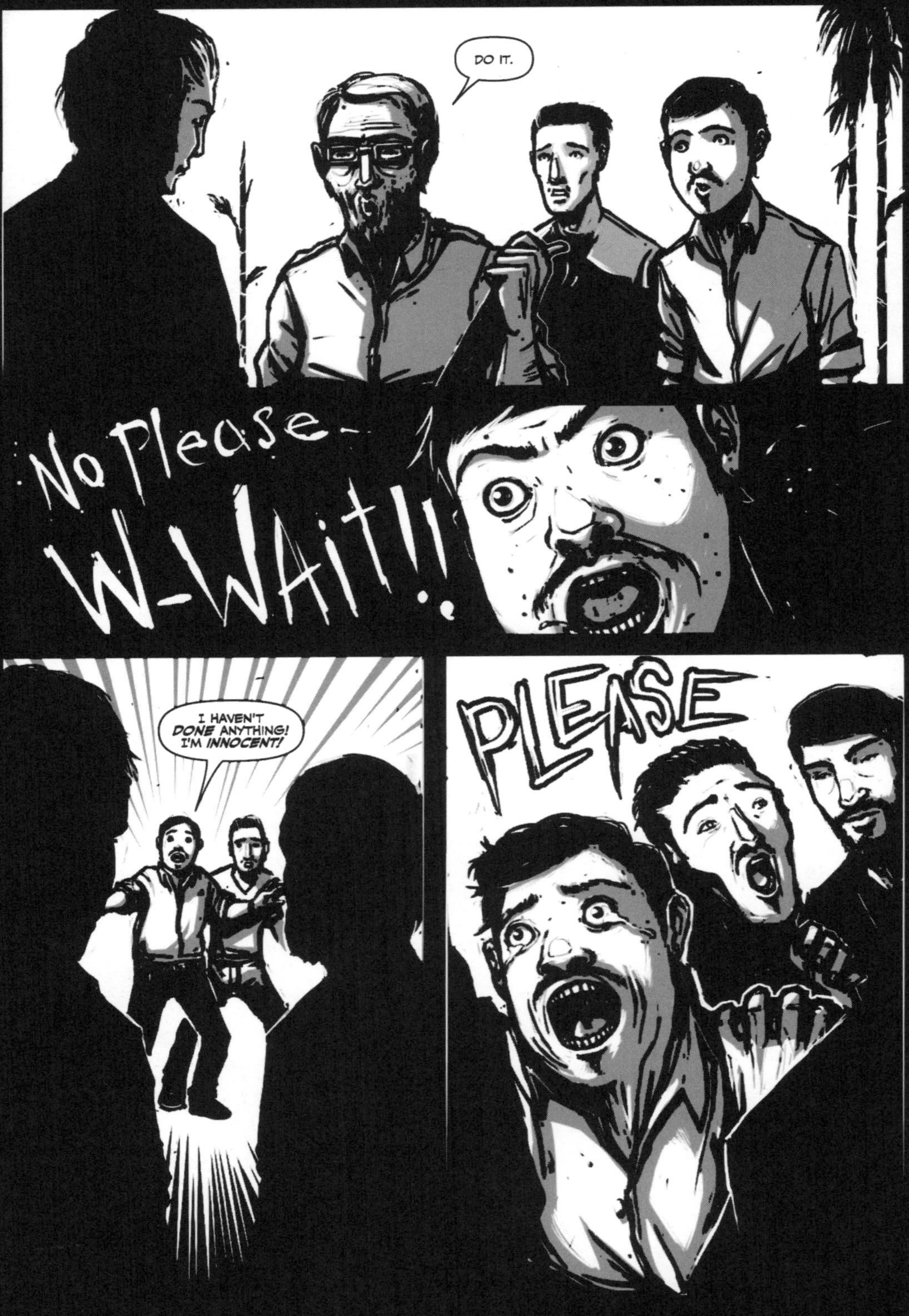
DO IT.
No Please-
W-WAIT!!
I HAVEN'T DONE ANYTHING! I'M INNOCENT!
PLEASE

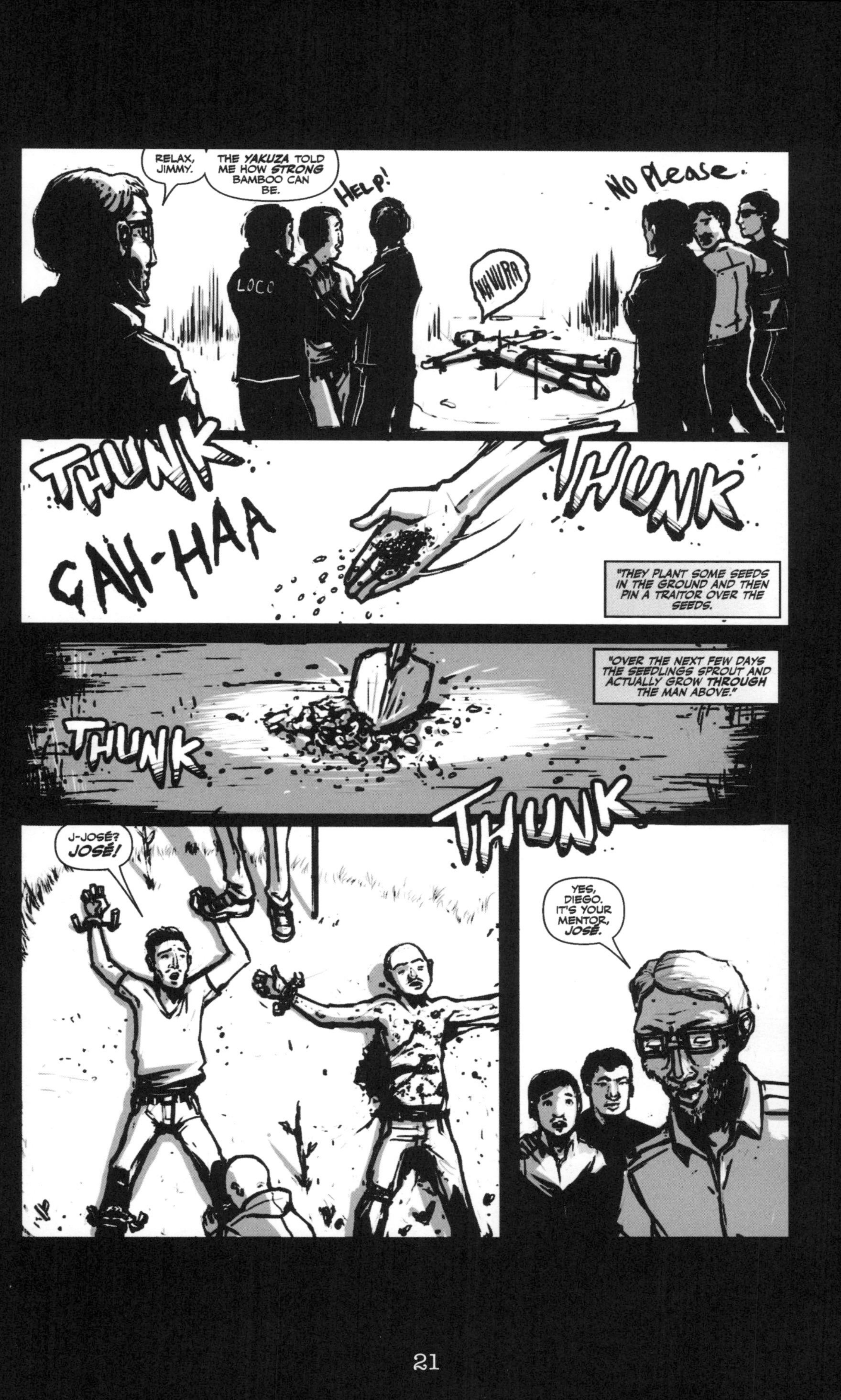

RELAX, JIMMY.
THE YAKUZA TOLD ME HOW STRONG BAMBOO CAN BE.
HELP!
NO PLEASE.
LOCO
THUNK
GAH-HAA
THUNK
"THEY PLANT SOME SEEDS IN THE GROUND AND THEN PIN A TRAITOR OVER THE SEEDS.
"OVER THE NEXT FEW DAYS THE SEEDLINGS SPROUT AND ACTUALLY GROW THROUGH THE MAN ABOVE."
THUNK
THUNK
J-JOSÉ? JOSÉ!
YES, DIEGO. IT'S YOUR MENTOR, JOSÉ.

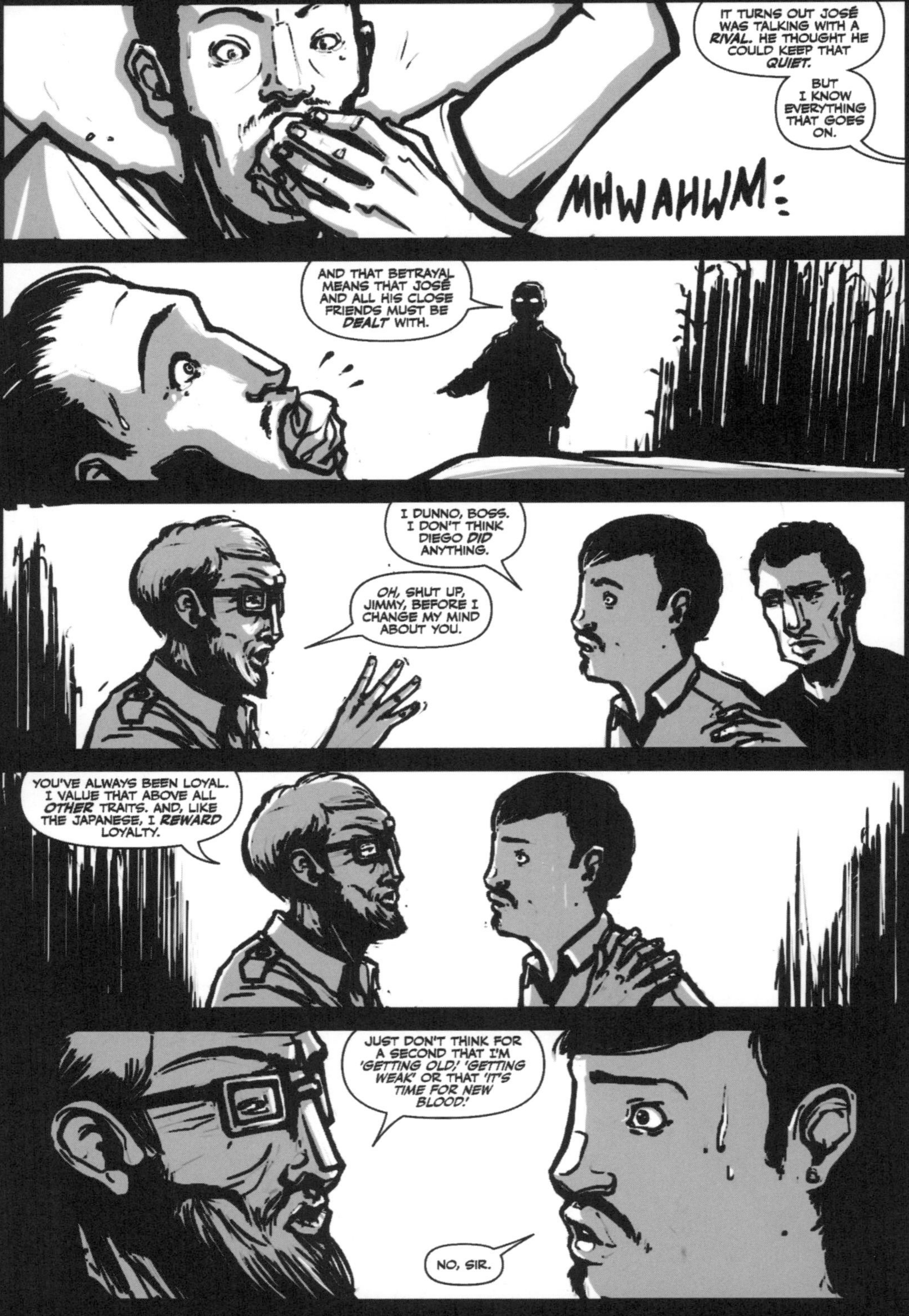
IT TURNS OUT JOSÉ WAS TALKING WITH A *RIVAL.* HE THOUGHT HE COULD KEEP THAT *QUIET.*
BUT I KNOW EVERYTHING THAT GOES ON.
MHWAHWM:
AND THAT BETRAYAL MEANS THAT JOSÉ AND ALL HIS CLOSE FRIENDS MUST BE *DEALT* WITH.
I DUNNO, BOSS. I DON'T THINK DIEGO *DID* ANYTHING.
OH, SHUT UP, JIMMY, BEFORE I CHANGE MY MIND ABOUT YOU.
YOU'VE ALWAYS BEEN LOYAL. I VALUE THAT ABOVE ALL *OTHER* TRAITS. AND, LIKE THE JAPANESE, I *REWARD* LOYALTY.
JUST DON'T THINK FOR A SECOND THAT I'M *'GETTING OLD,' 'GETTING WEAK'* OR THAT *'IT'S TIME FOR NEW BLOOD.'*
NO, SIR.

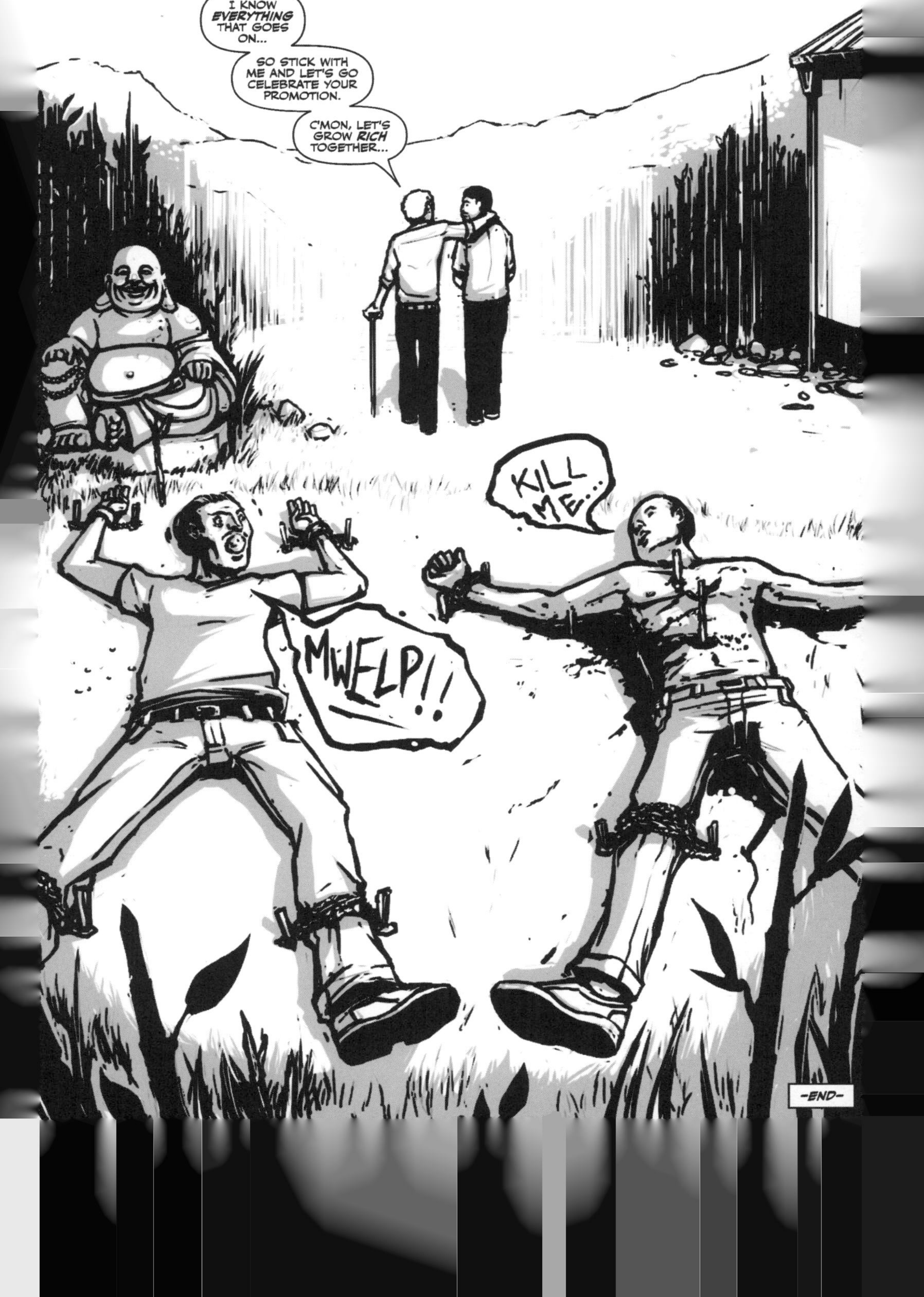
I KNOW EVERYTHING THAT GOES ON...
SO STICK WITH ME AND LET'S GO CELEBRATE YOUR PROMOTION.
C'MON, LET'S GROW RICH TOGETHER...
KILL ME...
MWELP!!
-END-

Love of my Life...

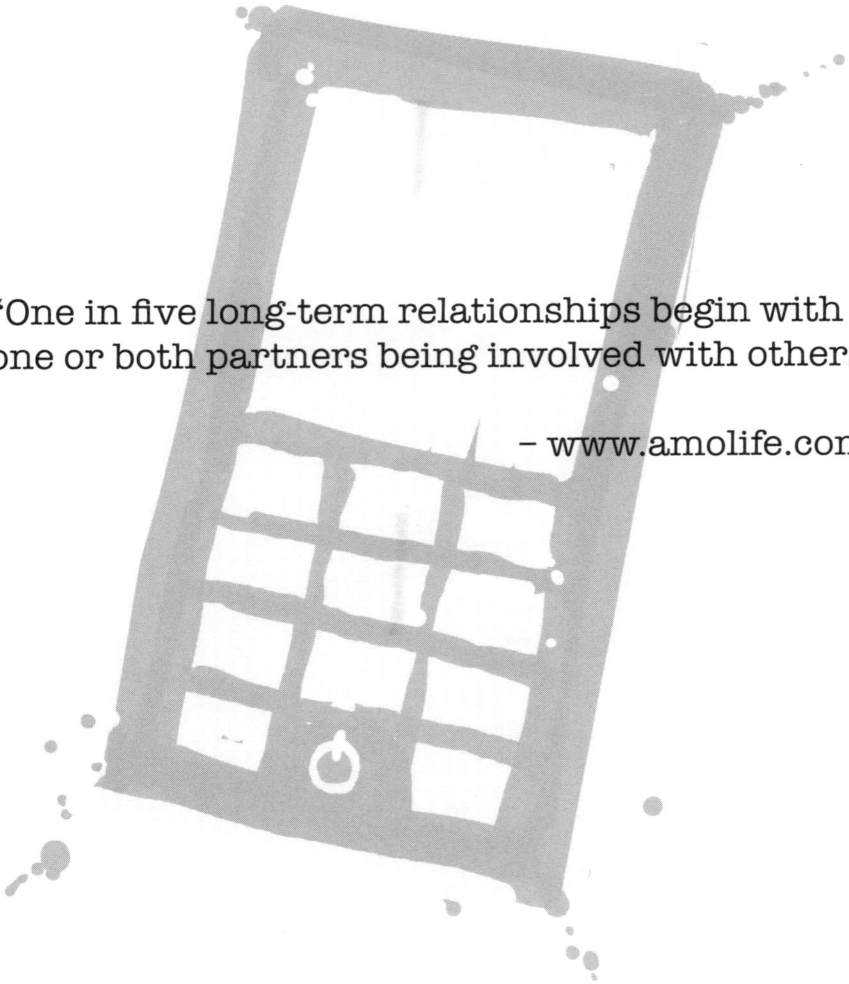

"One in five long-term relationships begin with one or both partners being involved with others."

– www.amolife.com

Writer/Creator
Neil Gibson

Illustrator
Jan Wijngaard

www.tpub.co.uk

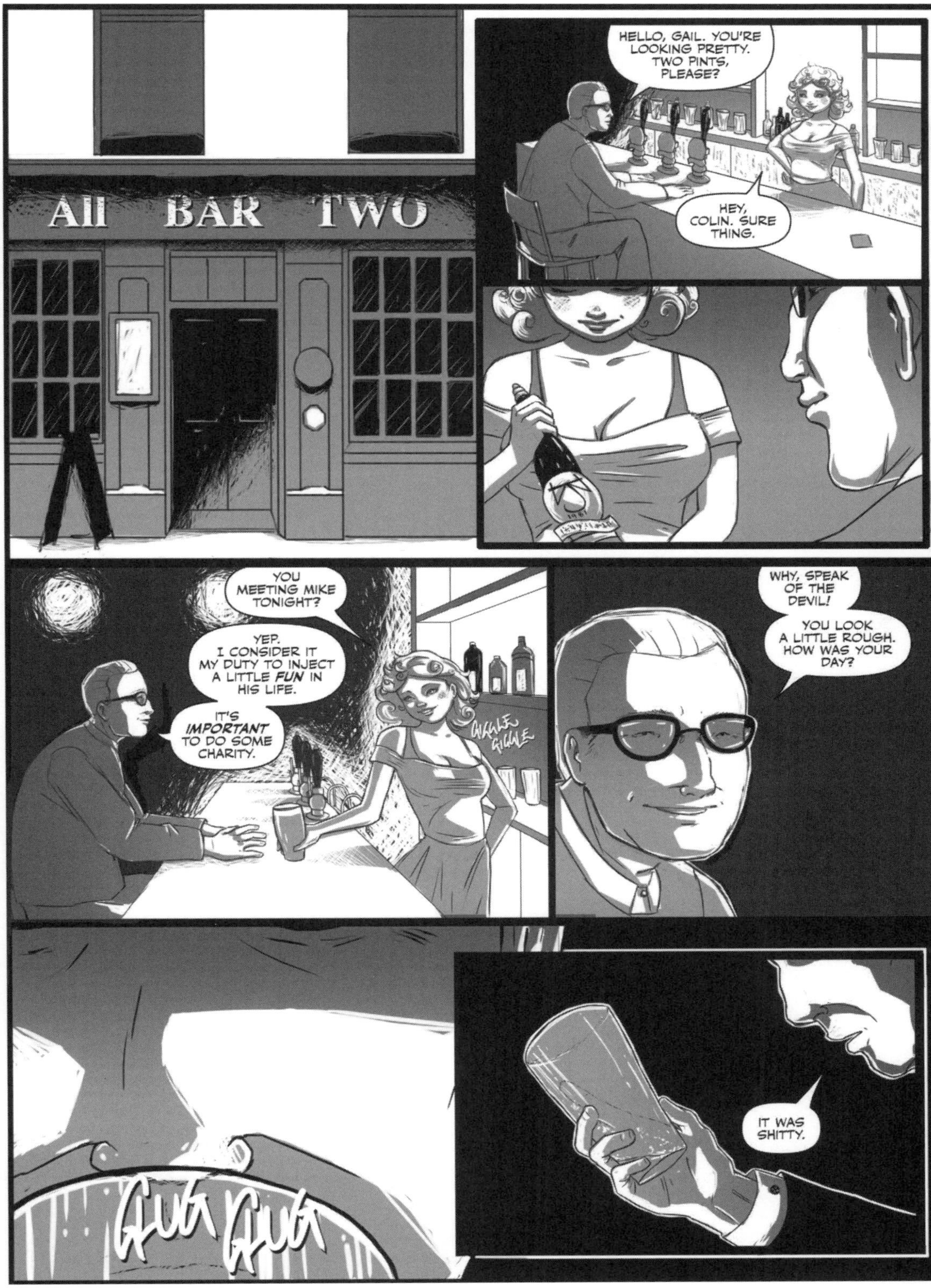
All BAR TWO
HELLO, GAIL. YOU'RE LOOKING PRETTY. TWO PINTS, PLEASE?
HEY, COLIN. SURE THING.
YOU MEETING MIKE TONIGHT?
YEP. I CONSIDER IT MY DUTY TO INJECT A LITTLE *FUN* IN HIS LIFE.
IT'S *IMPORTANT* TO DO SOME CHARITY.
GIGGLE GIGGLE
WHY, SPEAK OF THE DEVIL!
YOU LOOK A LITTLE ROUGH. HOW WAS YOUR DAY?
GUG GUG
IT WAS SHITTY.

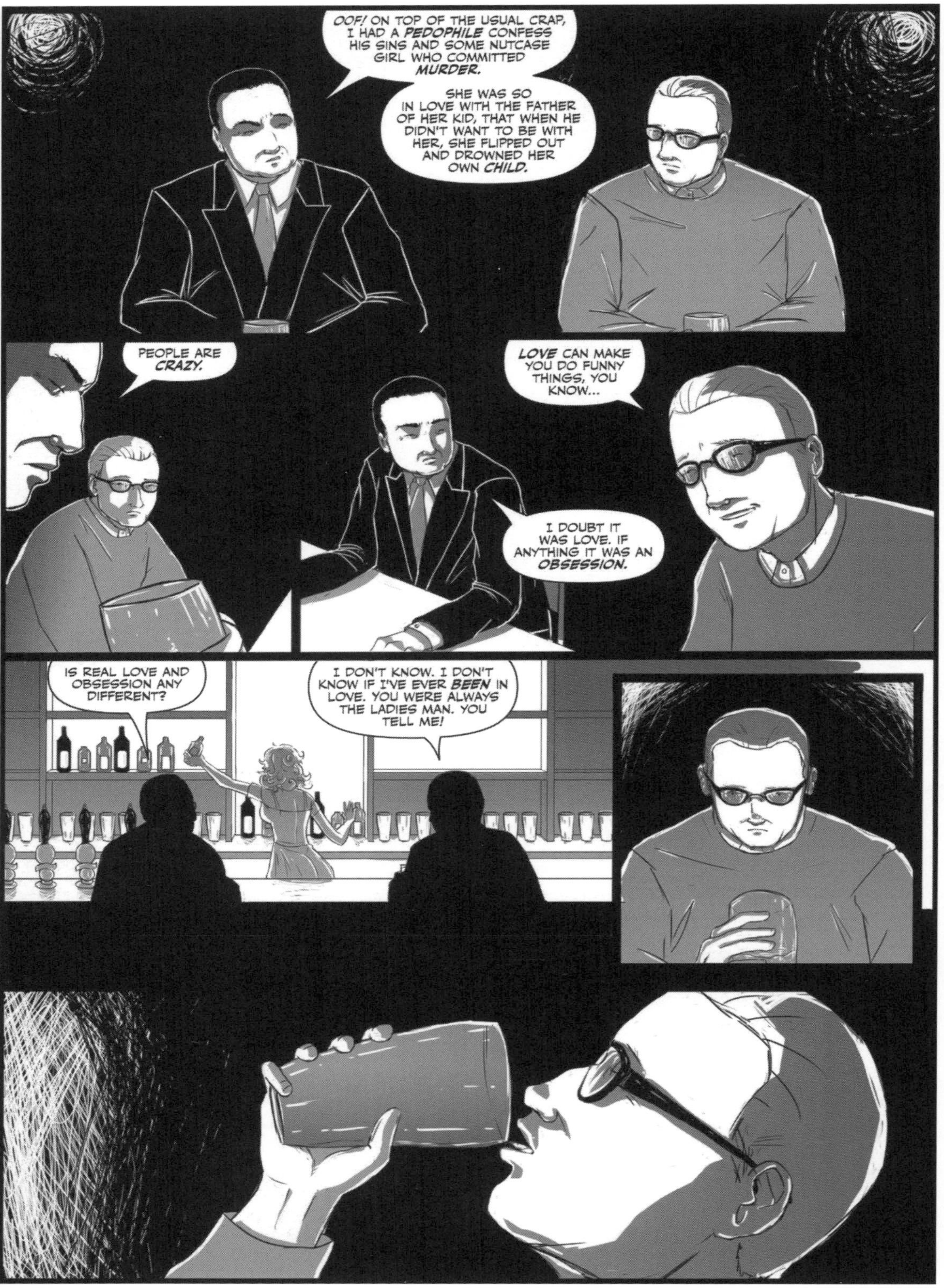
OOF! ON TOP OF THE USUAL CRAP, I HAD A PEDOPHILE CONFESS HIS SINS AND SOME NUTCASE GIRL WHO COMMITTED MURDER.
SHE WAS SO IN LOVE WITH THE FATHER OF HER KID, THAT WHEN HE DIDN'T WANT TO BE WITH HER, SHE FLIPPED OUT AND DROWNED HER OWN CHILD.
PEOPLE ARE CRAZY.
LOVE CAN MAKE YOU DO FUNNY THINGS, YOU KNOW...
I DOUBT IT WAS LOVE. IF ANYTHING IT WAS AN OBSESSION.
IS REAL LOVE AND OBSESSION ANY DIFFERENT?
I DON'T KNOW. I DON'T KNOW IF I'VE EVER BEEN IN LOVE. YOU WERE ALWAYS THE LADIES MAN. YOU TELL ME!

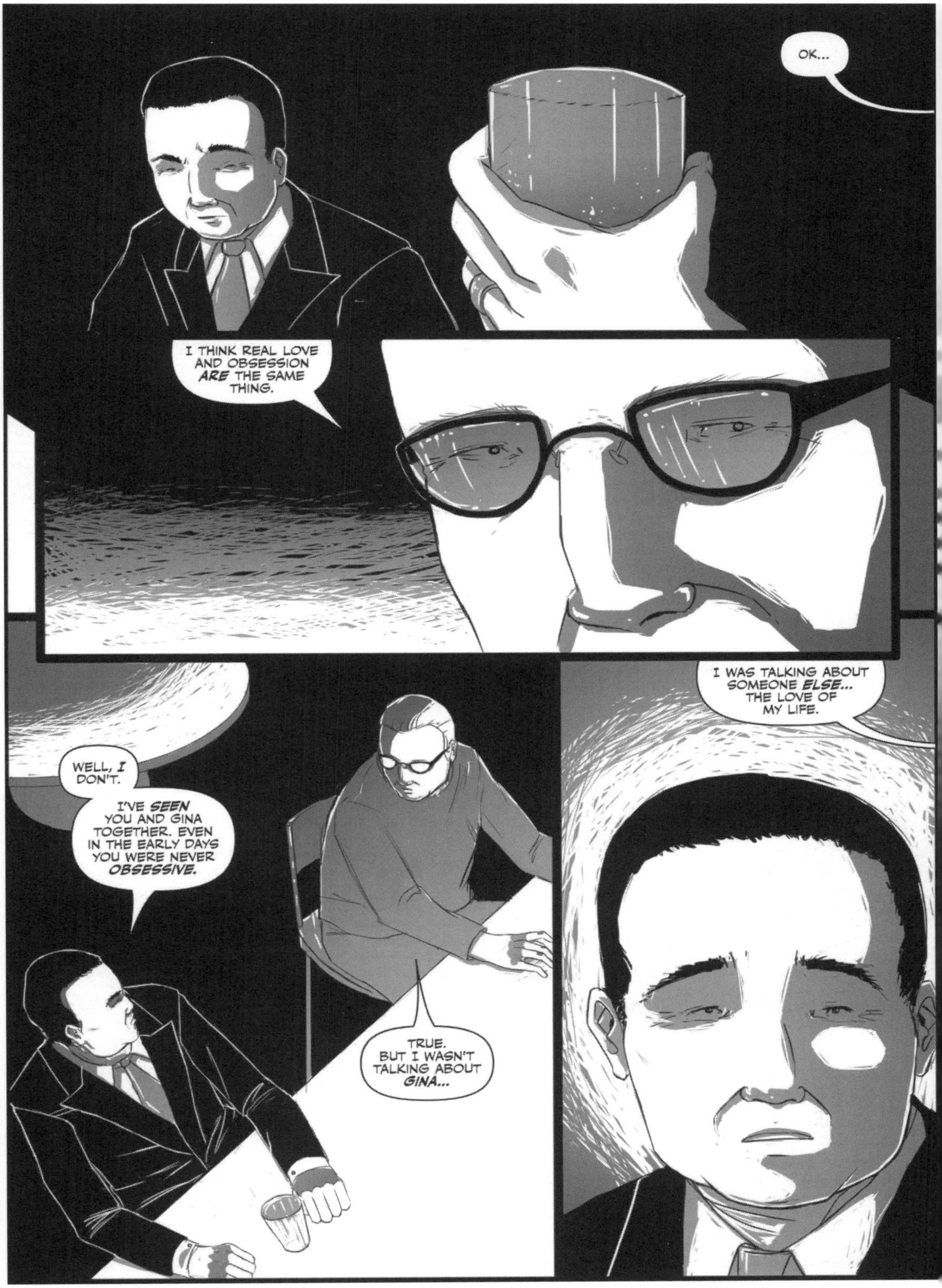
OK...
I THINK REAL LOVE AND OBSESSION ARE THE SAME THING.
WELL, I DON'T.
I'VE SEEN YOU AND GINA TOGETHER. EVEN IN THE EARLY DAYS YOU WERE NEVER OBSESSIVE.
TRUE. BUT I WASN'T TALKING ABOUT GINA...
I WAS TALKING ABOUT SOMEONE ELSE... THE LOVE OF MY LIFE.

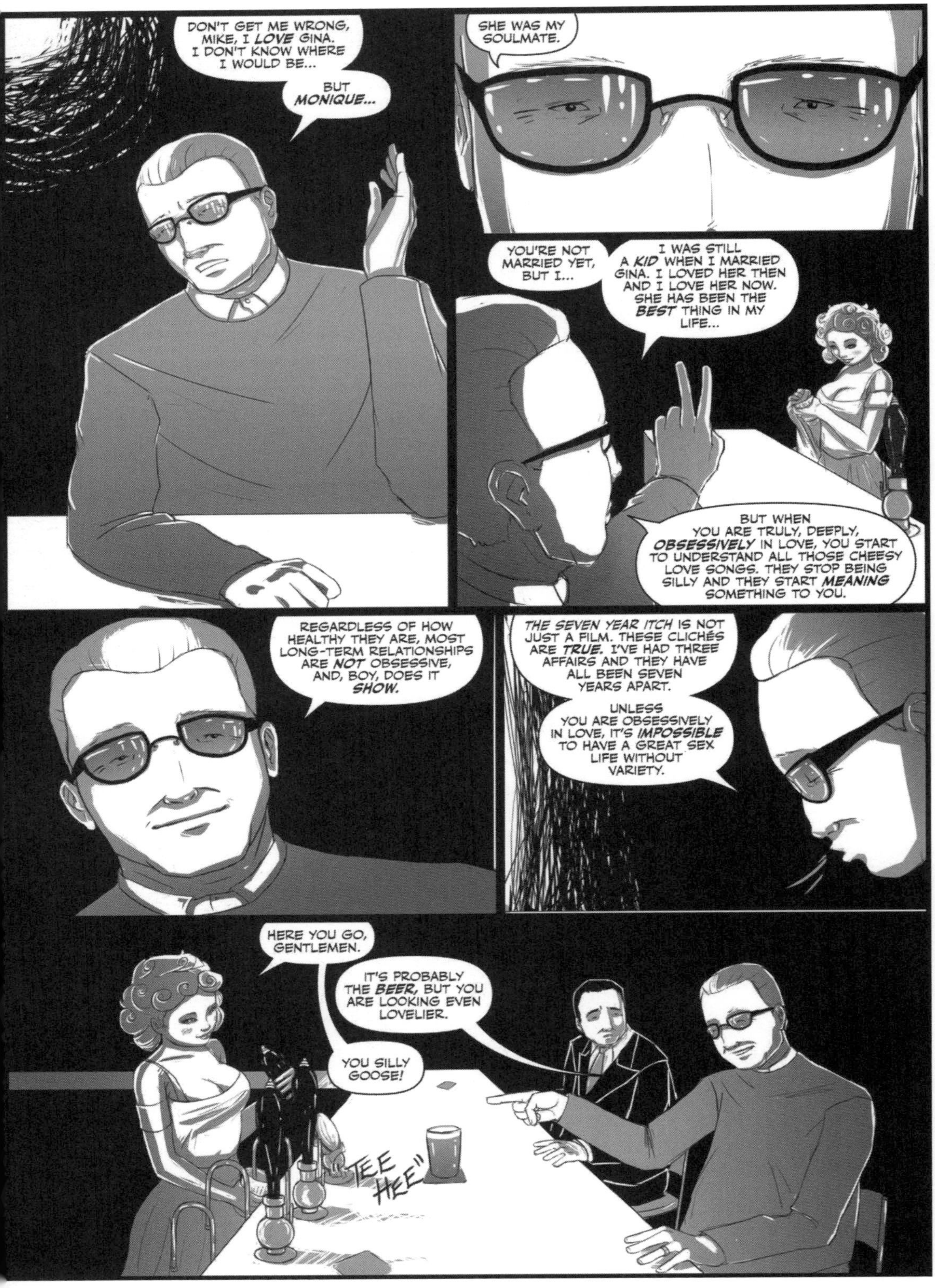
DON'T GET ME WRONG, MIKE, I LOVE GINA. I DON'T KNOW WHERE I WOULD BE...
BUT MONIQUE...
SHE WAS MY SOULMATE.
YOU'RE NOT MARRIED YET, BUT I...
I WAS STILL A KID WHEN I MARRIED GINA. I LOVED HER THEN AND I LOVE HER NOW. SHE HAS BEEN THE BEST THING IN MY LIFE...
BUT WHEN YOU ARE TRULY, DEEPLY, OBSESSIVELY IN LOVE, YOU START TO UNDERSTAND ALL THOSE CHEESY LOVE SONGS. THEY STOP BEING SILLY AND THEY START MEANING SOMETHING TO YOU.
REGARDLESS OF HOW HEALTHY THEY ARE, MOST LONG-TERM RELATIONSHIPS ARE NOT OBSESSIVE, AND, BOY, DOES IT SHOW.
THE SEVEN YEAR ITCH IS NOT JUST A FILM. THESE CLICHÉS ARE TRUE. I'VE HAD THREE AFFAIRS AND THEY HAVE ALL BEEN SEVEN YEARS APART.
UNLESS YOU ARE OBSESSIVELY IN LOVE, IT'S IMPOSSIBLE TO HAVE A GREAT SEX LIFE WITHOUT VARIETY.
HERE YOU GO, GENTLEMEN.
IT'S PROBABLY THE BEER, BUT YOU ARE LOOKING EVEN LOVELIER.
YOU SILLY GOOSE!
TEE HEE

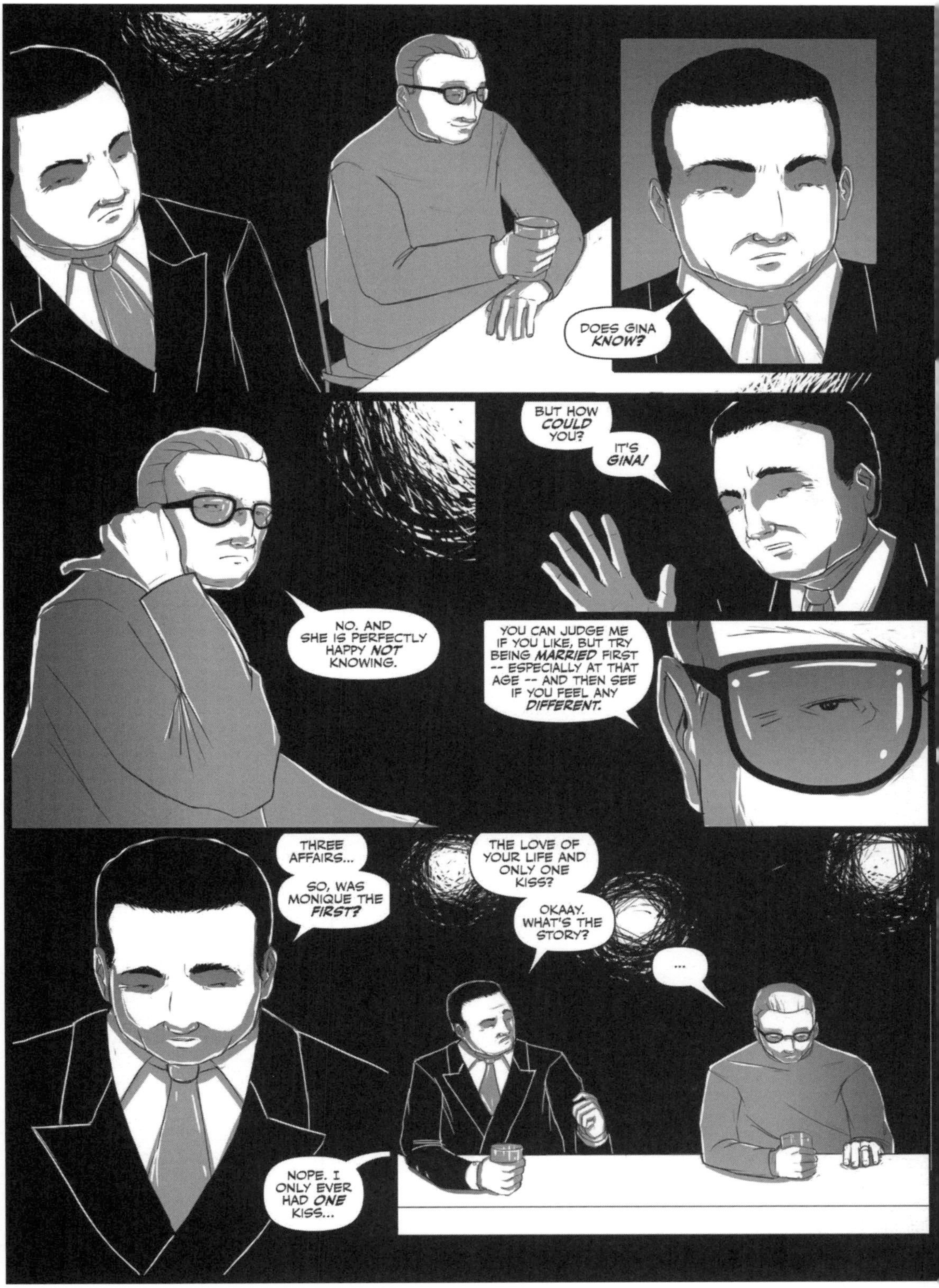
DOES GINA KNOW?
NO. AND SHE IS PERFECTLY HAPPY NOT KNOWING.
BUT HOW COULD YOU?
IT'S GINA!
YOU CAN JUDGE ME IF YOU LIKE, BUT TRY BEING MARRIED FIRST -- ESPECIALLY AT THAT AGE -- AND THEN SEE IF YOU FEEL ANY DIFFERENT.
THREE AFFAIRS...
SO, WAS MONIQUE THE FIRST?
NOPE. I ONLY EVER HAD ONE KISS...
THE LOVE OF YOUR LIFE AND ONLY ONE KISS?
OKAAY. WHAT'S THE STORY?
...

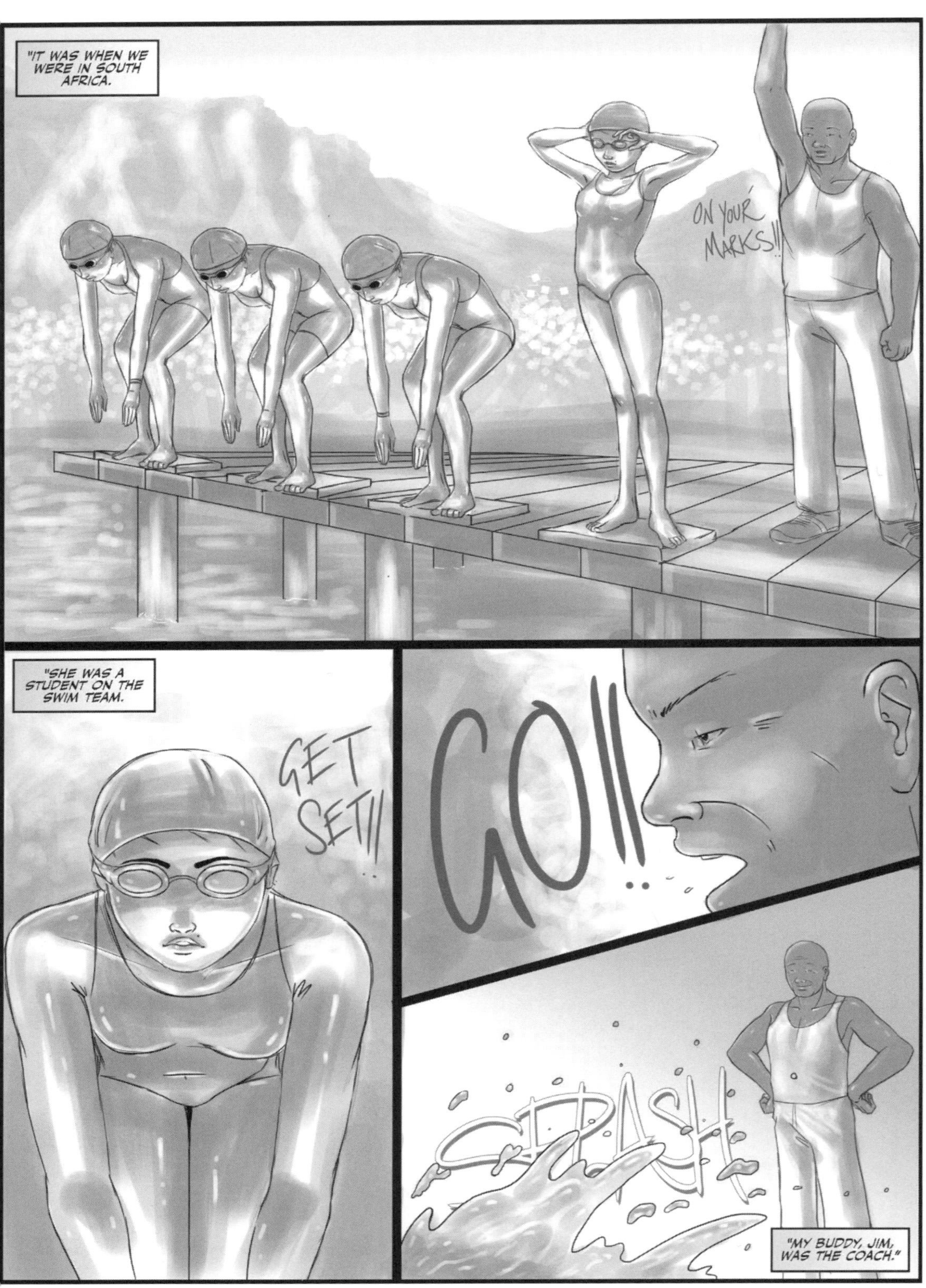
"IT WAS WHEN WE WERE IN SOUTH AFRICA.
ON YOUR MARKS!!
"SHE WAS A STUDENT ON THE SWIM TEAM.
GET SET!!
GO!!
SPLASH
"MY BUDDY, JIM, WAS THE COACH."

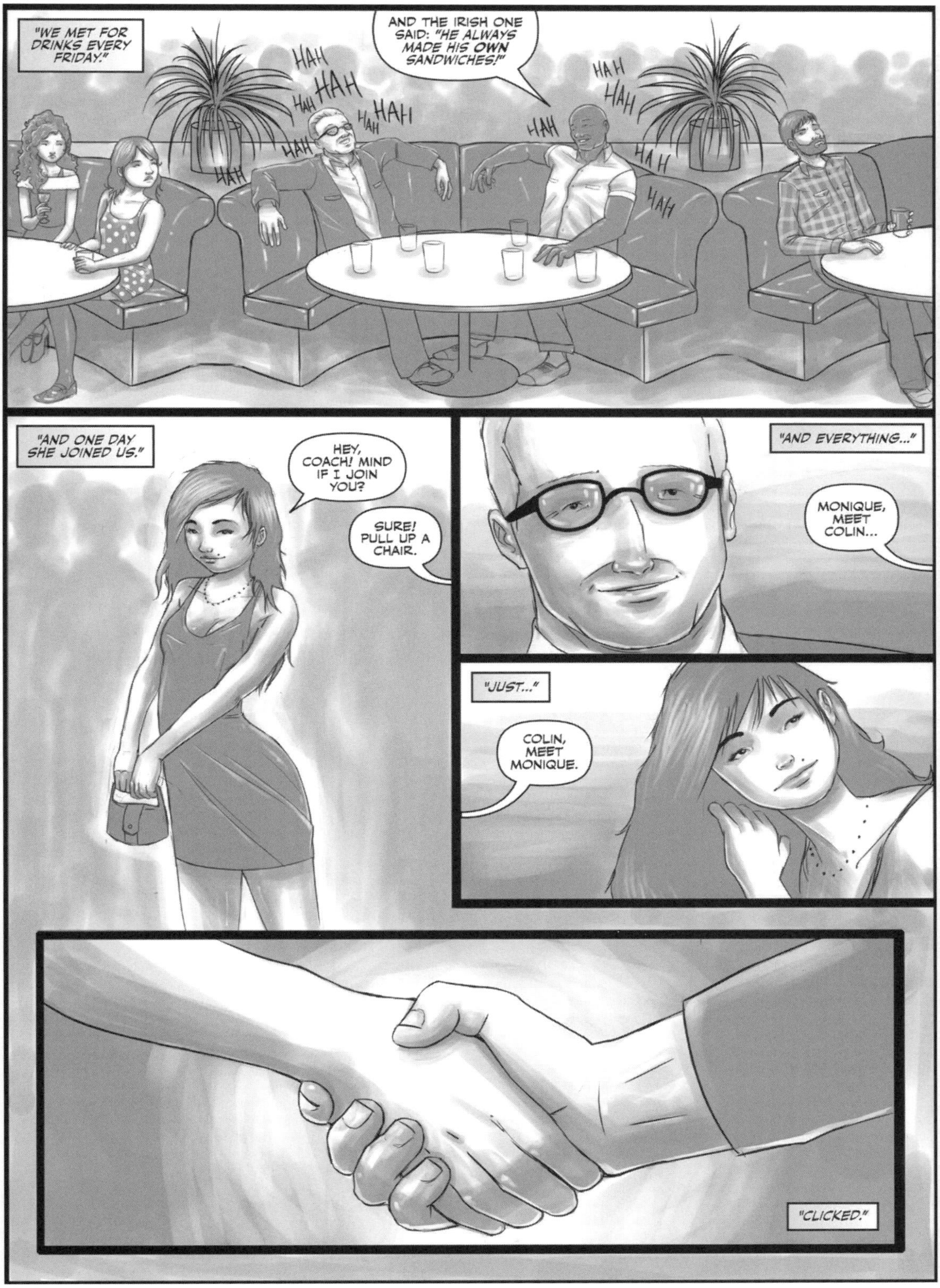

"WE MET FOR DRINKS EVERY FRIDAY."
AND THE IRISH ONE SAID: "HE ALWAYS MADE HIS OWN SANDWICHES!"
HAH HAH HAH HAH HAH HAH HAH HAH
HAH HAH HAH HAH HAH HAH
"AND ONE DAY SHE JOINED US."
HEY, COACH! MIND IF I JOIN YOU?
SURE! PULL UP A CHAIR.
"AND EVERYTHING..."
MONIQUE, MEET COLIN...
"JUST..."
COLIN, MEET MONIQUE.
"CLICKED."

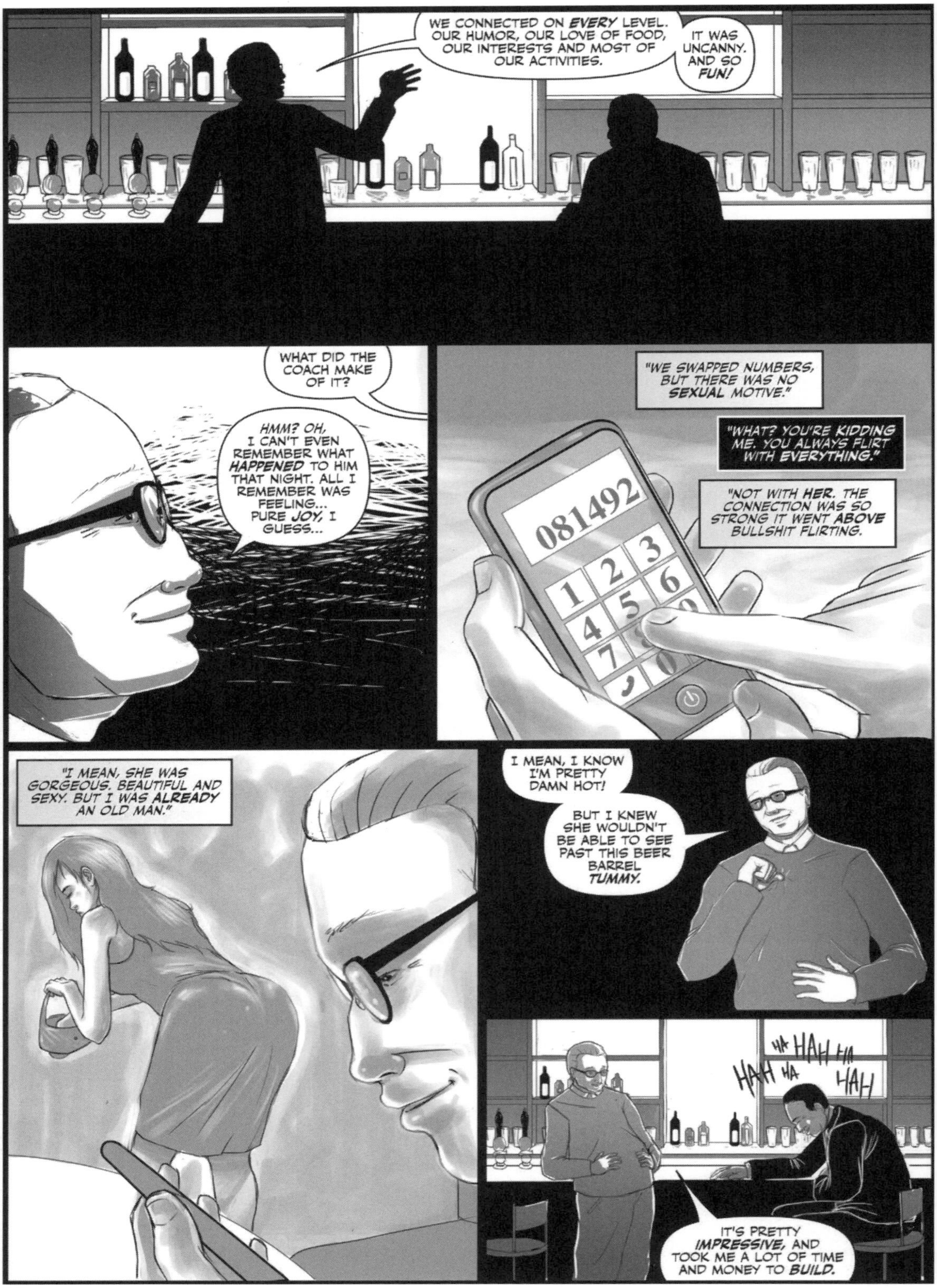
WE CONNECTED ON EVERY LEVEL. OUR HUMOR, OUR LOVE OF FOOD, OUR INTERESTS AND MOST OF OUR ACTIVITIES.
IT WAS UNCANNY. AND SO FUN!
WHAT DID THE COACH MAKE OF IT?
HMM? OH, I CAN'T EVEN REMEMBER WHAT HAPPENED TO HIM THAT NIGHT. ALL I REMEMBER WAS FEELING... PURE JOY, I GUESS...
"WE SWAPPED NUMBERS, BUT THERE WAS NO SEXUAL MOTIVE."
"WHAT? YOU'RE KIDDING ME. YOU ALWAYS FLIRT WITH EVERYTHING."
"NOT WITH HER. THE CONNECTION WAS SO STRONG IT WENT ABOVE BULLSHIT FLIRTING.
081492
"I MEAN, SHE WAS GORGEOUS, BEAUTIFUL AND SEXY. BUT I WAS ALREADY AN OLD MAN."
I MEAN, I KNOW I'M PRETTY DAMN HOT!
BUT I KNEW SHE WOULDN'T BE ABLE TO SEE PAST THIS BEER BARREL TUMMY.
HA HAH HA HAH HA HAH
IT'S PRETTY IMPRESSIVE, AND TOOK ME A LOT OF TIME AND MONEY TO BUILD.

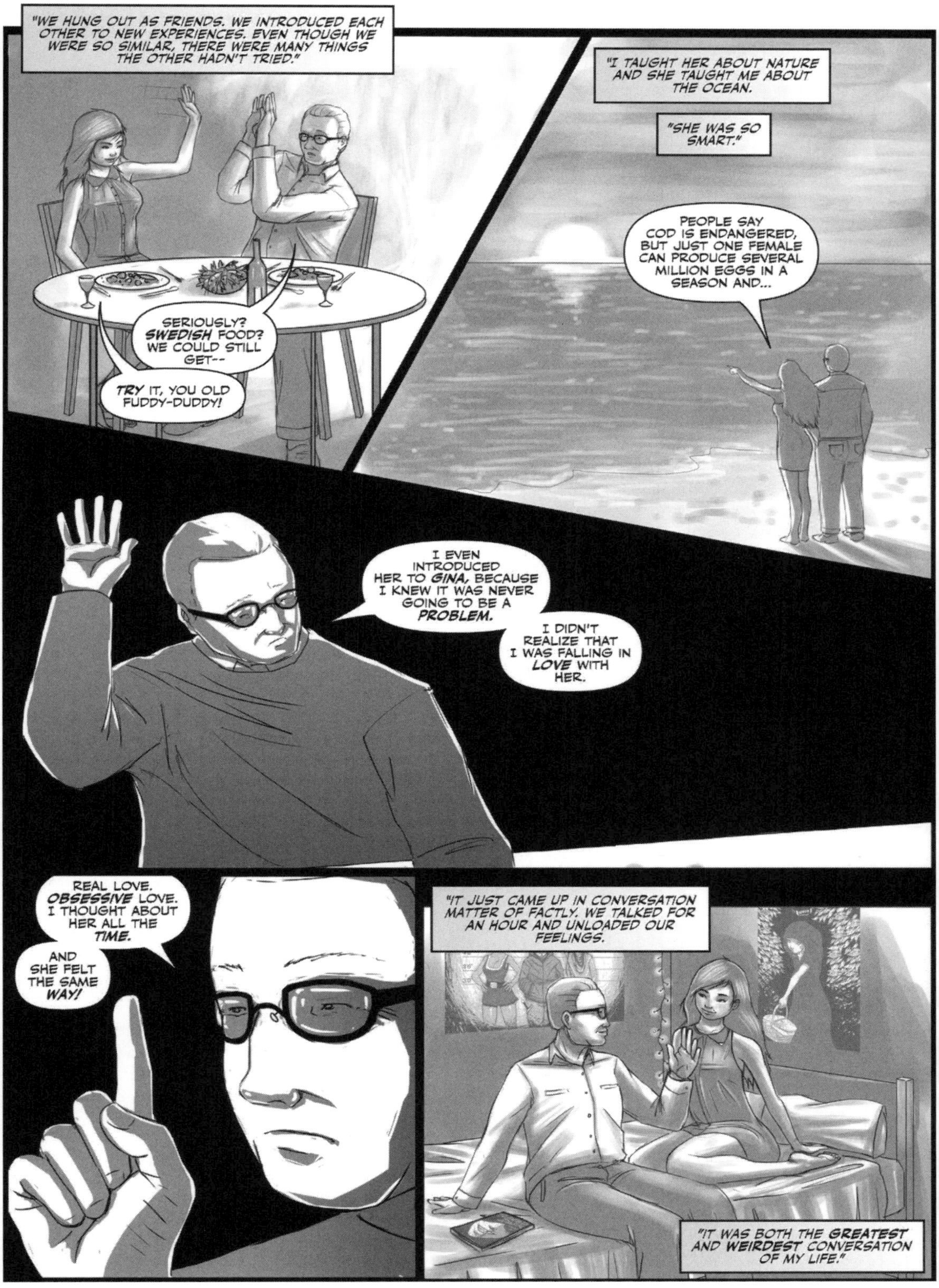
"WE HUNG OUT AS FRIENDS. WE INTRODUCED EACH OTHER TO NEW EXPERIENCES. EVEN THOUGH WE WERE SO SIMILAR, THERE WERE MANY THINGS THE OTHER HADN'T TRIED."
SERIOUSLY? SWEDISH FOOD? WE COULD STILL GET--
TRY IT, YOU OLD FUDDY-DUDDY!
"I TAUGHT HER ABOUT NATURE AND SHE TAUGHT ME ABOUT THE OCEAN.
"SHE WAS SO SMART."
PEOPLE SAY COD IS ENDANGERED, BUT JUST ONE FEMALE CAN PRODUCE SEVERAL MILLION EGGS IN A SEASON AND...
I EVEN INTRODUCED HER TO GINA, BECAUSE I KNEW IT WAS NEVER GOING TO BE A PROBLEM.
I DIDN'T REALIZE THAT I WAS FALLING IN LOVE WITH HER.
REAL LOVE. OBSESSIVE LOVE. I THOUGHT ABOUT HER ALL THE TIME.
AND SHE FELT THE SAME WAY!
"IT JUST CAME UP IN CONVERSATION MATTER OF FACTLY. WE TALKED FOR AN HOUR AND UNLOADED OUR FEELINGS.
"IT WAS BOTH THE GREATEST AND WEIRDEST CONVERSATION OF MY LIFE."

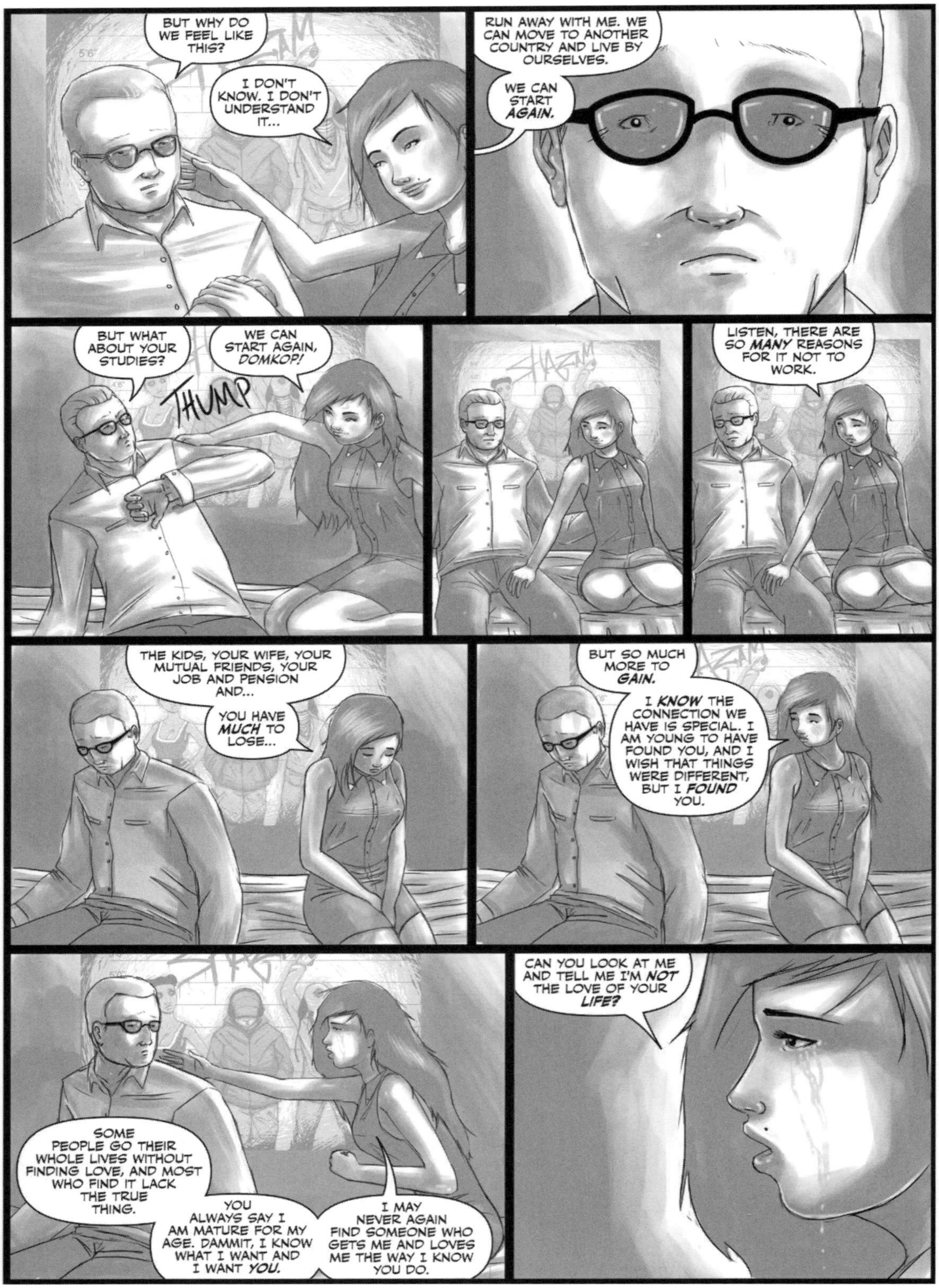
BUT WHY DO WE FEEL LIKE THIS?
I DON'T KNOW. I DON'T UNDERSTAND IT...
RUN AWAY WITH ME. WE CAN MOVE TO ANOTHER COUNTRY AND LIVE BY OURSELVES.
WE CAN START AGAIN.
BUT WHAT ABOUT YOUR STUDIES?
WE CAN START AGAIN, DOMKOP!
THUMP
LISTEN, THERE ARE SO MANY REASONS FOR IT NOT TO WORK.
THE KIDS, YOUR WIFE, YOUR MUTUAL FRIENDS, YOUR JOB AND PENSION AND...
YOU HAVE MUCH TO LOSE...
BUT SO MUCH MORE TO GAIN.
I KNOW THE CONNECTION WE HAVE IS SPECIAL. I AM YOUNG TO HAVE FOUND YOU, AND I WISH THAT THINGS WERE DIFFERENT, BUT I FOUND YOU.
SOME PEOPLE GO THEIR WHOLE LIVES WITHOUT FINDING LOVE, AND MOST WHO FIND IT LACK THE TRUE THING.
YOU ALWAYS SAY I AM MATURE FOR MY AGE. DAMMIT, I KNOW WHAT I WANT AND I WANT YOU.
I MAY NEVER AGAIN FIND SOMEONE WHO GETS ME AND LOVES ME THE WAY I KNOW YOU DO.
CAN YOU LOOK AT ME AND TELL ME I'M NOT THE LOVE OF YOUR LIFE?

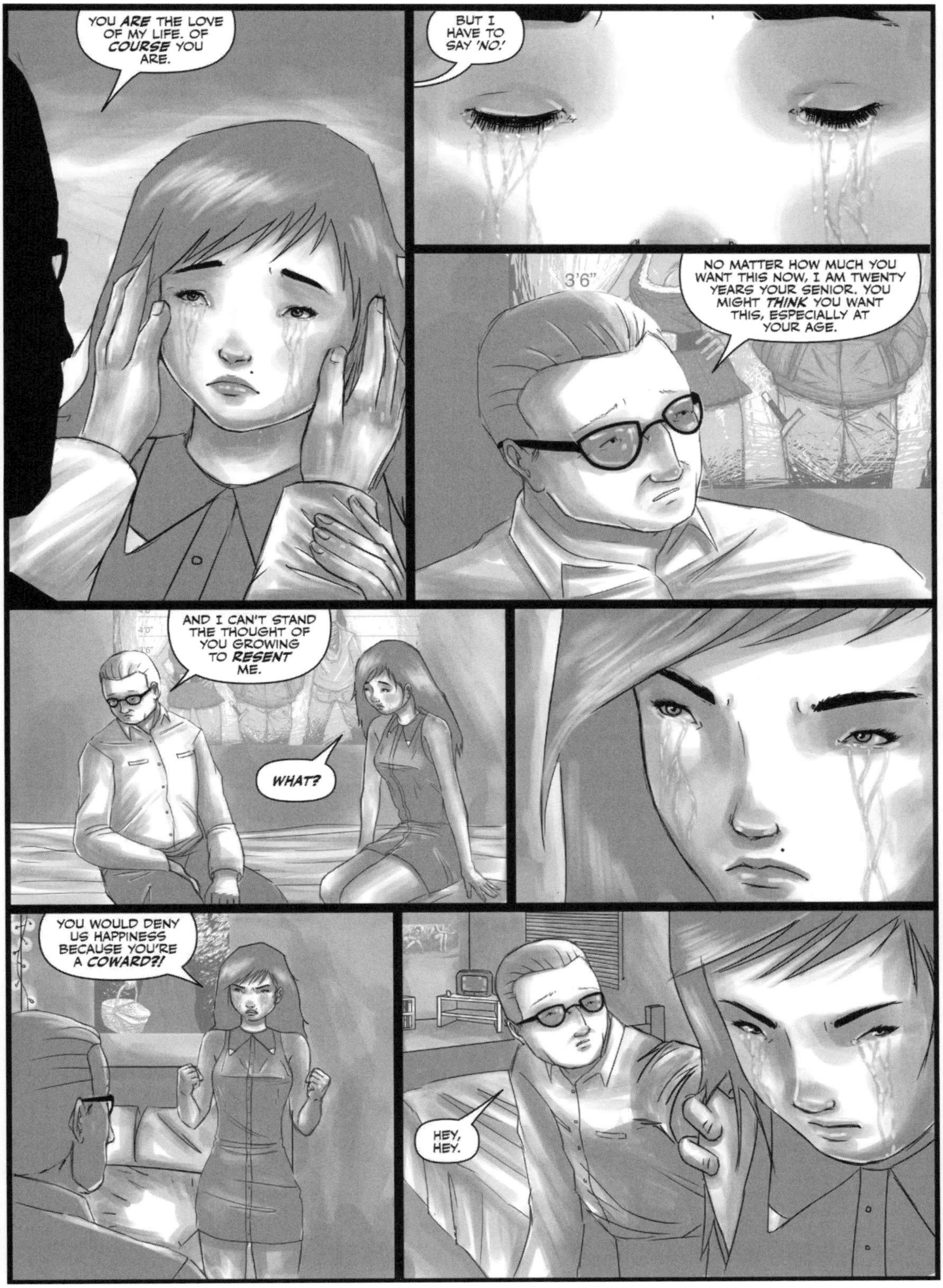
YOU ARE THE LOVE OF MY LIFE. OF COURSE YOU ARE.
BUT I HAVE TO SAY 'NO.'
3'6"
NO MATTER HOW MUCH YOU WANT THIS NOW, I AM TWENTY YEARS YOUR SENIOR. YOU MIGHT THINK YOU WANT THIS, ESPECIALLY AT YOUR AGE.
AND I CAN'T STAND THE THOUGHT OF YOU GROWING TO RESENT ME.
WHAT?
YOU WOULD DENY US HAPPINESS BECAUSE YOU'RE A COWARD?!
HEY, HEY.

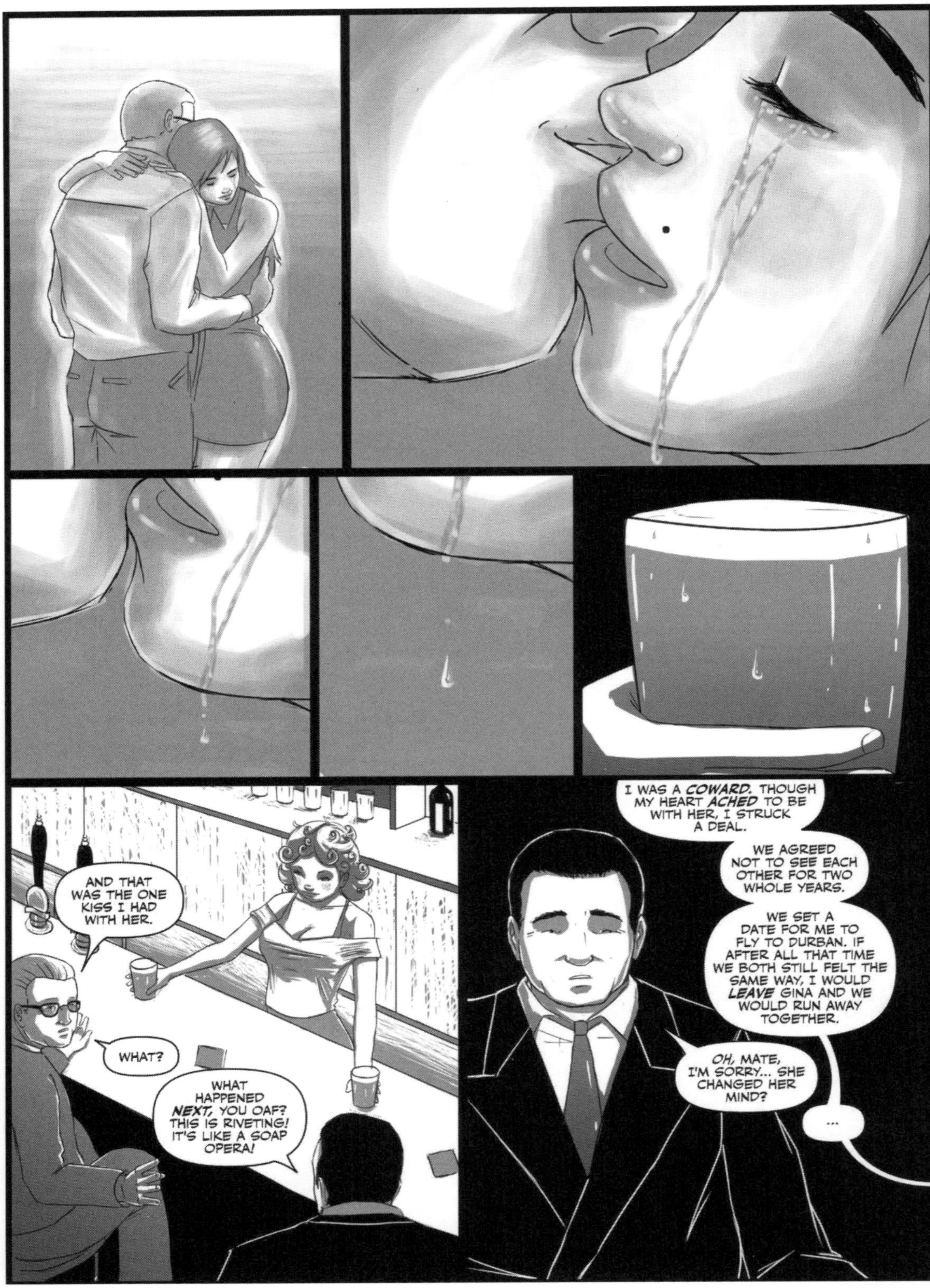
AND THAT WAS THE ONE KISS I HAD WITH HER.
WHAT?
WHAT HAPPENED NEXT, YOU OAF? THIS IS RIVETING! IT'S LIKE A SOAP OPERA!
I WAS A COWARD. THOUGH MY HEART ACHED TO BE WITH HER, I STRUCK A DEAL.
WE AGREED NOT TO SEE EACH OTHER FOR TWO WHOLE YEARS.
WE SET A DATE FOR ME TO FLY TO DURBAN. IF AFTER ALL THAT TIME WE BOTH STILL FELT THE SAME WAY, I WOULD LEAVE GINA AND WE WOULD RUN AWAY TOGETHER.
OH, MATE, I'M SORRY... SHE CHANGED HER MIND?
...

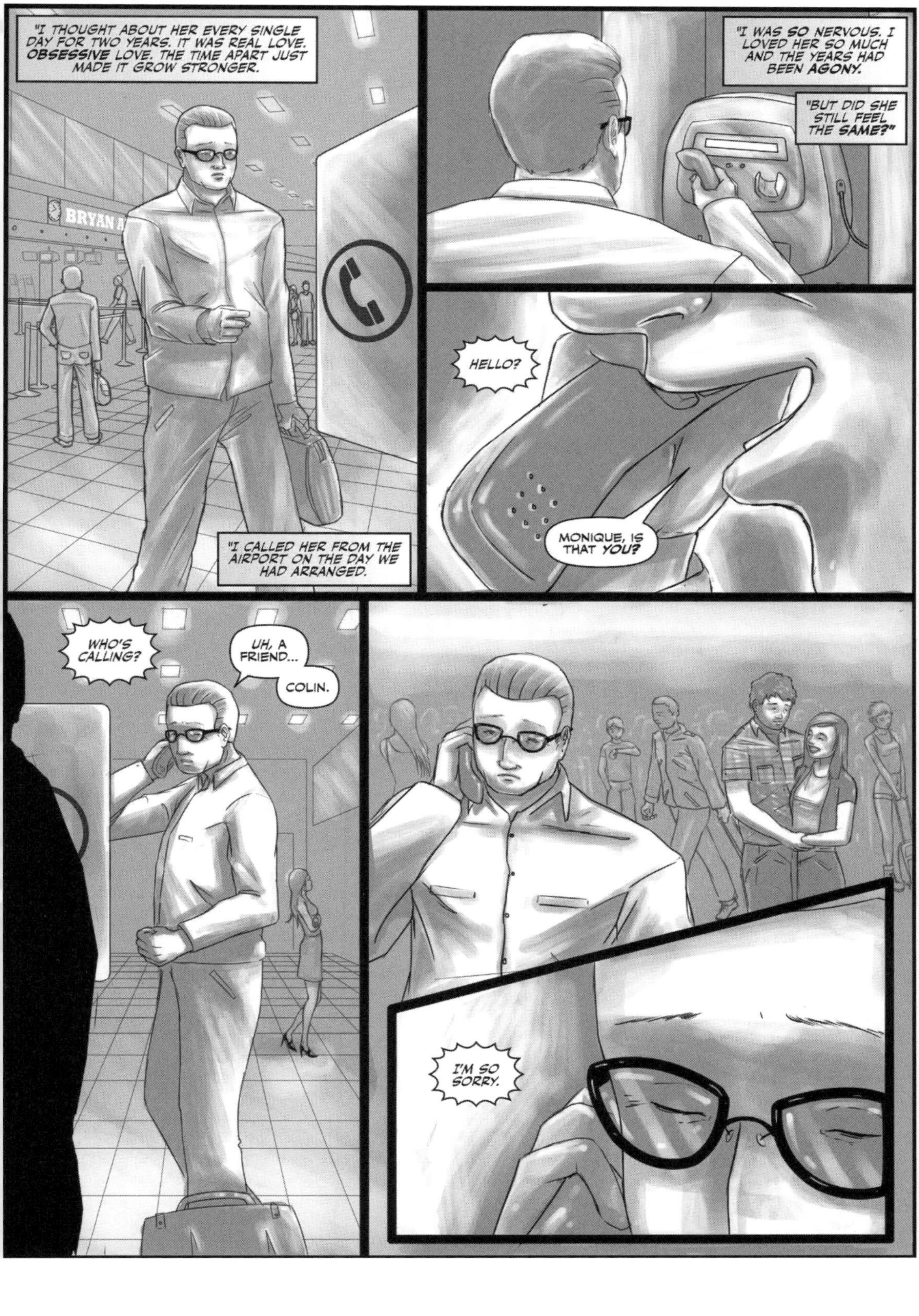
"I THOUGHT ABOUT HER EVERY SINGLE DAY FOR TWO YEARS. IT WAS REAL LOVE. OBSESSIVE LOVE. THE TIME APART JUST MADE IT GROW STRONGER.
BRYAN A
"I CALLED HER FROM THE AIRPORT ON THE DAY WE HAD ARRANGED.
"I WAS SO NERVOUS. I LOVED HER SO MUCH AND THE YEARS HAD BEEN AGONY.
"BUT DID SHE STILL FEEL THE SAME?"
HELLO?
MONIQUE, IS THAT YOU?
WHO'S CALLING?
UH, A FRIEND...
COLIN.
I'M SO SORRY.

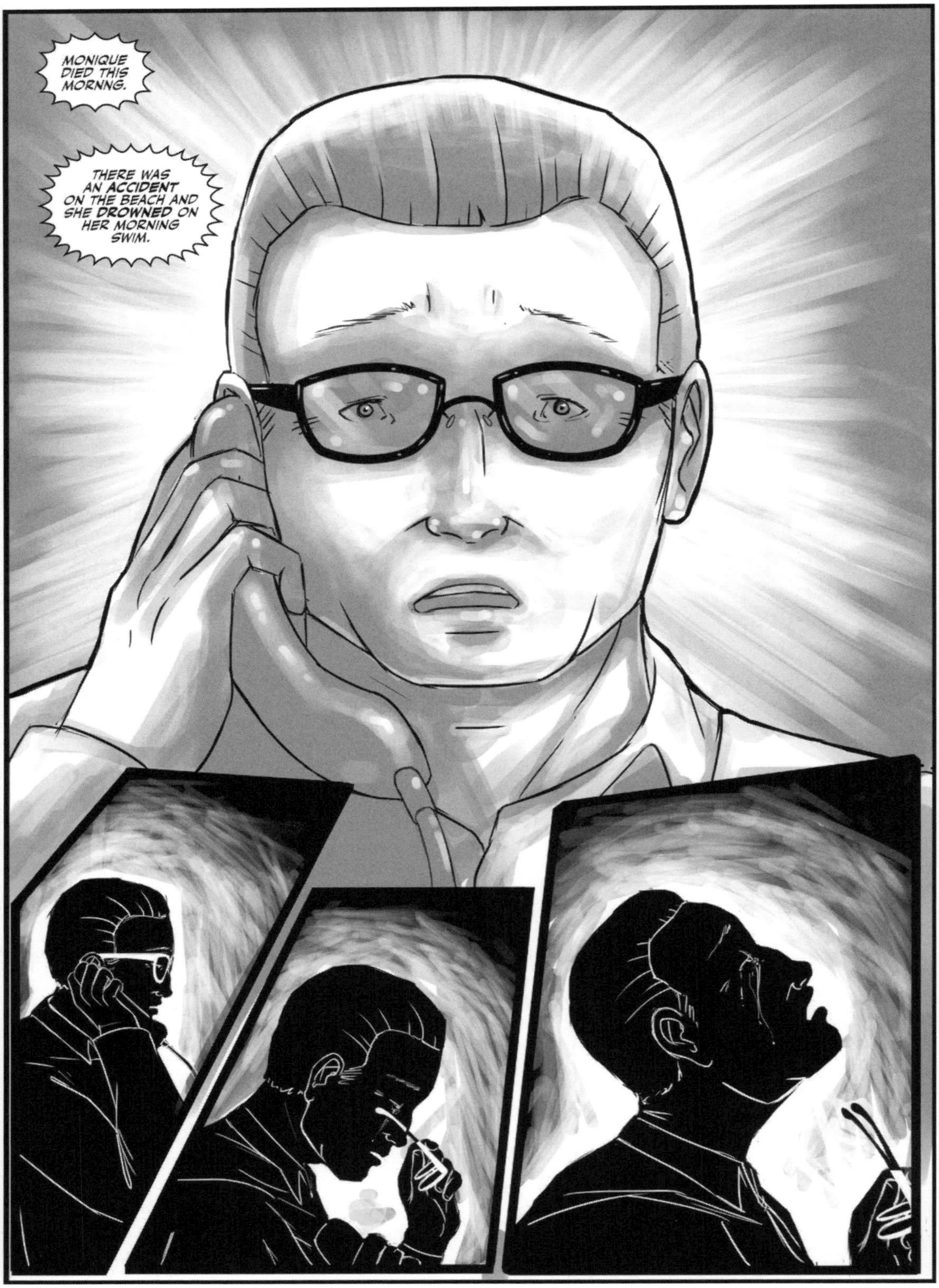
MONIQUE DIED THIS MORNNG.
THERE WAS AN ACCIDENT ON THE BEACH AND SHE DROWNED ON HER MORNING SWIM.

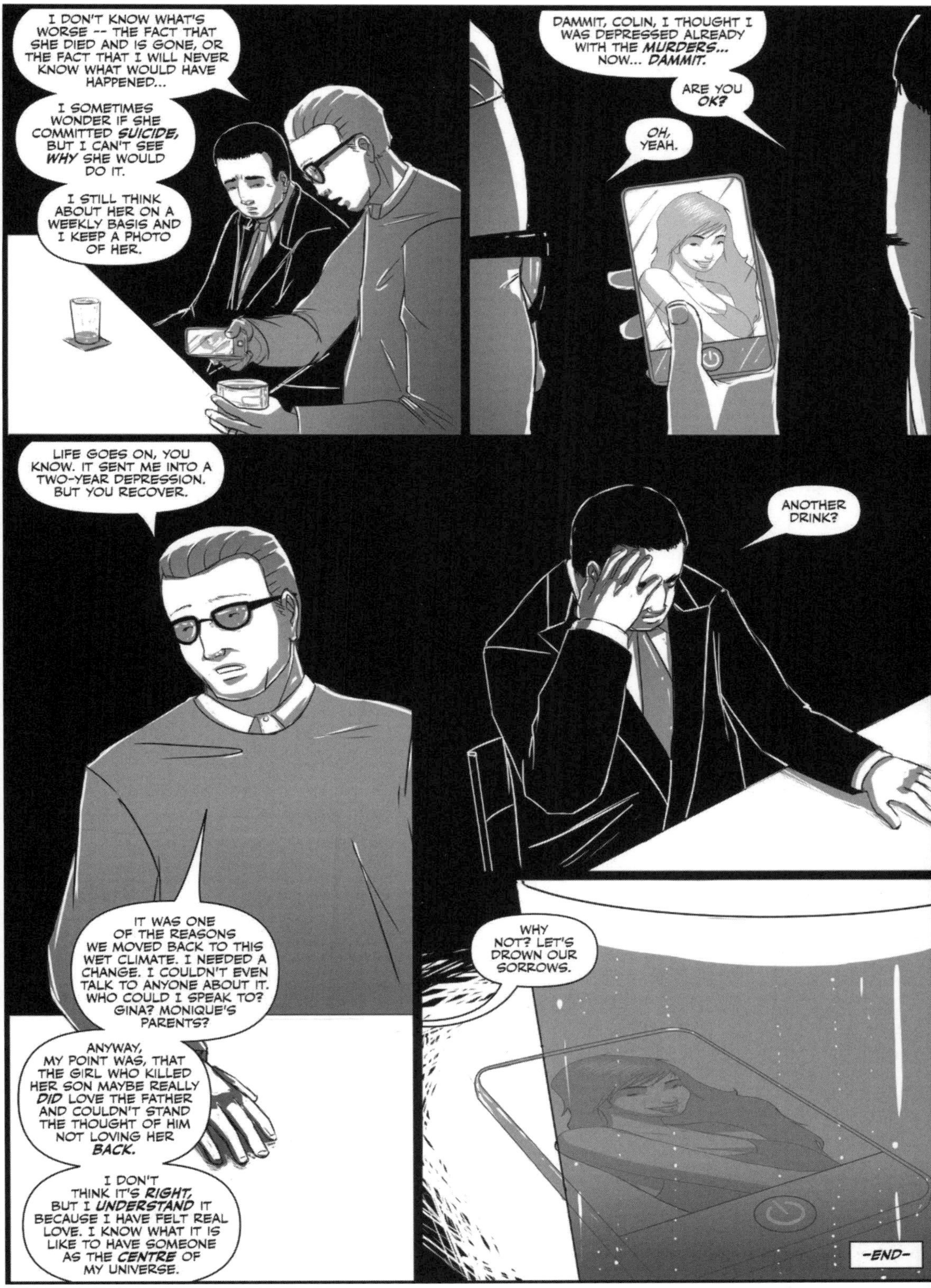
I DON'T KNOW WHAT'S WORSE -- THE FACT THAT SHE DIED AND IS GONE, OR THE FACT THAT I WILL NEVER KNOW WHAT WOULD HAVE HAPPENED...
I SOMETIMES WONDER IF SHE COMMITTED SUICIDE, BUT I CAN'T SEE WHY SHE WOULD DO IT.
I STILL THINK ABOUT HER ON A WEEKLY BASIS AND I KEEP A PHOTO OF HER.
DAMMIT, COLIN, I THOUGHT I WAS DEPRESSED ALREADY WITH THE MURDERS... NOW... DAMMIT.
ARE YOU OK?
OH, YEAH.
LIFE GOES ON, YOU KNOW. IT SENT ME INTO A TWO-YEAR DEPRESSION. BUT YOU RECOVER.
IT WAS ONE OF THE REASONS WE MOVED BACK TO THIS WET CLIMATE. I NEEDED A CHANGE. I COULDN'T EVEN TALK TO ANYONE ABOUT IT. WHO COULD I SPEAK TO? GINA? MONIQUE'S PARENTS?
ANYWAY, MY POINT WAS, THAT THE GIRL WHO KILLED HER SON MAYBE REALLY DID LOVE THE FATHER AND COULDN'T STAND THE THOUGHT OF HIM NOT LOVING HER BACK.
I DON'T THINK IT'S RIGHT, BUT I UNDERSTAND IT BECAUSE I HAVE FELT REAL LOVE. I KNOW WHAT IT IS LIKE TO HAVE SOMEONE AS THE CENTRE OF MY UNIVERSE.
ANOTHER DRINK?
WHY NOT? LET'S DROWN OUR SORROWS.
-END-

Drink Driving...

Drinking and driving is the number one criminal cause of death in Canada. Some of ICBC's most common excuses for drinking and driving include:

"I can handle my liquor."
"I'm more careful after a couple."
"I wasn't drinking / only smoked a joint."

Writer/Creator
Neil Gibson

Illustrator
Atula Siriwardane

www.tpub.co.uk

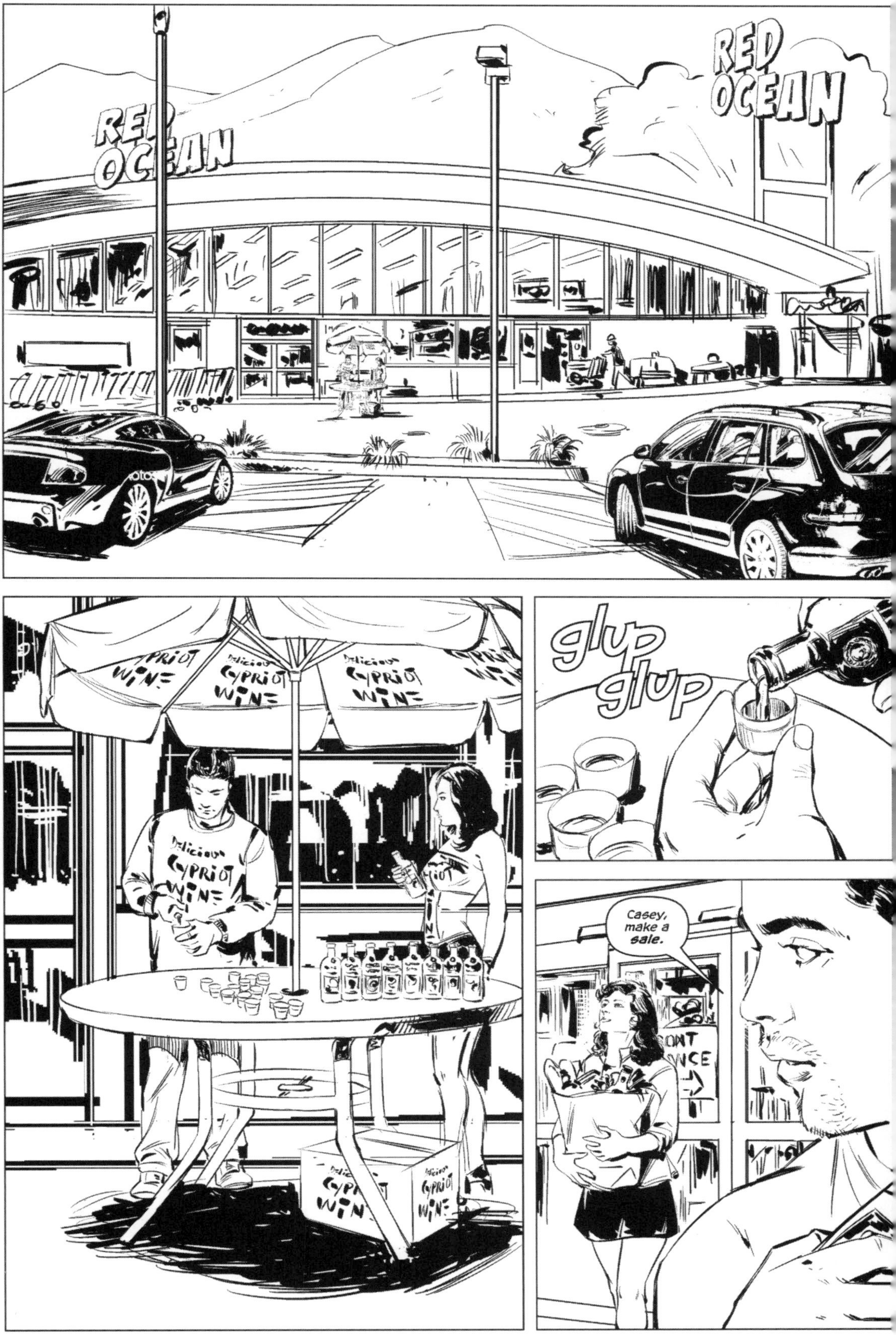
RED OCEAN
RED OCEAN
Delicious CYPRIOT WINE
glup glup
Casey, make a sale.

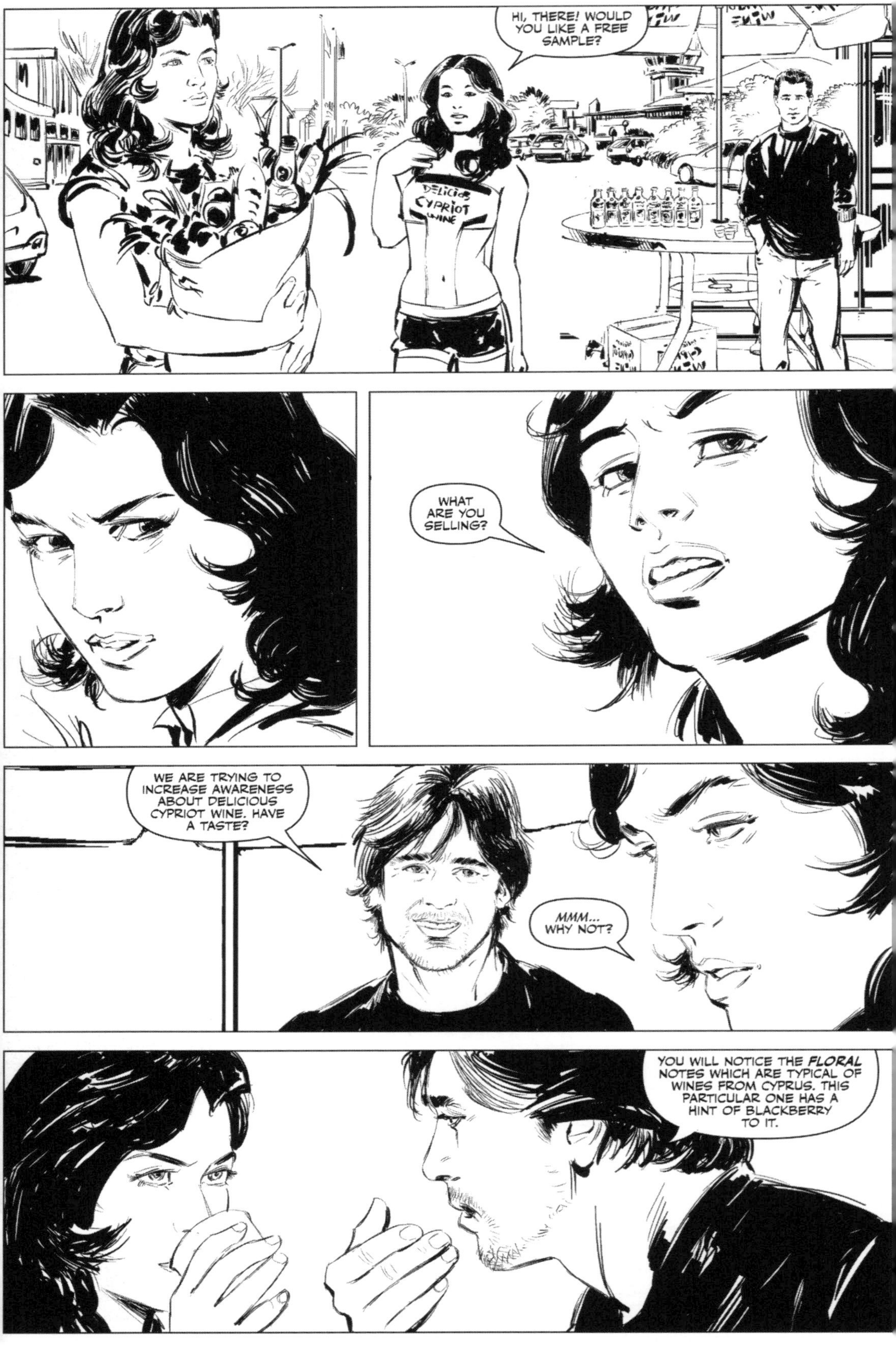
HI, THERE! WOULD YOU LIKE A FREE SAMPLE?
DELICIOS CYPRIOT WINE
WHAT ARE YOU SELLING?
WE ARE TRYING TO INCREASE AWARENESS ABOUT DELICIOUS CYPRIOT WINE. HAVE A TASTE?
MMM... WHY NOT?
YOU WILL NOTICE THE *FLORAL* NOTES WHICH ARE TYPICAL OF WINES FROM CYPRUS. THIS PARTICULAR ONE HAS A HINT OF BLACKBERRY TO IT.

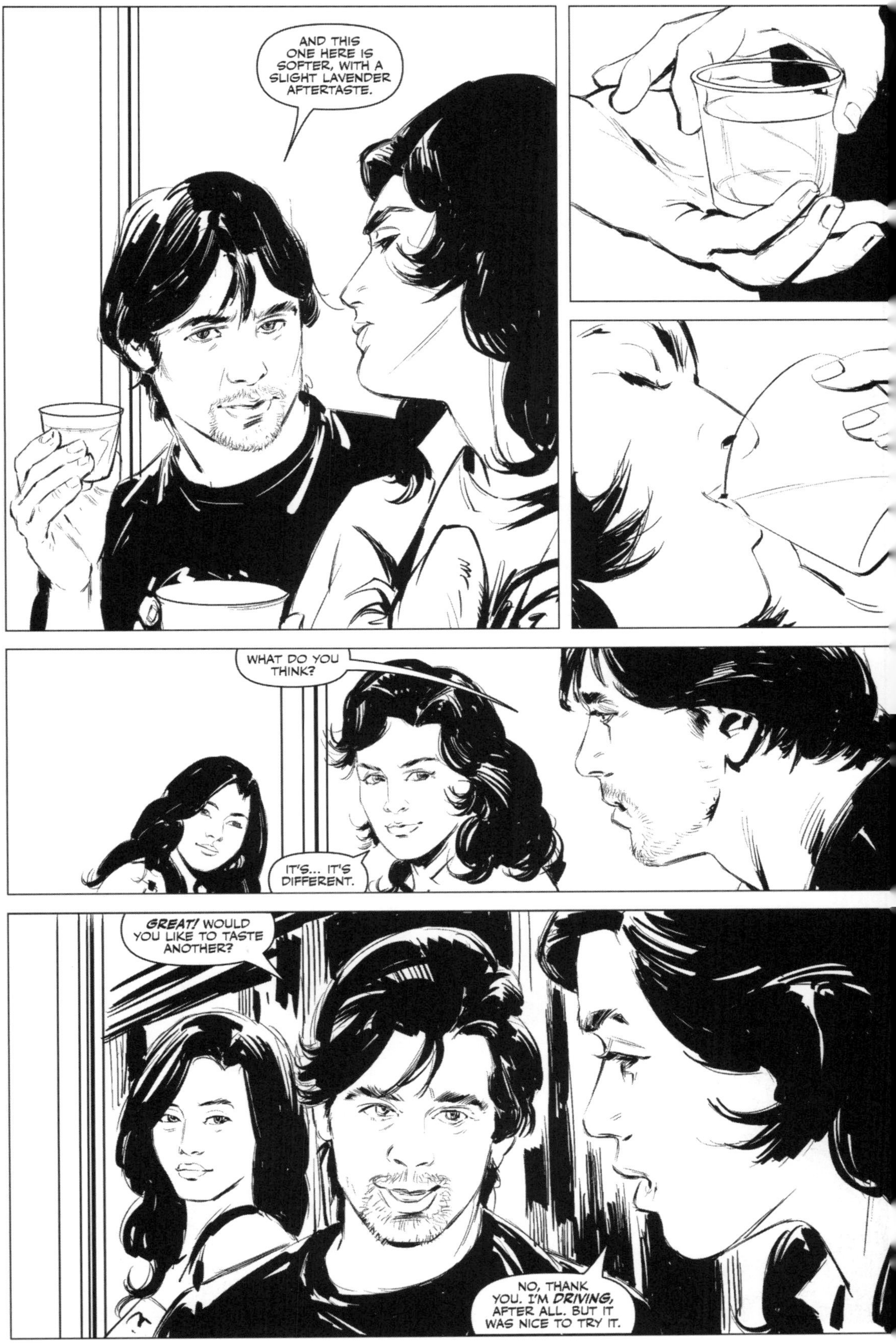
AND THIS ONE HERE IS SOFTER, WITH A SLIGHT LAVENDER AFTERTASTE.
WHAT DO YOU THINK?
IT'S... IT'S DIFFERENT.
GREAT! WOULD YOU LIKE TO TASTE ANOTHER?
NO, THANK YOU. I'M DRIVING, AFTER ALL. BUT IT WAS NICE TO TRY IT.

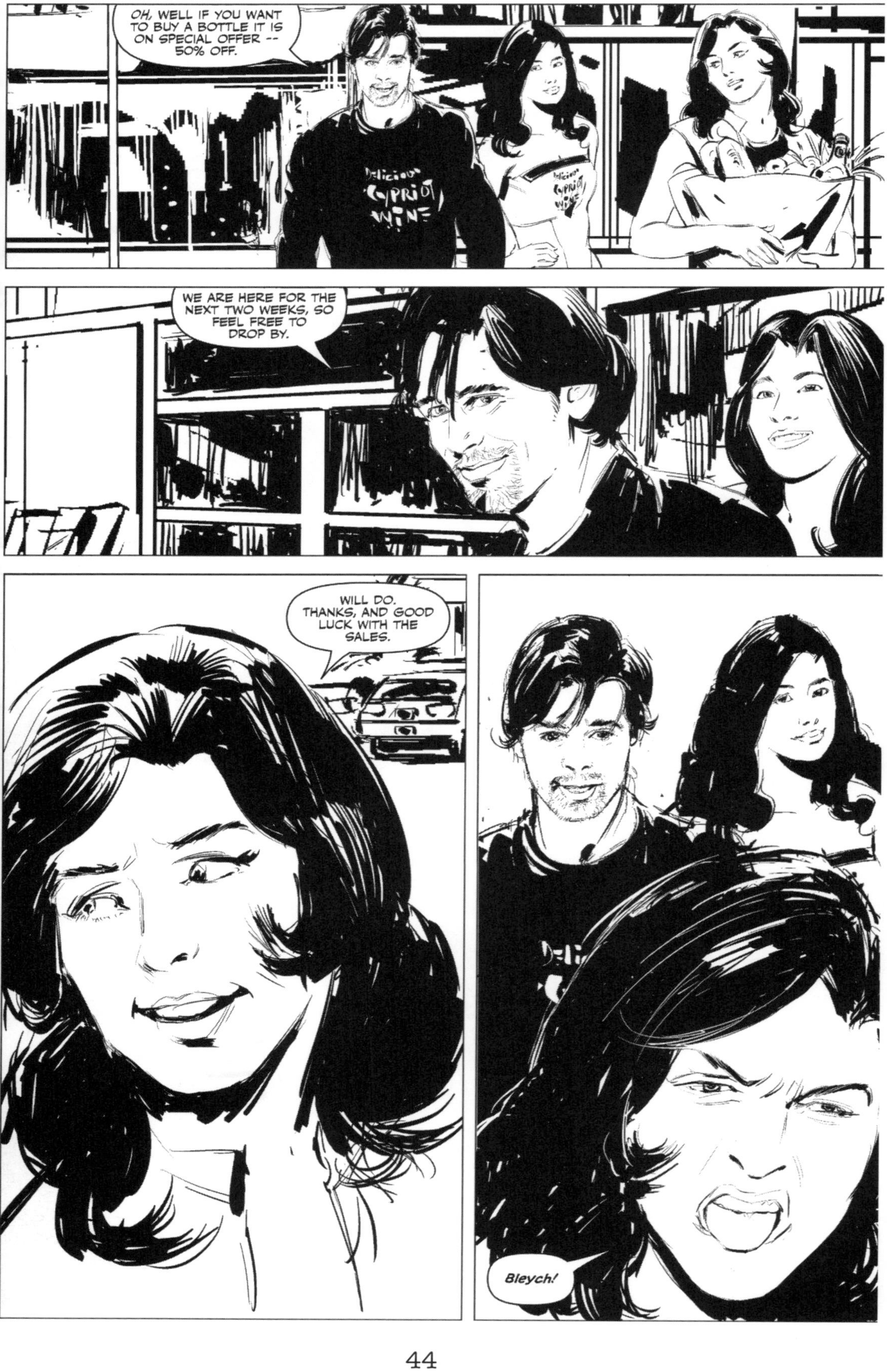
OH, WELL IF YOU WANT TO BUY A BOTTLE IT IS ON SPECIAL OFFER -- 50% OFF.
WE ARE HERE FOR THE NEXT TWO WEEKS, SO FEEL FREE TO DROP BY.
WILL DO. THANKS, AND GOOD LUCK WITH THE SALES.
Bleych!

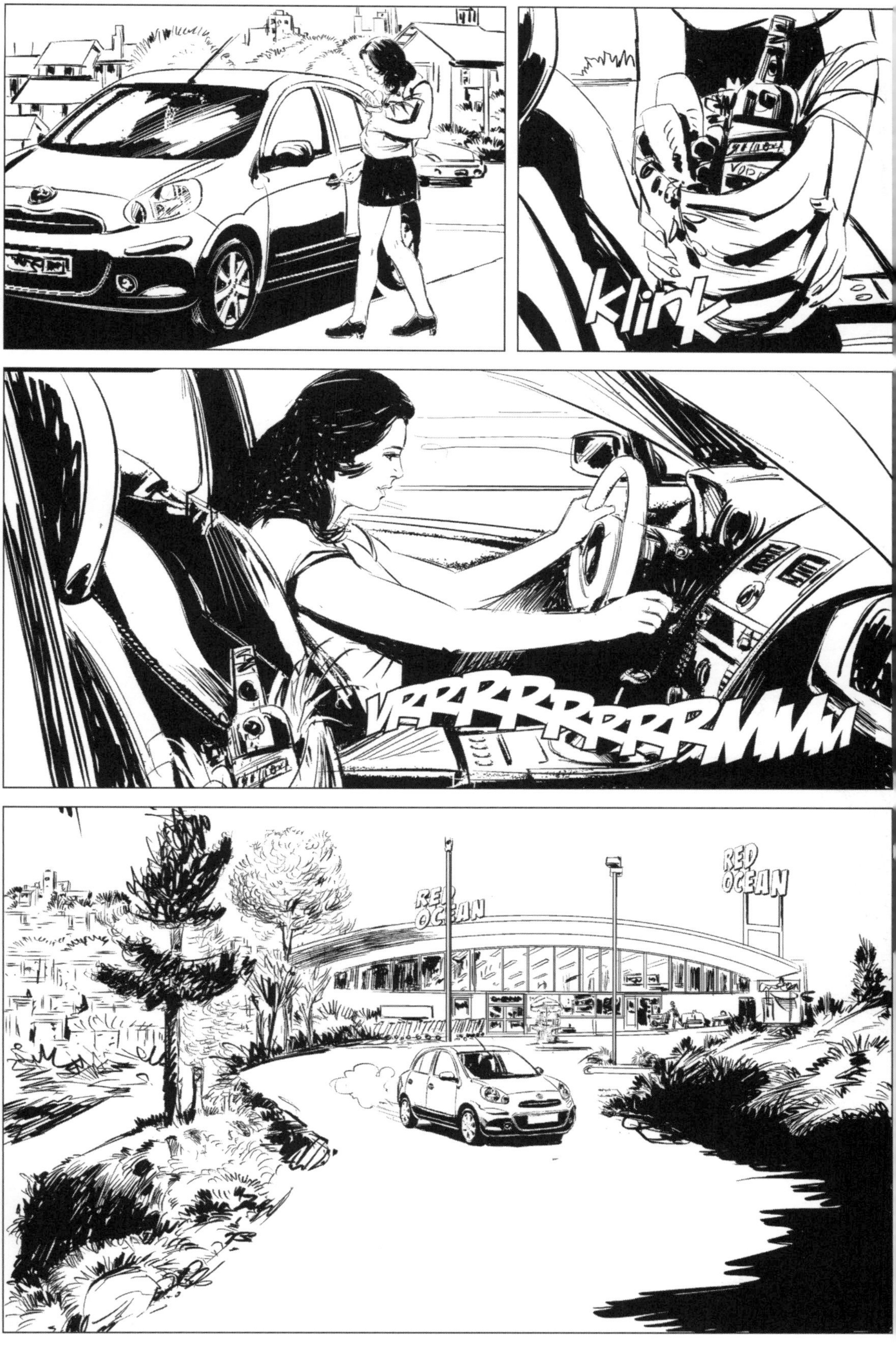
klink
VRRRRRRRRRMMMM
RED OCEAN
RED OCEAN

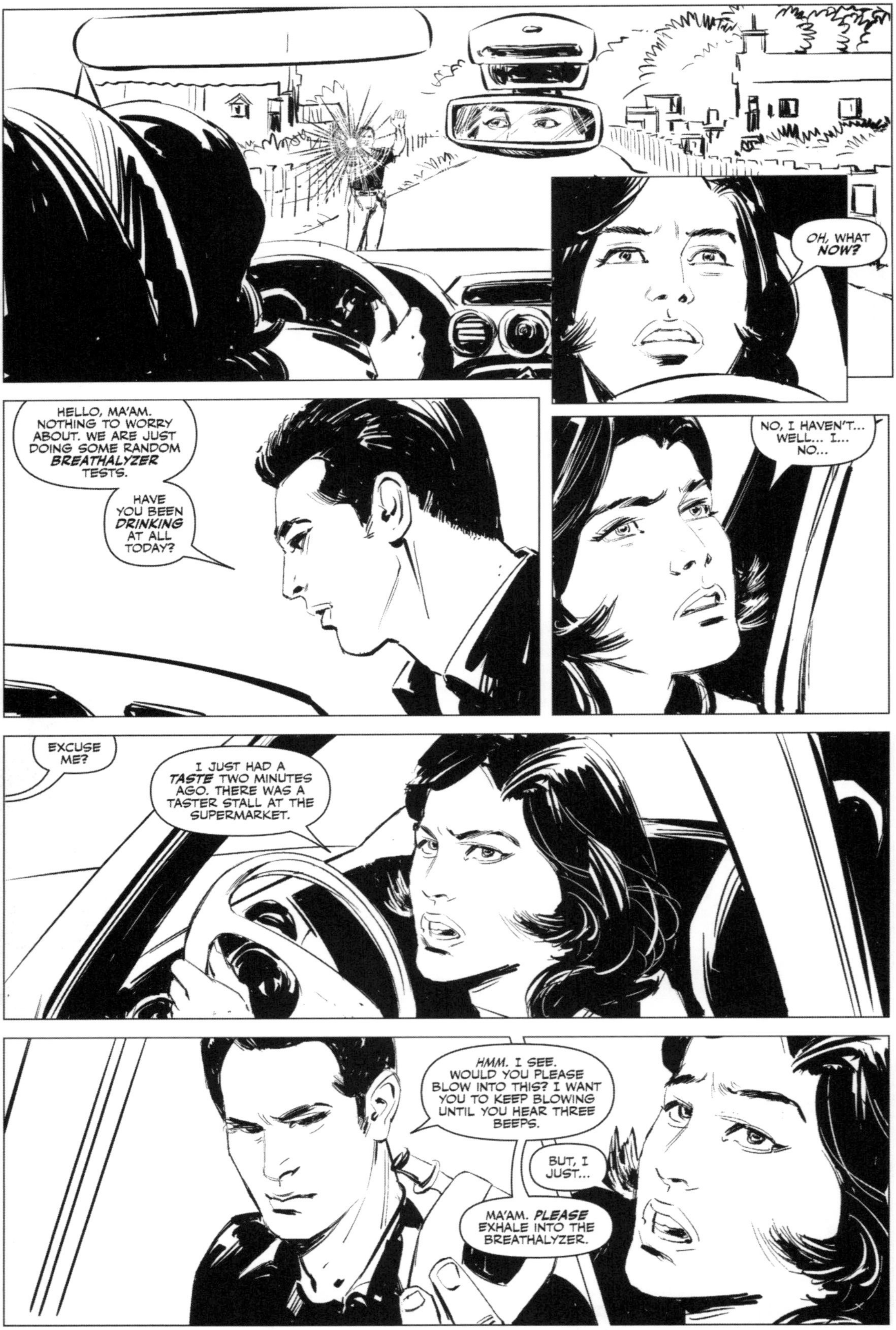
OH, WHAT *NOW?*
HELLO, MA'AM. NOTHING TO WORRY ABOUT. WE ARE JUST DOING SOME RANDOM *BREATHALYZER* TESTS.
HAVE YOU BEEN *DRINKING* AT ALL TODAY?
NO, I HAVEN'T... WELL... I... NO...
EXCUSE ME?
I JUST HAD A *TASTE* TWO MINUTES AGO. THERE WAS A TASTER STALL AT THE SUPERMARKET.
HMM. I SEE. WOULD YOU PLEASE BLOW INTO THIS? I WANT YOU TO KEEP BLOWING UNTIL YOU HEAR THREE BEEPS.
BUT, I JUST...
MA'AM. *PLEASE* EXHALE INTO THE BREATHALYZER.

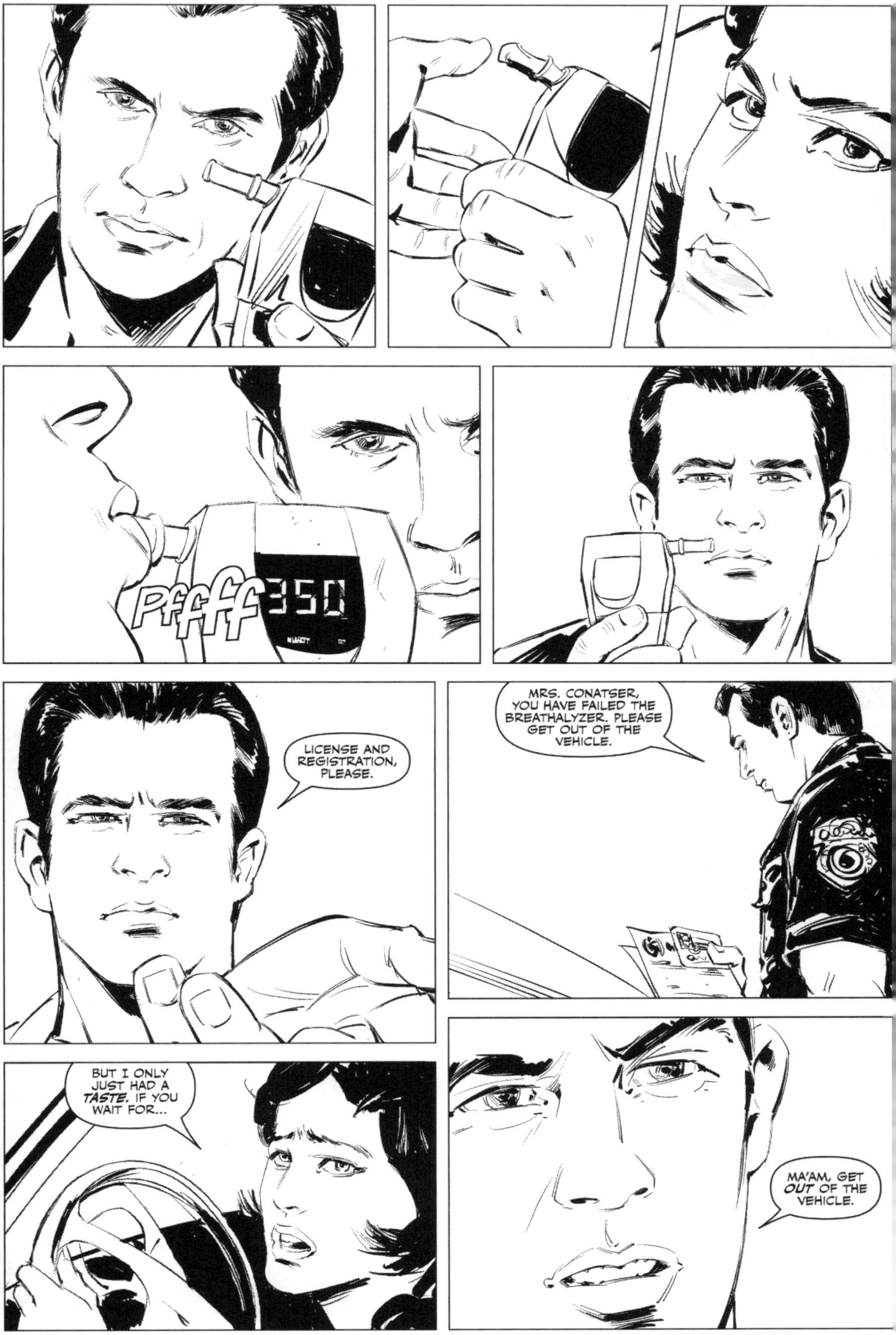
Pffff
350
LICENSE AND REGISTRATION, PLEASE.
MRS. CONATSER, YOU HAVE FAILED THE BREATHALYZER. PLEASE GET OUT OF THE VEHICLE.
BUT I ONLY JUST HAD A *TASTE.* IF YOU WAIT FOR...
MA'AM, GET *OUT* OF THE VEHICLE.

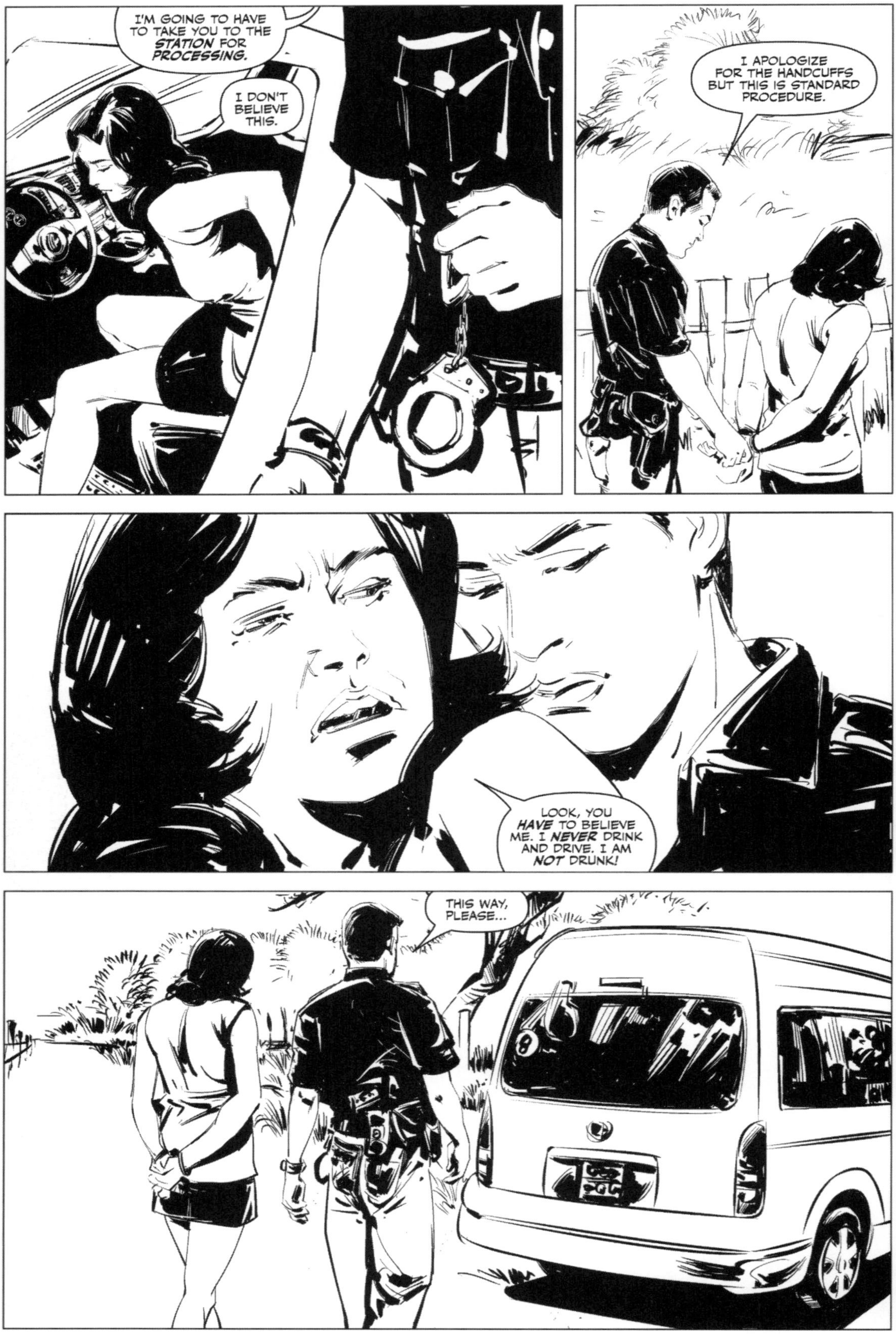
I'M GOING TO HAVE TO TAKE YOU TO THE *STATION* FOR *PROCESSING.*
I DON'T BELIEVE THIS.
I APOLOGIZE FOR THE HANDCUFFS BUT THIS IS STANDARD PROCEDURE.
LOOK, YOU *HAVE* TO BELIEVE ME. I *NEVER* DRINK AND DRIVE. I AM *NOT* DRUNK!
THIS WAY, PLEASE...

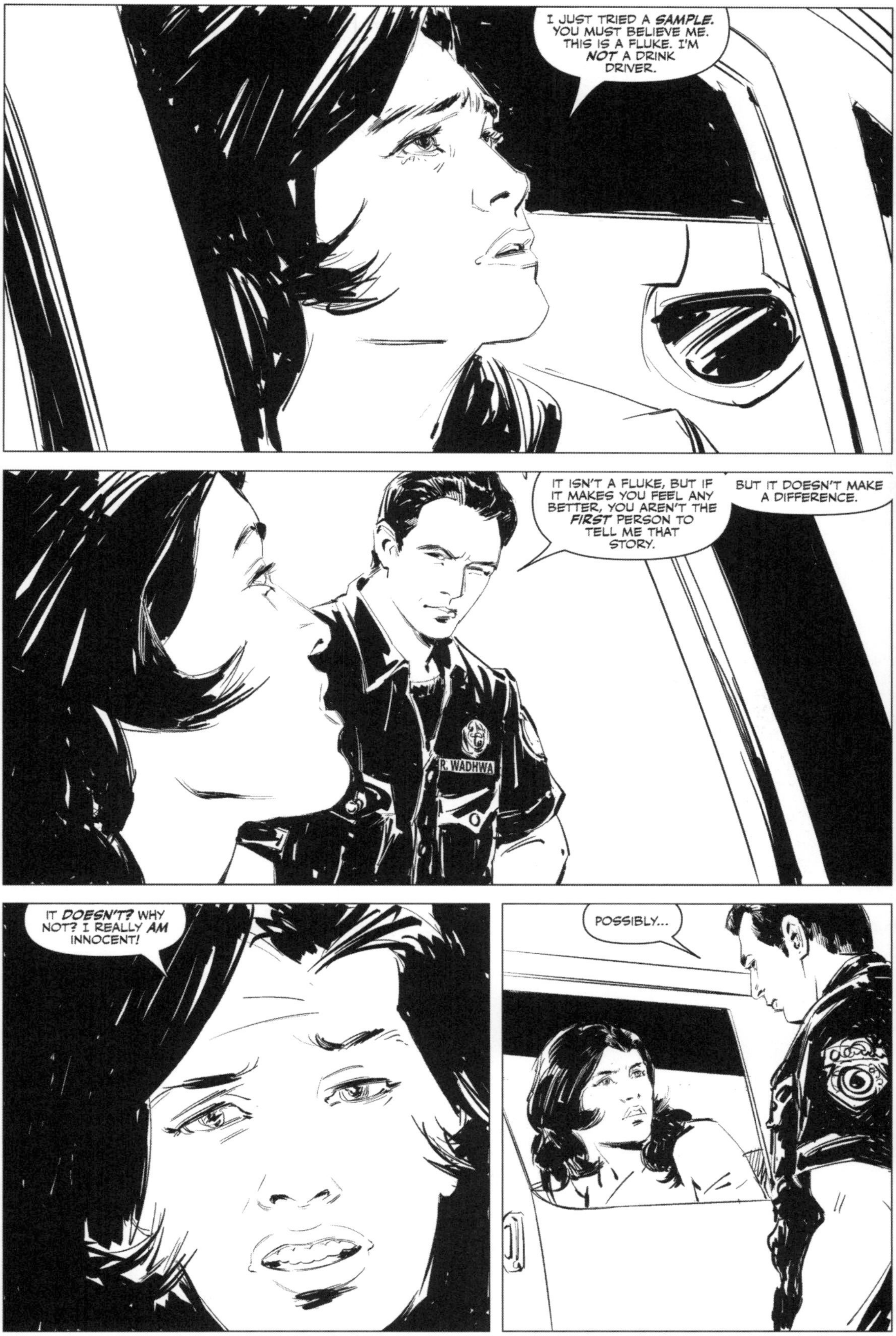
I JUST TRIED A SAMPLE. YOU MUST BELIEVE ME. THIS IS A FLUKE. I'M NOT A DRINK DRIVER.
IT ISN'T A FLUKE, BUT IF IT MAKES YOU FEEL ANY BETTER, YOU AREN'T THE FIRST PERSON TO TELL ME THAT STORY.
BUT IT DOESN'T MAKE A DIFFERENCE.
R. WADHWA
IT DOESN'T? WHY NOT? I REALLY AM INNOCENT!
POSSIBLY...

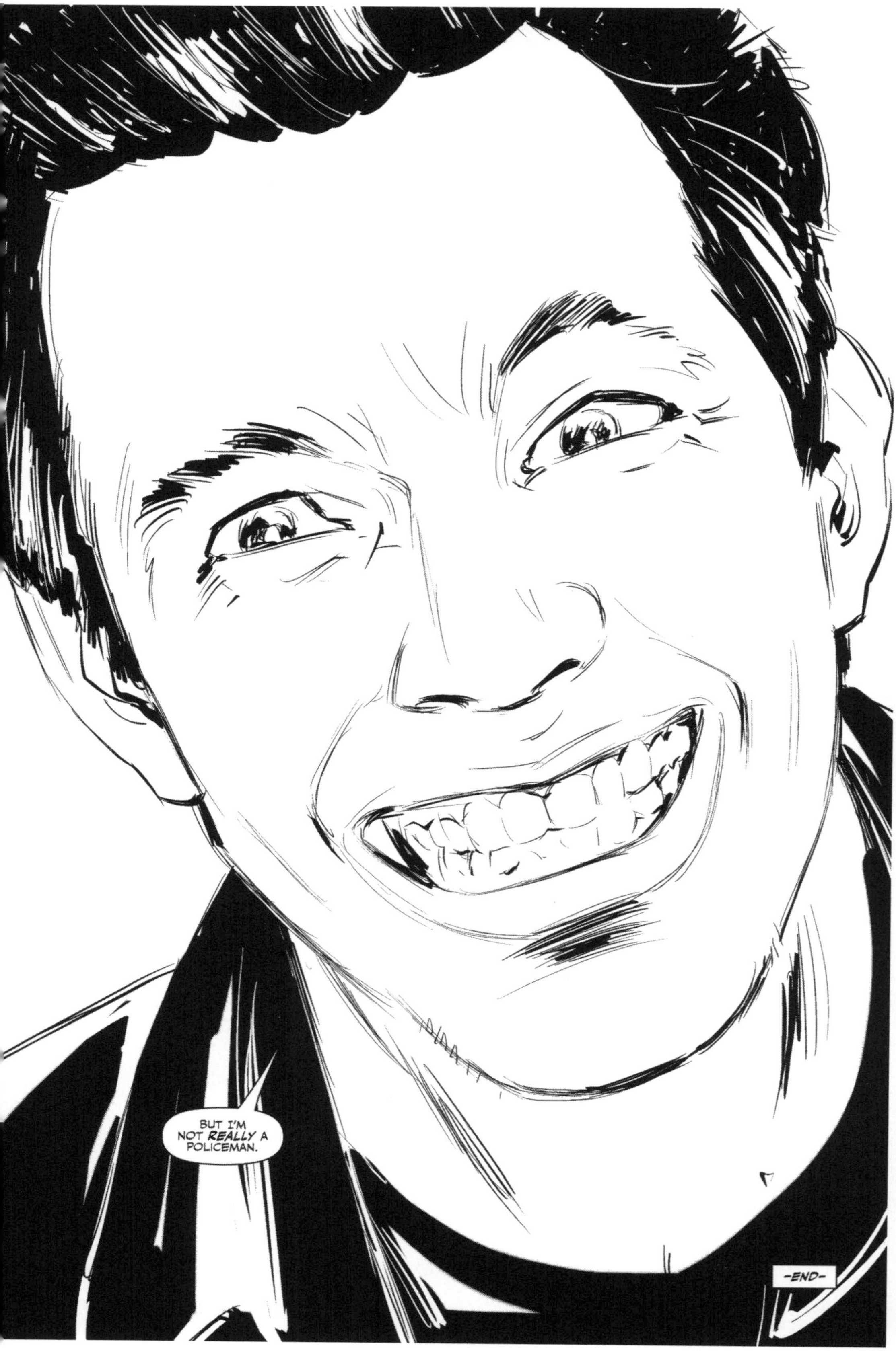
BUT I'M NOT *REALLY* A POLICEMAN.
-END-

Hitting Back

"Between 40,000 to 100,000 Nigerians are currently living in South Africa, of which only 4,000 have the legal right to be there. Nigerian criminal networks now dominate the ranks of the street dealers."

– Vermaat, E. (2010) The Problem with Africa: Illegal Immigrants, Crime, Terrorism, Polygamy and AIDS

Writer/Creator
Neil Gibson

Illustrator
Jake Elphick &
Caspar Wijngaard

www.tpub.co.uk

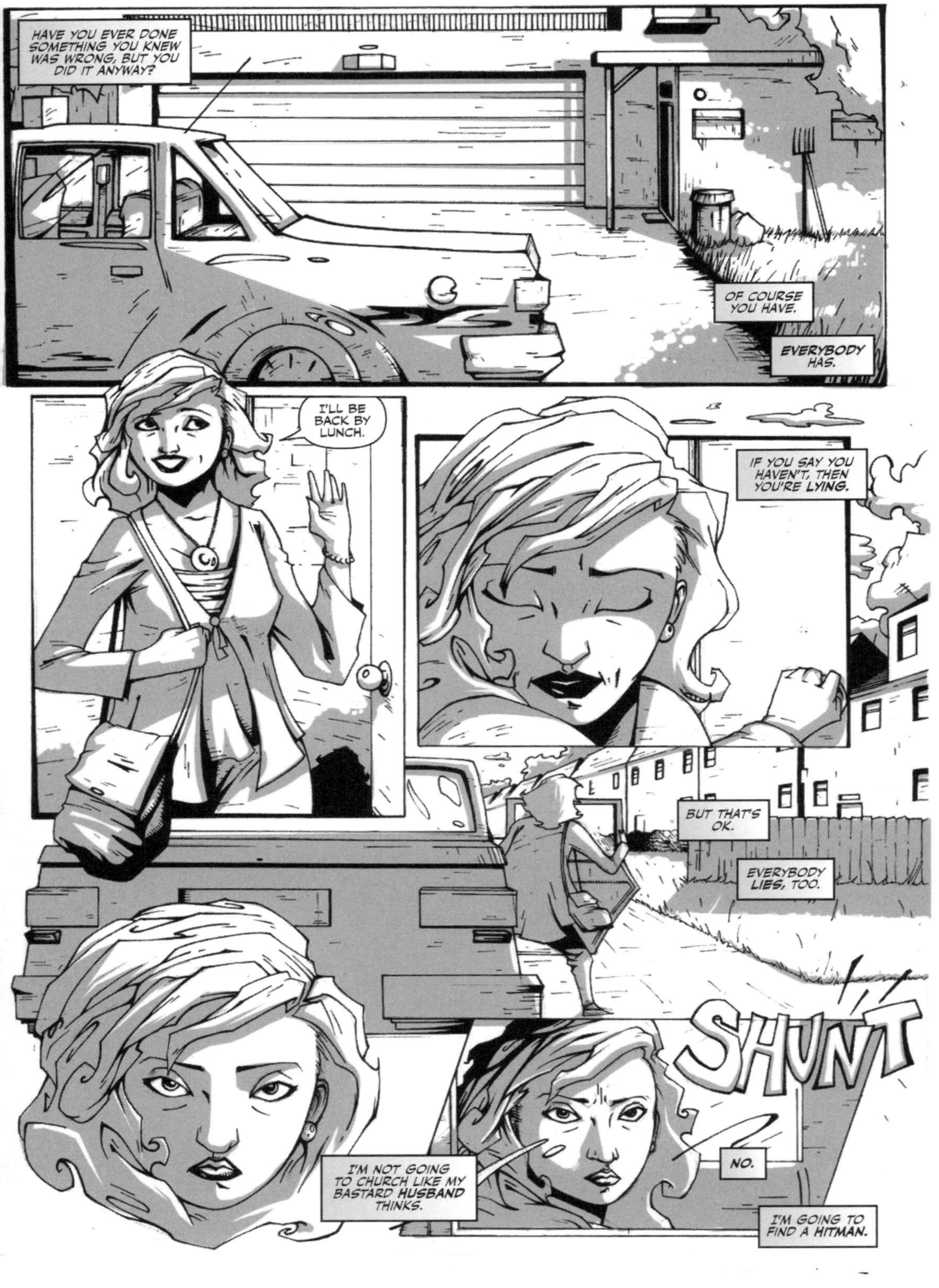
HAVE YOU EVER DONE SOMETHING YOU KNEW WAS WRONG, BUT YOU DID IT ANYWAY?
OF COURSE YOU HAVE.
EVERYBODY HAS.
I'LL BE BACK BY LUNCH.
IF YOU SAY YOU HAVEN'T, THEN YOU'RE LYING.
BUT THAT'S OK.
EVERYBODY LIES, TOO.
SHUNT
I'M NOT GOING TO CHURCH LIKE MY BASTARD HUSBAND THINKS.
NO.
I'M GOING TO FIND A HITMAN.

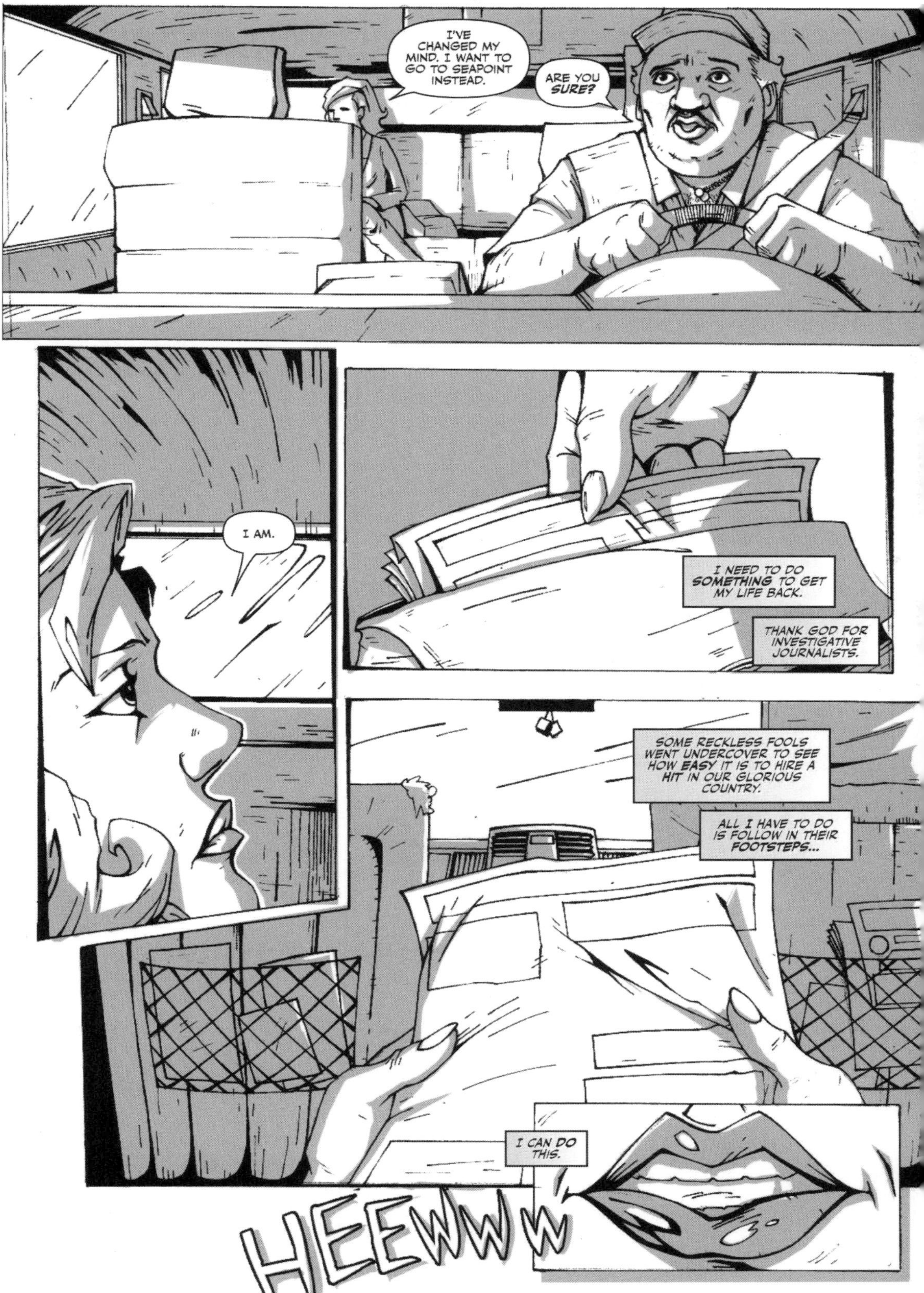
I'VE CHANGED MY MIND. I WANT TO GO TO SEAPOINT INSTEAD.
ARE YOU SURE?
I AM.
I NEED TO DO SOMETHING TO GET MY LIFE BACK.
THANK GOD FOR INVESTIGATIVE JOURNALISTS.
SOME RECKLESS FOOLS WENT UNDERCOVER TO SEE HOW EASY IT IS TO HIRE A HIT IN OUR GLORIOUS COUNTRY.
ALL I HAVE TO DO IS FOLLOW IN THEIR FOOTSTEPS...
I CAN DO THIS.
HEEWWW

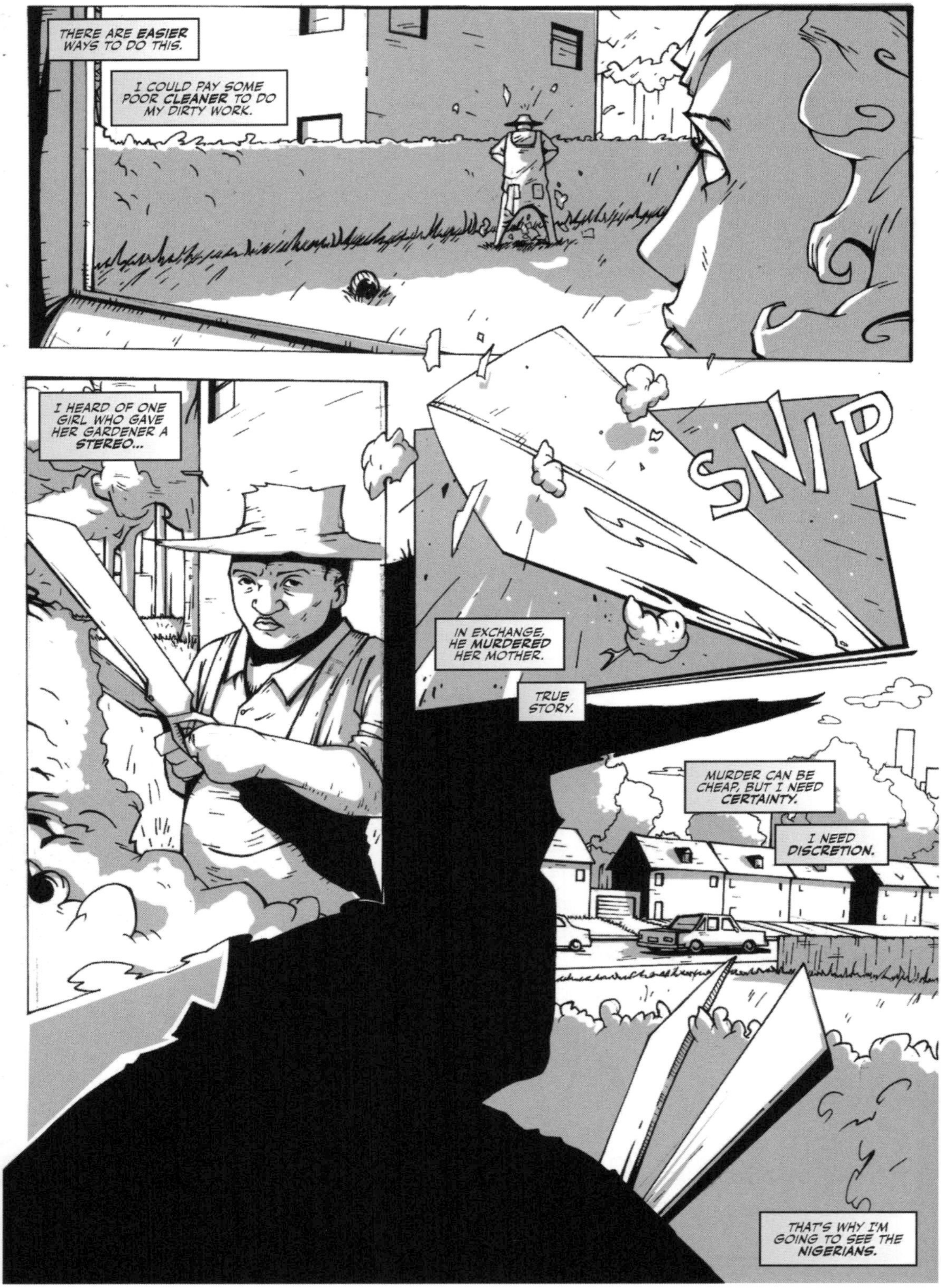
THERE ARE EASIER WAYS TO DO THIS.
I COULD PAY SOME POOR CLEANER TO DO MY DIRTY WORK.
I HEARD OF ONE GIRL WHO GAVE HER GARDENER A STEREO...
SNIP
IN EXCHANGE, HE MURDERED HER MOTHER.
TRUE STORY.
MURDER CAN BE CHEAP, BUT I NEED CERTAINTY.
I NEED DISCRETION.
THAT'S WHY I'M GOING TO SEE THE NIGERIANS.

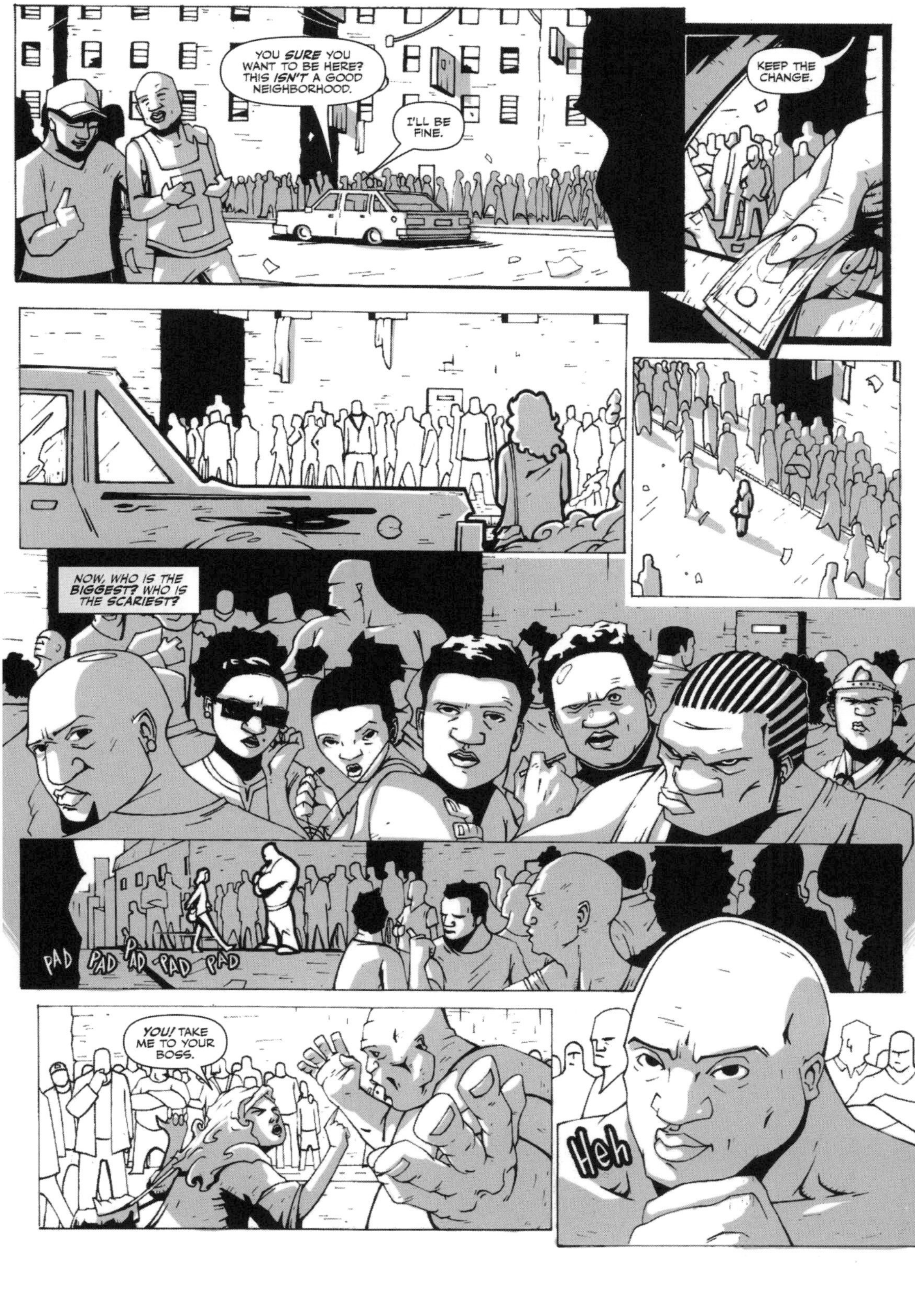

YOU SURE YOU WANT TO BE HERE? THIS ISN'T A GOOD NEIGHBORHOOD.
I'LL BE FINE.
KEEP THE CHANGE.
NOW, WHO IS THE BIGGEST? WHO IS THE SCARIEST?
PAD PAD PAD PAD PAD
YOU! TAKE ME TO YOUR BOSS.
Heh

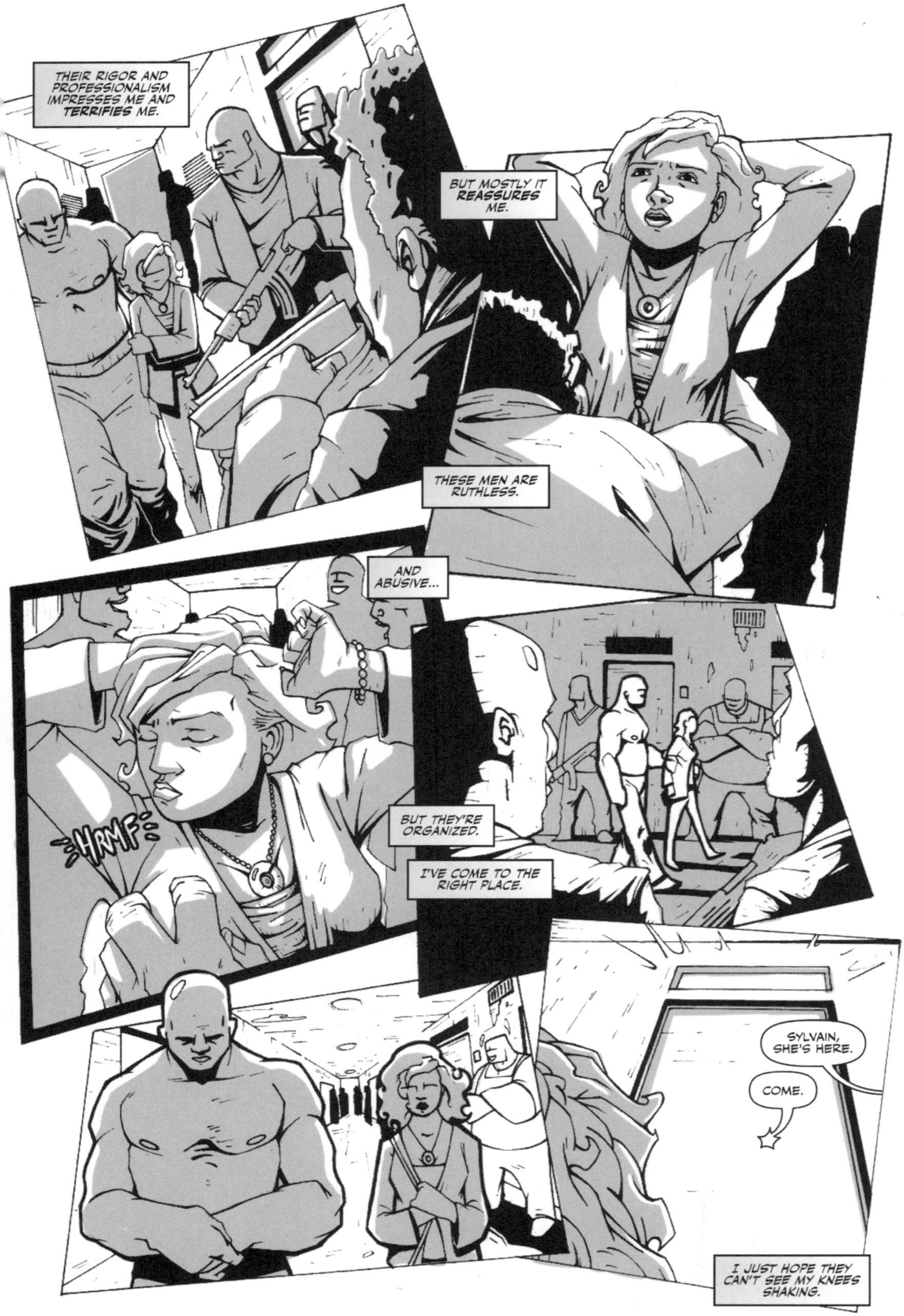
THEIR RIGOR AND PROFESSIONALISM IMPRESSES ME AND TERRIFIES ME.
BUT MOSTLY IT REASSURES ME.
THESE MEN ARE RUTHLESS.
AND ABUSIVE...
HRMF
BUT THEY'RE ORGANIZED.
I'VE COME TO THE RIGHT PLACE.
SYLVAIN, SHE'S HERE.
COME.
I JUST HOPE THEY CAN'T SEE MY KNEES SHAKING.

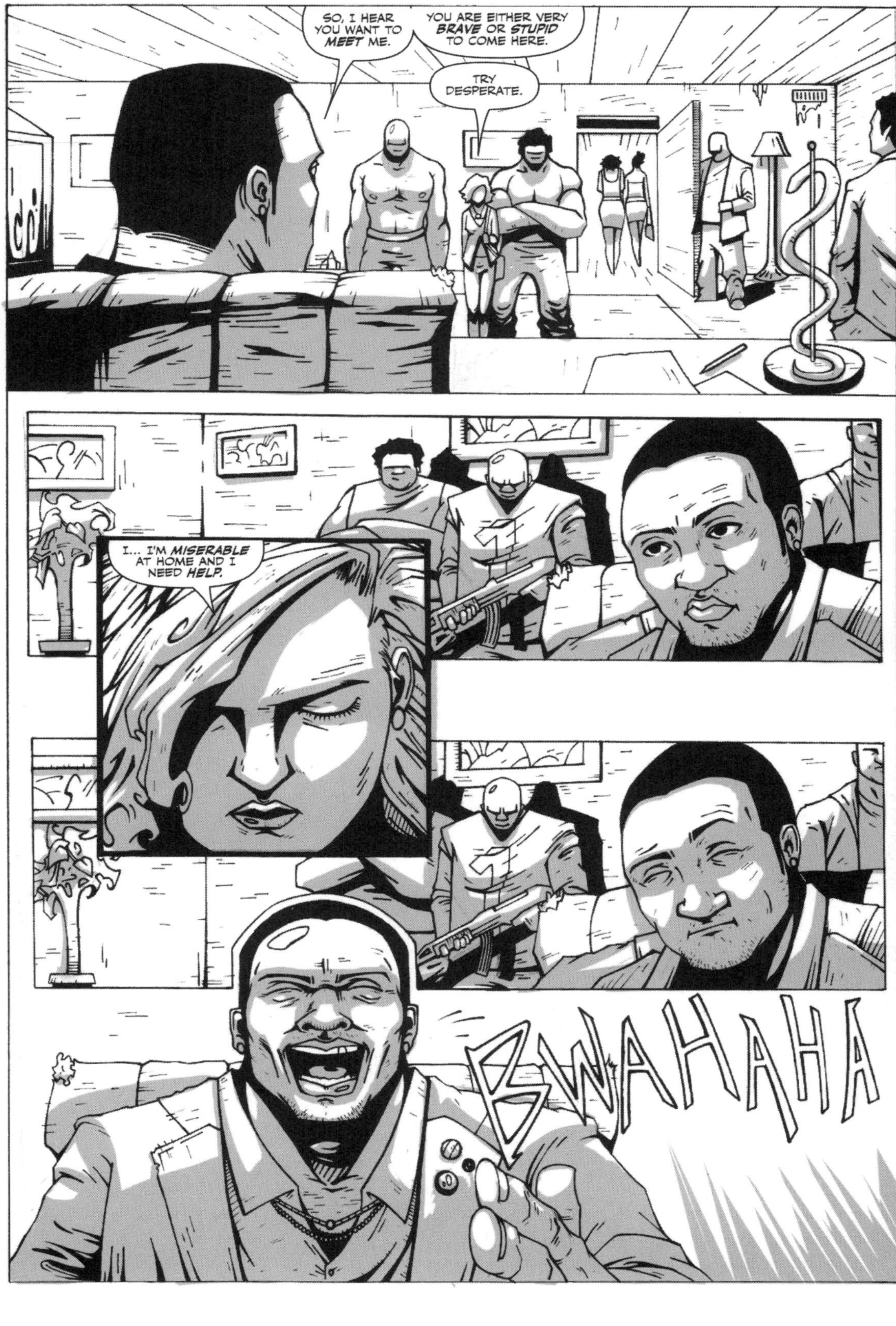
SO, I HEAR YOU WANT TO MEET ME.
YOU ARE EITHER VERY BRAVE OR STUPID TO COME HERE.
TRY DESPERATE.
I... I'M MISERABLE AT HOME AND I NEED HELP.
BWAHAHA

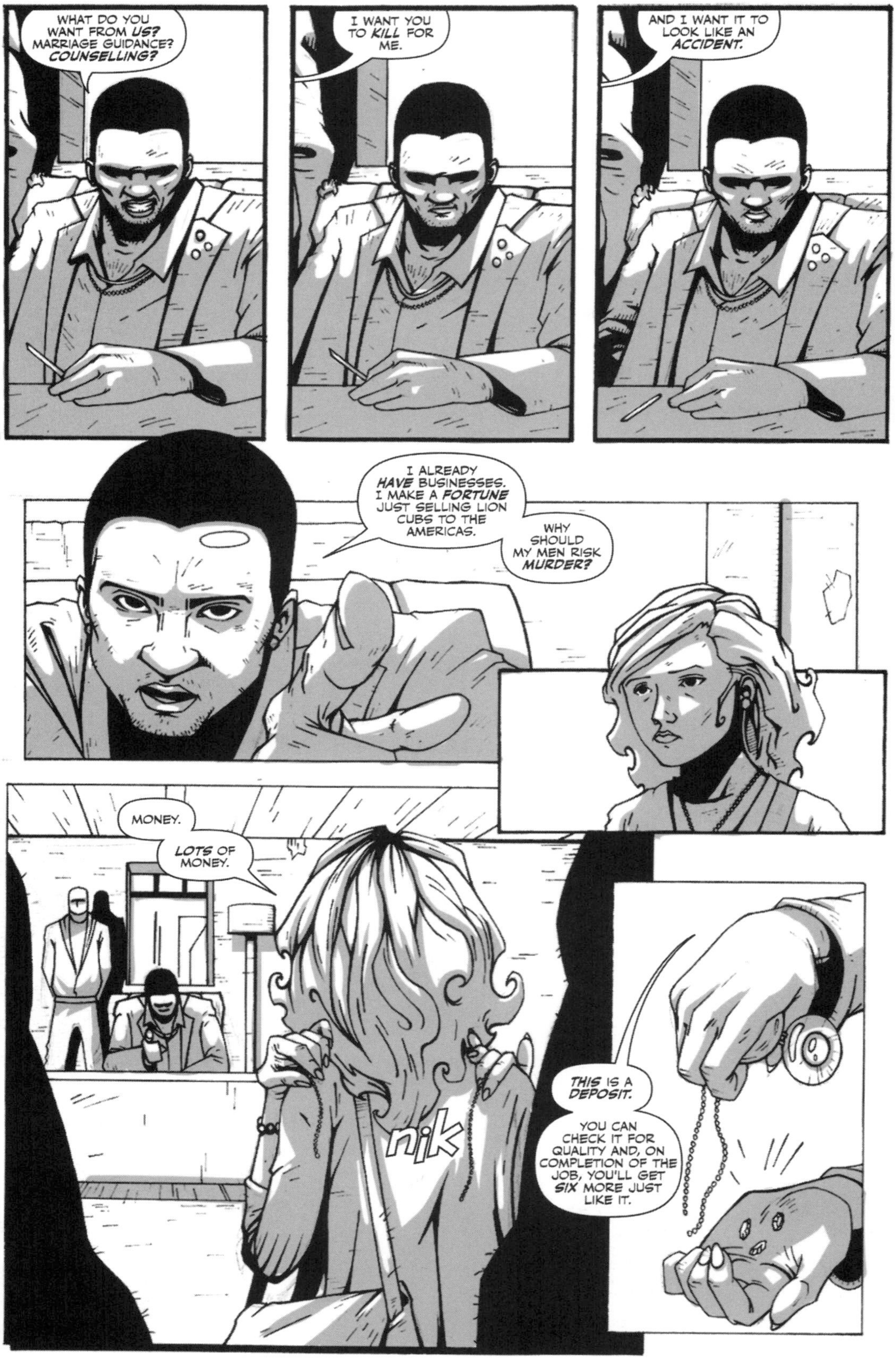
WHAT DO YOU WANT FROM US? MARRIAGE GUIDANCE? COUNSELLING?
I WANT YOU TO KILL FOR ME.
AND I WANT IT TO LOOK LIKE AN ACCIDENT.
I ALREADY HAVE BUSINESSES. I MAKE A FORTUNE JUST SELLING LION CUBS TO THE AMERICAS.
WHY SHOULD MY MEN RISK MURDER?
MONEY.
LOTS OF MONEY.
THIS IS A DEPOSIT.
YOU CAN CHECK IT FOR QUALITY AND, ON COMPLETION OF THE JOB, YOU'LL GET SIX MORE JUST LIKE IT.
nik

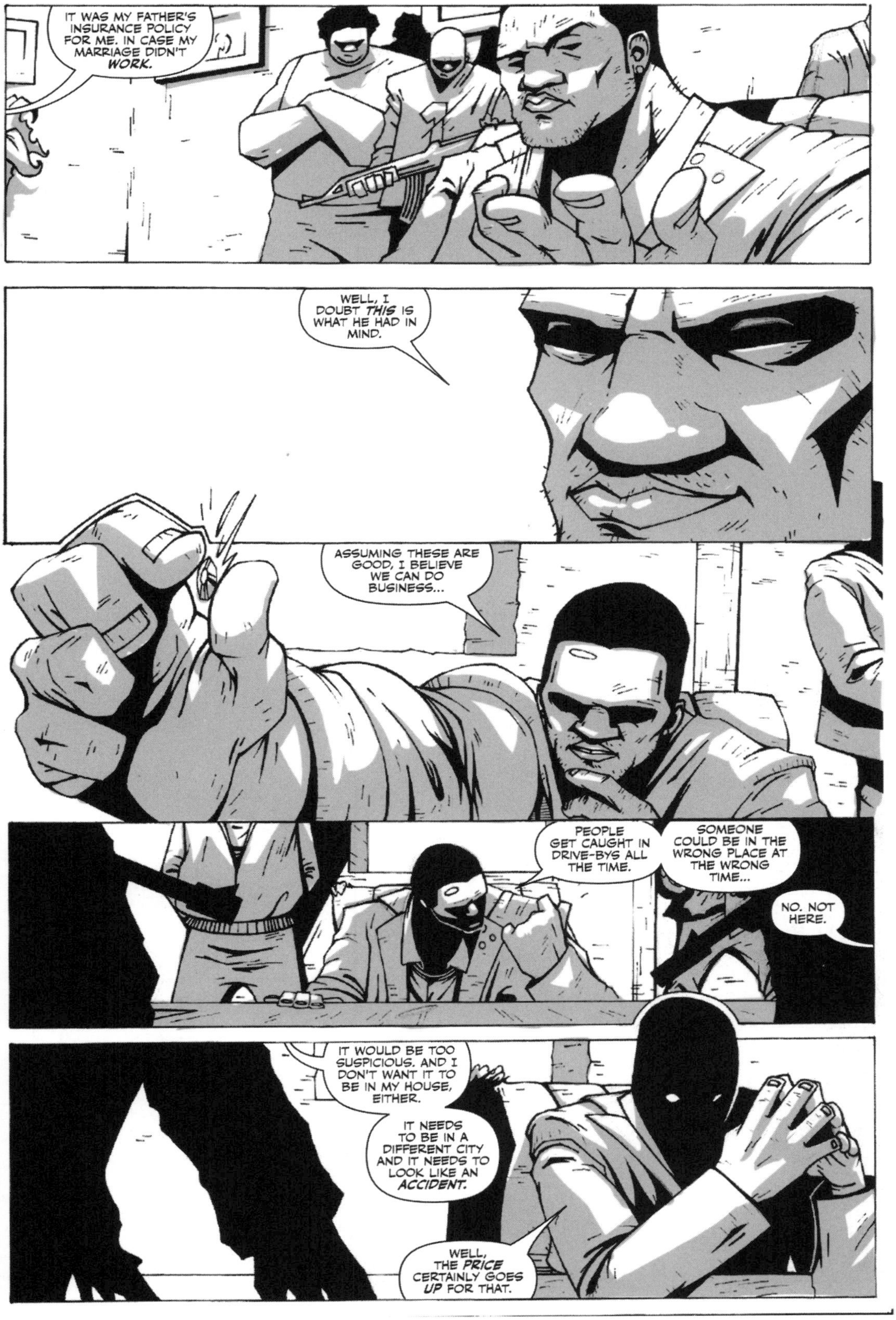

IT WAS MY FATHER'S INSURANCE POLICY FOR ME. IN CASE MY MARRIAGE DIDN'T *WORK.*
WELL, I DOUBT *THIS* IS WHAT HE HAD IN MIND.
ASSUMING THESE ARE GOOD, I BELIEVE WE CAN DO BUSINESS...
PEOPLE GET CAUGHT IN DRIVE-BYS ALL THE TIME.
SOMEONE COULD BE IN THE WRONG PLACE AT THE WRONG TIME...
NO. NOT HERE.
IT WOULD BE TOO SUSPICIOUS. AND I DON'T WANT IT TO BE IN MY HOUSE, EITHER.
IT NEEDS TO BE IN A DIFFERENT CITY AND IT NEEDS TO LOOK LIKE AN *ACCIDENT.*
WELL, THE *PRICE* CERTAINLY GOES *UP* FOR THAT.

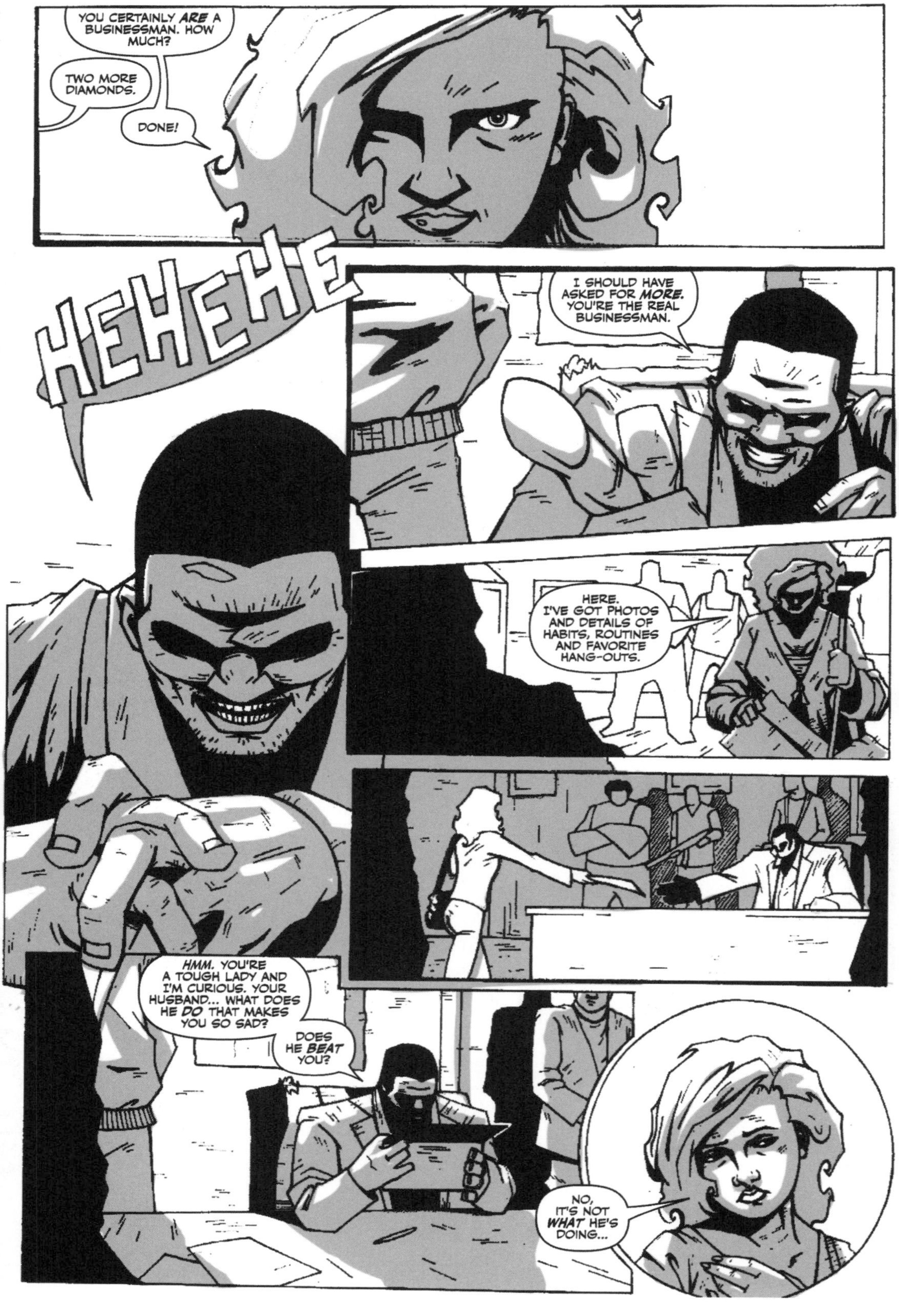
YOU CERTAINLY ARE A BUSINESSMAN. HOW MUCH?
TWO MORE DIAMONDS.
DONE!
HEHEHE
I SHOULD HAVE ASKED FOR MORE. YOU'RE THE REAL BUSINESSMAN.
HERE. I'VE GOT PHOTOS AND DETAILS OF HABITS, ROUTINES AND FAVORITE HANG-OUTS.
HMM. YOU'RE A TOUGH LADY AND I'M CURIOUS. YOUR HUSBAND... WHAT DOES HE DO THAT MAKES YOU SO SAD?
DOES HE BEAT YOU?
NO, IT'S NOT WHAT HE'S DOING...

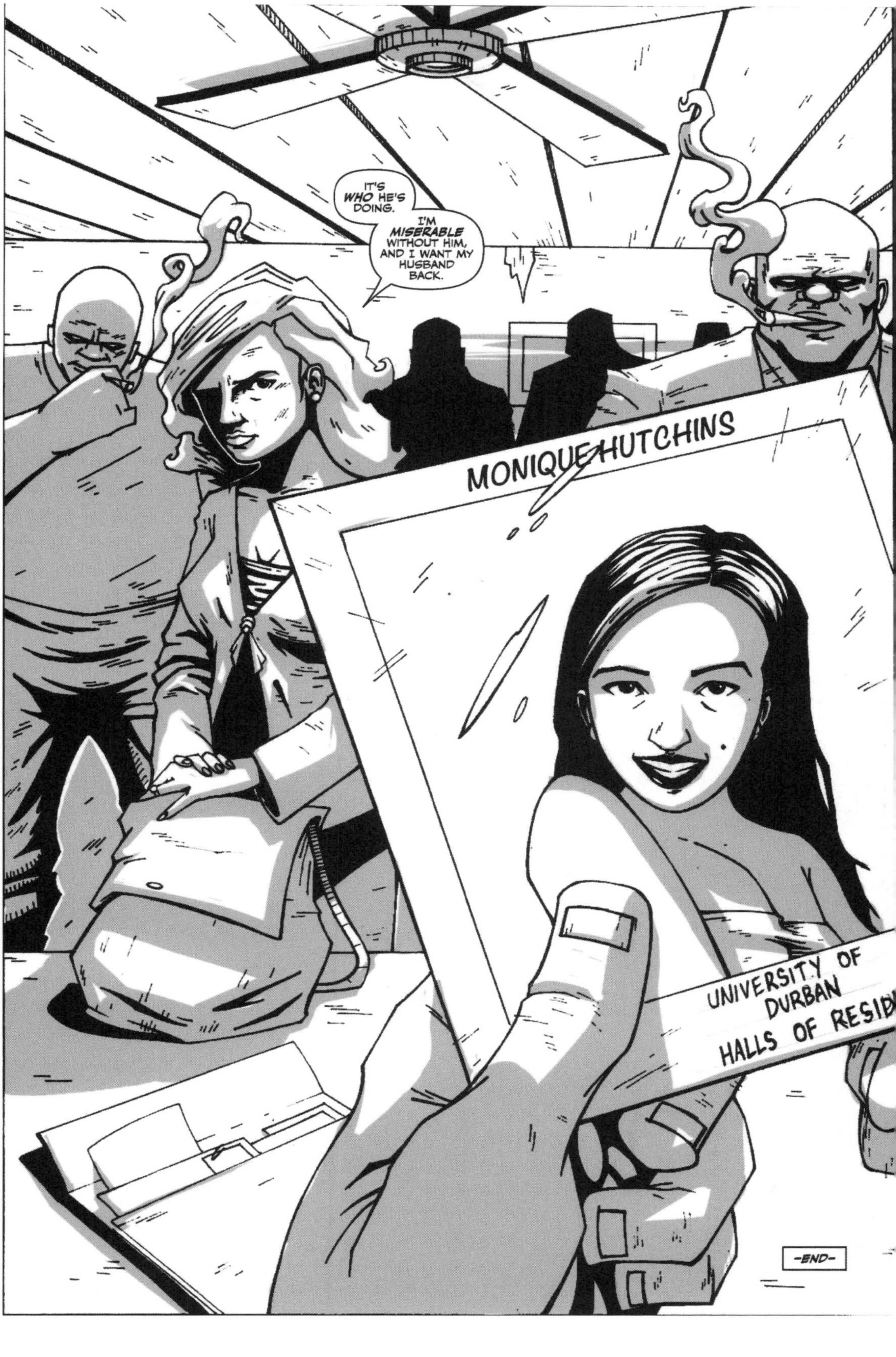
IT'S WHO HE'S DOING.
I'M MISERABLE WITHOUT HIM, AND I WANT MY HUSBAND BACK.
MONIQUE HUTCHINS
UNIVERSITY OF DURBAN HALLS OF RESID
-END-

Silent Justice...

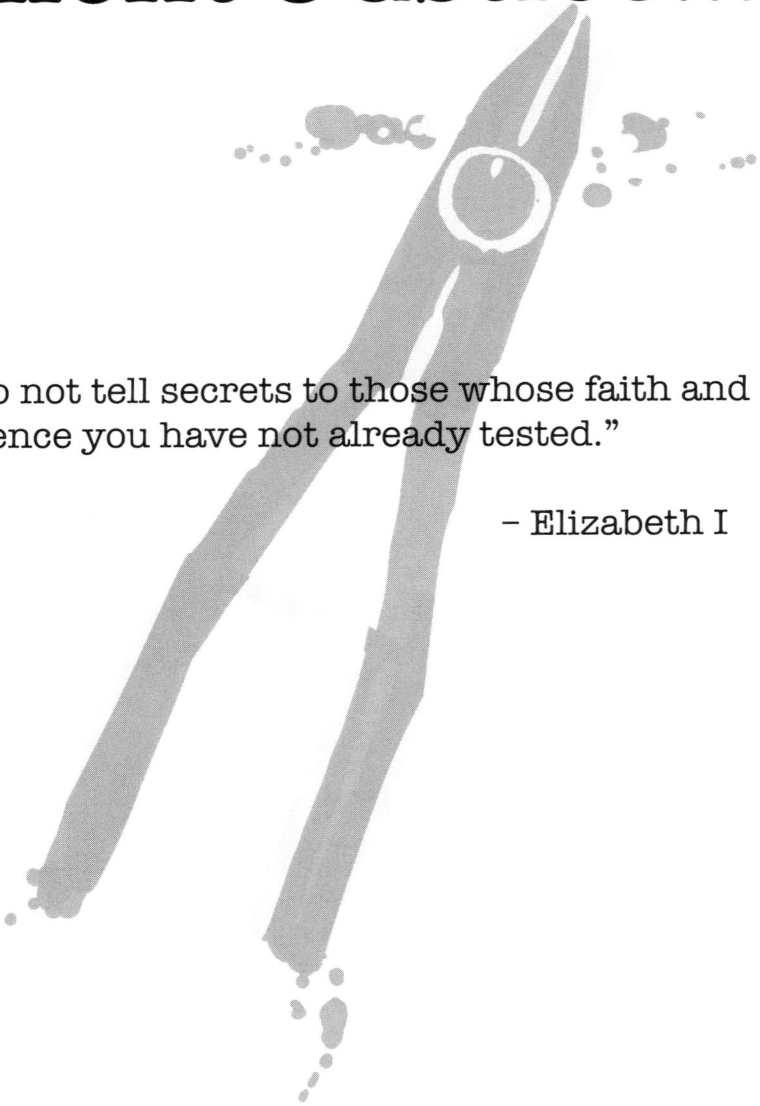

"Do not tell secrets to those whose faith and silence you have not already tested."

– Elizabeth I

Writer/Creator
Neil Gibson

Illustrator
Seb Antoniou

www.tpub.co.uk

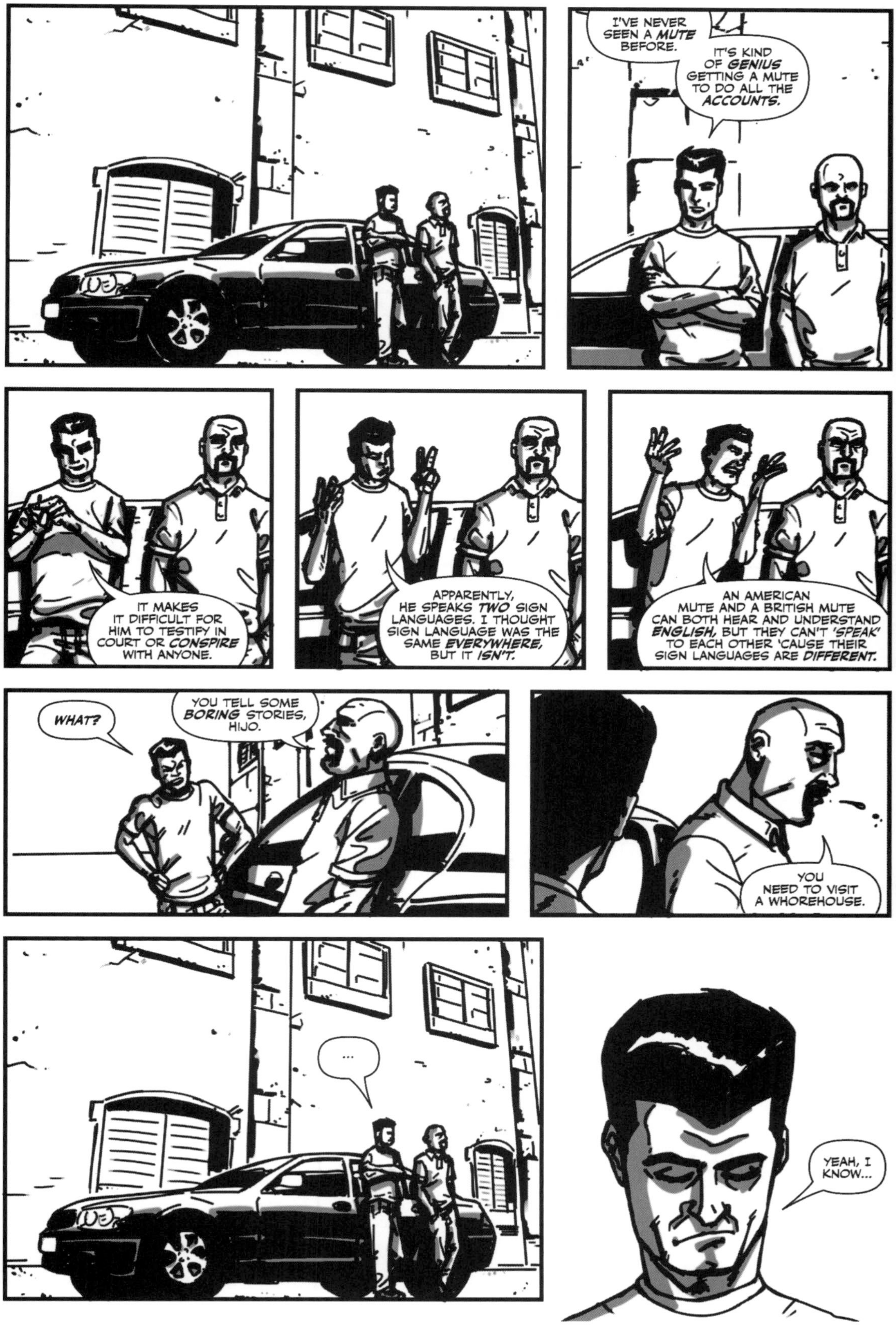
I'VE NEVER SEEN A MUTE BEFORE.
IT'S KIND OF GENIUS GETTING A MUTE TO DO ALL THE ACCOUNTS.
IT MAKES IT DIFFICULT FOR HIM TO TESTIFY IN COURT OR CONSPIRE WITH ANYONE.
APPARENTLY, HE SPEAKS TWO SIGN LANGUAGES. I THOUGHT SIGN LANGUAGE WAS THE SAME EVERYWHERE, BUT IT ISN'T.
AN AMERICAN MUTE AND A BRITISH MUTE CAN BOTH HEAR AND UNDERSTAND ENGLISH, BUT THEY CAN'T 'SPEAK' TO EACH OTHER 'CAUSE THEIR SIGN LANGUAGES ARE DIFFERENT.
YOU TELL SOME BORING STORIES, HIJO.
WHAT?
YOU NEED TO VISIT A WHOREHOUSE.
...
YEAH, I KNOW...

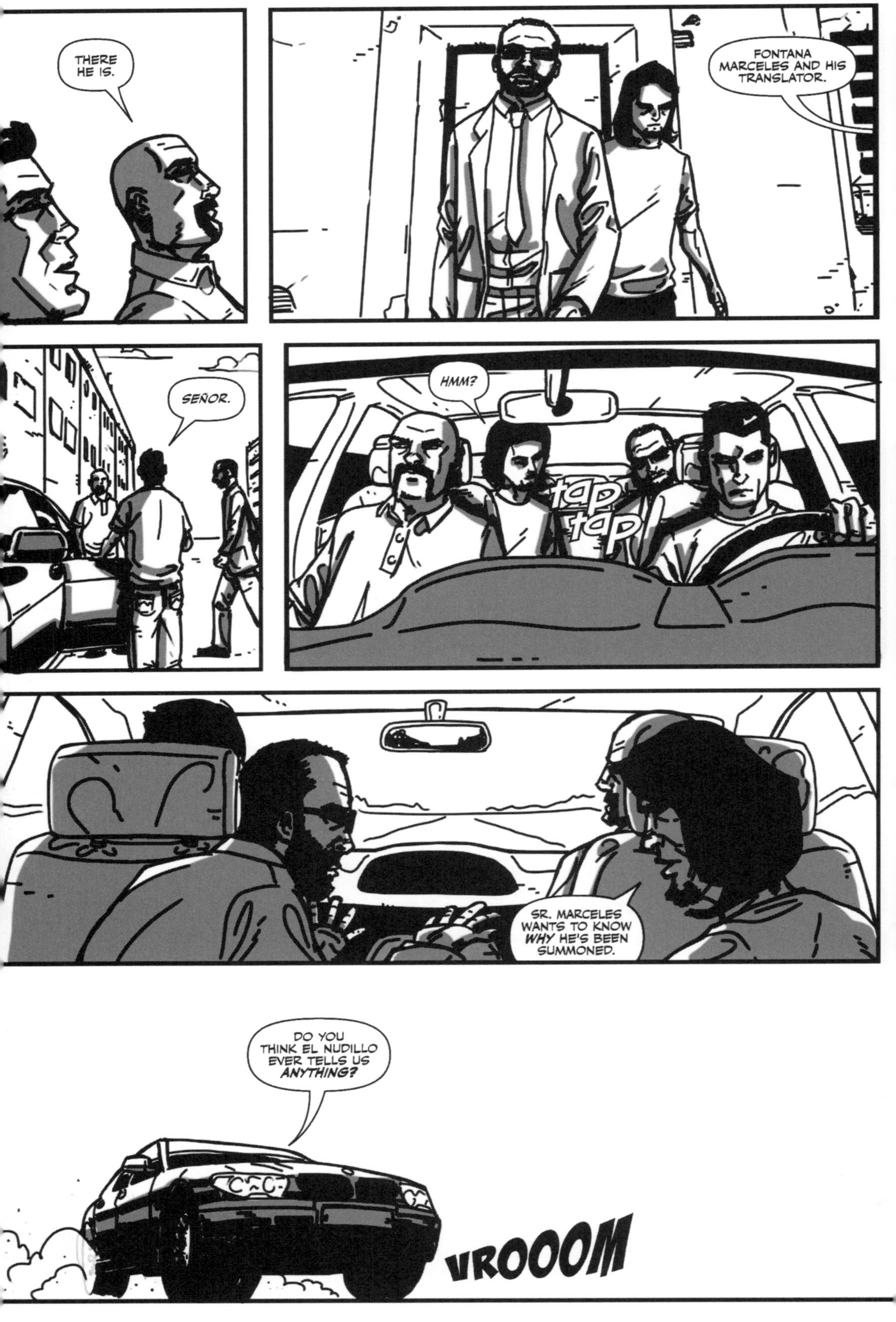
THERE HE IS.
FONTANA MARCELES AND HIS TRANSLATOR.
SEÑOR.
HMM?
tap tap
SR. MARCELES WANTS TO KNOW *WHY* HE'S BEEN SUMMONED.
DO YOU THINK EL NUDILLO EVER TELLS US *ANYTHING?*
VROOOM

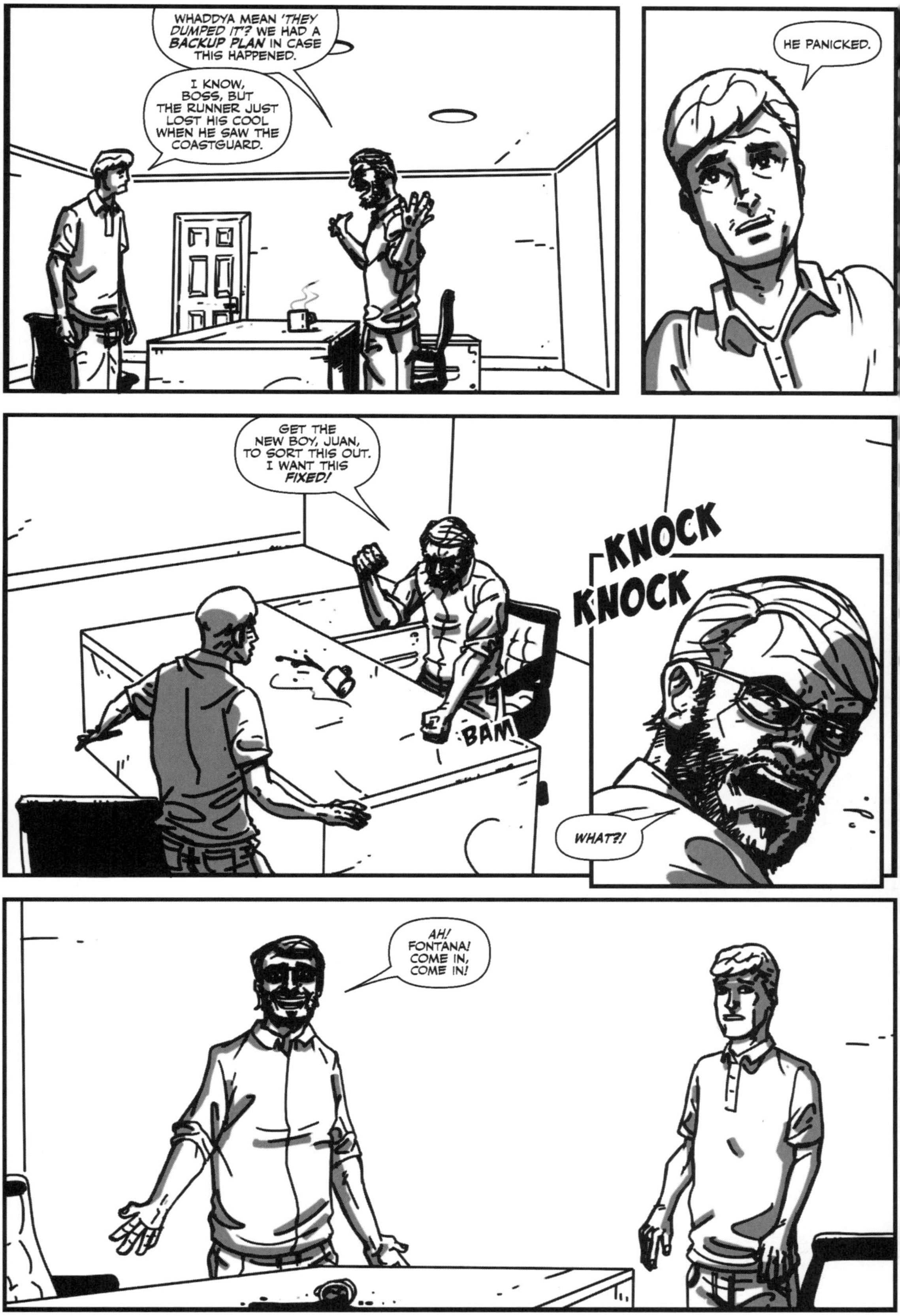
WHADDYA MEAN *'THEY DUMPED IT'*? WE HAD A **BACKUP PLAN** IN CASE THIS HAPPENED.
I KNOW, BOSS, BUT THE RUNNER JUST LOST HIS COOL WHEN HE SAW THE COASTGUARD.
HE PANICKED.
GET THE NEW BOY, JUAN, TO SORT THIS OUT. I WANT THIS ***FIXED!***
BAM
KNOCK
KNOCK
WHAT?!
AH! FONTANA! COME IN, COME IN!

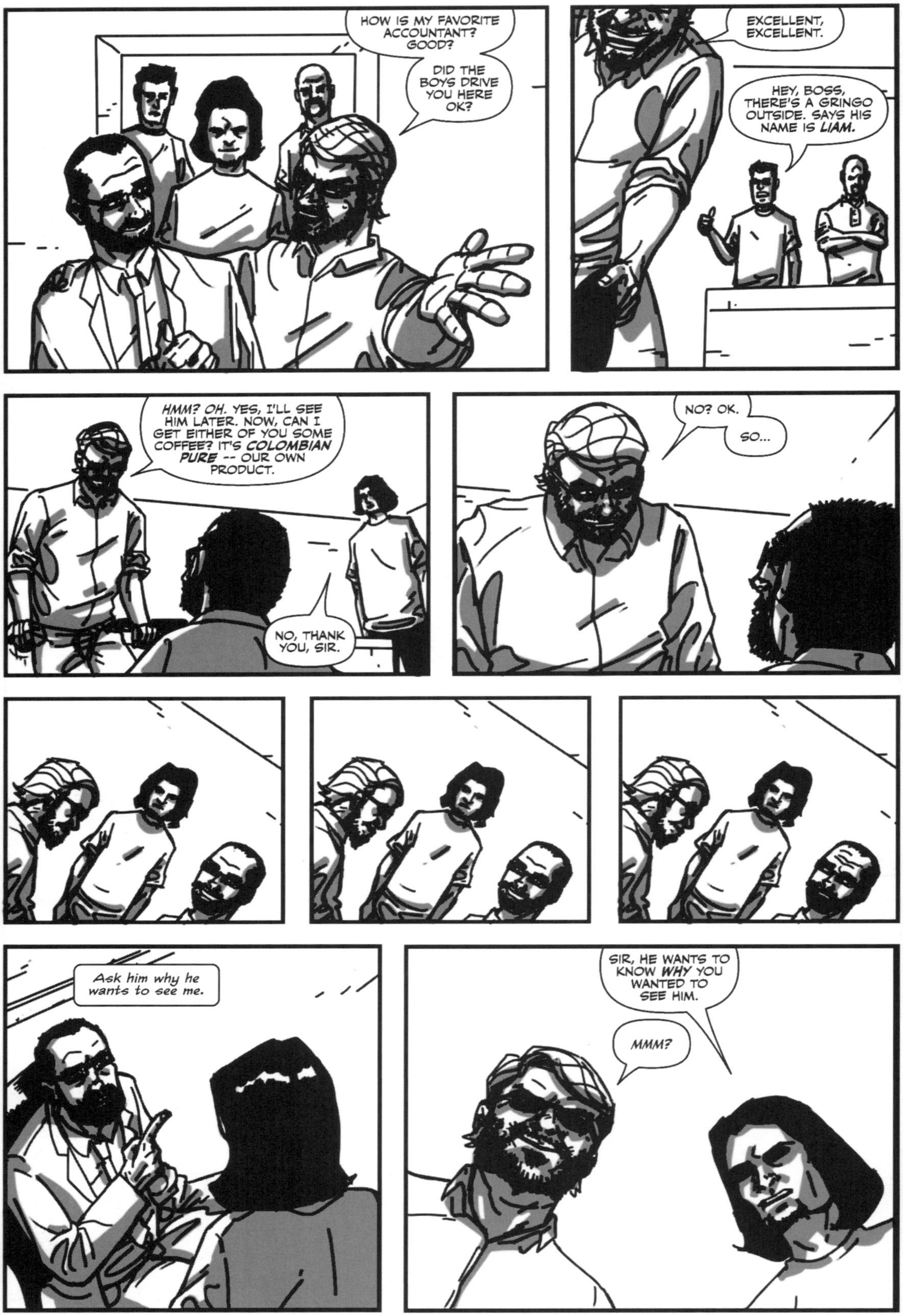

HOW IS MY FAVORITE ACCOUNTANT? GOOD?
DID THE BOYS DRIVE YOU HERE OK?
EXCELLENT, EXCELLENT.
HEY, BOSS, THERE'S A GRINGO OUTSIDE. SAYS HIS NAME IS *LIAM.*
HMM? OH. YES, I'LL SEE HIM LATER. NOW, CAN I GET EITHER OF YOU SOME COFFEE? IT'S ***COLOMBIAN PURE*** -- OUR OWN PRODUCT.
NO, THANK YOU, SIR.
NO? OK.
SO...
Ask him why he wants to see me.
SIR, HE WANTS TO KNOW ***WHY*** YOU WANTED TO SEE HIM.
MMM?

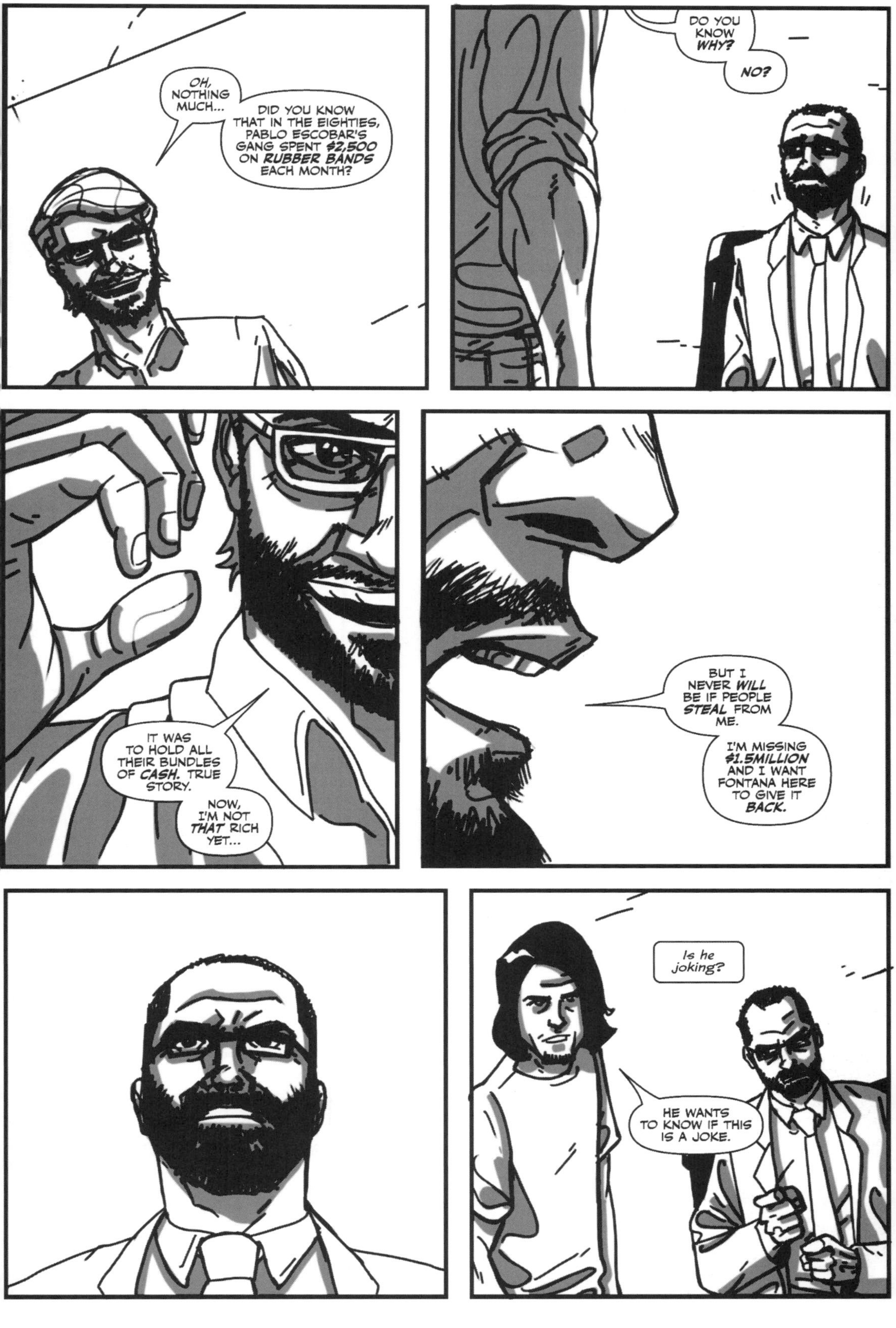

OH, NOTHING MUCH...
DID YOU KNOW THAT IN THE EIGHTIES, PABLO ESCOBAR'S GANG SPENT $2,500 ON RUBBER BANDS EACH MONTH?
DO YOU KNOW WHY?
NO?
IT WAS TO HOLD ALL THEIR BUNDLES OF CASH. TRUE STORY.
NOW, I'M NOT THAT RICH YET...
BUT I NEVER WILL BE IF PEOPLE STEAL FROM ME.
I'M MISSING $1.5MILLION AND I WANT FONTANA HERE TO GIVE IT BACK.
Is he joking?
HE WANTS TO KNOW IF THIS IS A JOKE.

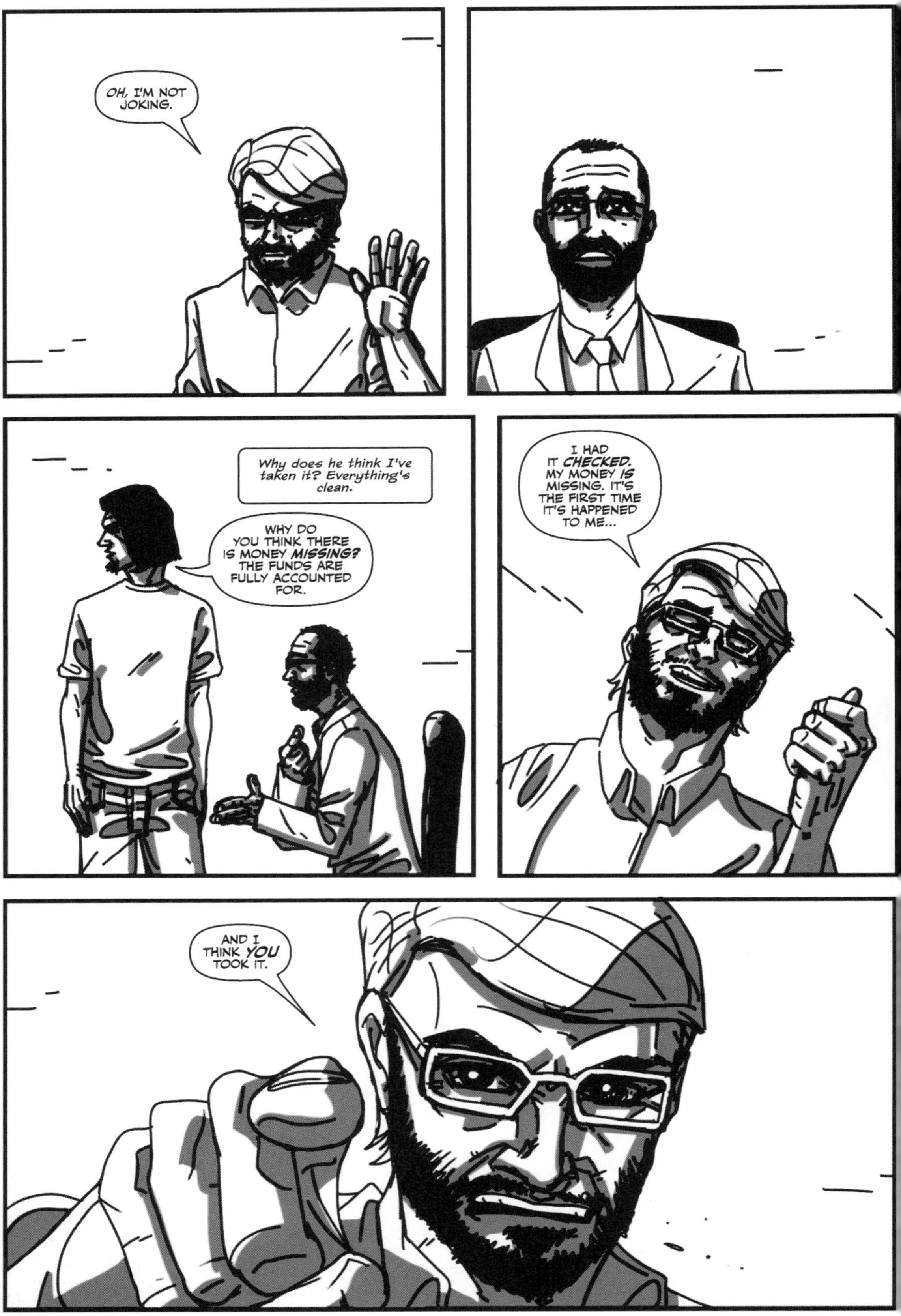
OH, I'M NOT JOKING.
Why does he think I've taken it? Everything's clean.
WHY DO YOU THINK THERE IS MONEY MISSING? THE FUNDS ARE FULLY ACCOUNTED FOR.
I HAD IT CHECKED. MY MONEY IS MISSING. IT'S THE FIRST TIME IT'S HAPPENED TO ME...
AND I THINK YOU TOOK IT.

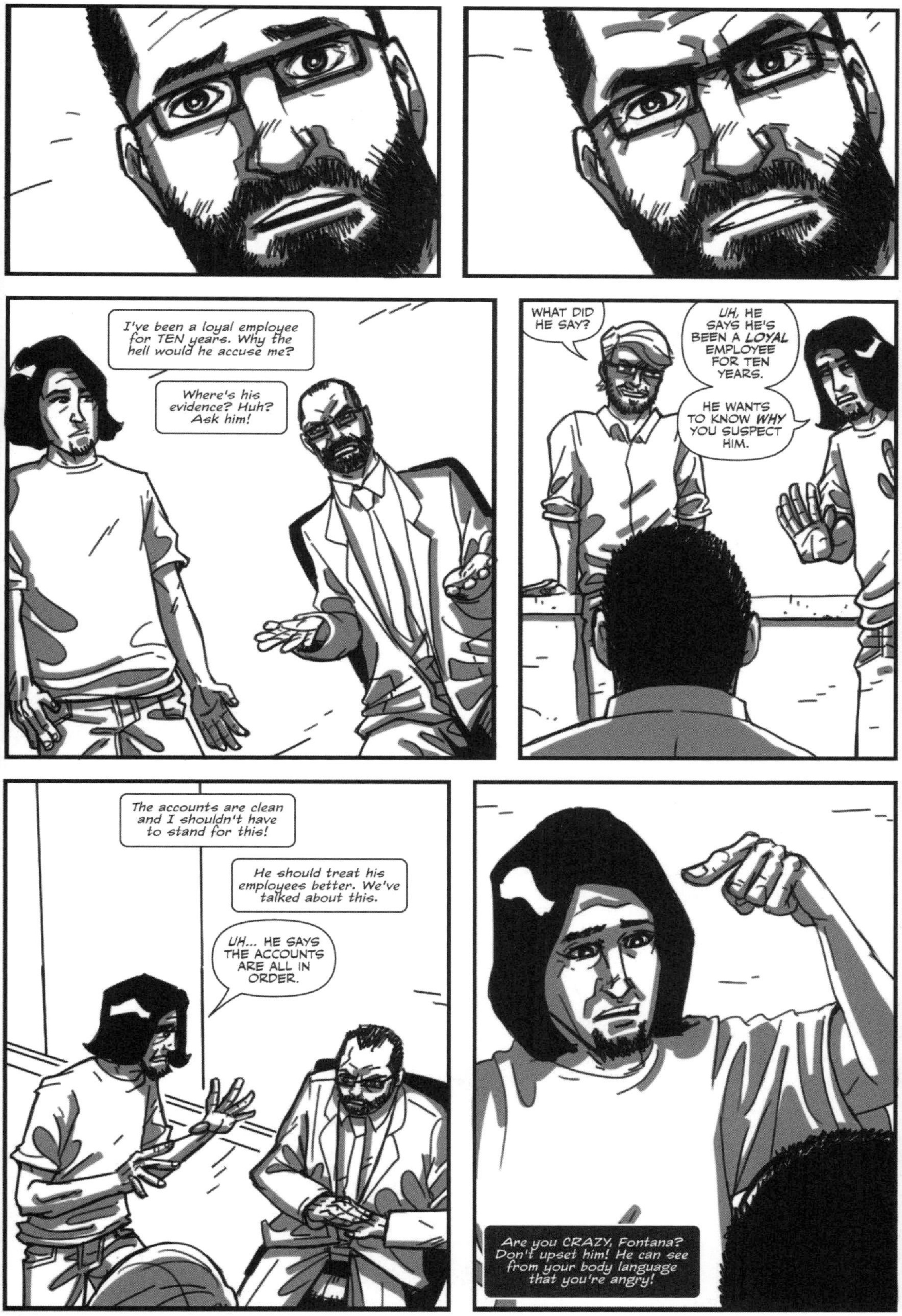
I've been a loyal employee for TEN years. Why the hell would he accuse me?
Where's his evidence? Huh? Ask him!
WHAT DID HE SAY?
UH, HE SAYS HE'S BEEN A LOYAL EMPLOYEE FOR TEN YEARS.
HE WANTS TO KNOW WHY YOU SUSPECT HIM.
The accounts are clean and I shouldn't have to stand for this!
He should treat his employees better. We've talked about this.
UH... HE SAYS THE ACCOUNTS ARE ALL IN ORDER.
Are you CRAZY, Fontana? Don't upset him! He can see from your body language that you're angry!

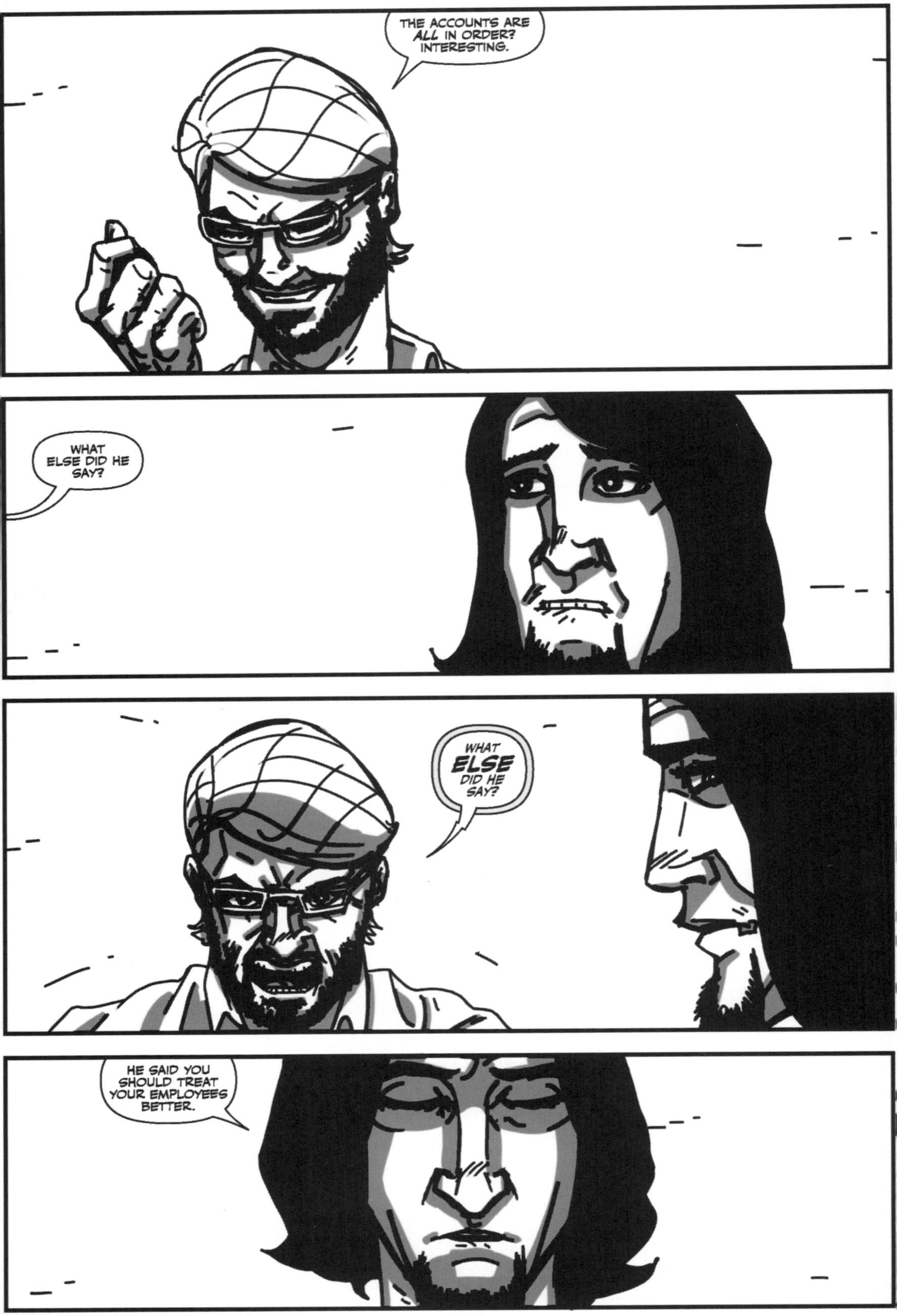
THE ACCOUNTS ARE ALL IN ORDER? INTERESTING.
WHAT ELSE DID HE SAY?
WHAT ELSE DID HE SAY?
HE SAID YOU SHOULD TREAT YOUR EMPLOYEES BETTER.

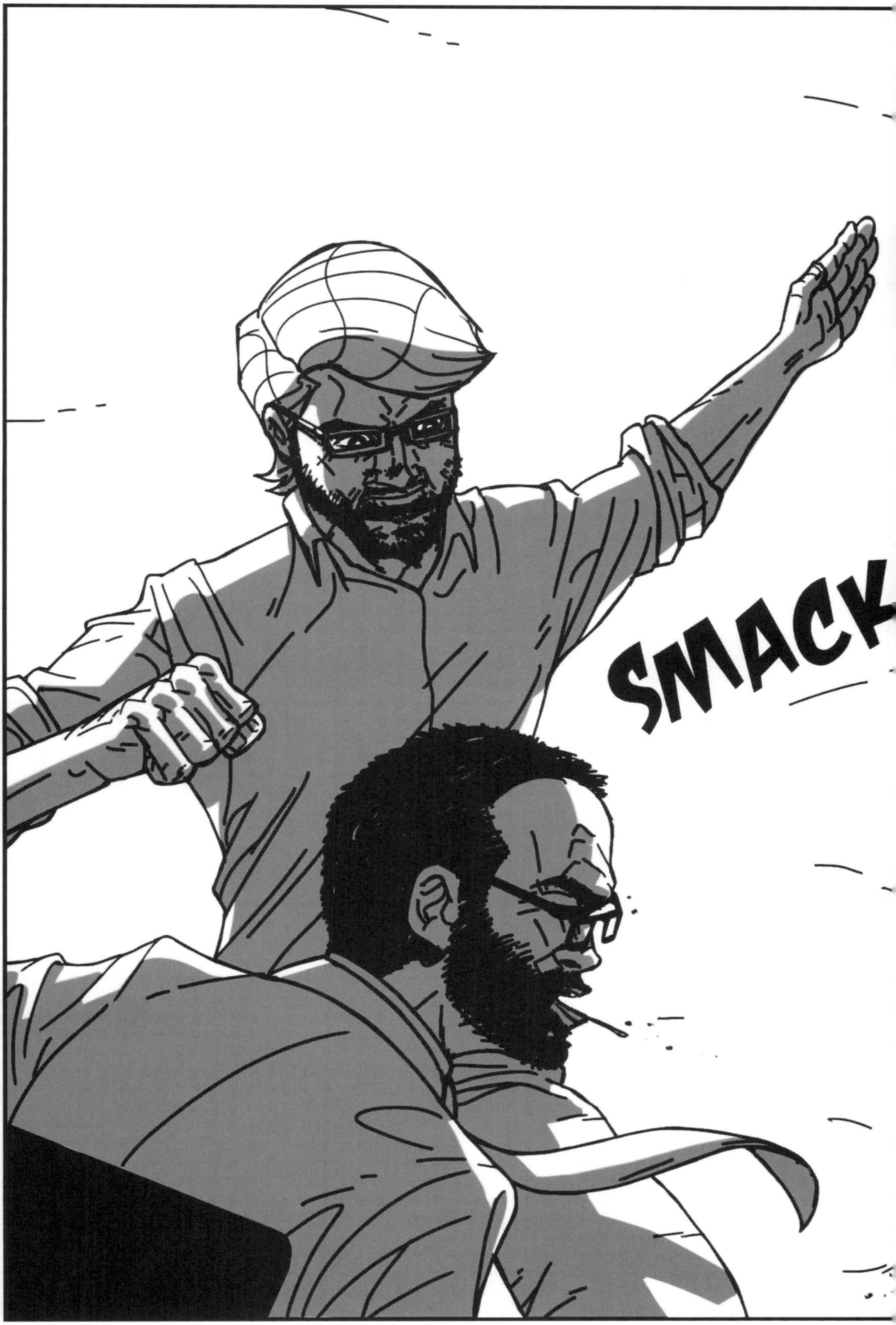
SMACK

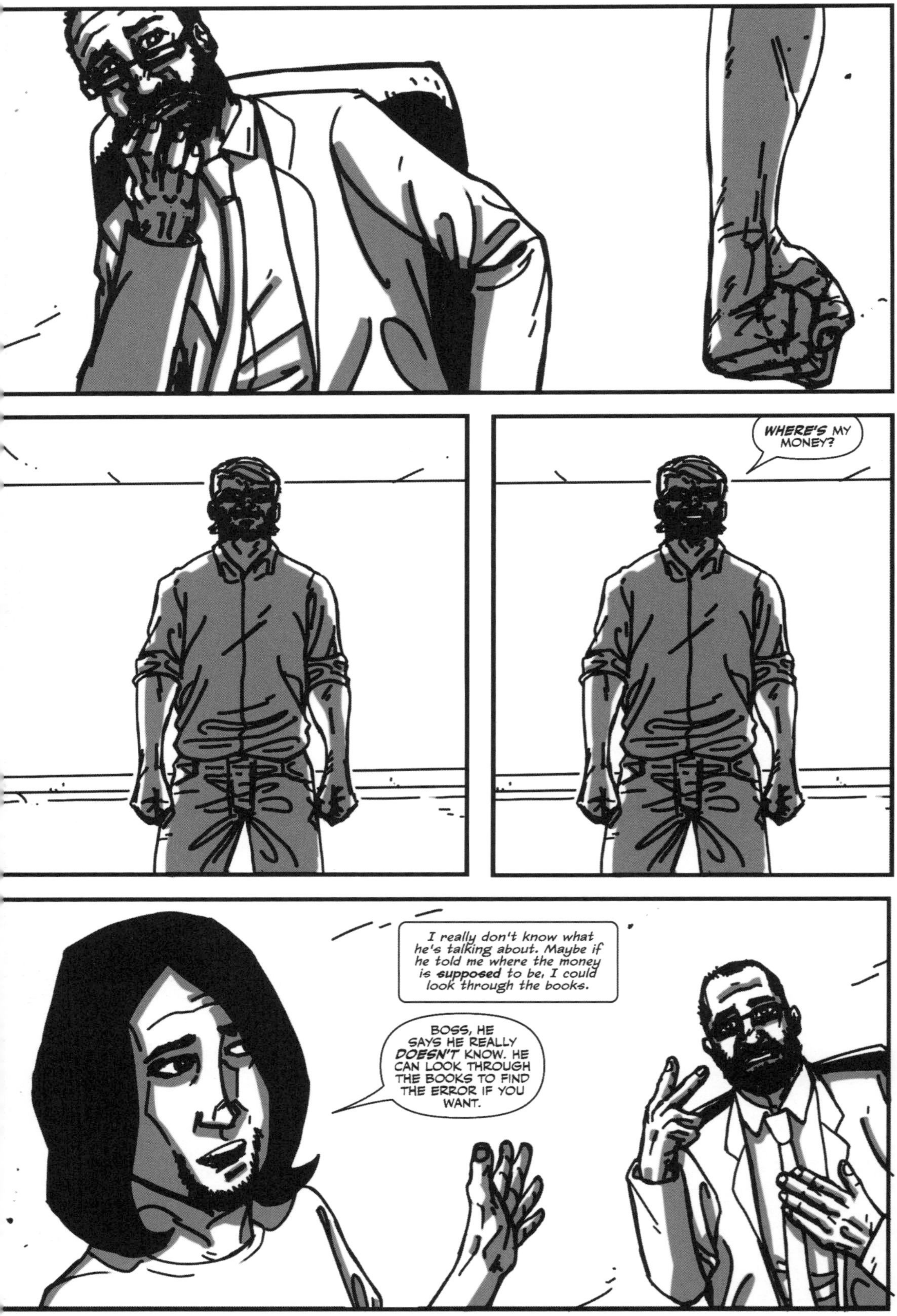
WHERE'S MY MONEY?
I really don't know what he's talking about. Maybe if he told me where the money is supposed to be, I could look through the books.
BOSS, HE SAYS HE REALLY DOESN'T KNOW. HE CAN LOOK THROUGH THE BOOKS TO FIND THE ERROR IF YOU WANT.

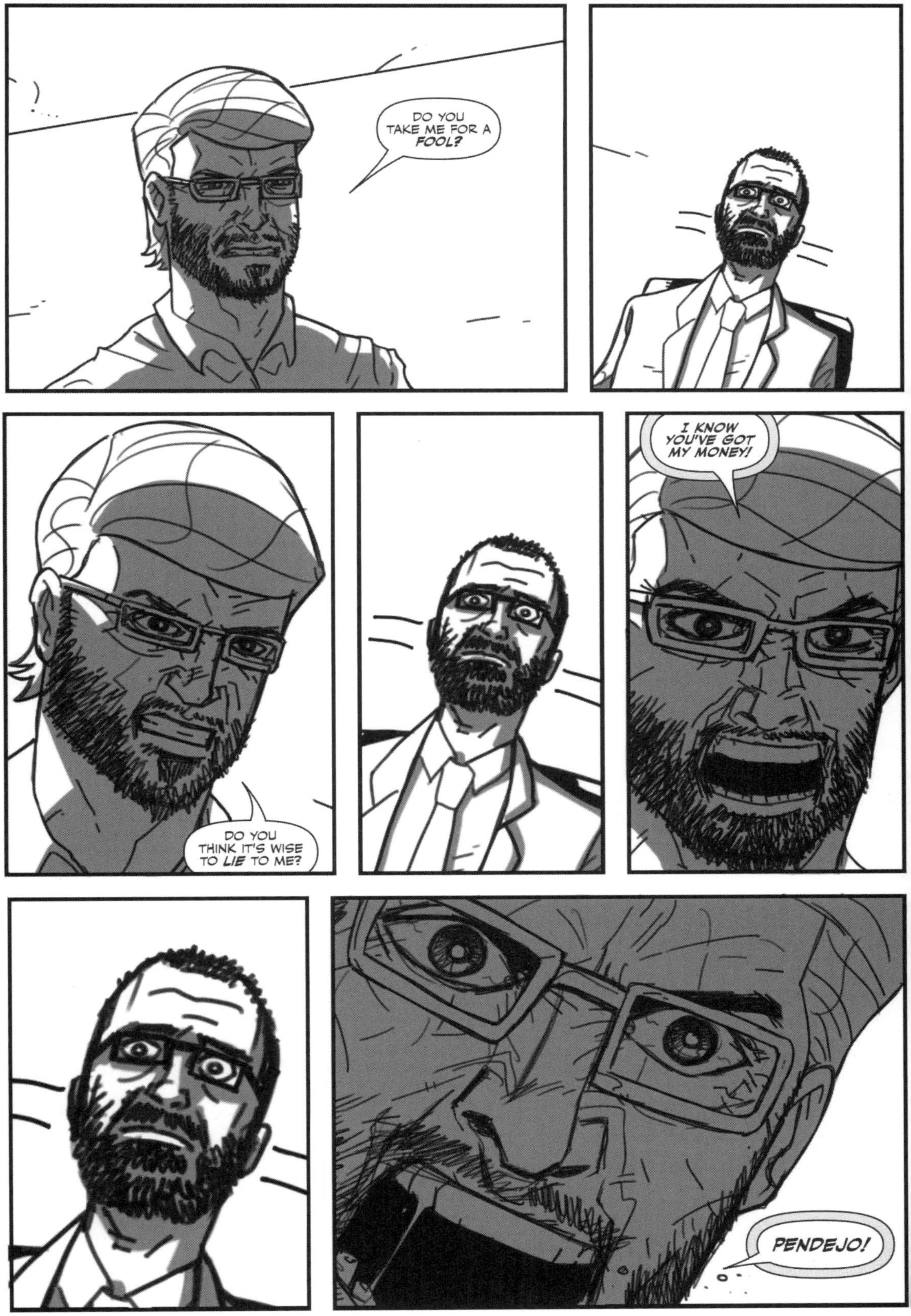
DO YOU TAKE ME FOR A FOOL?
DO YOU THINK IT'S WISE TO LIE TO ME?
I KNOW YOU'VE GOT MY MONEY!
PENDEJO!

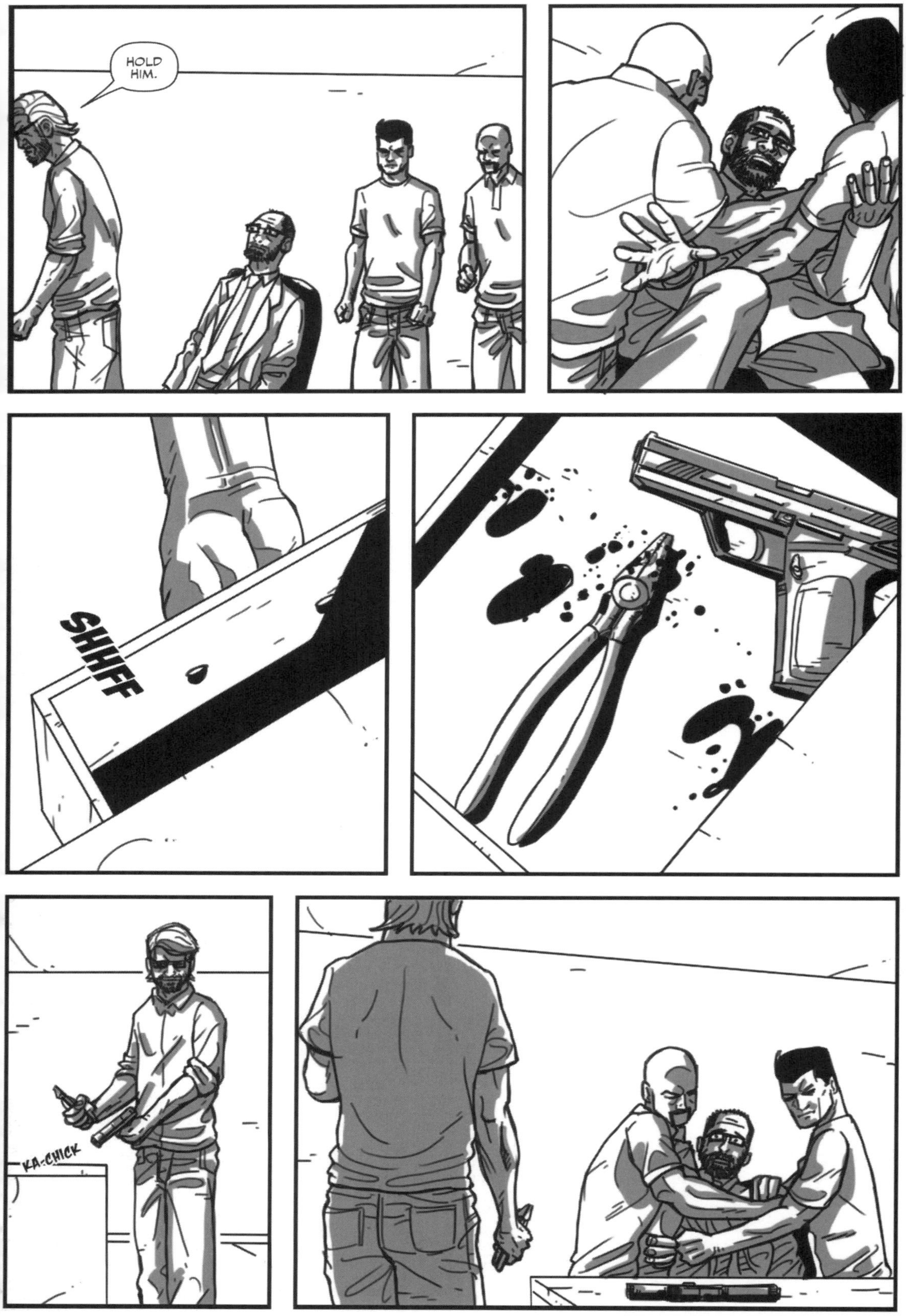
HOLD HIM.
SHHFF
KA-CHICK

DO YOU KNOW *WHY* I'M CALLED *EL NUDILLO?*

OF COURSE YOU DO. I WANT *EVERYONE* TO KNOW.

BMMFF

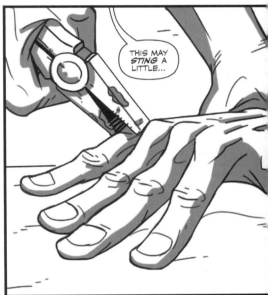

THIS MAY *STING* A LITTLE...

CCRRUNCH

NGGG

75

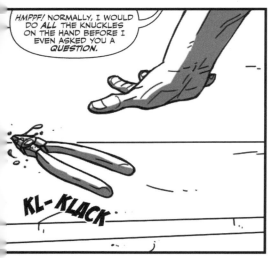

HMPPF! NORMALLY, I WOULD DO *ALL* THE KNUCKLES ON THE HAND BEFORE I EVEN ASKED YOU A *QUESTION.*

KL- KLACK

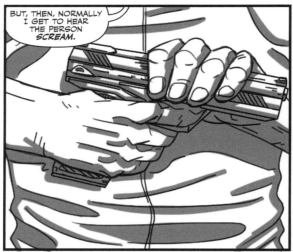

BUT, THEN, NORMALLY I GET TO HEAR THE PERSON *SCREAM.*

AND, SADLY, YOU NEED YOUR *HANDS* TO TALK.

SO I'M GOING TO ASK ONE FUCKING *LAST* TIME -- WHERE'S MY *MONEY?*

AND IF I DON'T FIND OUT, I'M JUST GONNA BLOW YOUR *BRAINS* OUT.

76

OK, OK, I have the money.

One million is in an old Pan Am suitcase in the janitor's cupboard in my apartment block. The rest is in various banks.

But if he lets me go, not only will I give him back all the money, I'll also tell him which of his six captains have been siphoning a little for themselves.

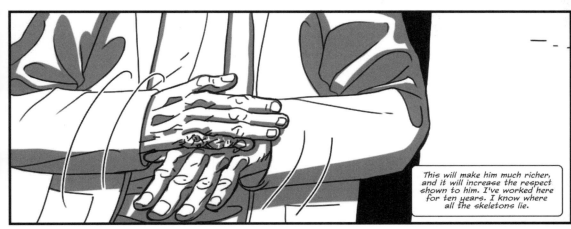

This will make him much richer, and it will increase the respect shown to him. I've worked here for ten years. I know where all the skeletons lie.

I can **help** him. He needs me to stop his captains stealing from him.

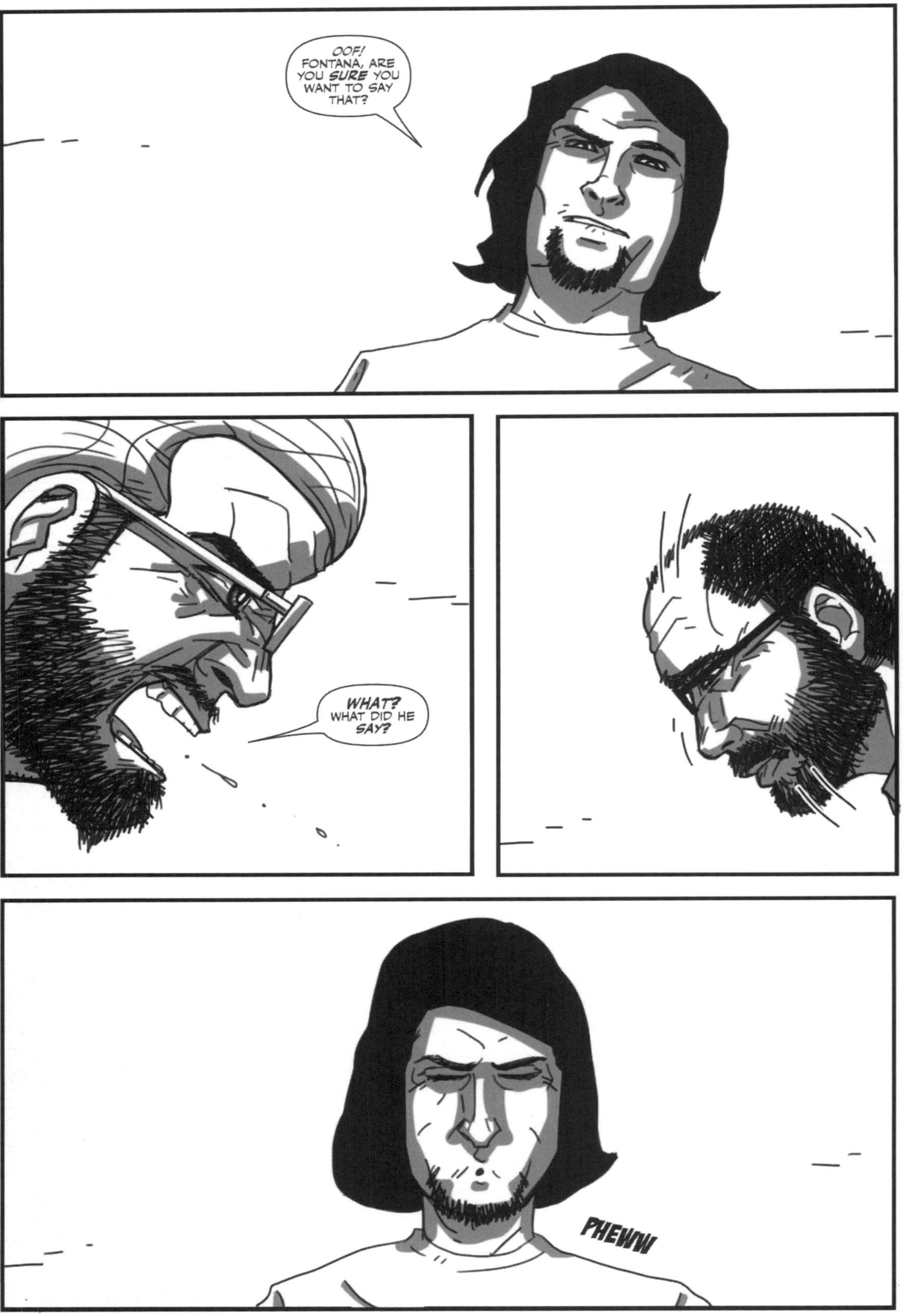
OOF! FONTANA, ARE YOU SURE YOU WANT TO SAY THAT?
WHAT? WHAT DID HE SAY?
PHEWW

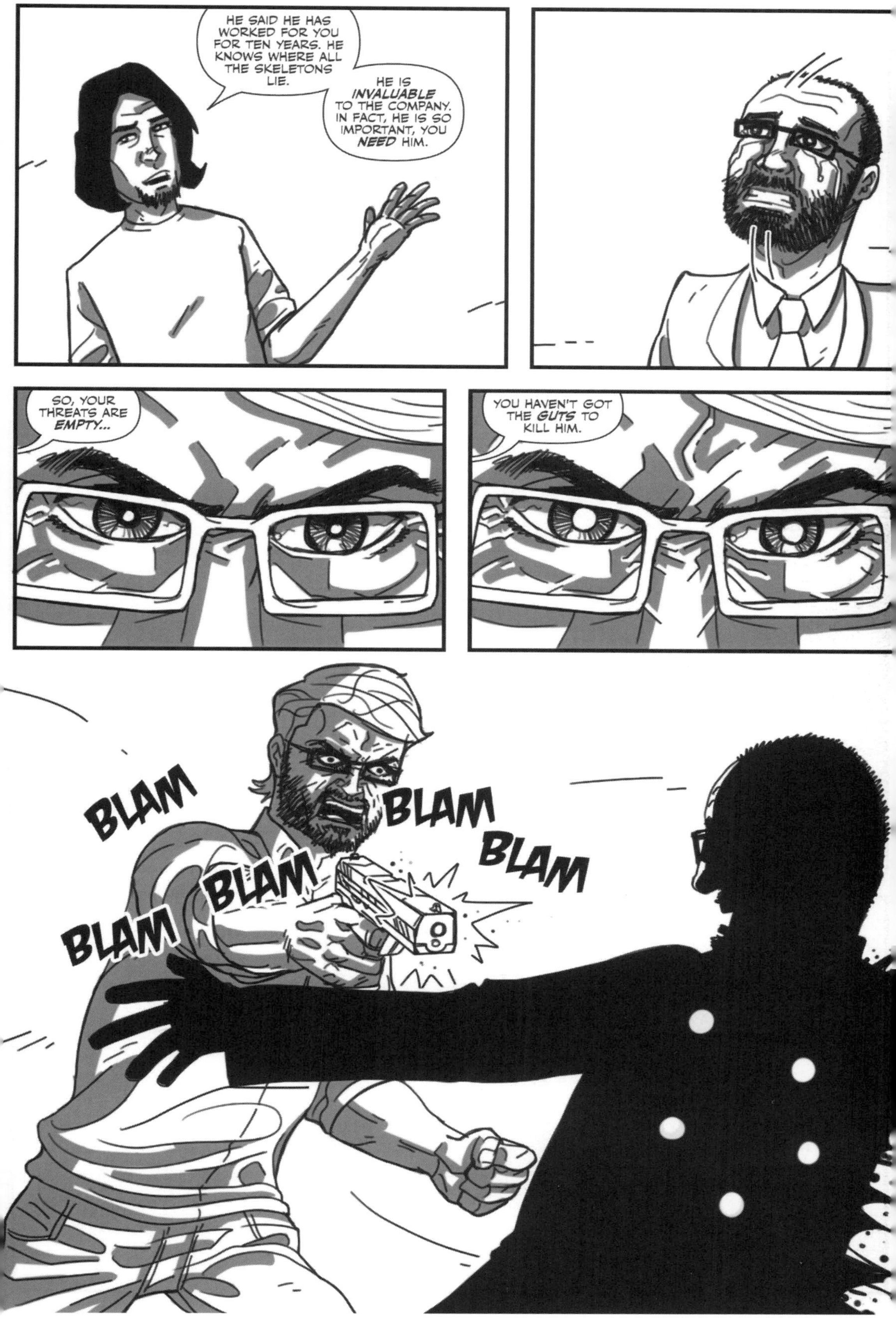
HE SAID HE HAS WORKED FOR YOU FOR TEN YEARS. HE KNOWS WHERE ALL THE SKELETONS LIE.
HE IS *INVALUABLE* TO THE COMPANY. IN FACT, HE IS SO IMPORTANT, YOU *NEED* HIM.
SO, YOUR THREATS ARE *EMPTY...*
YOU HAVEN'T GOT THE *GUTS* TO KILL HIM.
BLAM
BLAM
BLAM
BLAM
BLAM

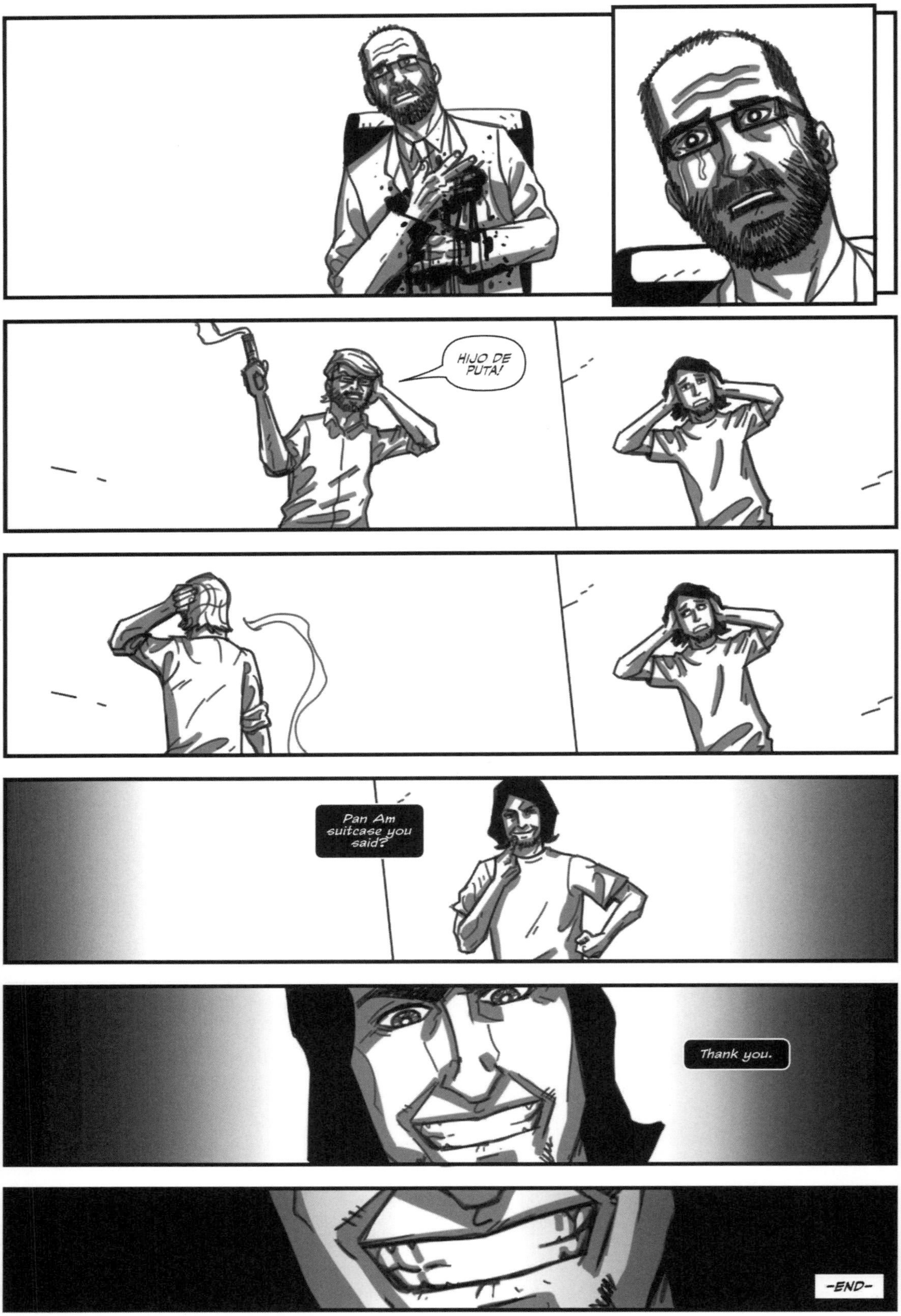
HIJO DE PUTA!
Pan Am suitcase you said?
Thank you.
-END-

Career Choice...

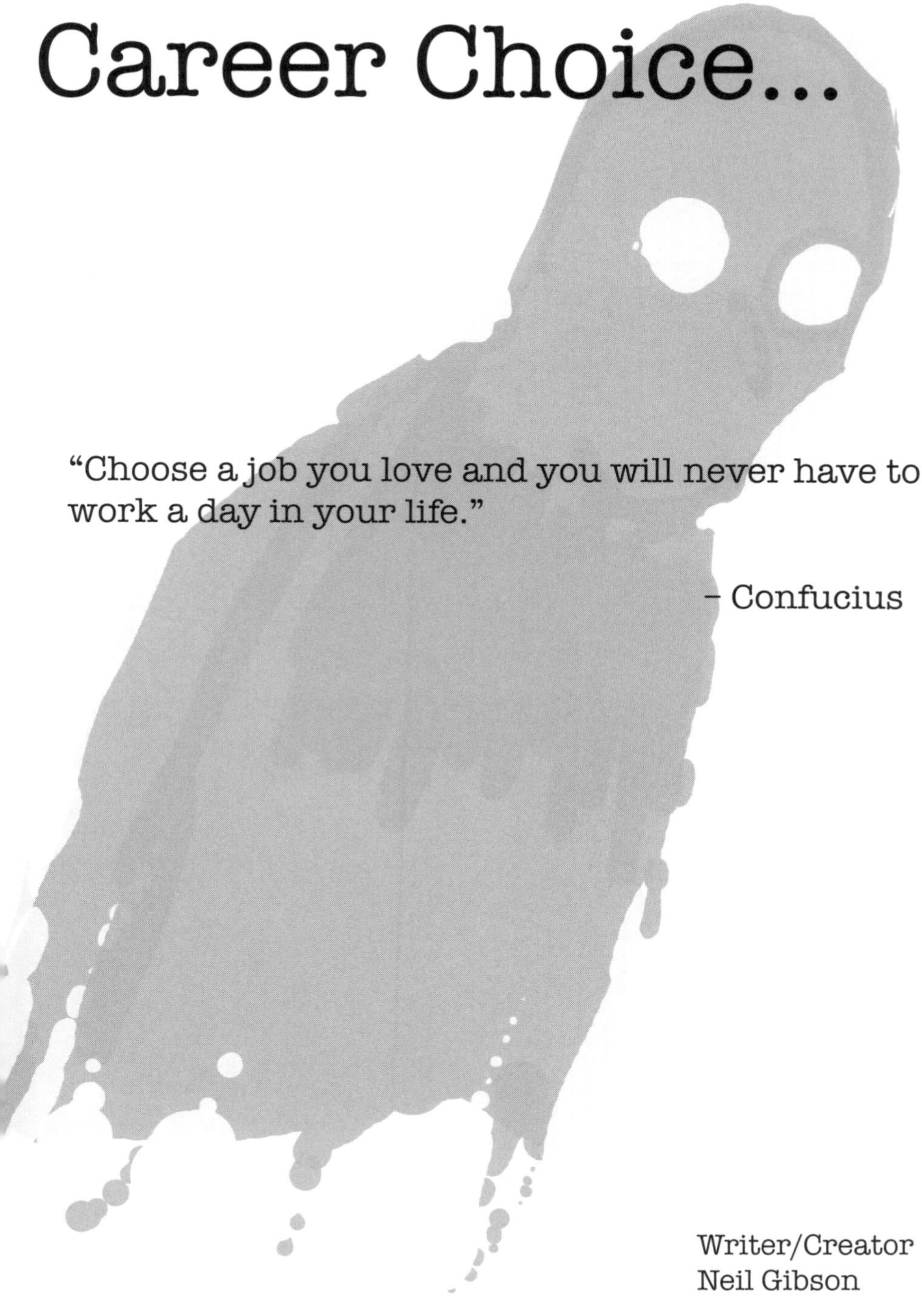

"Choose a job you love and you will never have to work a day in your life."

– Confucius

Writer/Creator
Neil Gibson

Illustrator
Leonardo Gonzalez

www.tpub.co.uk

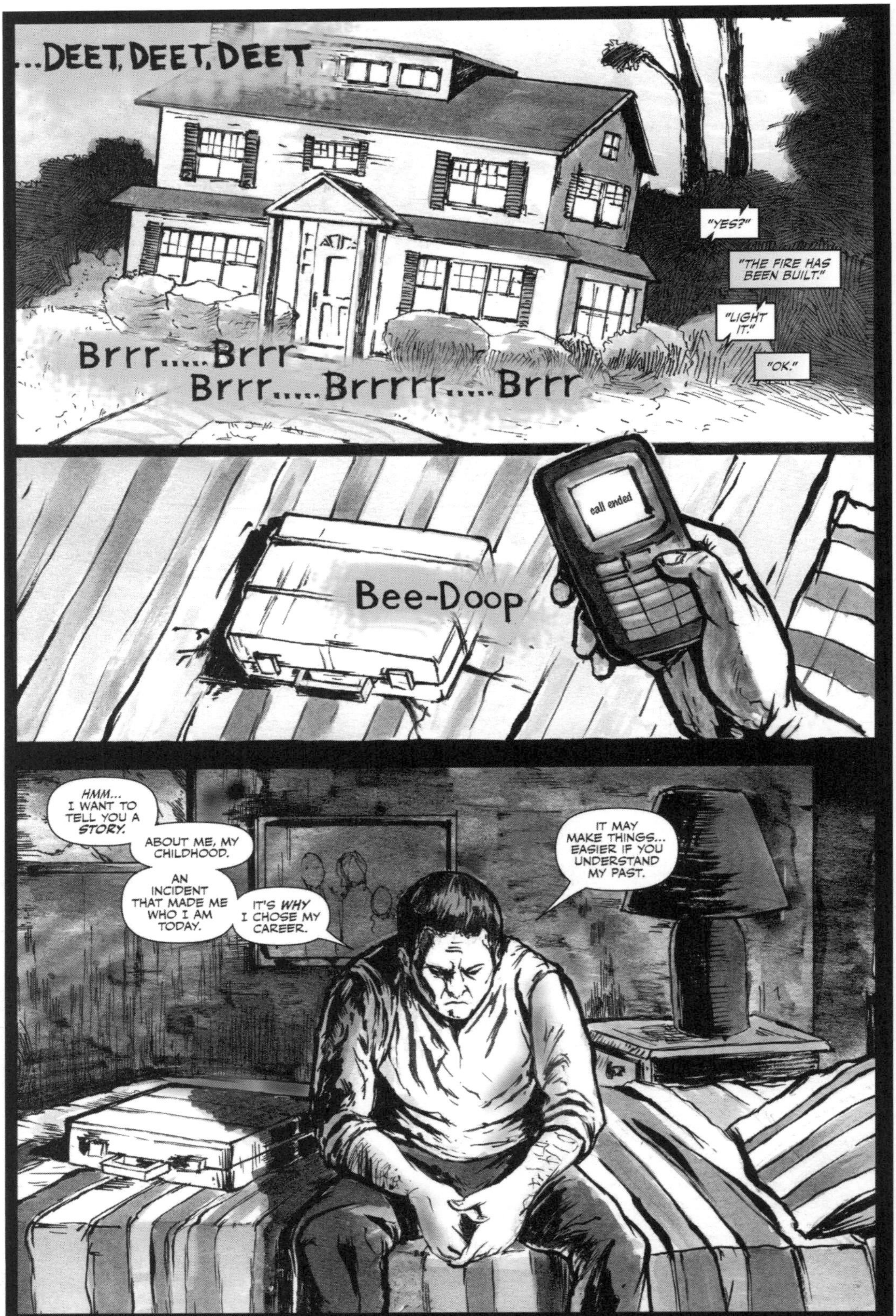
...DEET, DEET, DEET
Brrr.....Brrr
Brrr.....Brrrrr.....Brrr
"YES?"
"THE FIRE HAS BEEN BUILT."
"LIGHT IT."
"OK."
call ended
Bee-Doop
HMM... I WANT TO TELL YOU A STORY.
ABOUT ME, MY CHILDHOOD.
AN INCIDENT THAT MADE ME WHO I AM TODAY.
IT'S WHY I CHOSE MY CAREER.
IT MAY MAKE THINGS... EASIER IF YOU UNDERSTAND MY PAST.

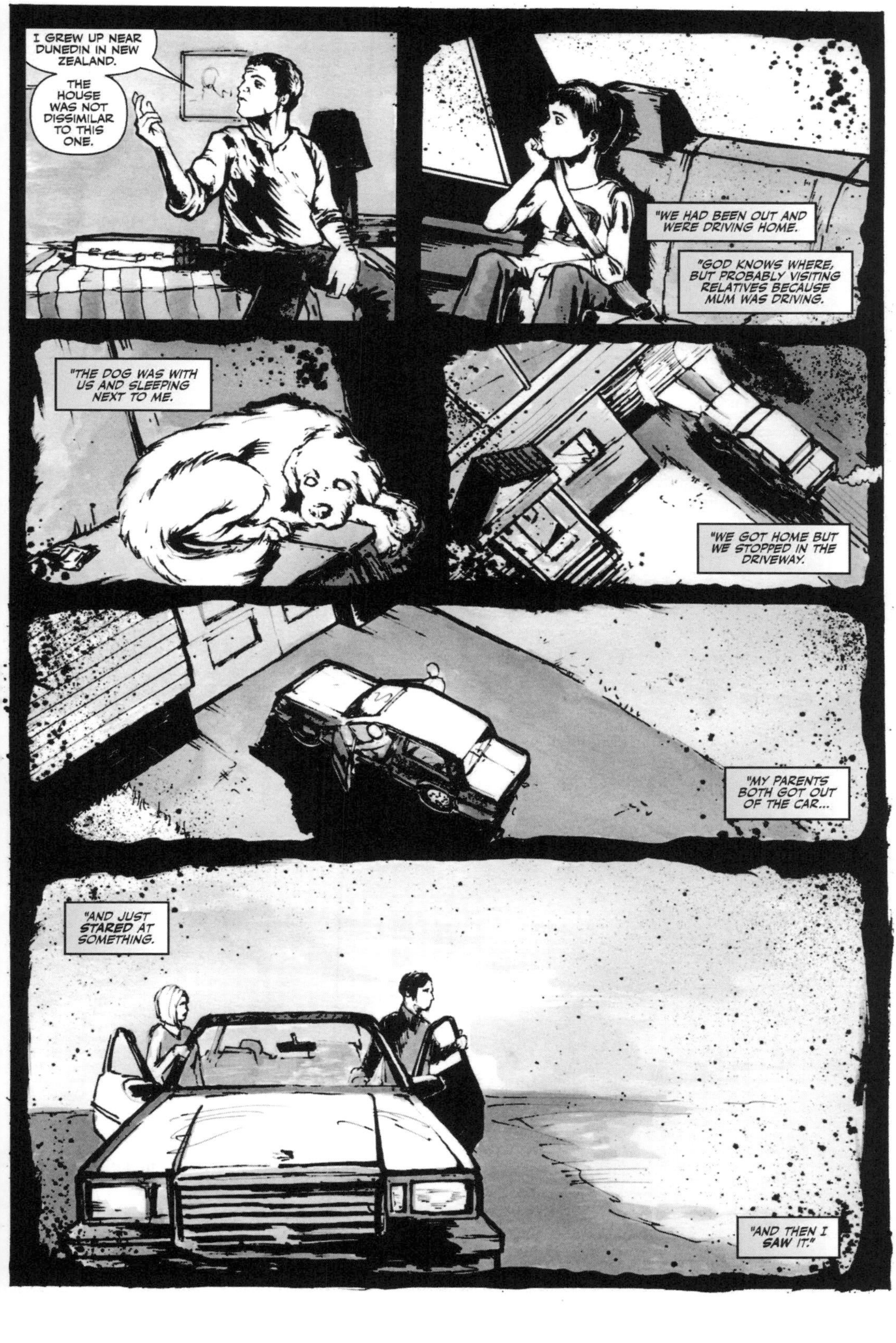

I GREW UP NEAR DUNEDIN IN NEW ZEALAND.
THE HOUSE WAS NOT DISSIMILAR TO THIS ONE.
"WE HAD BEEN OUT AND WERE DRIVING HOME.
"GOD KNOWS WHERE, BUT PROBABLY VISITING RELATIVES BECAUSE MUM WAS DRIVING.
"THE DOG WAS WITH US AND SLEEPING NEXT TO ME.
"WE GOT HOME BUT WE STOPPED IN THE DRIVEWAY.
"MY PARENTS BOTH GOT OUT OF THE CAR...
"AND JUST STARED AT SOMETHING.
"AND THEN I SAW IT."

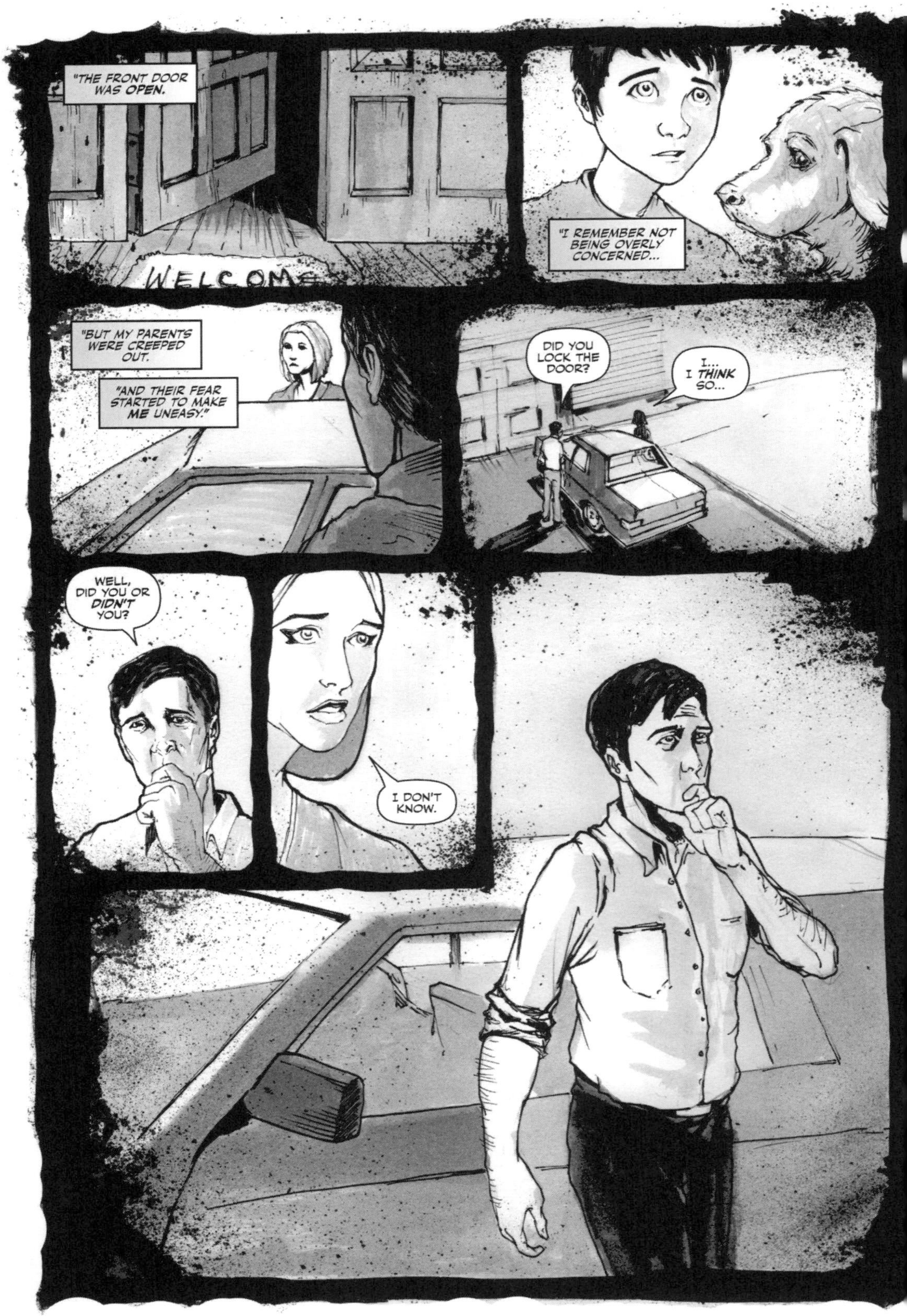
"THE FRONT DOOR WAS OPEN.
WELCOME
"I REMEMBER NOT BEING OVERLY CONCERNED...
"BUT MY PARENTS WERE CREEPED OUT.
"AND THEIR FEAR STARTED TO MAKE ME UNEASY."
DID YOU LOCK THE DOOR?
I... I THINK SO...
WELL, DID YOU OR DIDN'T YOU?
I DON'T KNOW.

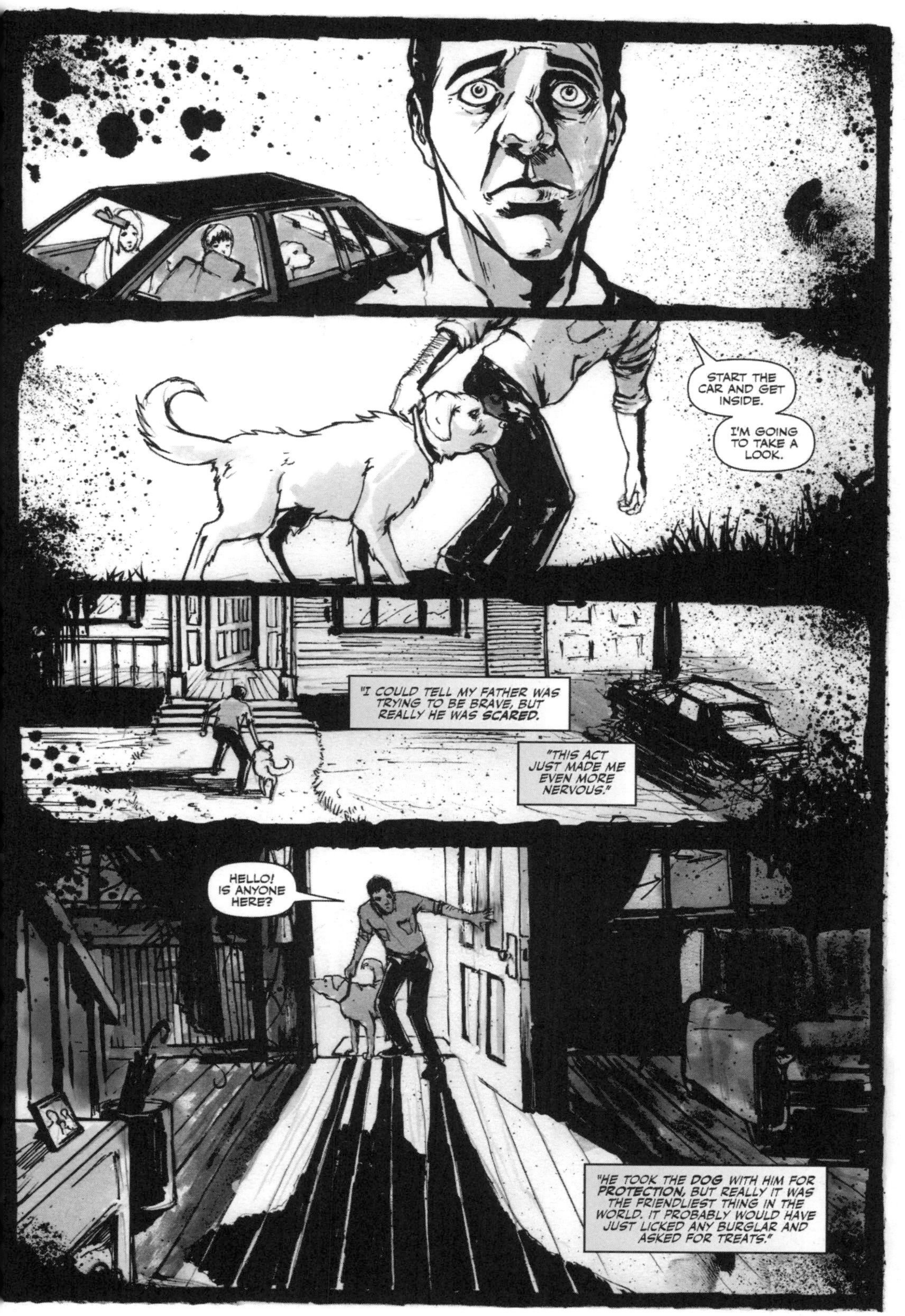
START THE CAR AND GET INSIDE.
I'M GOING TO TAKE A LOOK.
"I COULD TELL MY FATHER WAS TRYING TO BE BRAVE, BUT REALLY HE WAS SCARED.
"THIS ACT JUST MADE ME EVEN MORE NERVOUS."
HELLO! IS ANYONE HERE?
"HE TOOK THE DOG WITH HIM FOR PROTECTION, BUT REALLY IT WAS THE FRIENDLIEST THING IN THE WORLD. IT PROBABLY WOULD HAVE JUST LICKED ANY BURGLAR AND ASKED FOR TREATS."

SHHHHSK

"HE STARTED SEARCHING THE HOUSE, ALWAYS MAKING SURE HE LEFT AN EXIT FOR ANY BURGLAR TO ESCAPE THROUGH."

HELLO?

"'A CORNERED ANIMAL HAS NO CHOICE LEFT BUT TO ATTACK...' HE ALWAYS USED TO TELL US."

"IT FELT LIKE HE WAS GONE AN AGE."

I THINK IT'S ALL CLEAR.

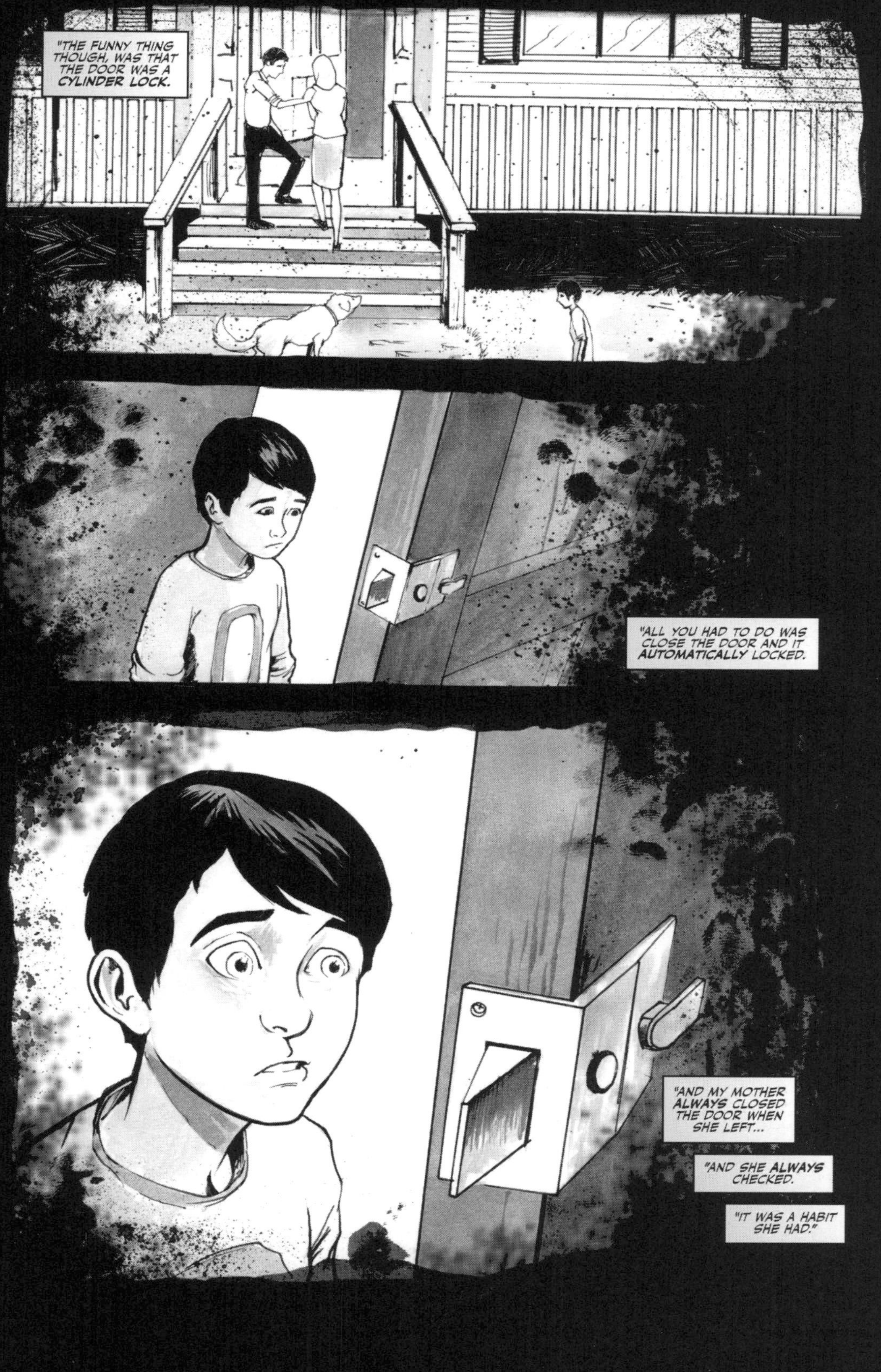
"THE FUNNY THING THOUGH, WAS THAT THE DOOR WAS A CYLINDER LOCK.
"ALL YOU HAD TO DO WAS CLOSE THE DOOR AND IT AUTOMATICALLY LOCKED.
"AND MY MOTHER ALWAYS CLOSED THE DOOR WHEN SHE LEFT...
"AND SHE ALWAYS CHECKED.
"IT WAS A HABIT SHE HAD."

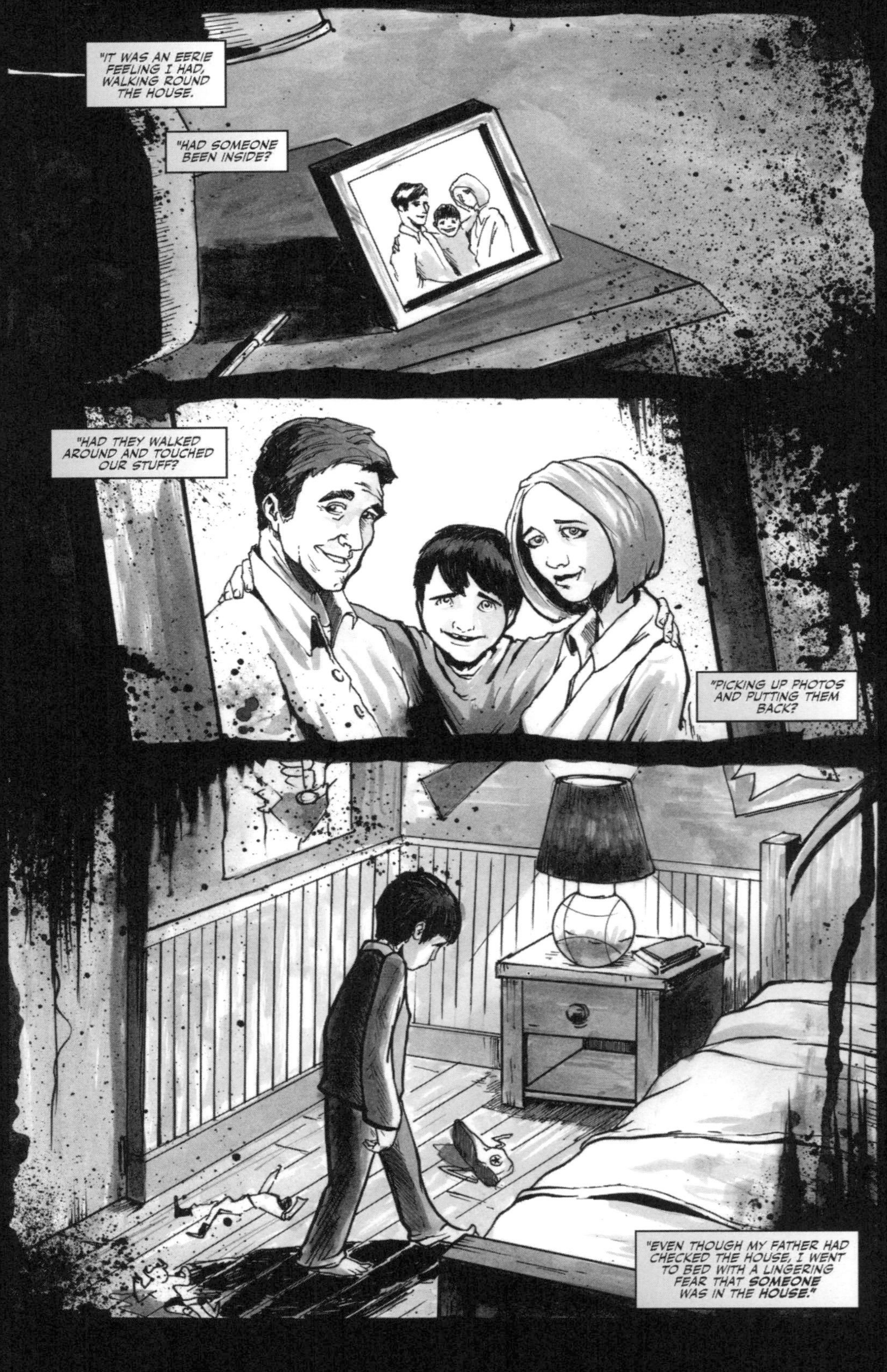
"IT WAS AN EERIE FEELING I HAD, WALKING ROUND THE HOUSE.
"HAD SOMEONE BEEN INSIDE?
"HAD THEY WALKED AROUND AND TOUCHED OUR STUFF?
"PICKING UP PHOTOS AND PUTTING THEM BACK?
"EVEN THOUGH MY FATHER HAD CHECKED THE HOUSE, I WENT TO BED WITH A LINGERING FEAR THAT SOMEONE WAS IN THE HOUSE."

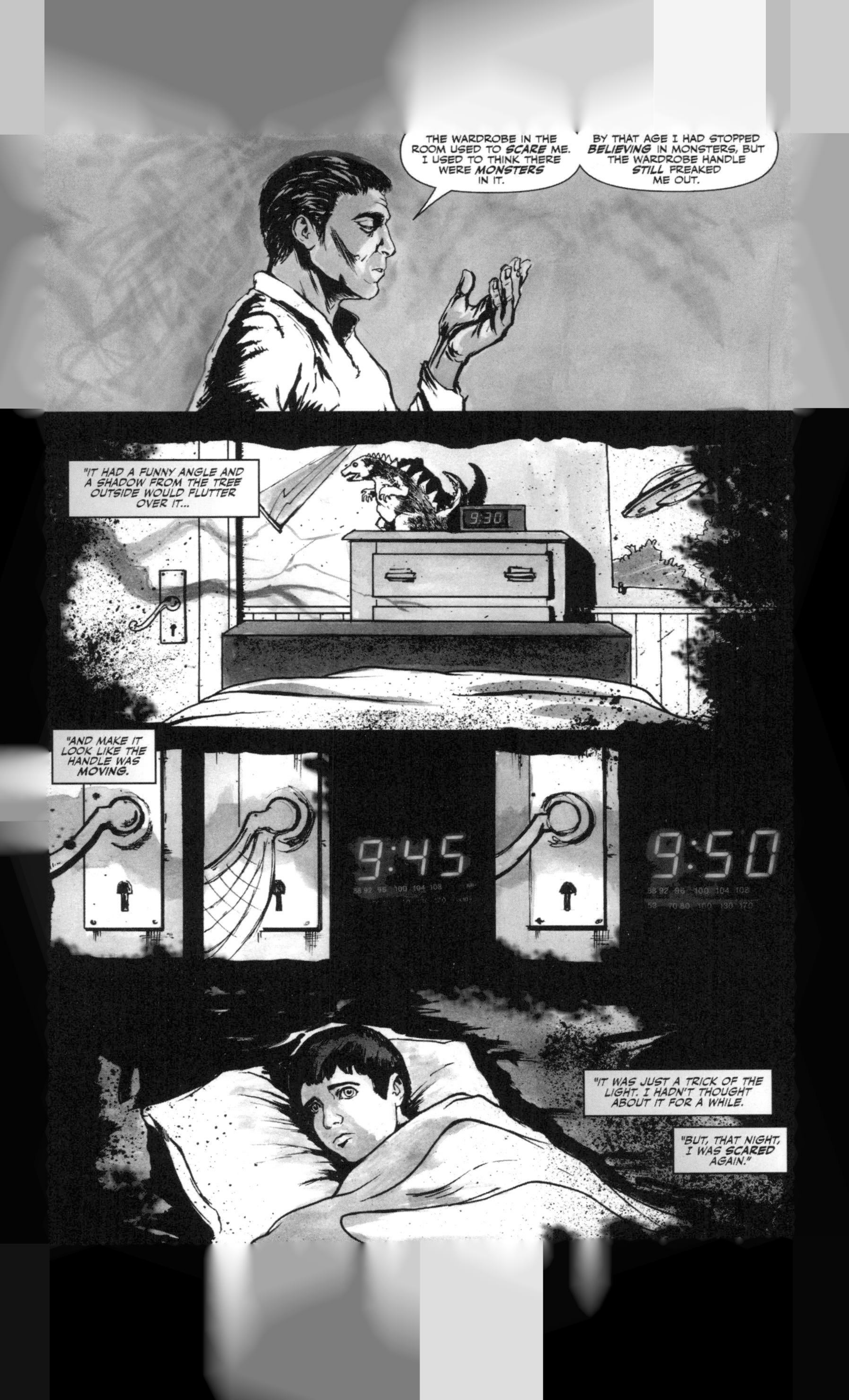

THE WARDROBE IN THE ROOM USED TO SCARE ME. I USED TO THINK THERE WERE MONSTERS IN IT.
BY THAT AGE I HAD STOPPED BELIEVING IN MONSTERS, BUT THE WARDROBE HANDLE STILL FREAKED ME OUT.
"IT HAD A FUNNY ANGLE AND A SHADOW FROM THE TREE OUTSIDE WOULD FLUTTER OVER IT...
9:30
"AND MAKE IT LOOK LIKE THE HANDLE WAS MOVING.
9:45
9:50
"IT WAS JUST A TRICK OF THE LIGHT. I HADN'T THOUGHT ABOUT IT FOR A WHILE.
"BUT, THAT NIGHT, I WAS SCARED AGAIN."

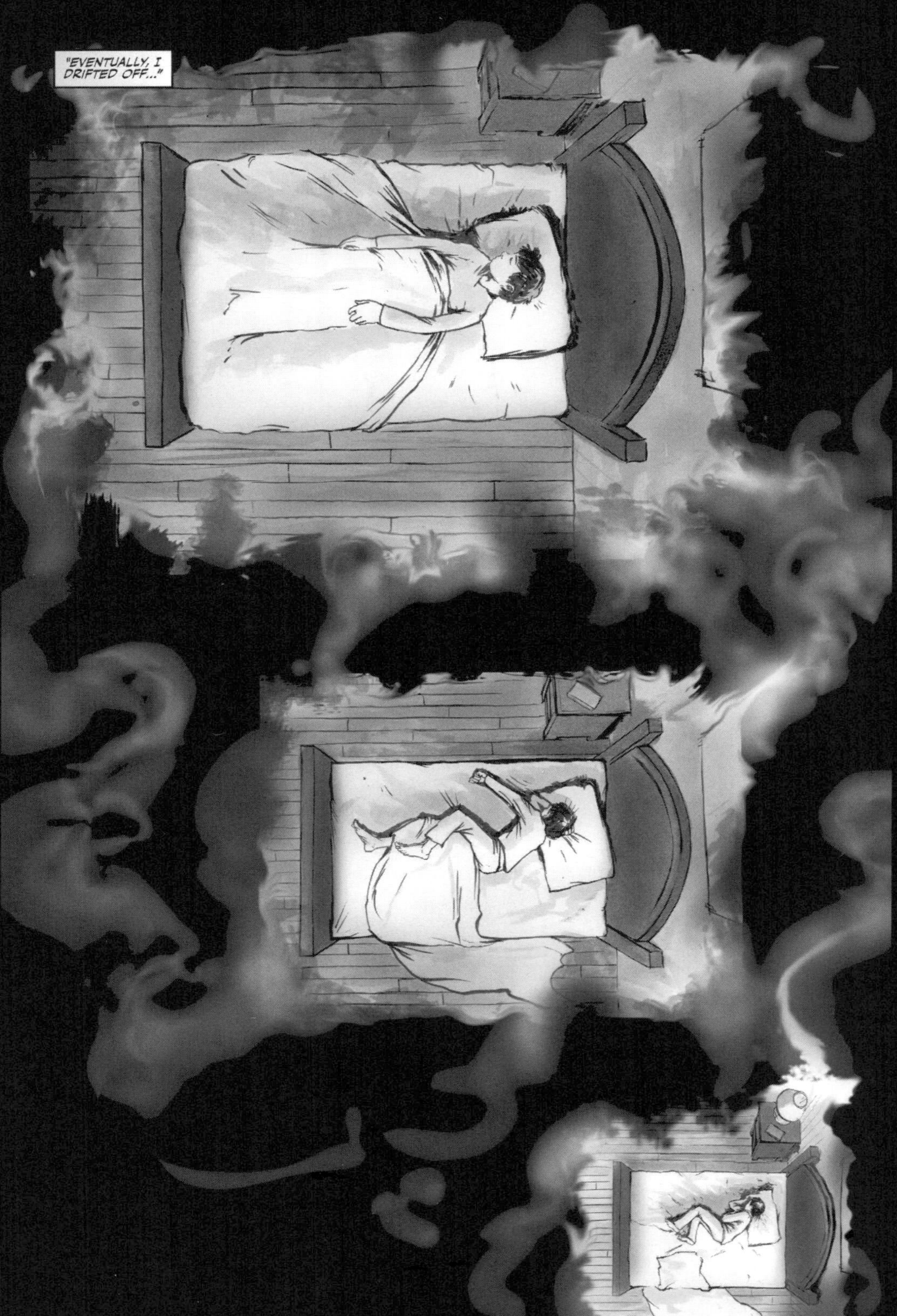
"EVENTUALLY, I DRIFTED OFF..."

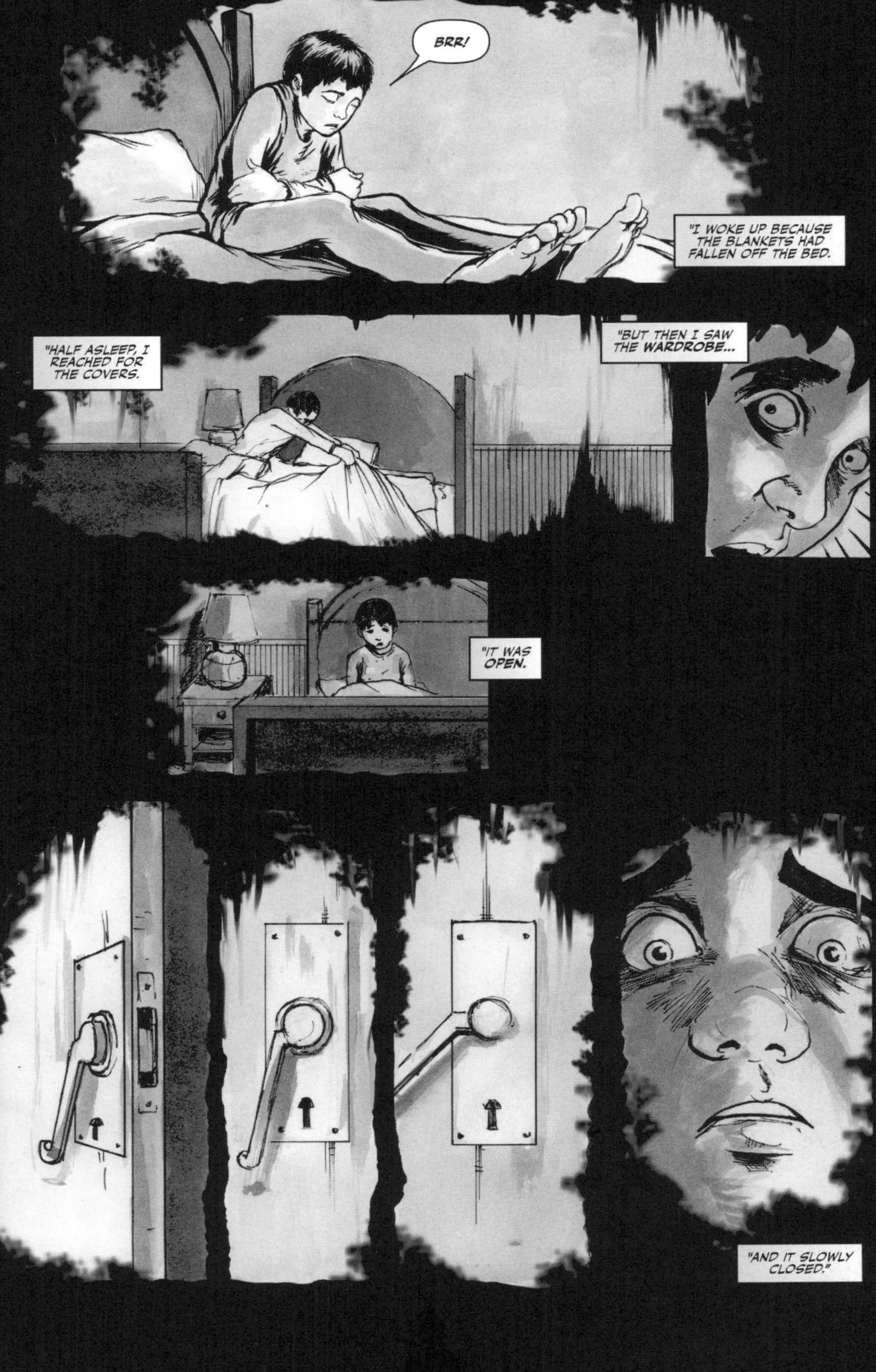
BRR!
"I WOKE UP BECAUSE THE BLANKETS HAD FALLEN OFF THE BED.
"HALF ASLEEP, I REACHED FOR THE COVERS.
"BUT THEN I SAW THE WARDROBE...
"IT WAS OPEN.
"AND IT SLOWLY CLOSED."

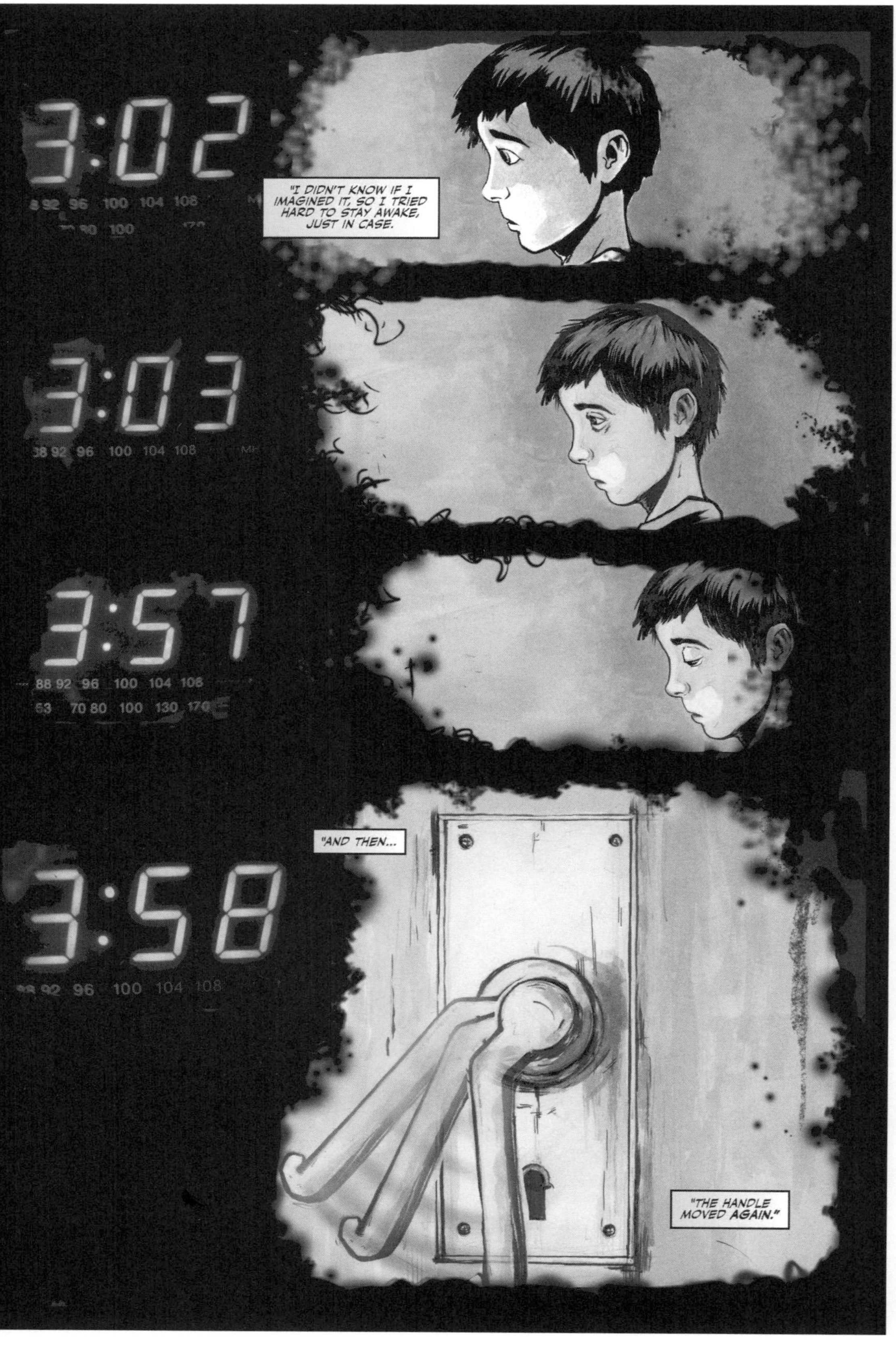
3:02
"I DIDN'T KNOW IF I IMAGINED IT, SO I TRIED HARD TO STAY AWAKE, JUST IN CASE.
3:03
3:57
3:58
"AND THEN...
"THE HANDLE MOVED AGAIN."

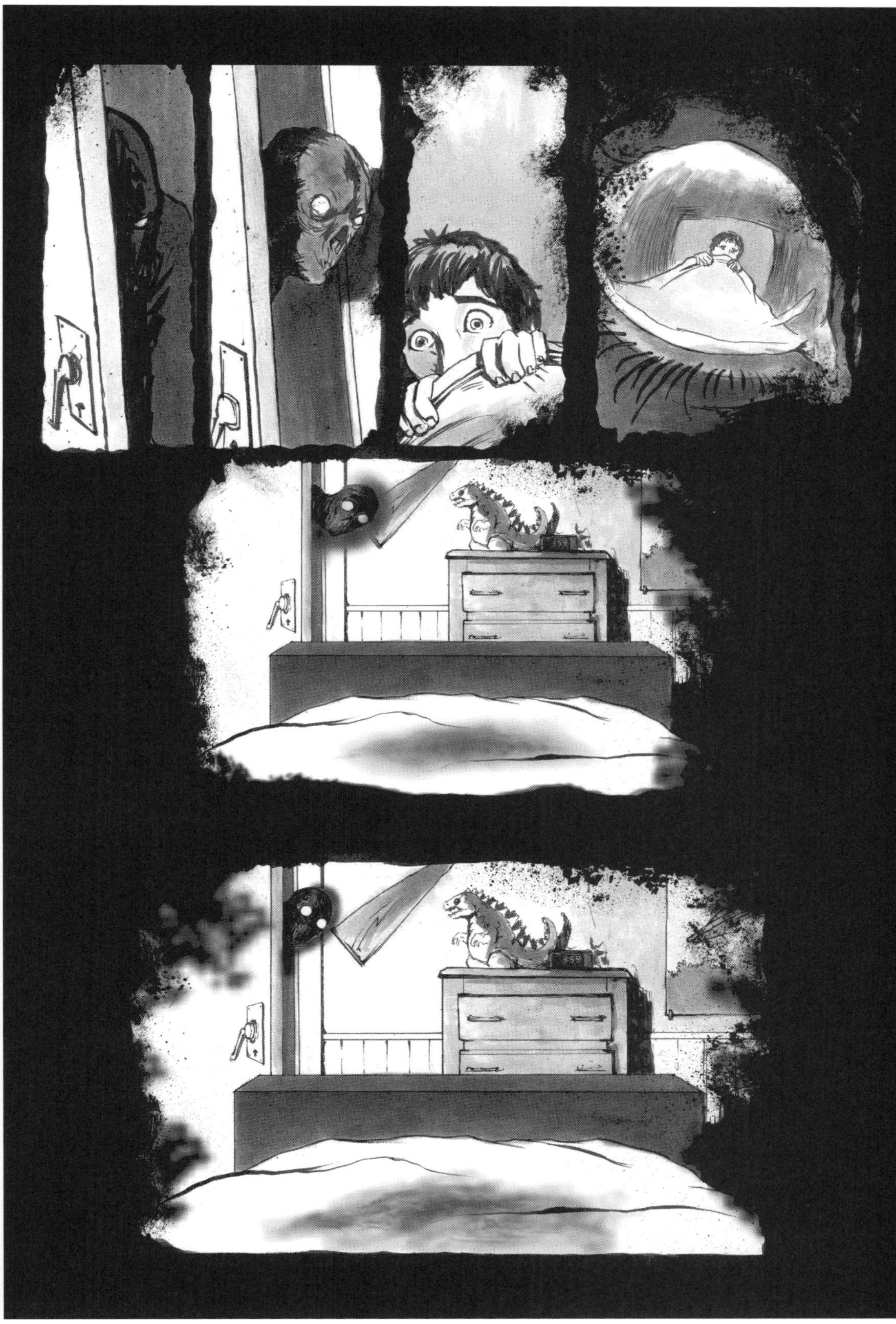

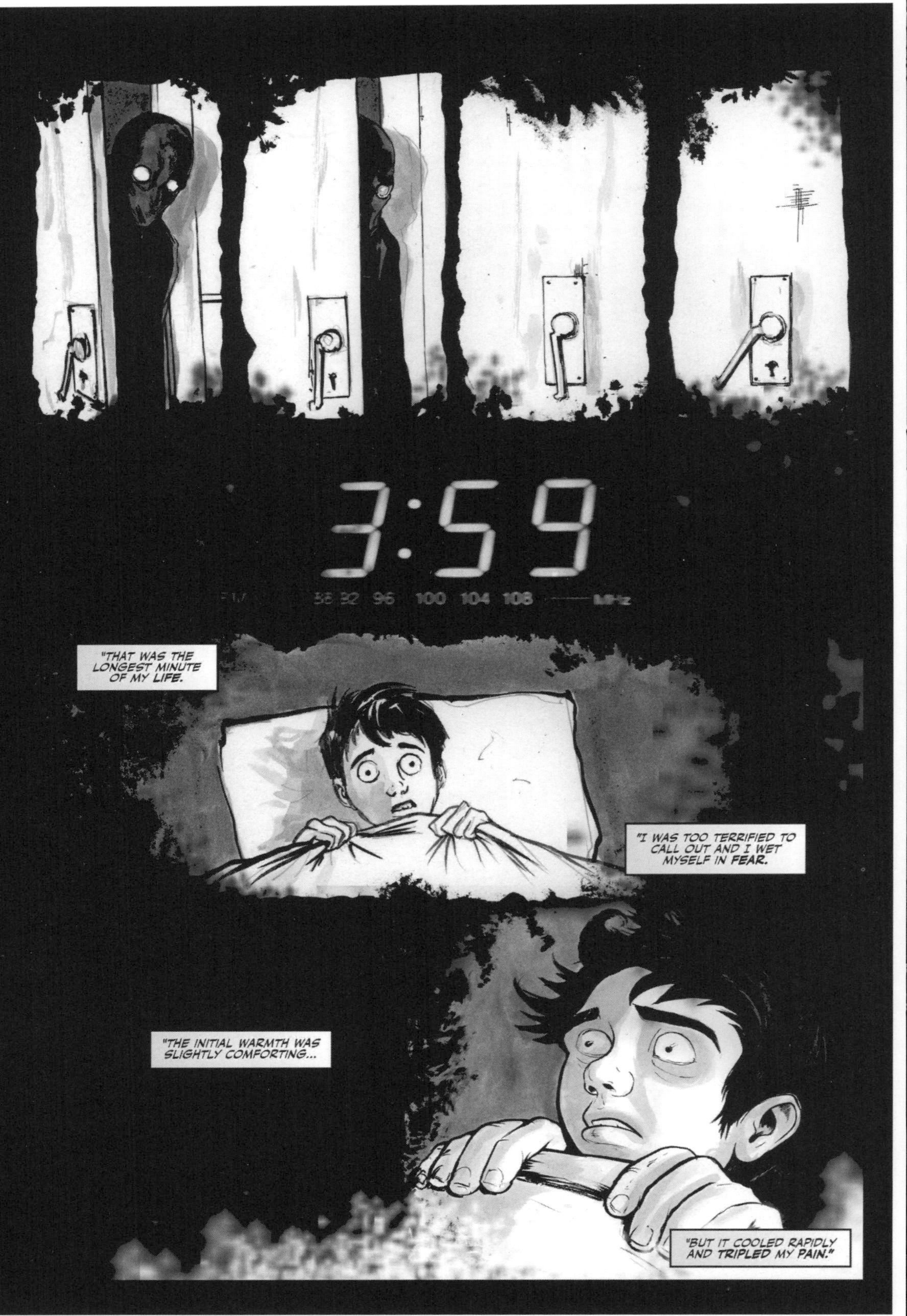
3:59
FM 88 92 96 100 104 108 MHz
"THAT WAS THE LONGEST MINUTE OF MY LIFE.
"I WAS TOO TERRIFIED TO CALL OUT AND I WET MYSELF IN FEAR.
"THE INITIAL WARMTH WAS SLIGHTLY COMFORTING...
"BUT IT COOLED RAPIDLY AND TRIPLED MY PAIN."

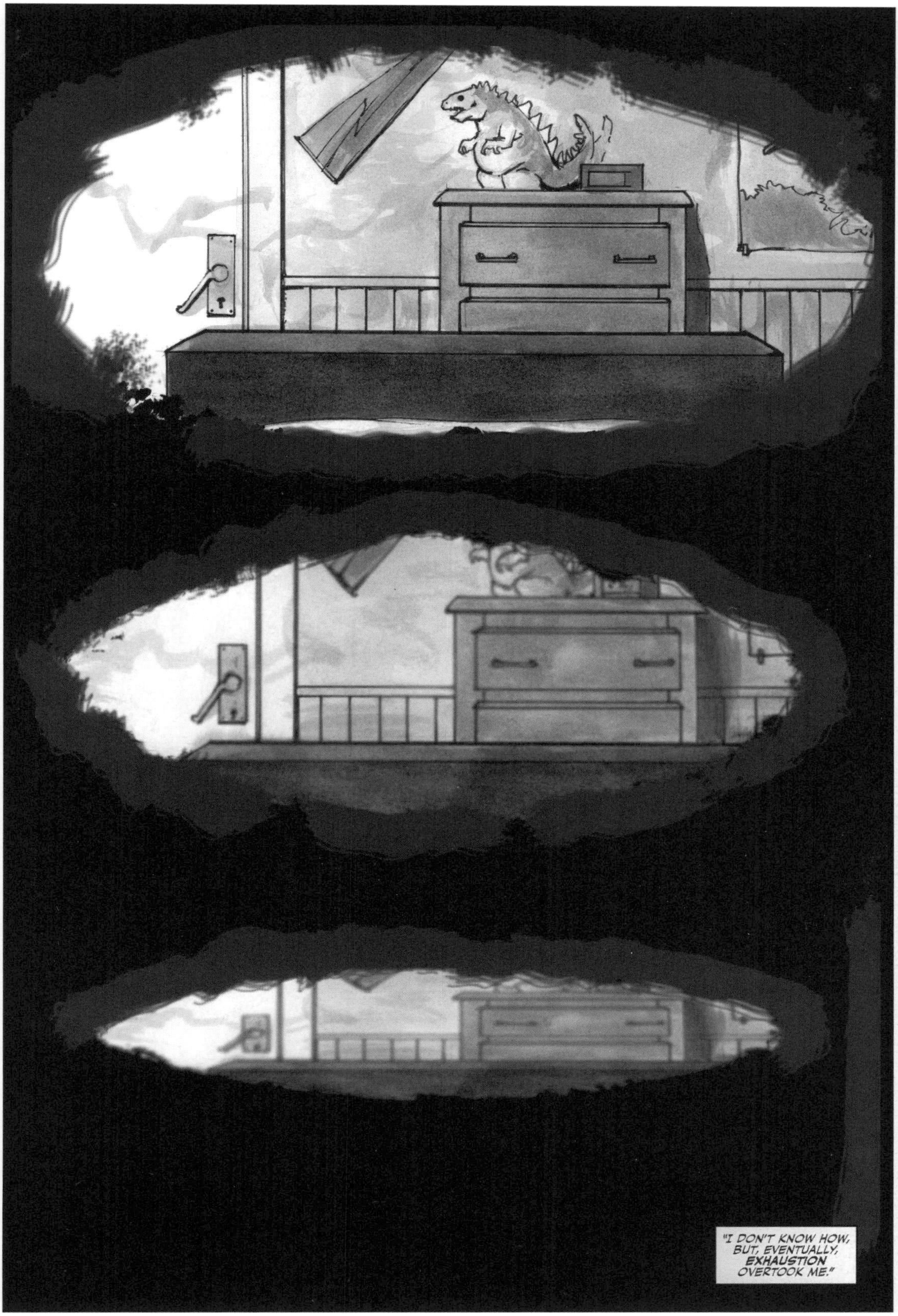
"I DON'T KNOW HOW, BUT, EVENTUALLY, EXHAUSTION OVERTOOK ME."

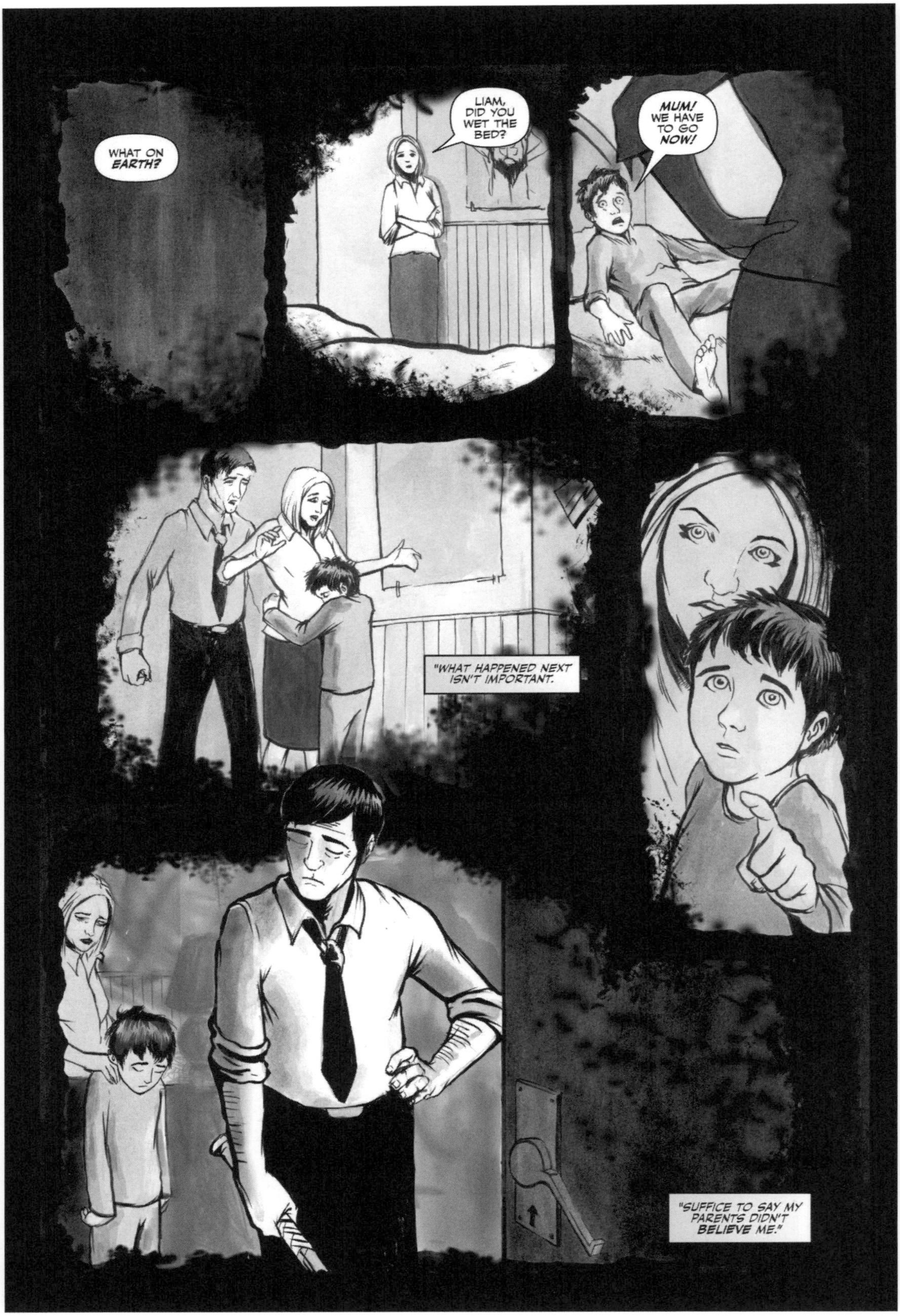
WHAT ON EARTH?
LIAM, DID YOU WET THE BED?
MUM! WE HAVE TO GO NOW!
"WHAT HAPPENED NEXT ISN'T IMPORTANT.
"SUFFICE TO SAY MY PARENTS DIDN'T BELIEVE ME."

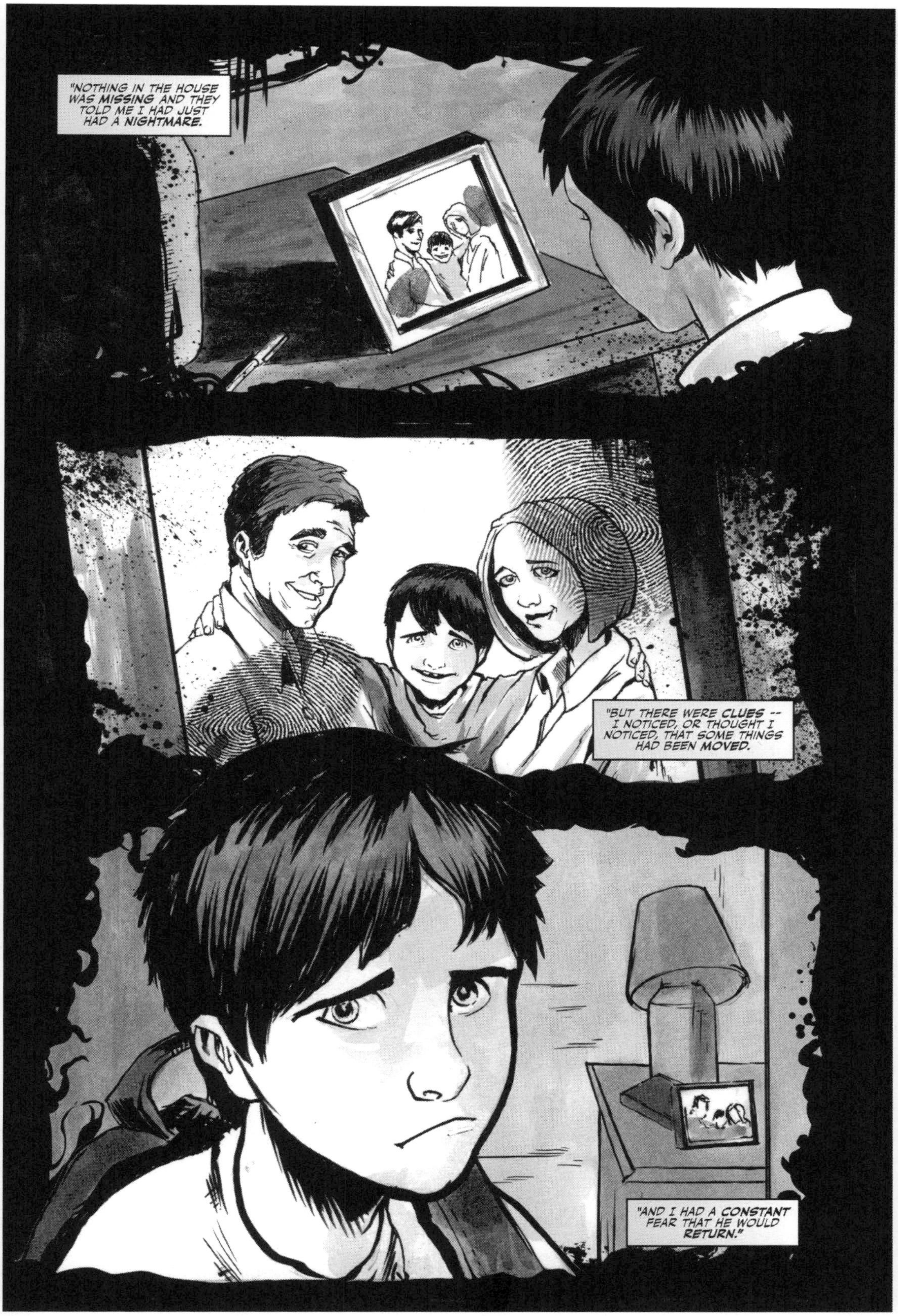
"NOTHING IN THE HOUSE WAS MISSING AND THEY TOLD ME I HAD JUST HAD A NIGHTMARE.
"BUT THERE WERE CLUES -- I NOTICED, OR THOUGHT I NOTICED, THAT SOME THINGS HAD BEEN MOVED.
"AND I HAD A CONSTANT FEAR THAT HE WOULD RETURN."

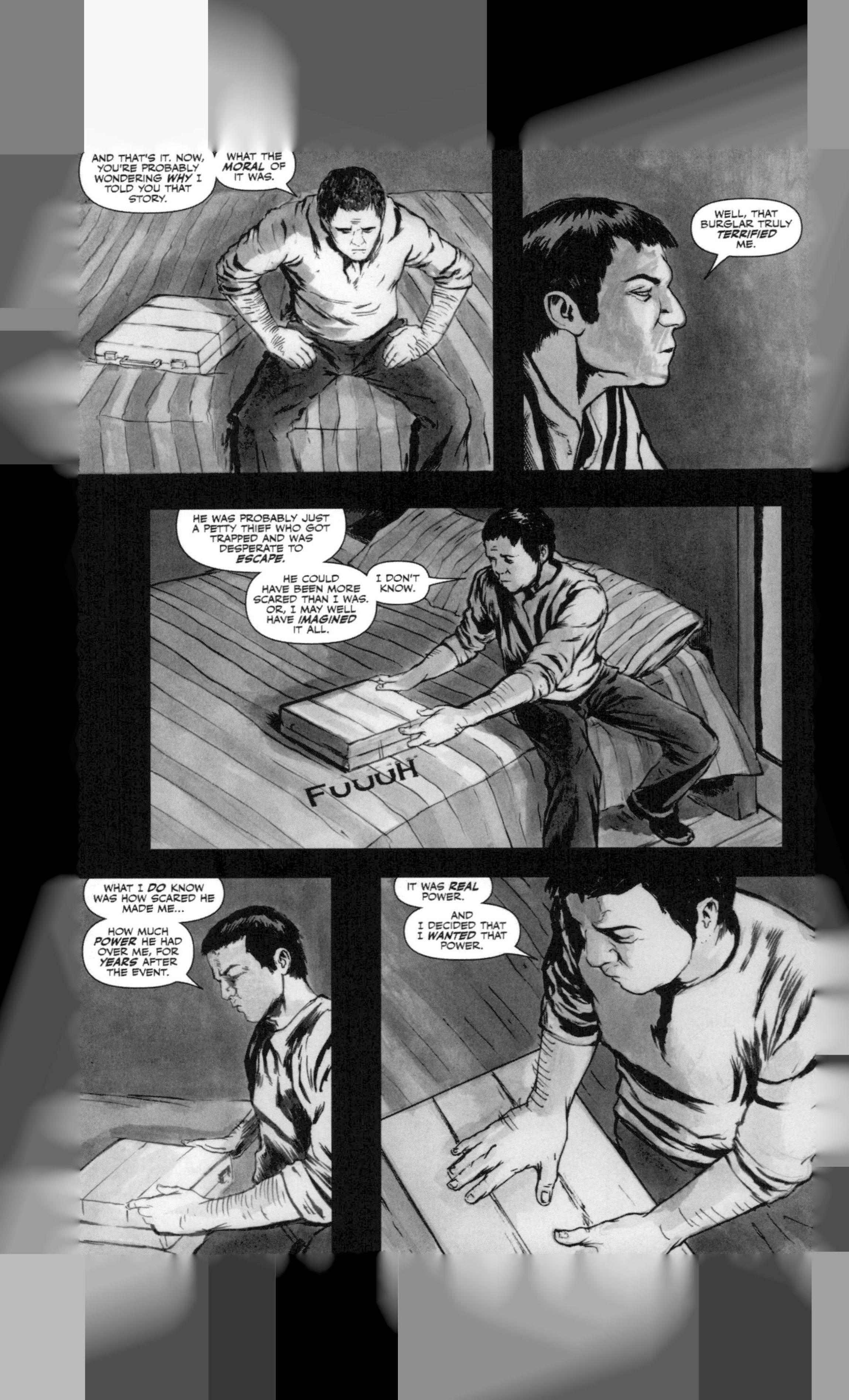

AND THAT'S IT. NOW, YOU'RE PROBABLY WONDERING WHY I TOLD YOU THAT STORY.
WHAT THE MORAL OF IT WAS.
WELL, THAT BURGLAR TRULY TERRIFIED ME.
HE WAS PROBABLY JUST A PETTY THIEF WHO GOT TRAPPED AND WAS DESPERATE TO ESCAPE.
HE COULD HAVE BEEN MORE SCARED THAN I WAS. OR, I MAY WELL HAVE IMAGINED IT ALL.
I DON'T KNOW.
FUUUH
WHAT I DO KNOW WAS HOW SCARED HE MADE ME...
HOW MUCH POWER HE HAD OVER ME, FOR YEARS AFTER THE EVENT.
IT WAS REAL POWER.
AND I DECIDED THAT I WANTED THAT POWER.

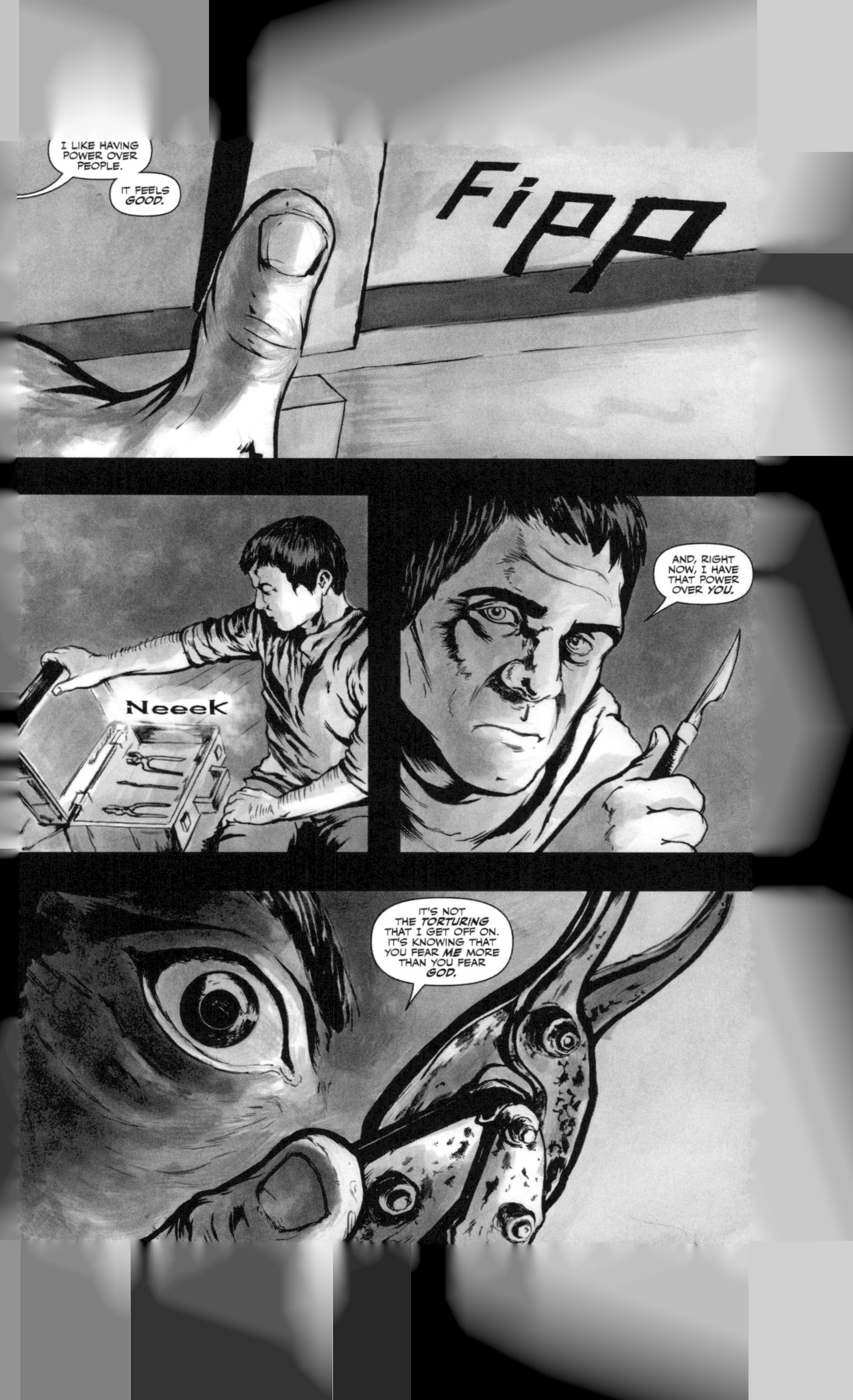
I LIKE HAVING POWER OVER PEOPLE.
IT FEELS GOOD.
FIPP
NeeeK
AND, RIGHT NOW, I HAVE THAT POWER OVER YOU.
IT'S NOT THE TORTURING THAT I GET OFF ON. IT'S KNOWING THAT YOU FEAR ME MORE THAN YOU FEAR GOD.

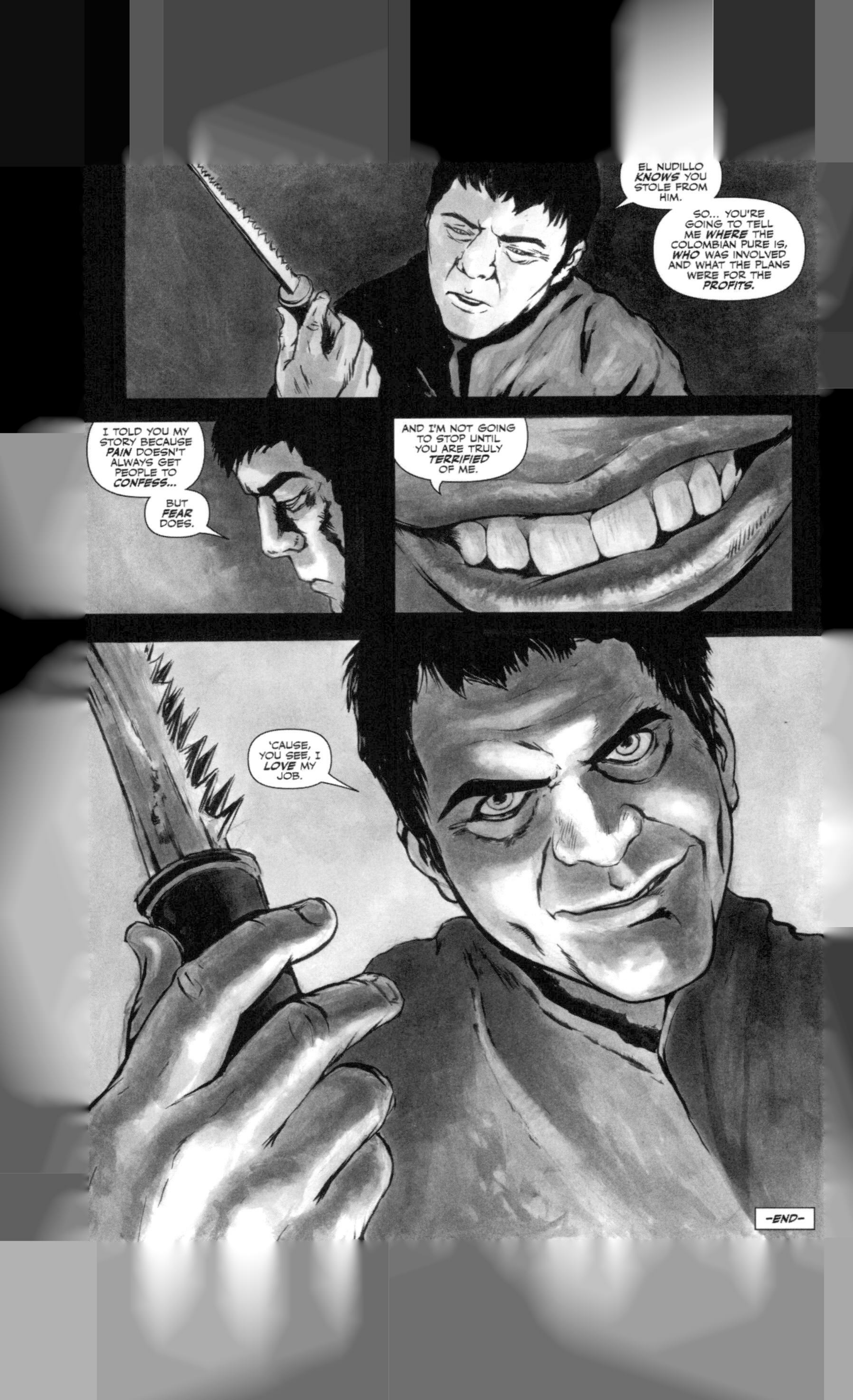
EL NUDILLO KNOWS YOU STOLE FROM HIM.
SO... YOU'RE GOING TO TELL ME WHERE THE COLOMBIAN PURE IS, WHO WAS INVOLVED AND WHAT THE PLANS WERE FOR THE PROFITS.
I TOLD YOU MY STORY BECAUSE PAIN DOESN'T ALWAYS GET PEOPLE TO CONFESS...
BUT FEAR DOES.
AND I'M NOT GOING TO STOP UNTIL YOU ARE TRULY TERRIFIED OF ME.
'CAUSE, YOU SEE, I LOVE MY JOB.
-END-

Perfection...

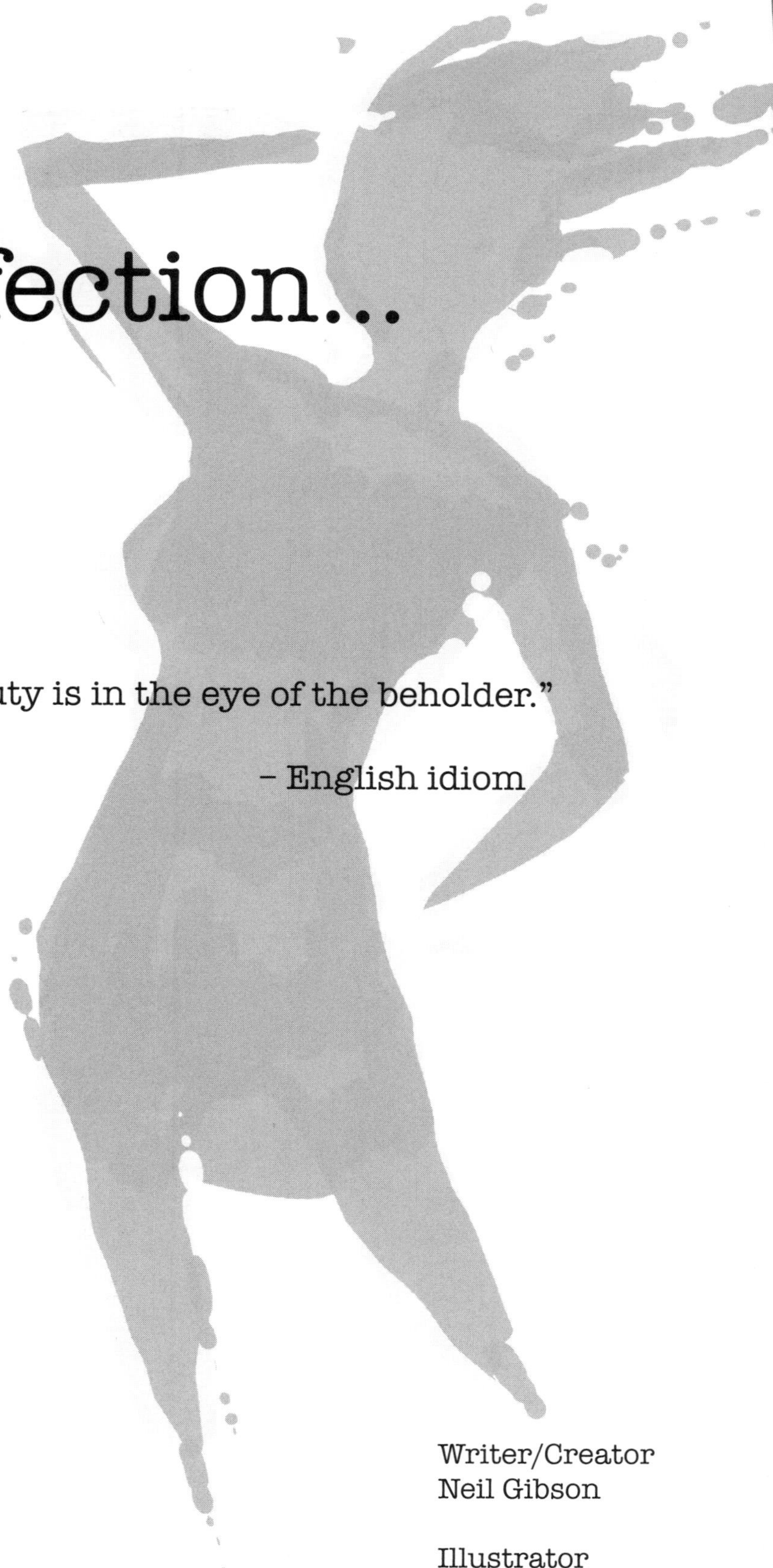

"Beauty is in the eye of the beholder."

– English idiom

Writer/Creator
Neil Gibson

Illustrator
Caspar Wijngaard

www.tpub.co.uk

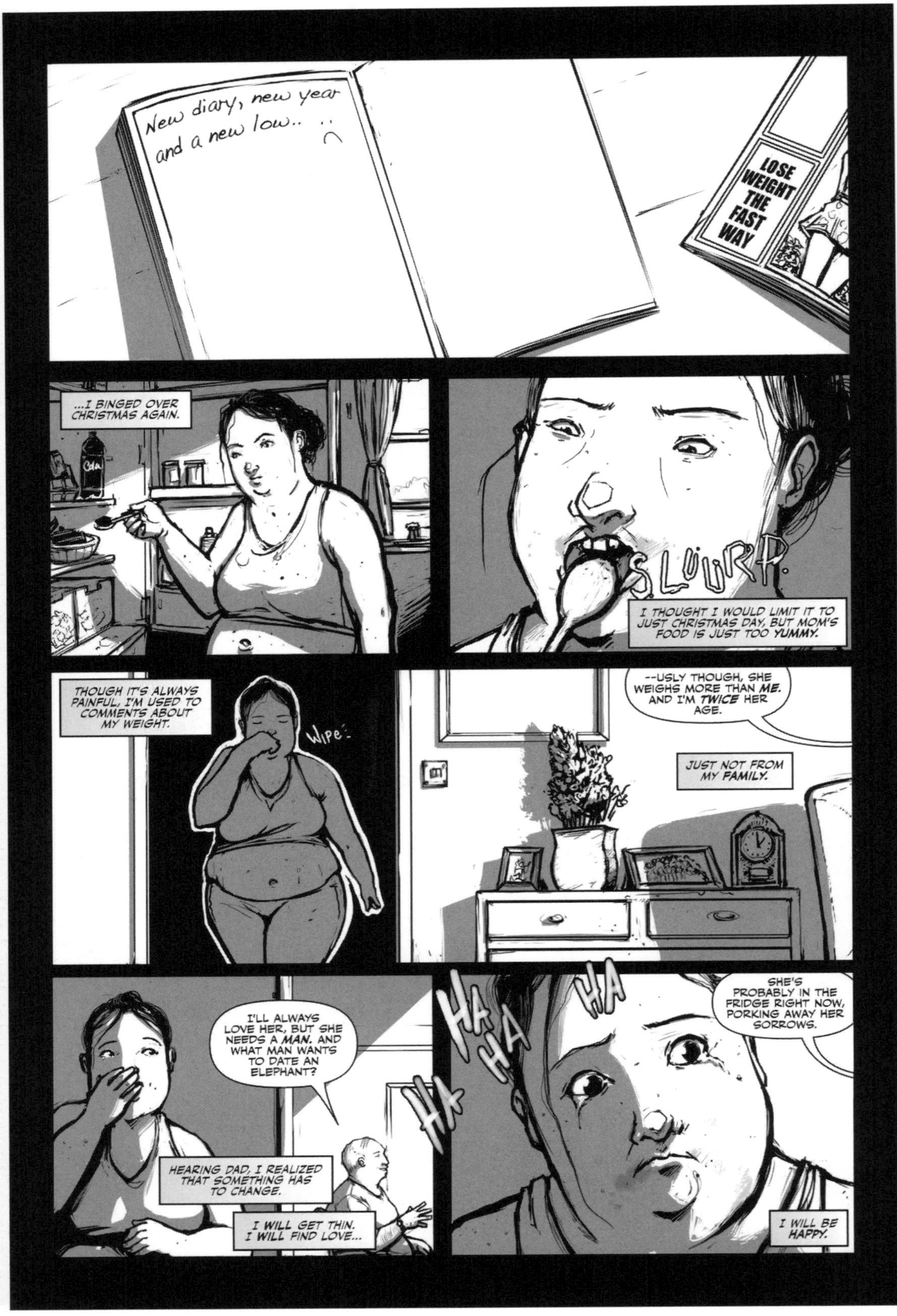
New diary, new year
and a new low.. :(
LOSE WEIGHT THE FAST WAY
...I BINGED OVER CHRISTMAS AGAIN.
Cola
SLURRP.
I THOUGHT I WOULD LIMIT IT TO JUST CHRISTMAS DAY, BUT MOM'S FOOD IS JUST TOO YUMMY.
THOUGH IT'S ALWAYS PAINFUL, I'M USED TO COMMENTS ABOUT MY WEIGHT.
WIPE
--USLY THOUGH, SHE WEIGHS MORE THAN ME. AND I'M TWICE HER AGE.
JUST NOT FROM MY FAMILY.
I'LL ALWAYS LOVE HER, BUT SHE NEEDS A MAN. AND WHAT MAN WANTS TO DATE AN ELEPHANT?
HEARING DAD, I REALIZED THAT SOMETHING HAS TO CHANGE.
I WILL GET THIN. I WILL FIND LOVE...
HA HA HA HA HA
SHE'S PROBABLY IN THE FRIDGE RIGHT NOW, PORKING AWAY HER SORROWS.
I WILL BE HAPPY.

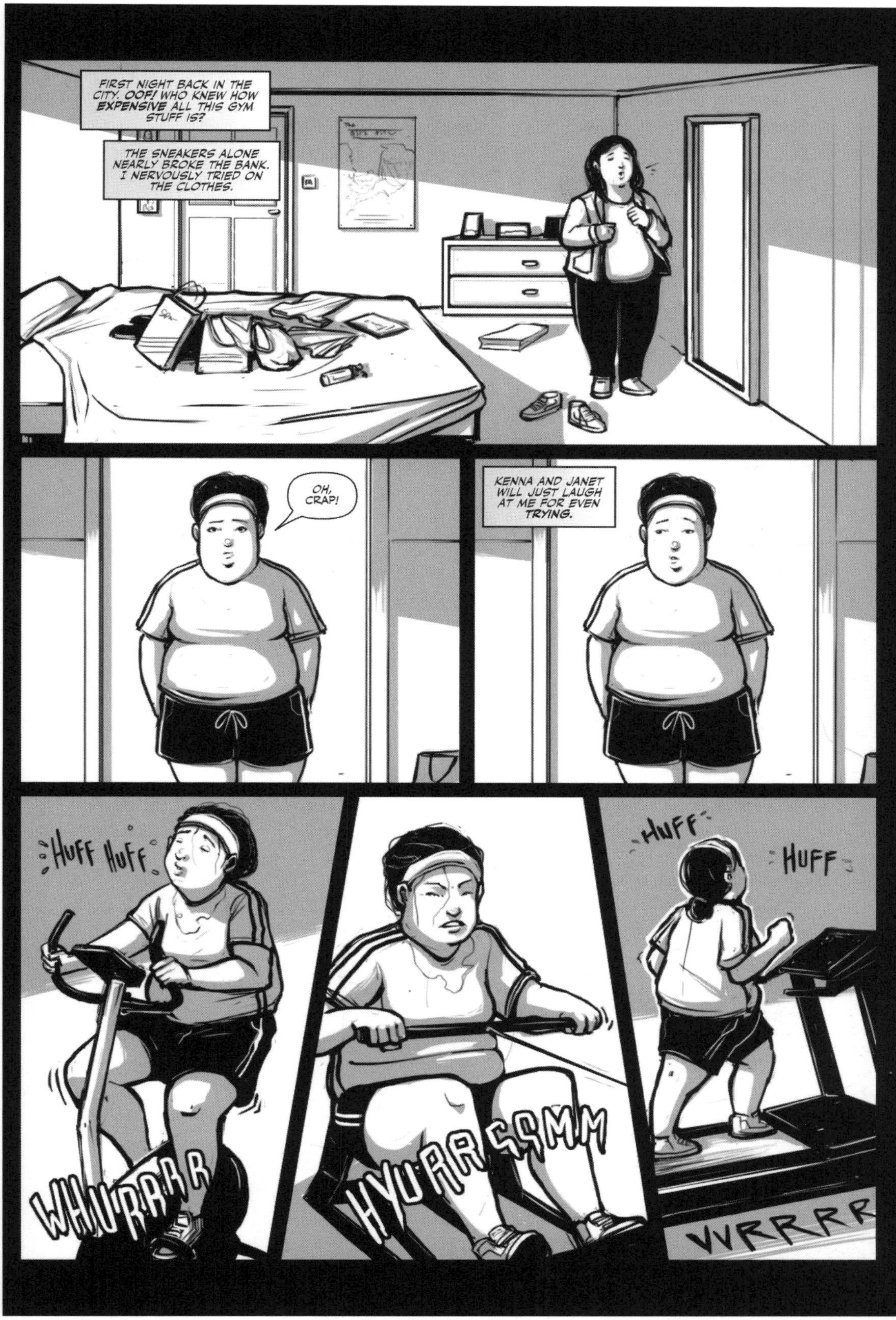
FIRST NIGHT BACK IN THE CITY. OOF! WHO KNEW HOW EXPENSIVE ALL THIS GYM STUFF IS?
THE SNEAKERS ALONE NEARLY BROKE THE BANK. I NERVOUSLY TRIED ON THE CLOTHES.
OH, CRAP!
KENNA AND JANET WILL JUST LAUGH AT ME FOR EVEN TRYING.
HUFF HUFF
WHURRRR
HYURRSSMM
HUFF
HUFF
VVRRRR

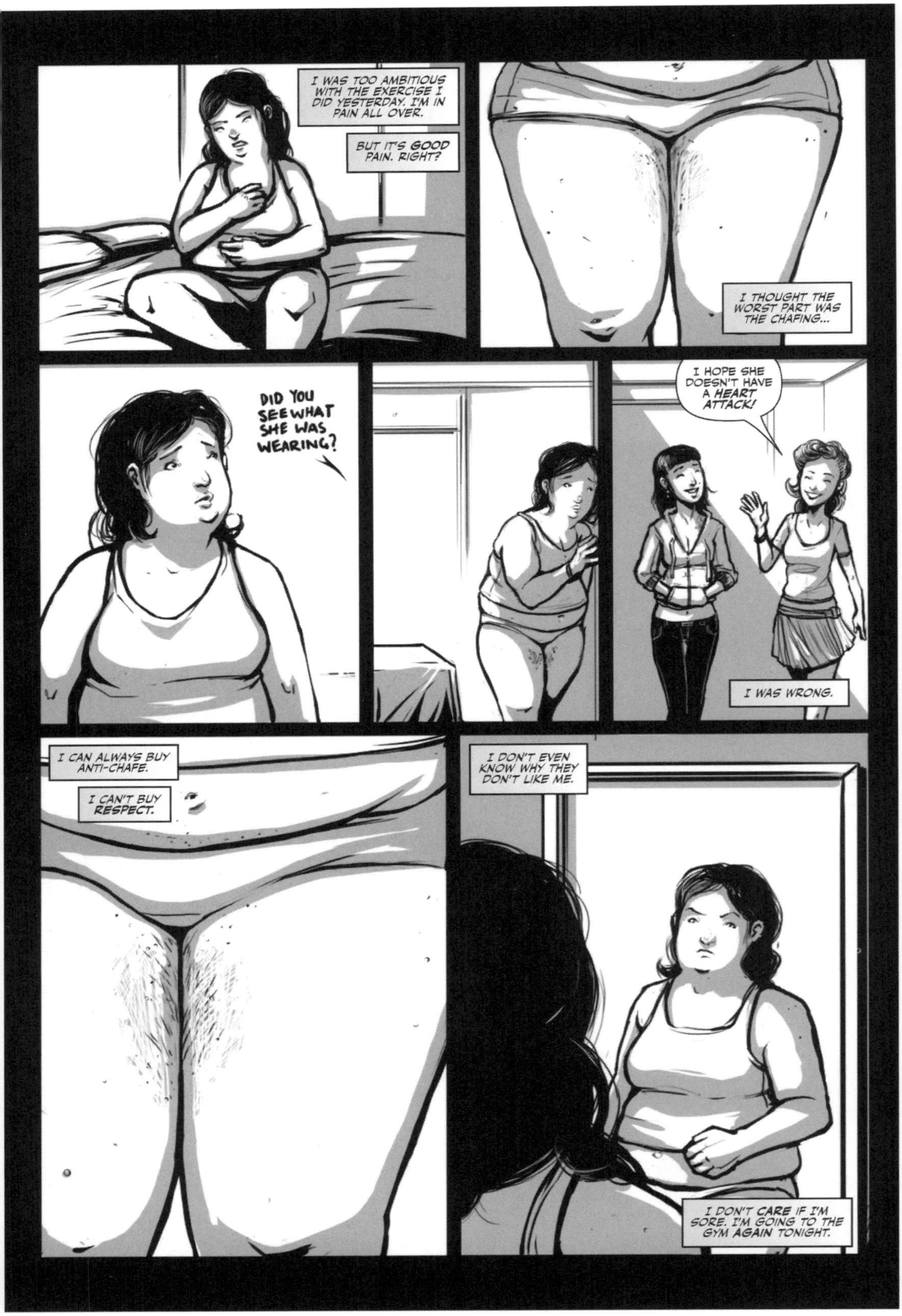
I WAS TOO AMBITIOUS WITH THE EXERCISE I DID YESTERDAY. I'M IN PAIN ALL OVER.
BUT IT'S GOOD PAIN. RIGHT?
I THOUGHT THE WORST PART WAS THE CHAFING...
DID YOU SEE WHAT SHE WAS WEARING?
I HOPE SHE DOESN'T HAVE A HEART ATTACK!
I WAS WRONG.
I CAN ALWAYS BUY ANTI-CHAFE.
I CAN'T BUY RESPECT.
I DON'T EVEN KNOW WHY THEY DON'T LIKE ME.
I DON'T CARE IF I'M SORE. I'M GOING TO THE GYM AGAIN TONIGHT.

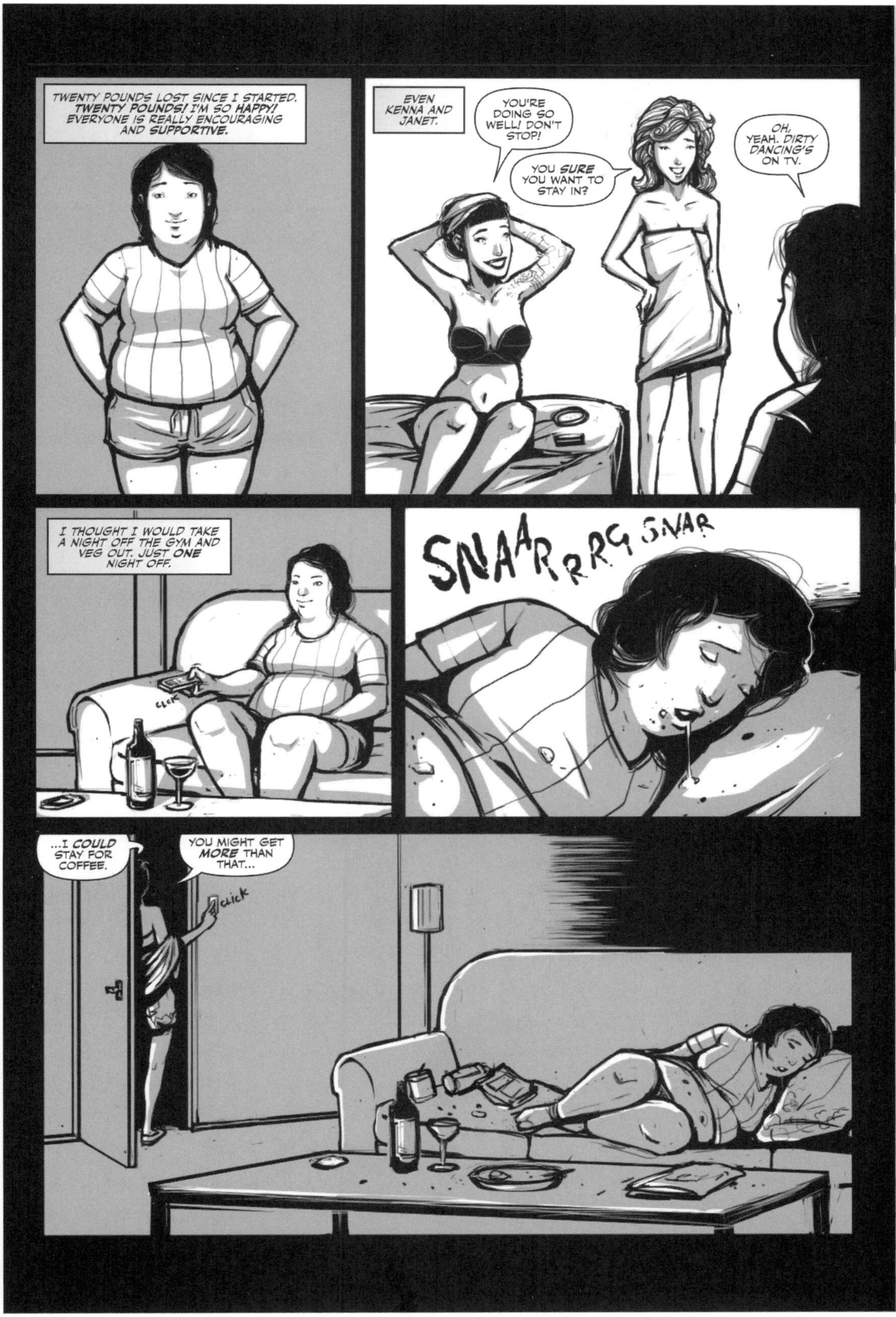
TWENTY POUNDS LOST SINCE I STARTED. TWENTY POUNDS! I'M SO HAPPY! EVERYONE IS REALLY ENCOURAGING AND SUPPORTIVE.
EVEN KENNA AND JANET.
YOU'RE DOING SO WELL! DON'T STOP!
YOU SURE YOU WANT TO STAY IN?
OH, YEAH. DIRTY DANCING'S ON TV.
I THOUGHT I WOULD TAKE A NIGHT OFF THE GYM AND VEG OUT. JUST ONE NIGHT OFF.
CLICK
SNAARRRG SNAR
...I COULD STAY FOR COFFEE.
YOU MIGHT GET MORE THAN THAT...
CLICK

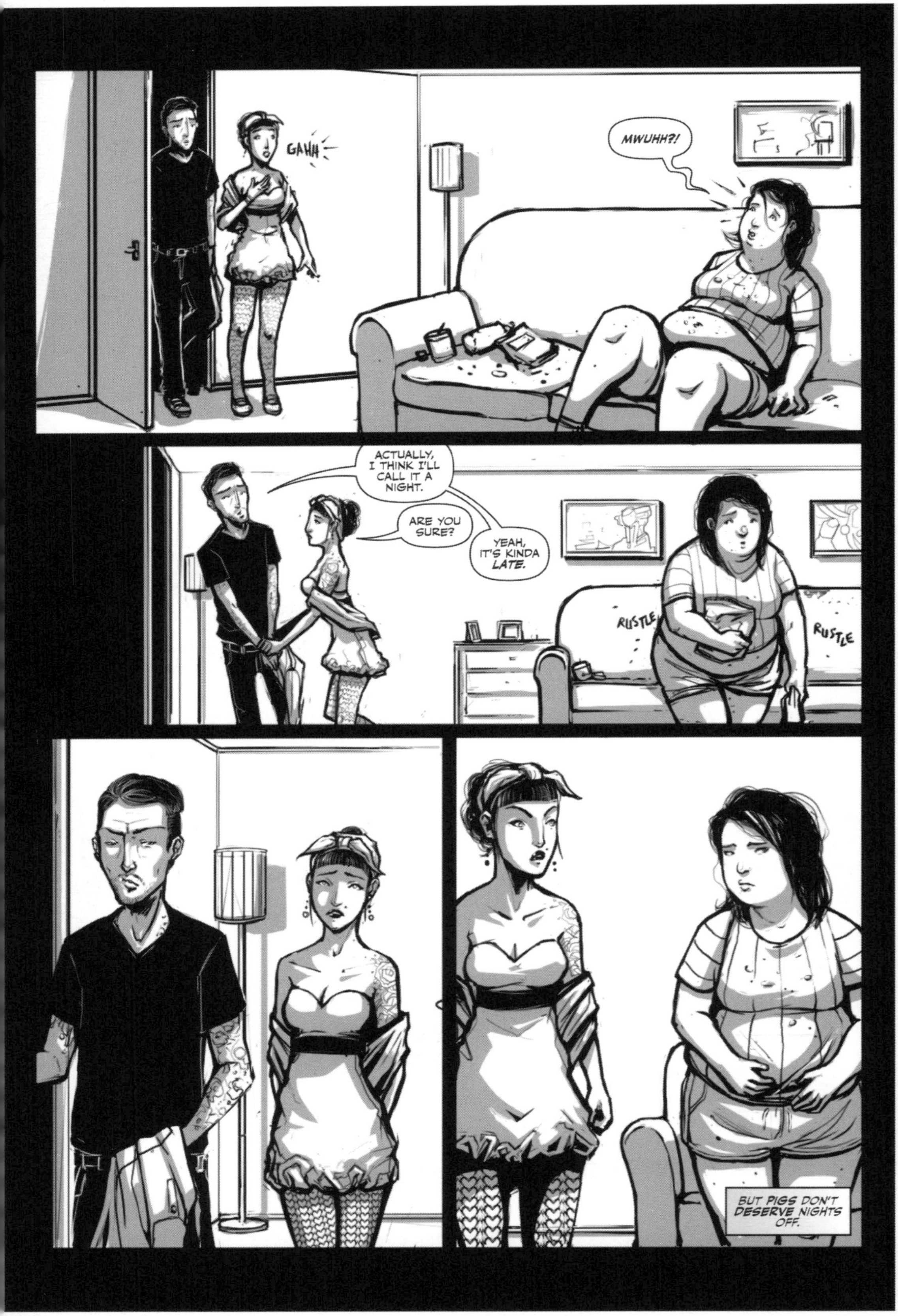
GAHH
MWUHH?!
ACTUALLY, I THINK I'LL CALL IT A NIGHT.
ARE YOU SURE?
YEAH, IT'S KINDA LATE.
RUSTLE
RUSTLE
BUT PIGS DON'T DESERVE NIGHTS OFF.

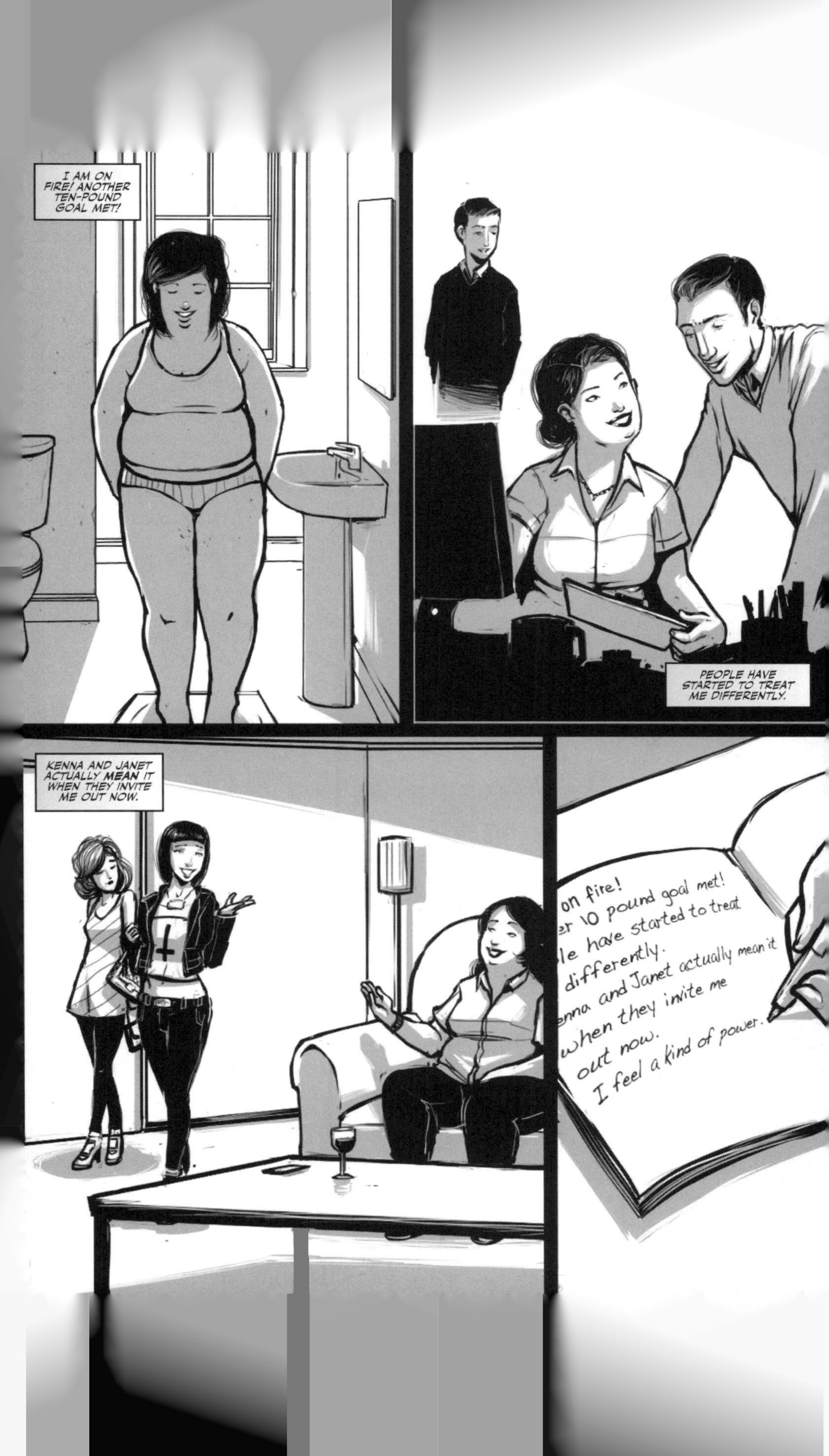
I AM ON FIRE! ANOTHER TEN-POUND GOAL MET!
PEOPLE HAVE STARTED TO TREAT ME DIFFERENTLY.
KENNA AND JANET ACTUALLY **MEAN** IT WHEN THEY INVITE ME OUT NOW.
on fire!
er 10 pound goal met!
le have started to treat
differently.
enna and Janet actually mean it
when they invite me
out now.
I feel a kind of power.

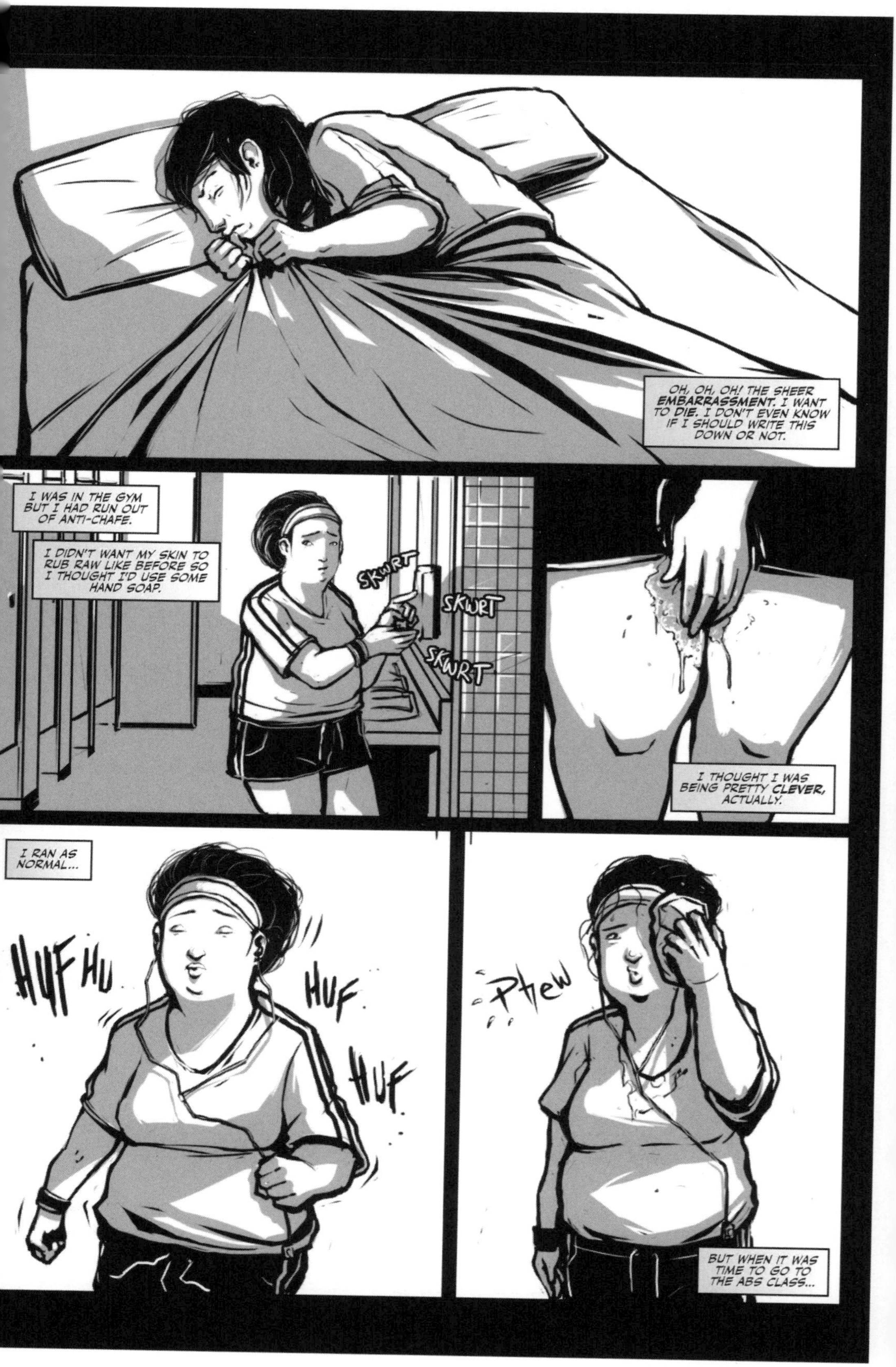
OH, OH, OH! THE SHEER EMBARRASSMENT. I WANT TO DIE. I DON'T EVEN KNOW IF I SHOULD WRITE THIS DOWN OR NOT.
I WAS IN THE GYM BUT I HAD RUN OUT OF ANTI-CHAFE.
I DIDN'T WANT MY SKIN TO RUB RAW LIKE BEFORE SO I THOUGHT I'D USE SOME HAND SOAP.
SKWRT
SKWRT
SKWRT
I THOUGHT I WAS BEING PRETTY CLEVER, ACTUALLY.
I RAN AS NORMAL...
HUF HU
HUF
HUF
Phew
BUT WHEN IT WAS TIME TO GO TO THE ABS CLASS...

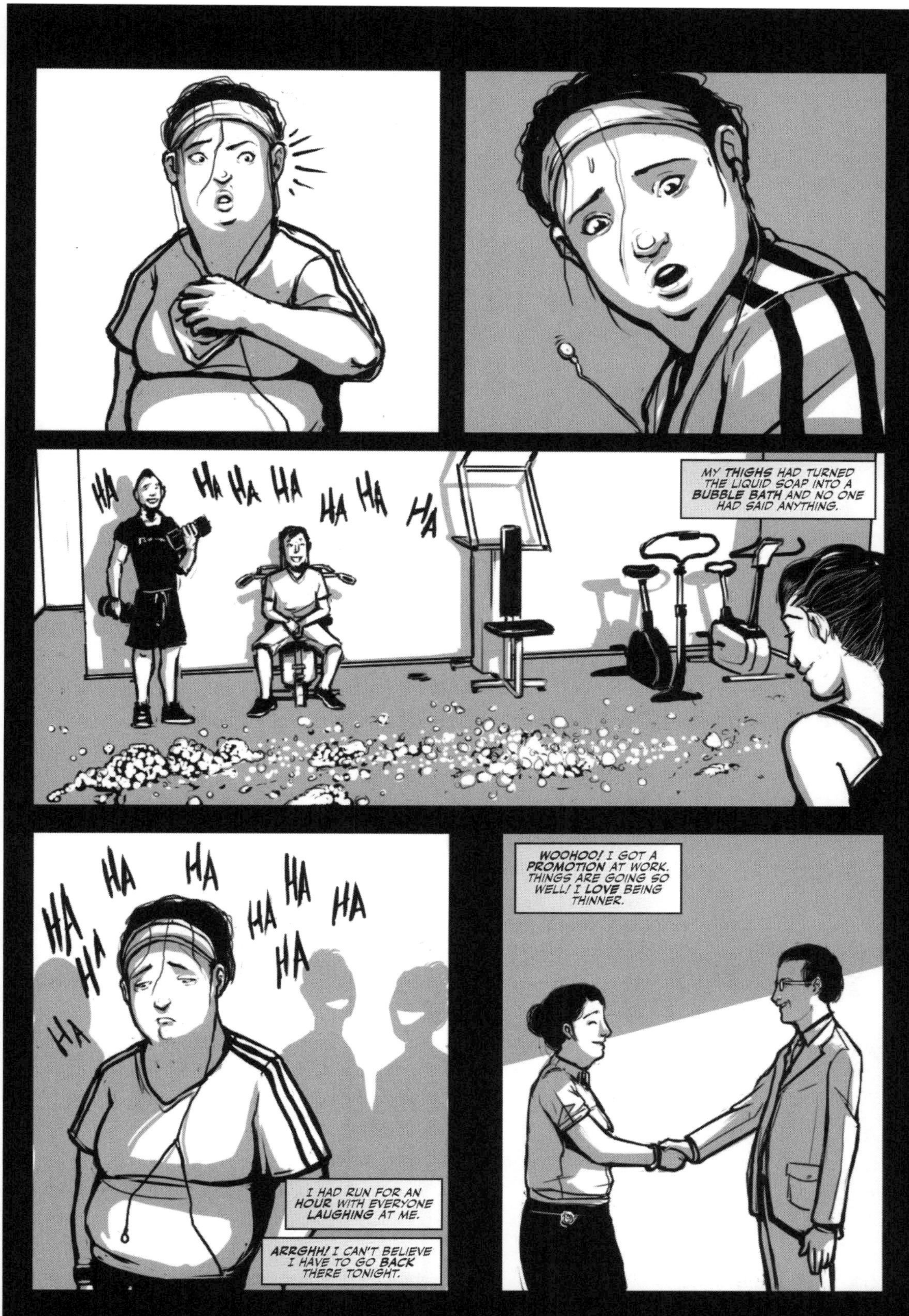
HA HA HA HA HA HA HA HA
MY THIGHS HAD TURNED THE LIQUID SOAP INTO A BUBBLE BATH AND NO ONE HAD SAID ANYTHING.
HA HA HA HA HA HA HA HA HA
I HAD RUN FOR AN HOUR WITH EVERYONE LAUGHING AT ME.
ARRGHH! I CAN'T BELIEVE I HAVE TO GO BACK THERE TONIGHT.
WOOHOO! I GOT A PROMOTION AT WORK. THINGS ARE GOING SO WELL! I LOVE BEING THINNER.

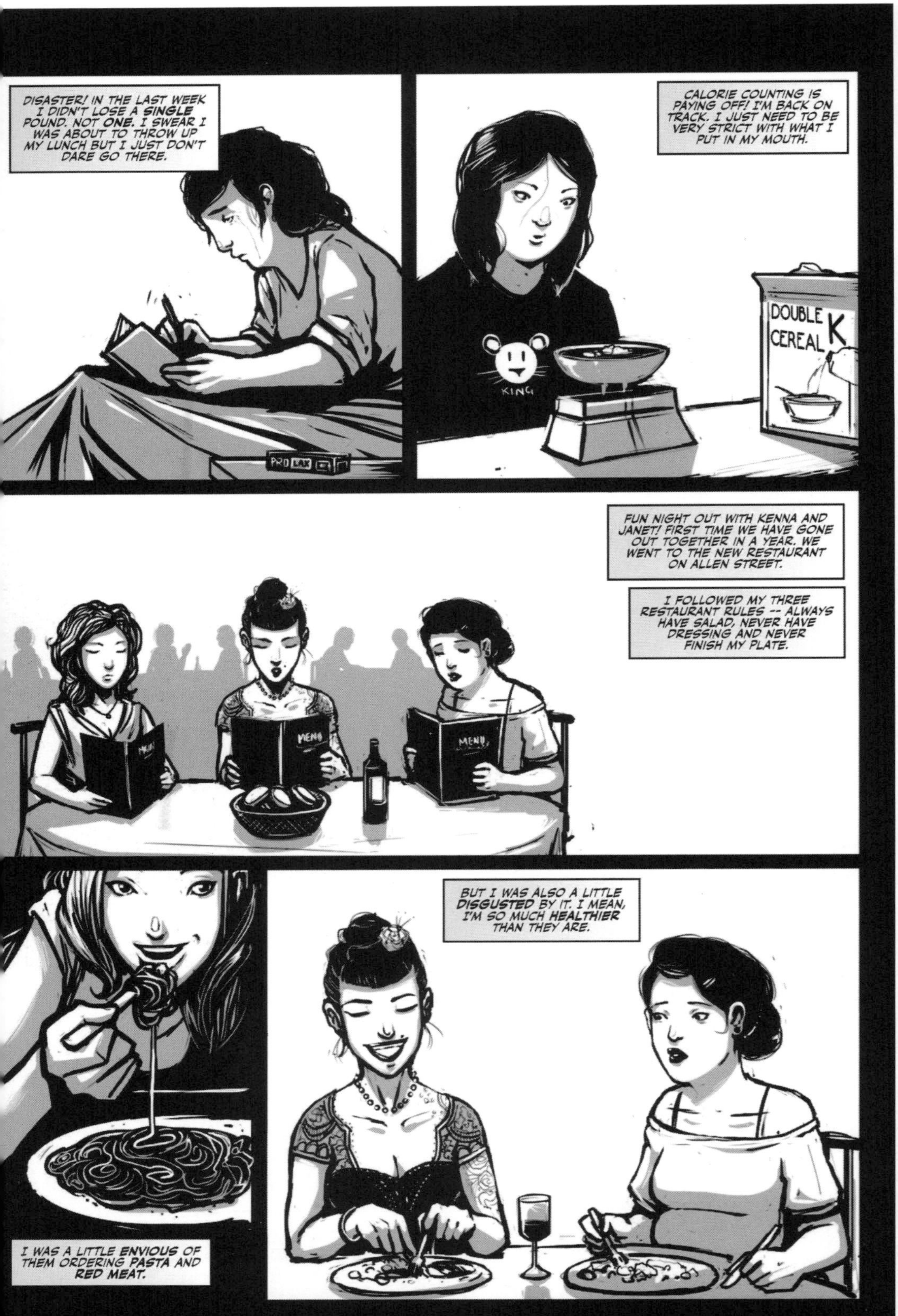
DISASTER! IN THE LAST WEEK I DIDN'T LOSE A SINGLE POUND. NOT ONE. I SWEAR I WAS ABOUT TO THROW UP MY LUNCH BUT I JUST DON'T DARE GO THERE.
PRO LAX
CALORIE COUNTING IS PAYING OFF! I'M BACK ON TRACK. I JUST NEED TO BE VERY STRICT WITH WHAT I PUT IN MY MOUTH.
KING
DOUBLE K CEREAL
FUN NIGHT OUT WITH KENNA AND JANET! FIRST TIME WE HAVE GONE OUT TOGETHER IN A YEAR. WE WENT TO THE NEW RESTAURANT ON ALLEN STREET.
I FOLLOWED MY THREE RESTAURANT RULES -- ALWAYS HAVE SALAD, NEVER HAVE DRESSING AND NEVER FINISH MY PLATE.
MENU
MENU
I WAS A LITTLE ENVIOUS OF THEM ORDERING PASTA AND RED MEAT.
BUT I WAS ALSO A LITTLE DISGUSTED BY IT. I MEAN, I'M SO MUCH HEALTHIER THAN THEY ARE.

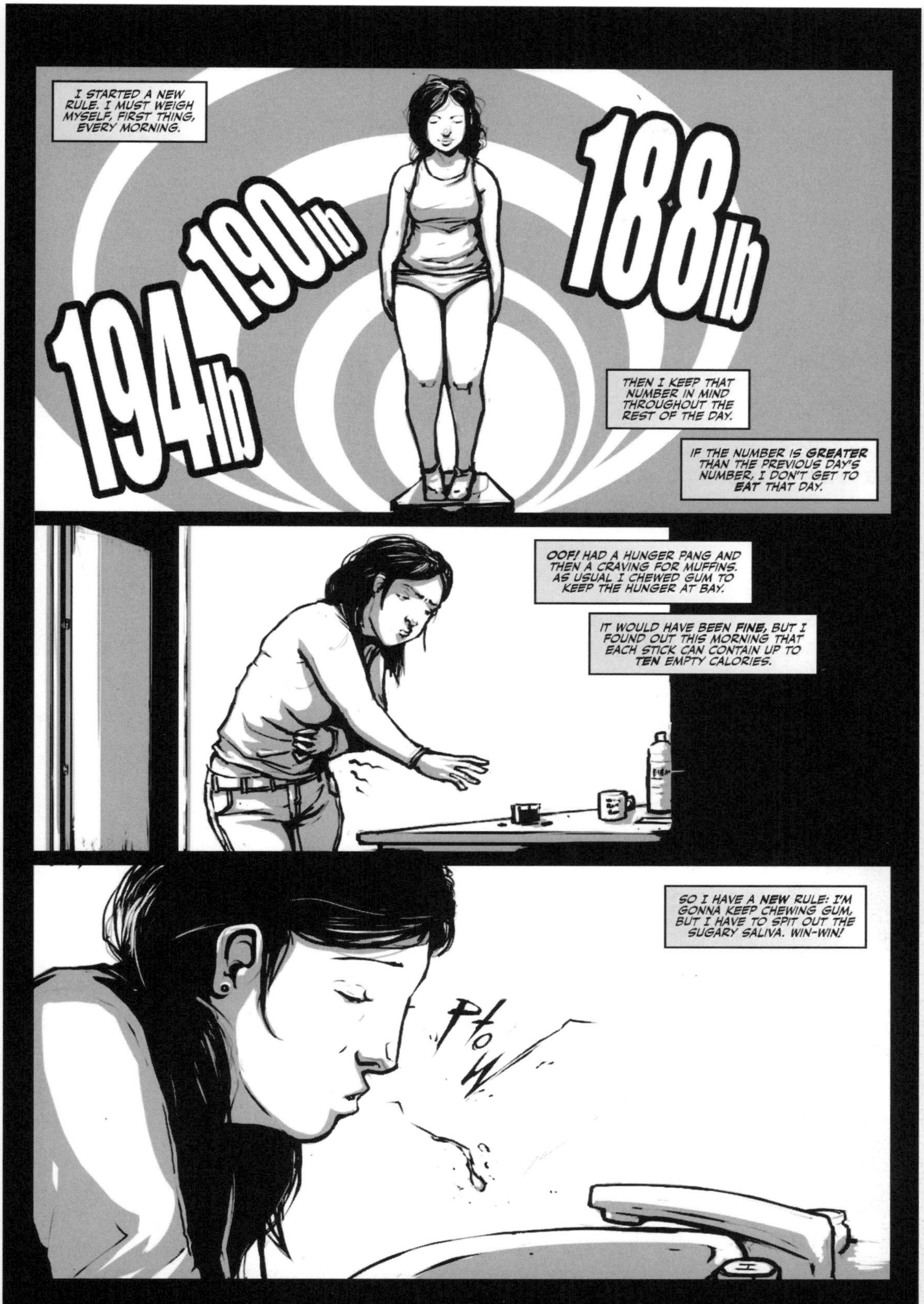
I STARTED A NEW RULE. I MUST WEIGH MYSELF, FIRST THING, EVERY MORNING.
194lb
190lb
188lb
THEN I KEEP THAT NUMBER IN MIND THROUGHOUT THE REST OF THE DAY.
IF THE NUMBER IS GREATER THAN THE PREVIOUS DAY'S NUMBER, I DON'T GET TO EAT THAT DAY.
OOF! HAD A HUNGER PANG AND THEN A CRAVING FOR MUFFINS. AS USUAL I CHEWED GUM TO KEEP THE HUNGER AT BAY.
IT WOULD HAVE BEEN FINE, BUT I FOUND OUT THIS MORNING THAT EACH STICK CAN CONTAIN UP TO TEN EMPTY CALORIES.
SO I HAVE A NEW RULE: I'M GONNA KEEP CHEWING GUM, BUT I HAVE TO SPIT OUT THE SUGARY SALIVA. WIN-WIN!
PTOW

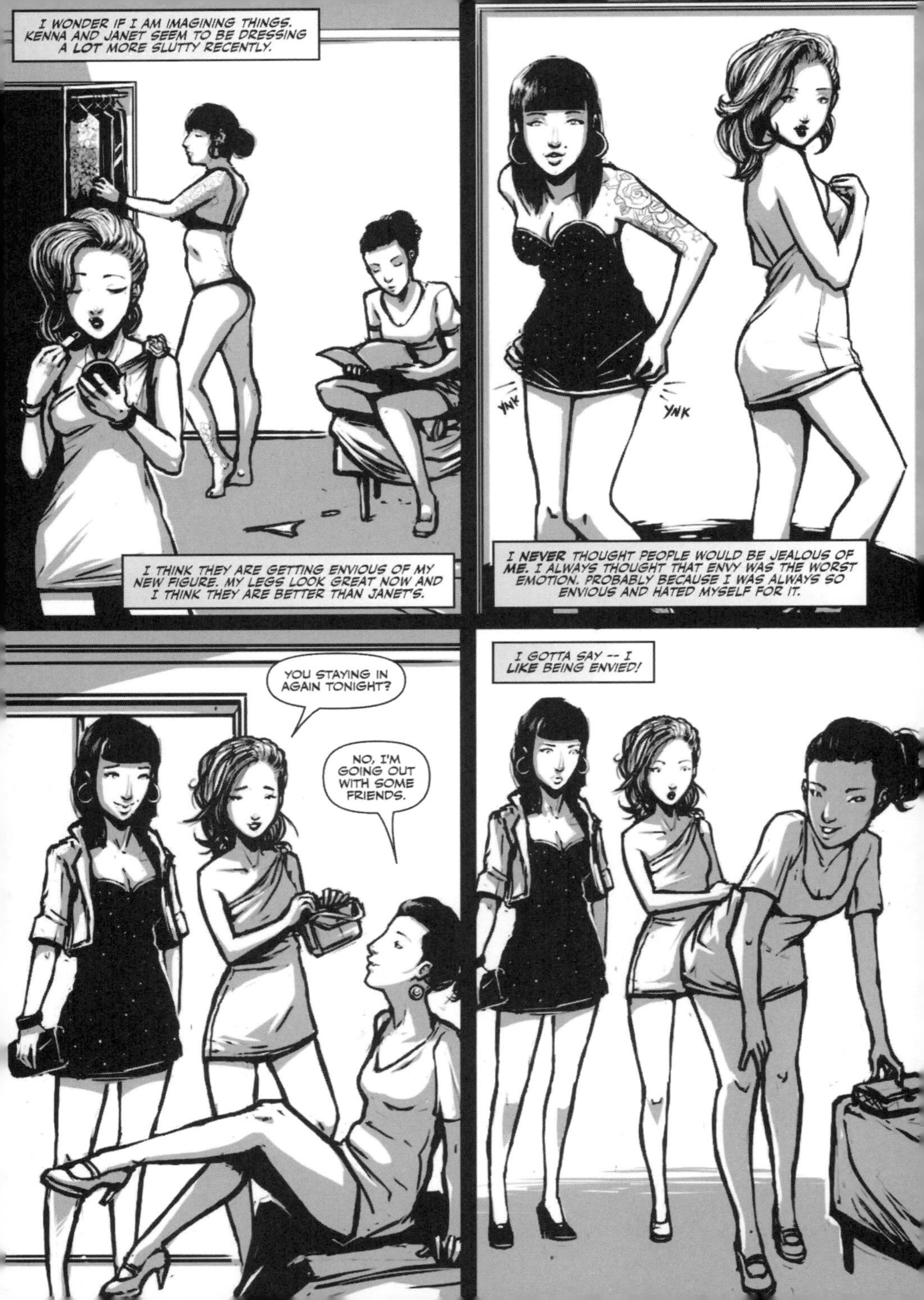
I WONDER IF I AM IMAGINING THINGS. KENNA AND JANET SEEM TO BE DRESSING A LOT MORE SLUTTY RECENTLY.
I THINK THEY ARE GETTING ENVIOUS OF MY NEW FIGURE. MY LEGS LOOK GREAT NOW AND I THINK THEY ARE BETTER THAN JANET'S.
YNK
YNK
I NEVER THOUGHT PEOPLE WOULD BE JEALOUS OF ME. I ALWAYS THOUGHT THAT ENVY WAS THE WORST EMOTION. PROBABLY BECAUSE I WAS ALWAYS SO ENVIOUS AND HATED MYSELF FOR IT.
YOU STAYING IN AGAIN TONIGHT?
NO, I'M GOING OUT WITH SOME FRIENDS.
I GOTTA SAY -- I LIKE BEING ENVIED!

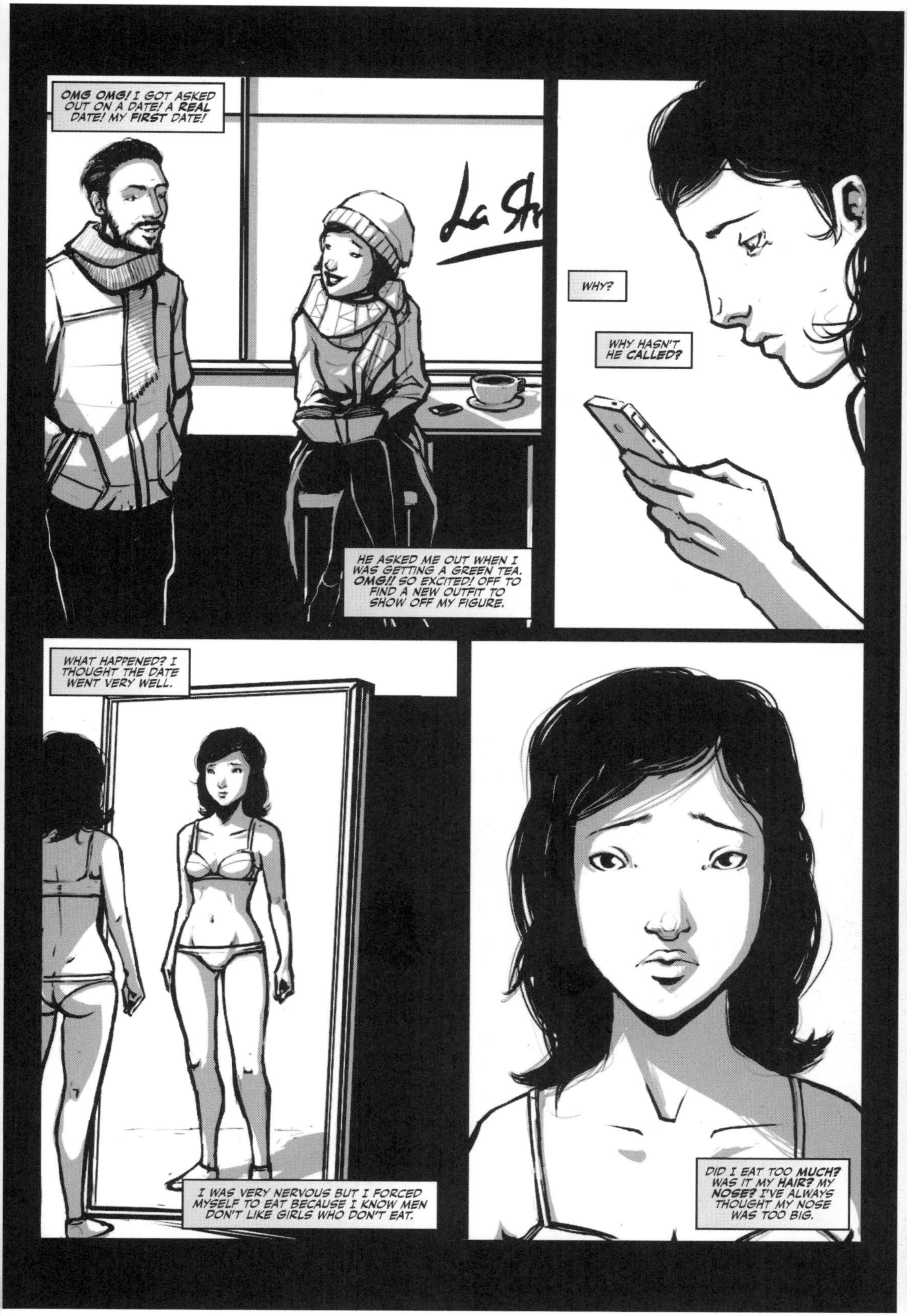
OMG OMG! I GOT ASKED OUT ON A DATE! A REAL DATE! MY FIRST DATE!
HE ASKED ME OUT WHEN I WAS GETTING A GREEN TEA. OMG!! SO EXCITED! OFF TO FIND A NEW OUTFIT TO SHOW OFF MY FIGURE.
WHY?
WHY HASN'T HE CALLED?
WHAT HAPPENED? I THOUGHT THE DATE WENT VERY WELL.
I WAS VERY NERVOUS BUT I FORCED MYSELF TO EAT BECAUSE I KNOW MEN DON'T LIKE GIRLS WHO DON'T EAT.
DID I EAT TOO MUCH? WAS IT MY HAIR? MY NOSE? I'VE ALWAYS THOUGHT MY NOSE WAS TOO BIG.

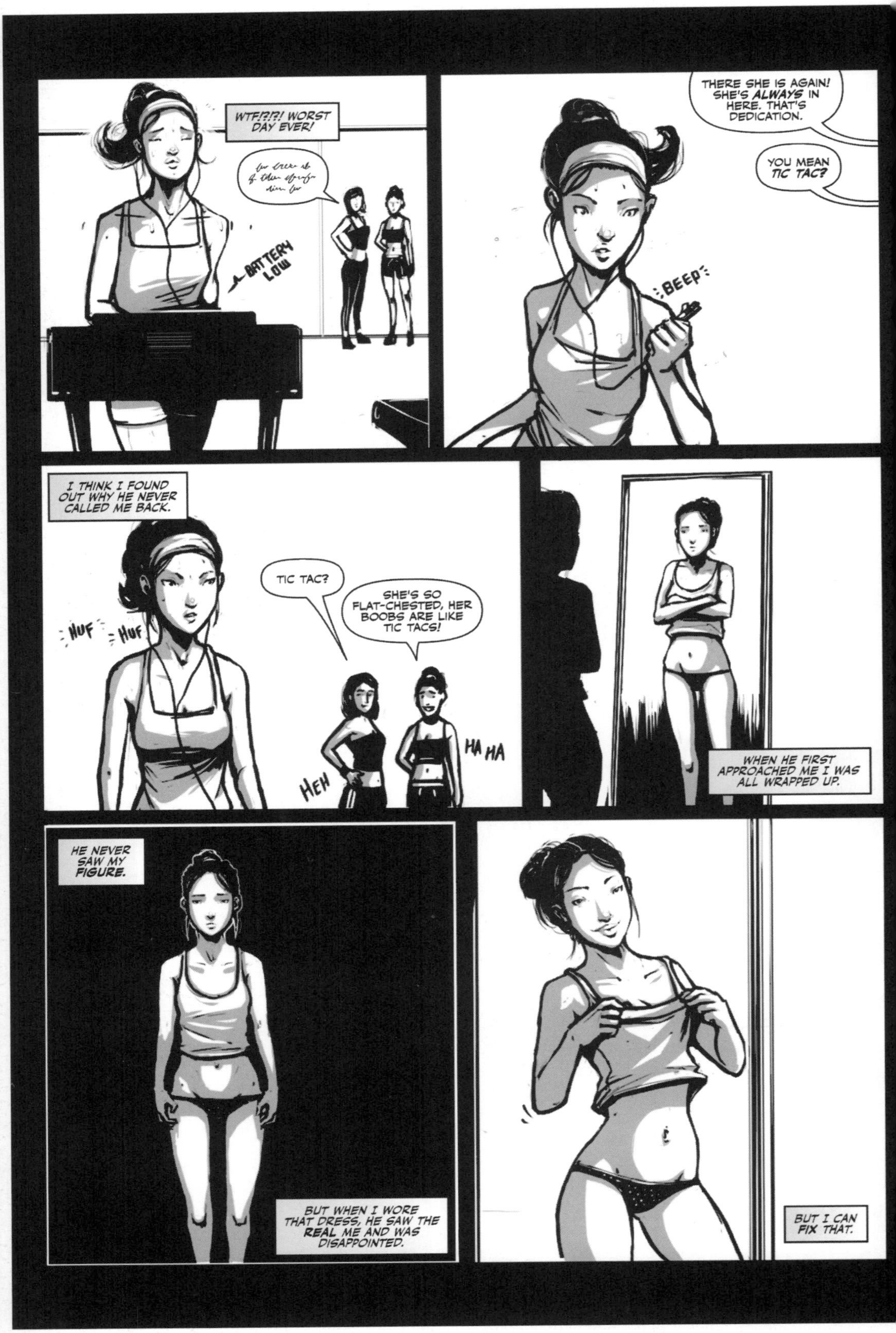
WTF!?!?! WORST DAY EVER!
BATTERY LOW
THERE SHE IS AGAIN! SHE'S ALWAYS IN HERE. THAT'S DEDICATION.
YOU MEAN TIC TAC?
BEEP
I THINK I FOUND OUT WHY HE NEVER CALLED ME BACK.
HUF HUF
TIC TAC?
SHE'S SO FLAT-CHESTED, HER BOOBS ARE LIKE TIC TACS!
HEH
HA HA
WHEN HE FIRST APPROACHED ME I WAS ALL WRAPPED UP.
HE NEVER SAW MY FIGURE.
BUT WHEN I WORE THAT DRESS, HE SAW THE REAL ME AND WAS DISAPPOINTED.
BUT I CAN FIX THAT.

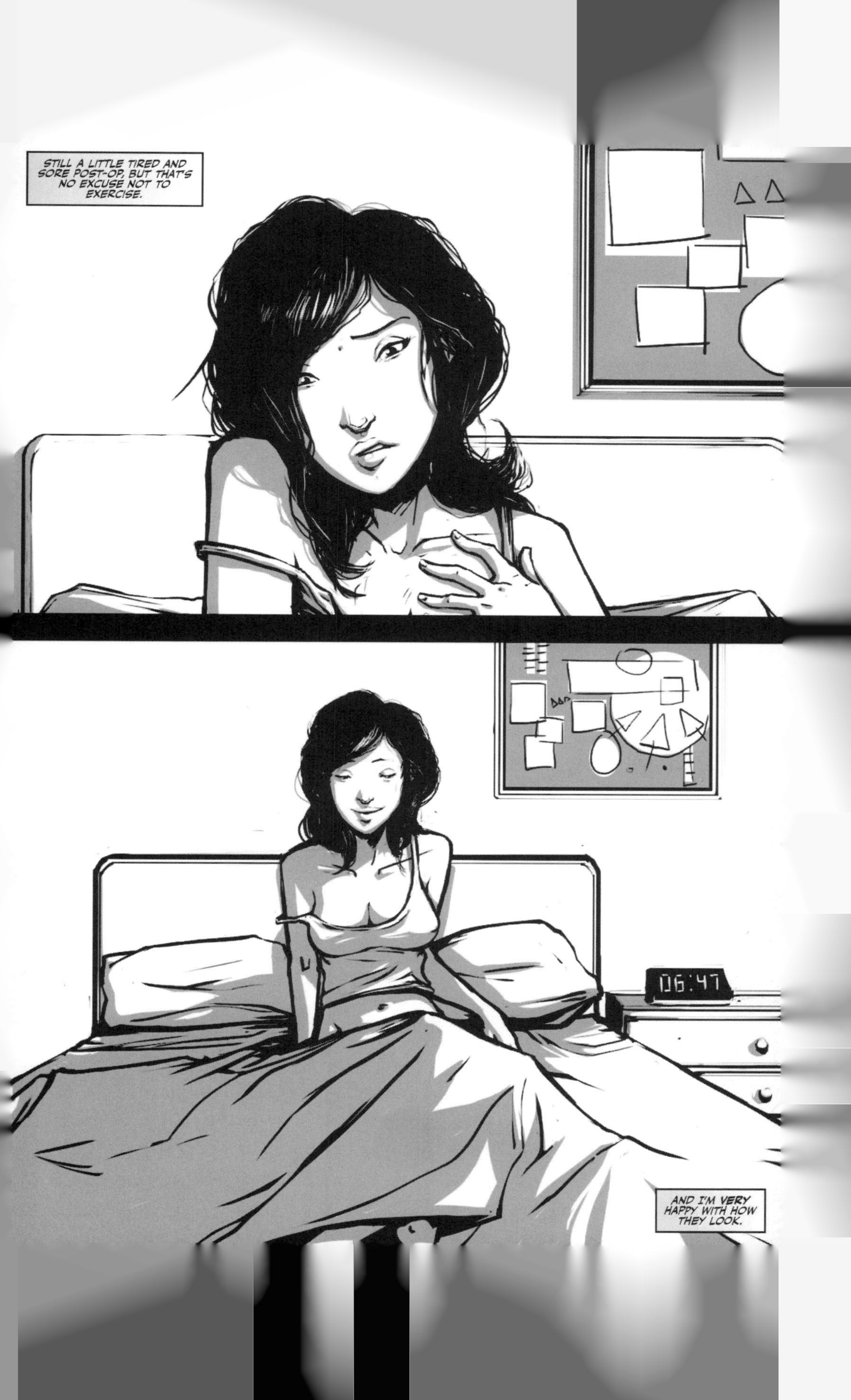
STILL A LITTLE TIRED AND SORE POST-OP, BUT THAT'S NO EXCUSE NOT TO EXERCISE.
06:47
AND I'M VERY HAPPY WITH HOW THEY LOOK.

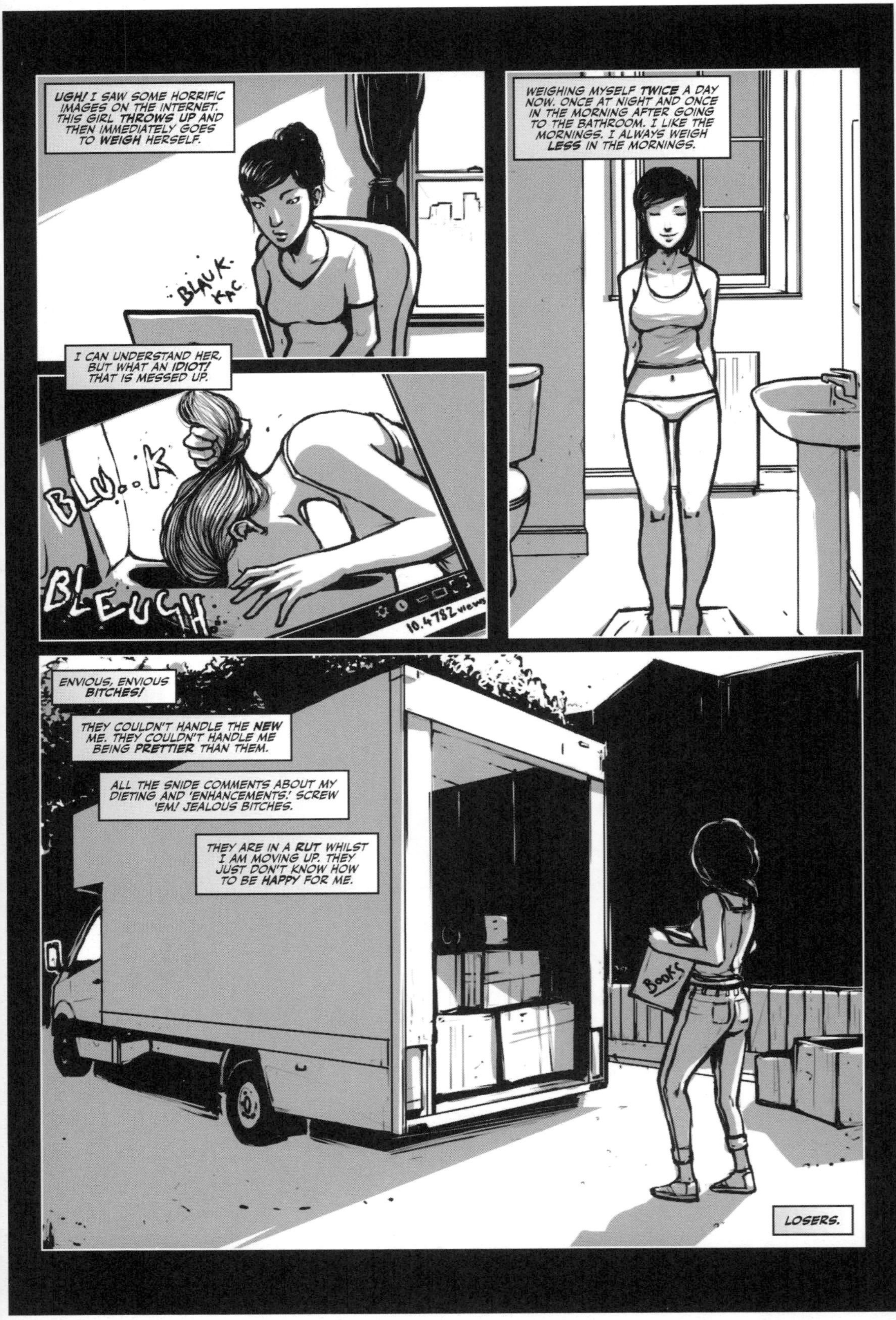
UGH! I SAW SOME HORRIFIC IMAGES ON THE INTERNET. THIS GIRL THROWS UP AND THEN IMMEDIATELY GOES TO WEIGH HERSELF.
BLAUK KAC
I CAN UNDERSTAND HER, BUT WHAT AN IDIOT! THAT IS MESSED UP.
BLU..K
BLEUGH
10.4782 views
WEIGHING MYSELF TWICE A DAY NOW. ONCE AT NIGHT AND ONCE IN THE MORNING AFTER GOING TO THE BATHROOM. I LIKE THE MORNINGS. I ALWAYS WEIGH LESS IN THE MORNINGS.
ENVIOUS, ENVIOUS BITCHES!
THEY COULDN'T HANDLE THE NEW ME. THEY COULDN'T HANDLE ME BEING PRETTIER THAN THEM.
ALL THE SNIDE COMMENTS ABOUT MY DIETING AND 'ENHANCEMENTS.' SCREW 'EM! JEALOUS BITCHES.
THEY ARE IN A RUT WHILST I AM MOVING UP. THEY JUST DON'T KNOW HOW TO BE HAPPY FOR ME.
BOOKS
LOSERS.

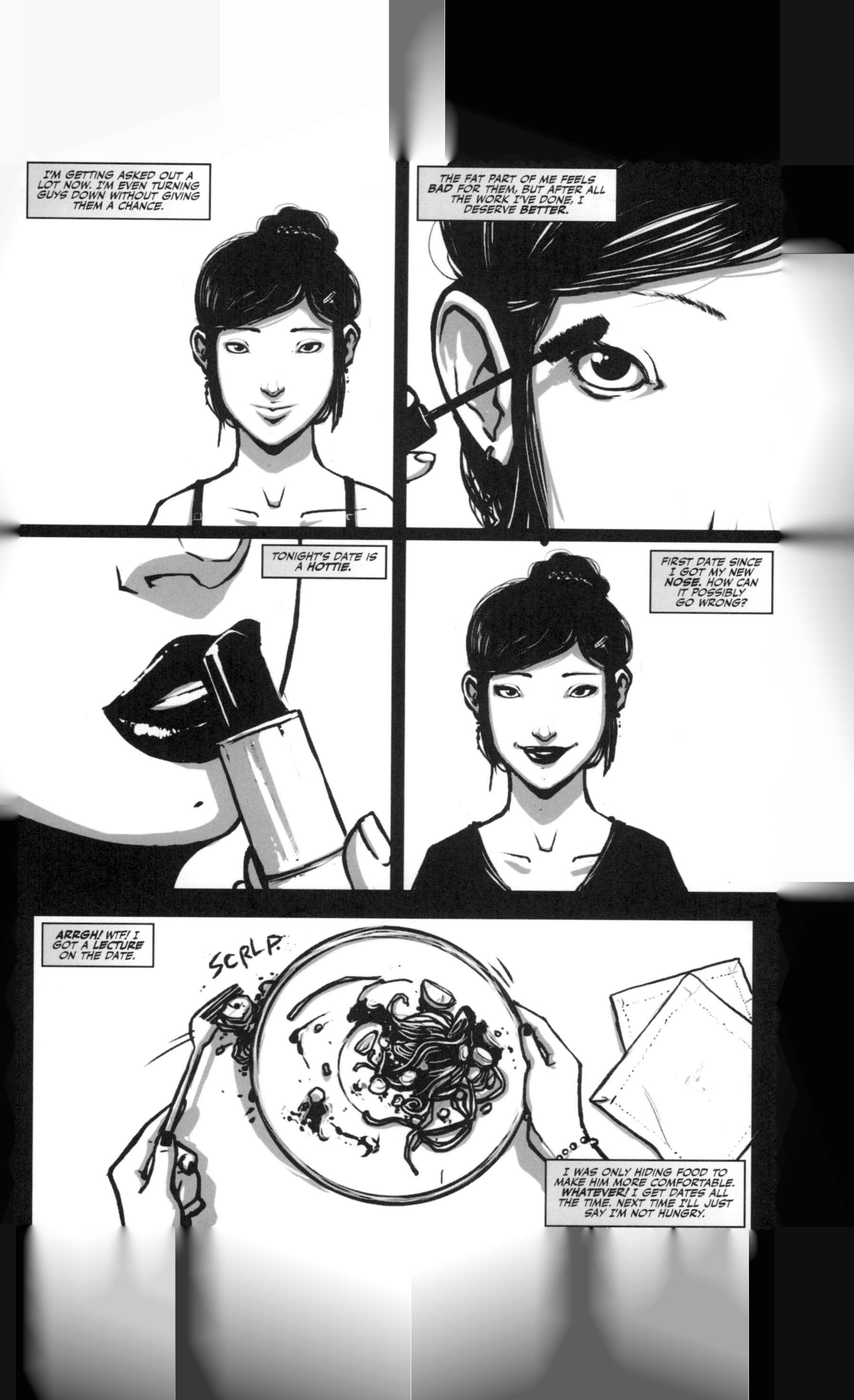

I'M GETTING ASKED OUT A LOT NOW. I'M EVEN TURNING GUYS DOWN WITHOUT GIVING THEM A CHANCE.
THE FAT PART OF ME FEELS BAD FOR THEM, BUT AFTER ALL THE WORK I'VE DONE, I DESERVE BETTER.
TONIGHT'S DATE IS A HOTTIE.
FIRST DATE SINCE I GOT MY NEW NOSE. HOW CAN IT POSSIBLY GO WRONG?
ARRGH! WTF! I GOT A LECTURE ON THE DATE.
SCRLP.
I WAS ONLY HIDING FOOD TO MAKE HIM MORE COMFORTABLE. WHATEVER! I GET DATES ALL THE TIME. NEXT TIME I'LL JUST SAY I'M NOT HUNGRY.

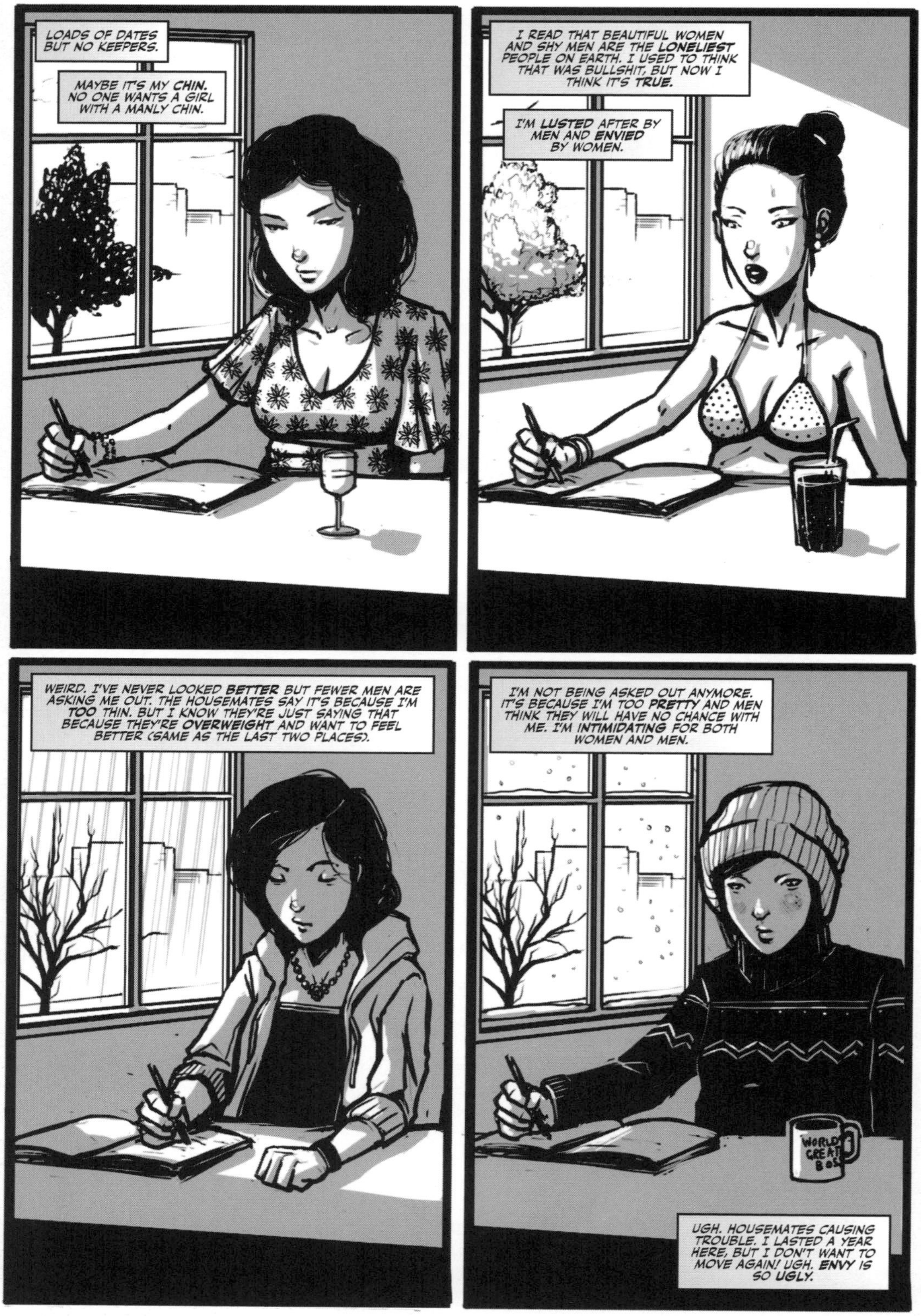

LOADS OF DATES BUT NO KEEPERS.
MAYBE IT'S MY CHIN. NO ONE WANTS A GIRL WITH A MANLY CHIN.
I READ THAT BEAUTIFUL WOMEN AND SHY MEN ARE THE LONELIEST PEOPLE ON EARTH. I USED TO THINK THAT WAS BULLSHIT, BUT NOW I THINK IT'S TRUE.
I'M LUSTED AFTER BY MEN AND ENVIED BY WOMEN.
WEIRD. I'VE NEVER LOOKED BETTER BUT FEWER MEN ARE ASKING ME OUT. THE HOUSEMATES SAY IT'S BECAUSE I'M TOO THIN. BUT I KNOW THEY'RE JUST SAYING THAT BECAUSE THEY'RE OVERWEIGHT AND WANT TO FEEL BETTER (SAME AS THE LAST TWO PLACES).
I'M NOT BEING ASKED OUT ANYMORE. IT'S BECAUSE I'M TOO PRETTY AND MEN THINK THEY WILL HAVE NO CHANCE WITH ME. I'M INTIMIDATING FOR BOTH WOMEN AND MEN.
UGH. HOUSEMATES CAUSING TROUBLE. I LASTED A YEAR HERE, BUT I DON'T WANT TO MOVE AGAIN! UGH. ENVY IS SO UGLY.

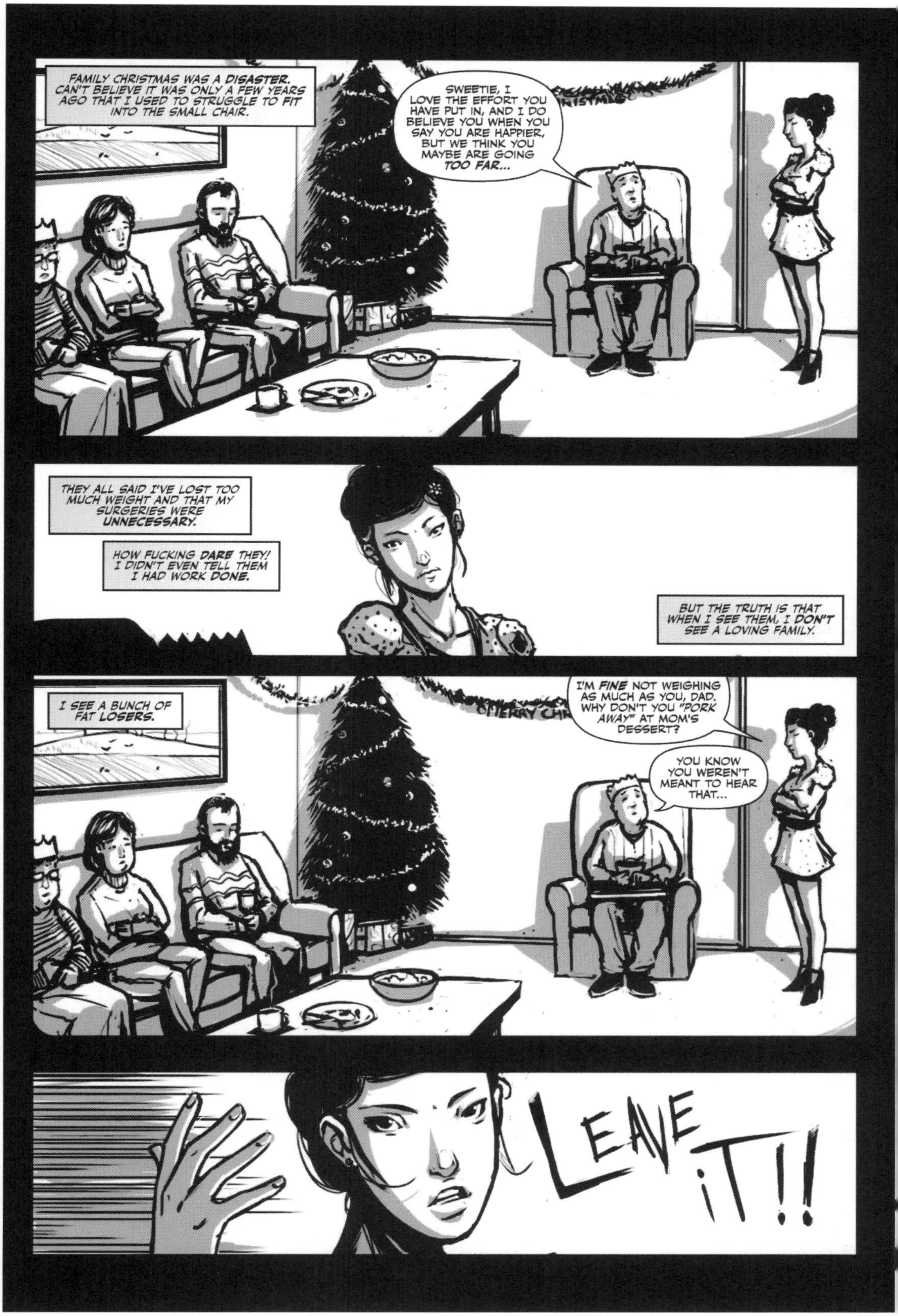
FAMILY CHRISTMAS WAS A DISASTER. CAN'T BELIEVE IT WAS ONLY A FEW YEARS AGO THAT I USED TO STRUGGLE TO FIT INTO THE SMALL CHAIR.
SWEETIE, I LOVE THE EFFORT YOU HAVE PUT IN, AND I DO BELIEVE YOU WHEN YOU SAY YOU ARE HAPPIER, BUT WE THINK YOU MAYBE ARE GOING TOO FAR...
THEY ALL SAID I'VE LOST TOO MUCH WEIGHT AND THAT MY SURGERIES WERE UNNECESSARY.
HOW FUCKING DARE THEY! I DIDN'T EVEN TELL THEM I HAD WORK DONE.
BUT THE TRUTH IS THAT WHEN I SEE THEM, I DON'T SEE A LOVING FAMILY.
I SEE A BUNCH OF FAT LOSERS.
I'M FINE NOT WEIGHING AS MUCH AS YOU, DAD. WHY DON'T YOU "PORK AWAY" AT MOM'S DESSERT?
YOU KNOW YOU WEREN'T MEANT TO HEAR THAT...
LEAVE IT!!

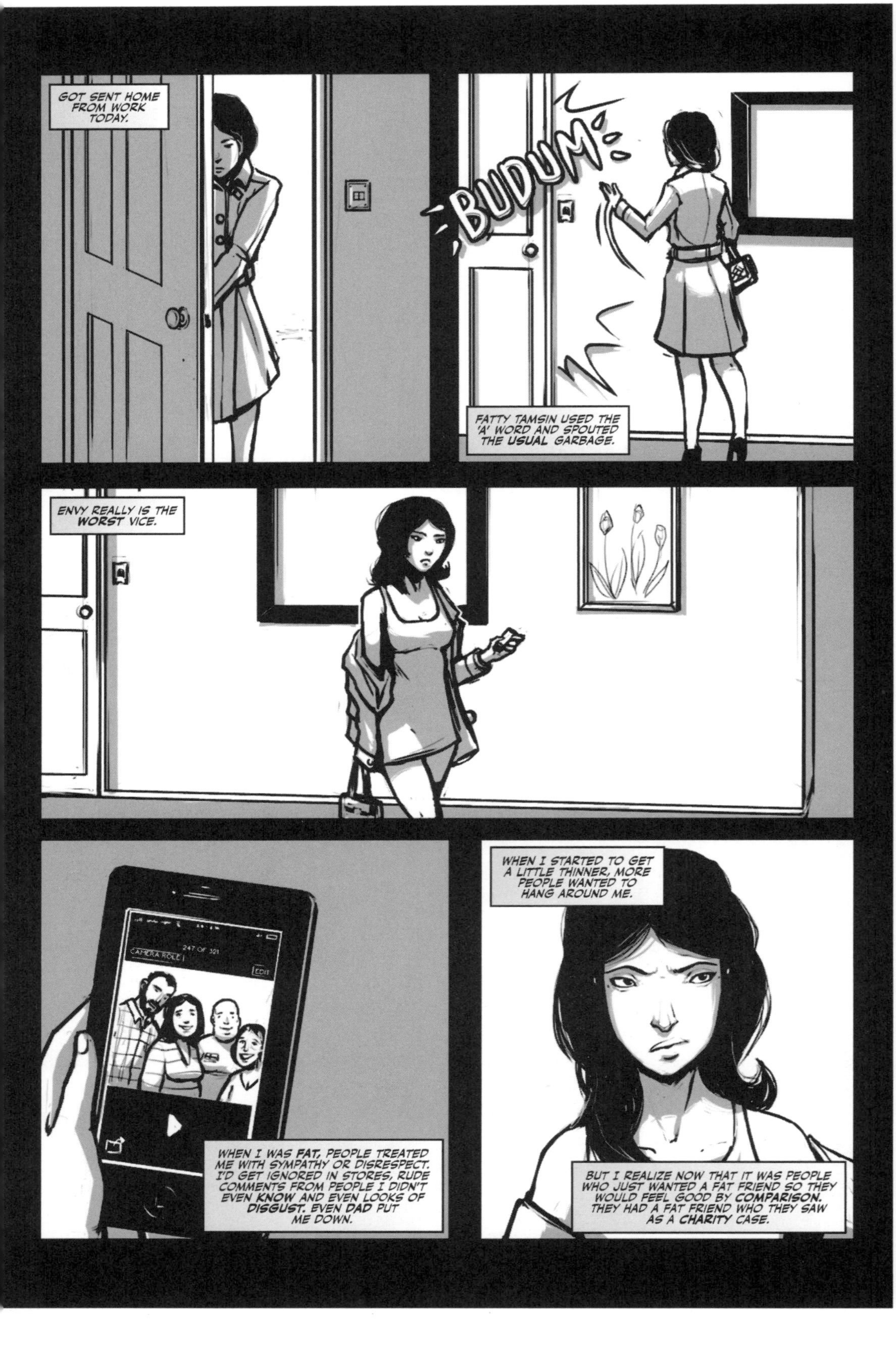
GOT SENT HOME FROM WORK TODAY.
BUDUM
FATTY TAMSIN USED THE 'A' WORD AND SPOUTED THE **USUAL** GARBAGE.
ENVY REALLY IS THE **WORST** VICE.
247 OF 321
CAMERA ROLE
EDIT
WHEN I WAS **FAT**, PEOPLE TREATED ME WITH SYMPATHY OR DISRESPECT. I'D GET IGNORED IN STORES, RUDE COMMENTS FROM PEOPLE I DIDN'T EVEN **KNOW** AND EVEN LOOKS OF **DISGUST**. EVEN **DAD** PUT ME DOWN.
WHEN I STARTED TO GET A LITTLE THINNER, MORE PEOPLE WANTED TO HANG AROUND ME.
BUT I REALIZE NOW THAT IT WAS PEOPLE WHO JUST WANTED A FAT FRIEND SO THEY WOULD FEEL GOOD BY **COMPARISON**. THEY HAD A FAT FRIEND WHO THEY SAW AS A **CHARITY** CASE.

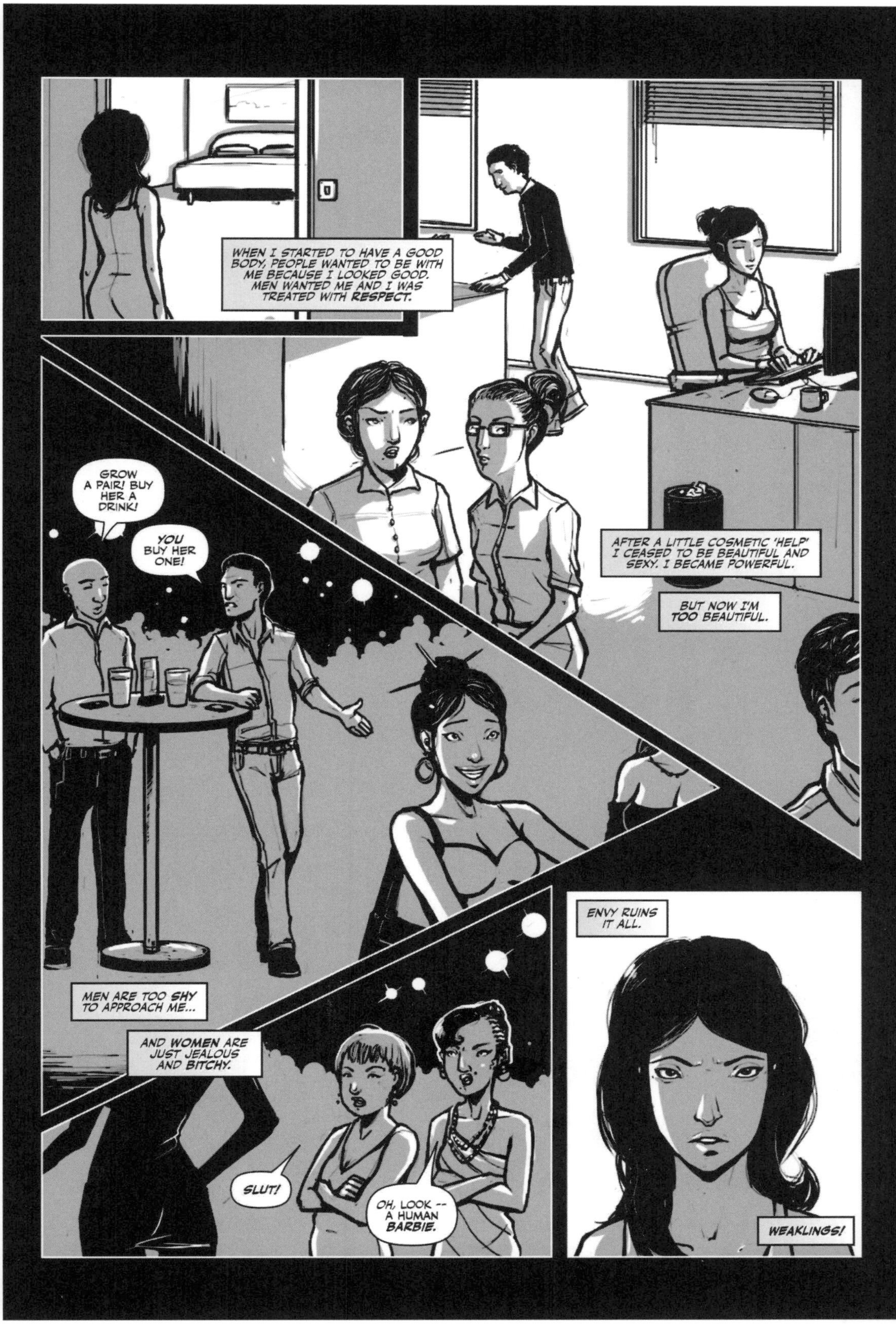
WHEN I STARTED TO HAVE A GOOD BODY, PEOPLE WANTED TO BE WITH ME BECAUSE I LOOKED GOOD. MEN WANTED ME AND I WAS TREATED WITH RESPECT.
AFTER A LITTLE COSMETIC 'HELP' I CEASED TO BE BEAUTIFUL AND SEXY. I BECAME POWERFUL.
BUT NOW I'M TOO BEAUTIFUL.
GROW A PAIR! BUY HER A DRINK!
YOU BUY HER ONE!
MEN ARE TOO SHY TO APPROACH ME...
AND WOMEN ARE JUST JEALOUS AND BITCHY.
SLUT!
OH, LOOK -- A HUMAN BARBIE.
ENVY RUINS IT ALL.
WEAKLINGS!

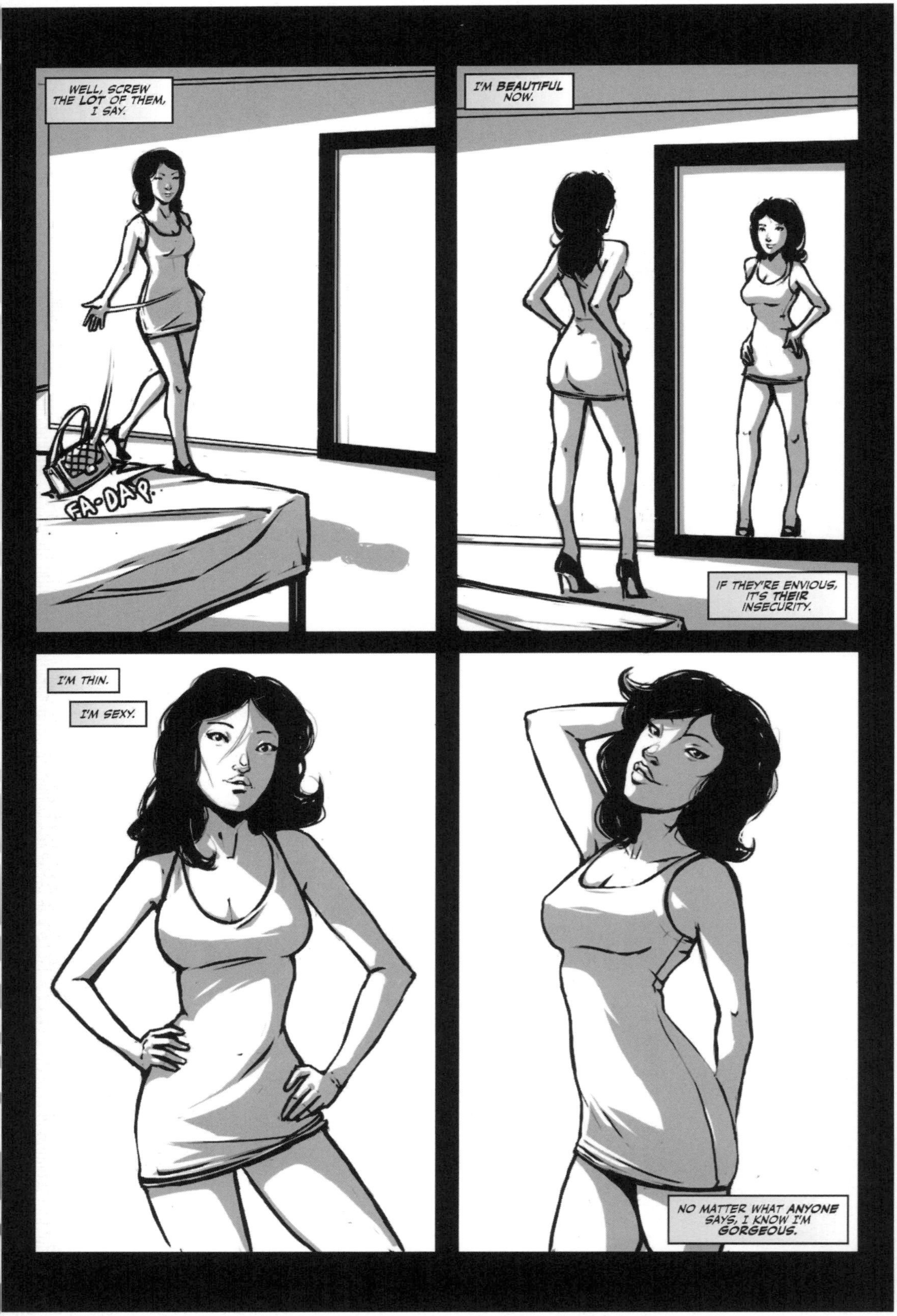
WELL, SCREW THE LOT OF THEM, I SAY.
FA-DAP
I'M BEAUTIFUL NOW.
IF THEY'RE ENVIOUS, IT'S THEIR INSECURITY.
I'M THIN.
I'M SEXY.
NO MATTER WHAT ANYONE SAYS, I KNOW I'M GORGEOUS.

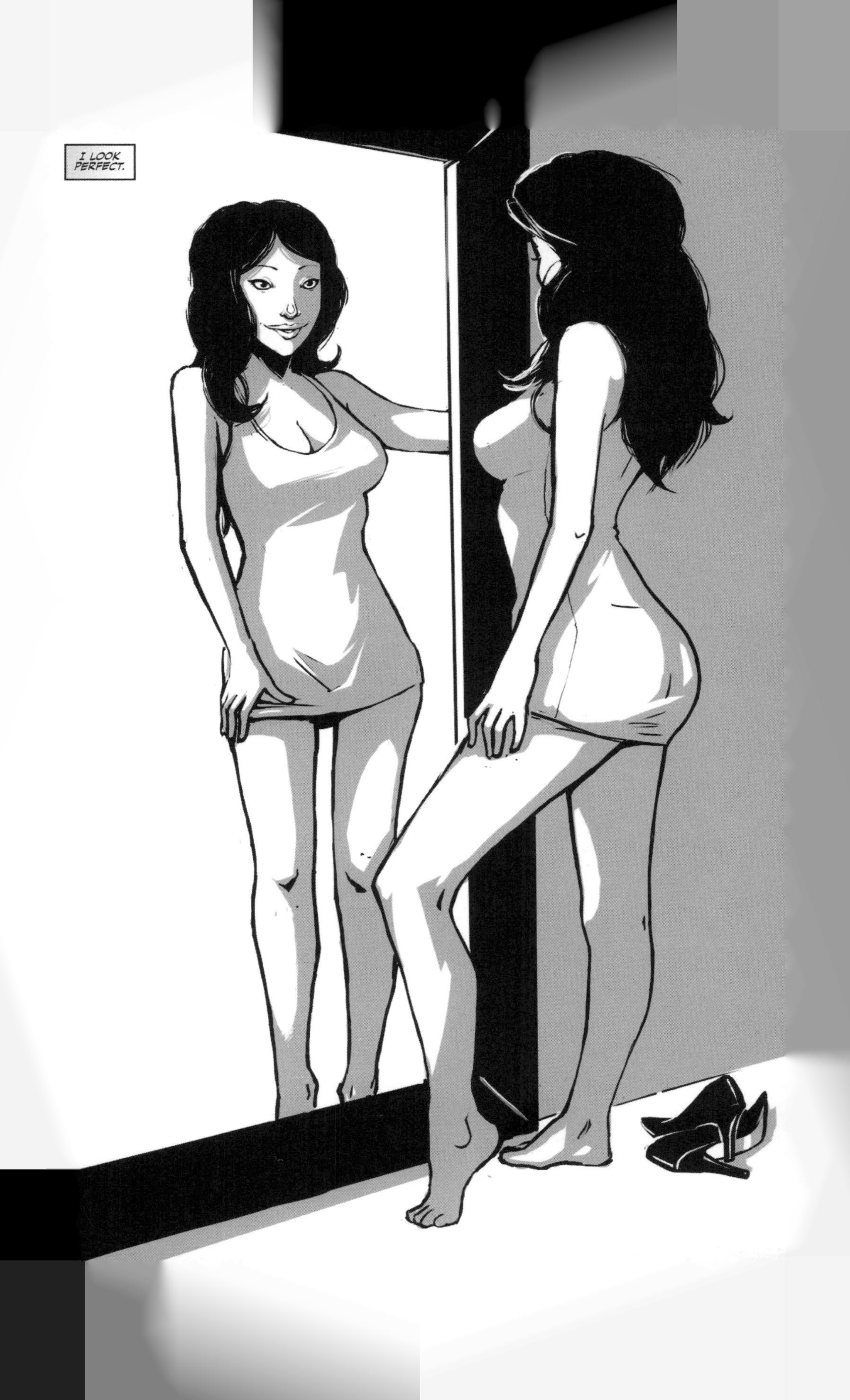
I LOOK PERFECT.

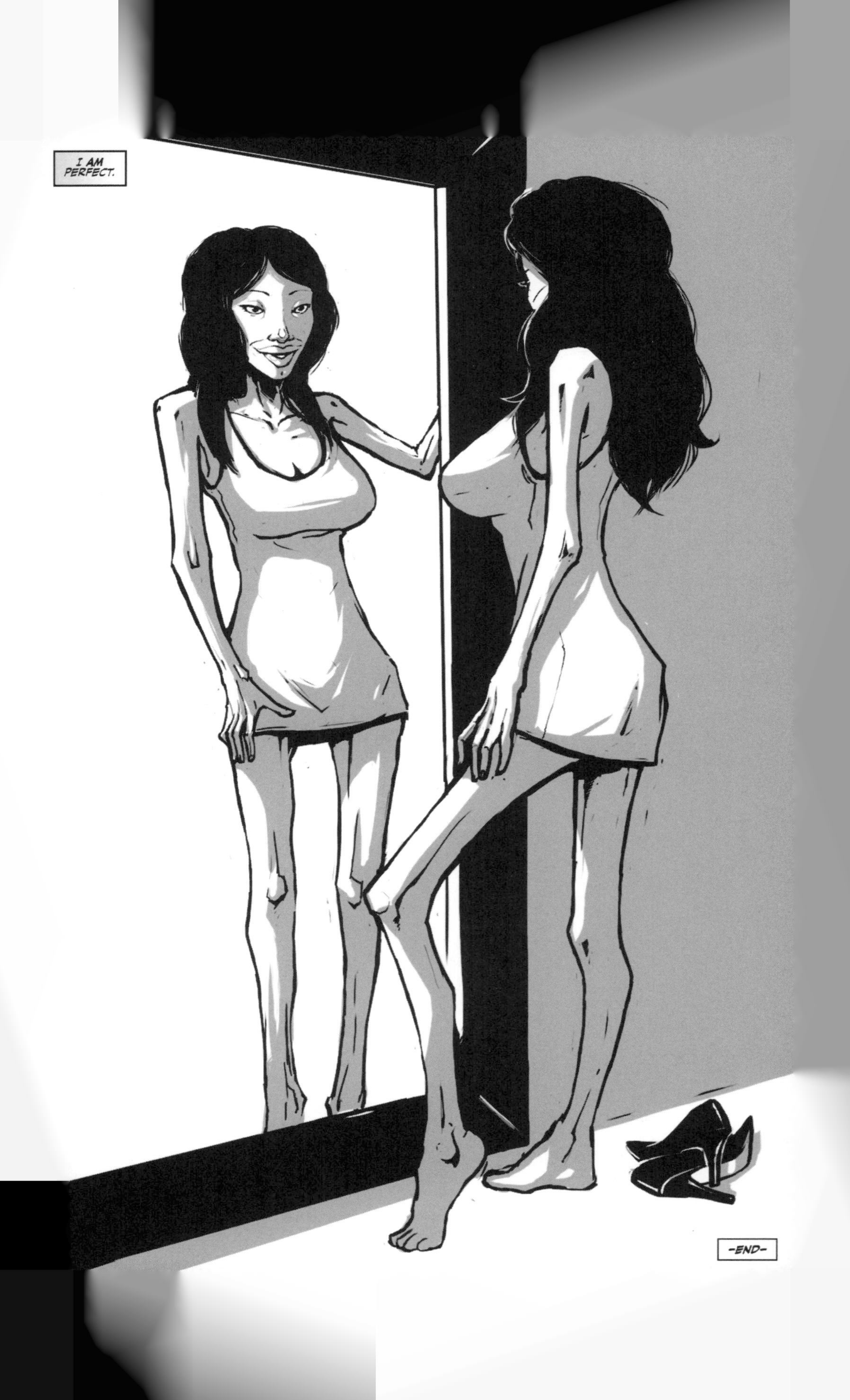
I AM PERFECT.
-END-

The Bid...

Named after its designer, engineer Gustav Eiffel, the Eiffel Tower was built as the entrance arch to the 1889 World's Fair. A global icon of France and one of the most recognizable structures in the world, it is the tallest building in Paris and ascended by millions every year.

Writer/Creator
Neil Gibson

Illustrator
Hugo Wijngaard

www.tpub.co.uk

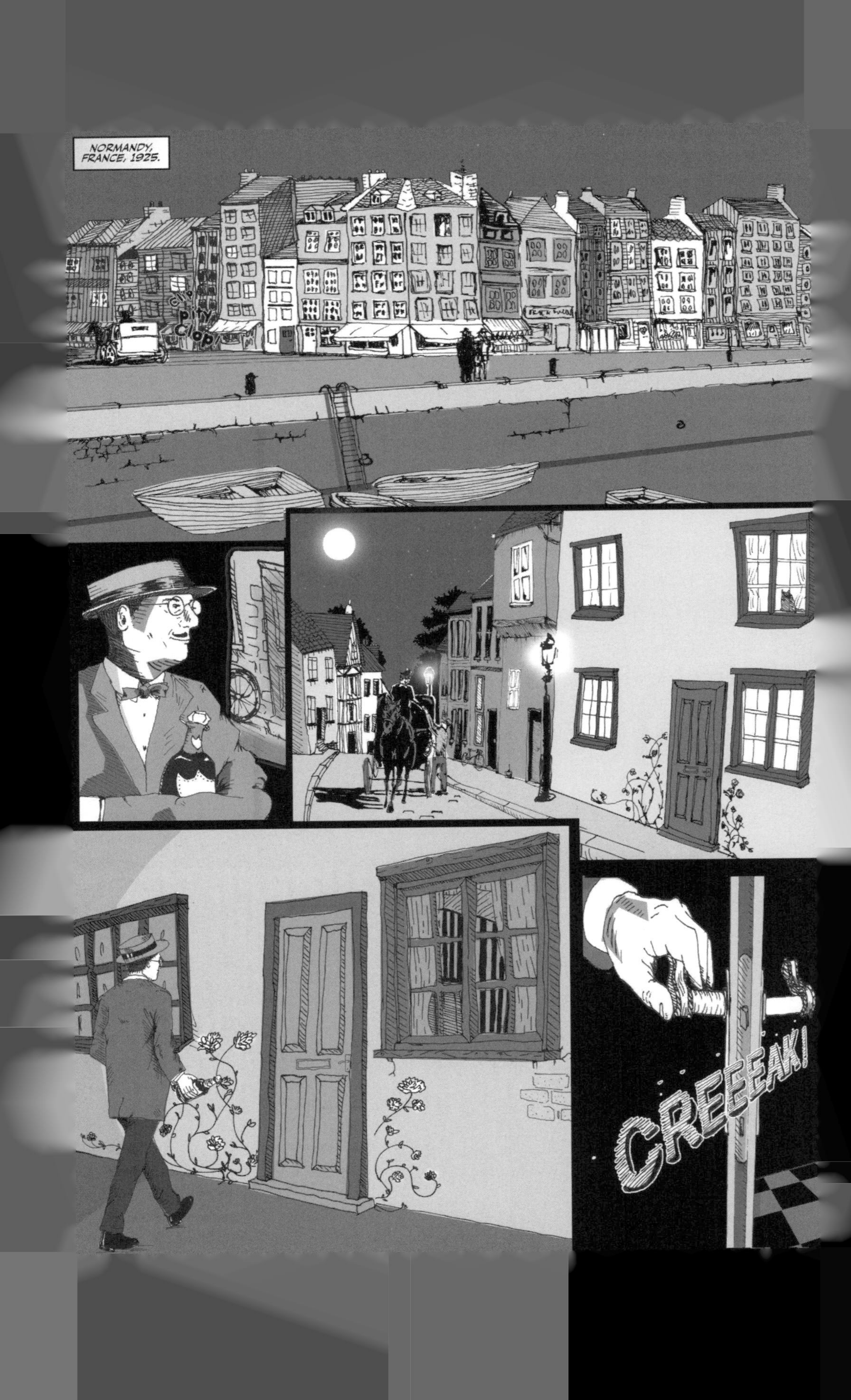
NORMANDY, FRANCE, 1925.
clip pity clop
CREEEAK!

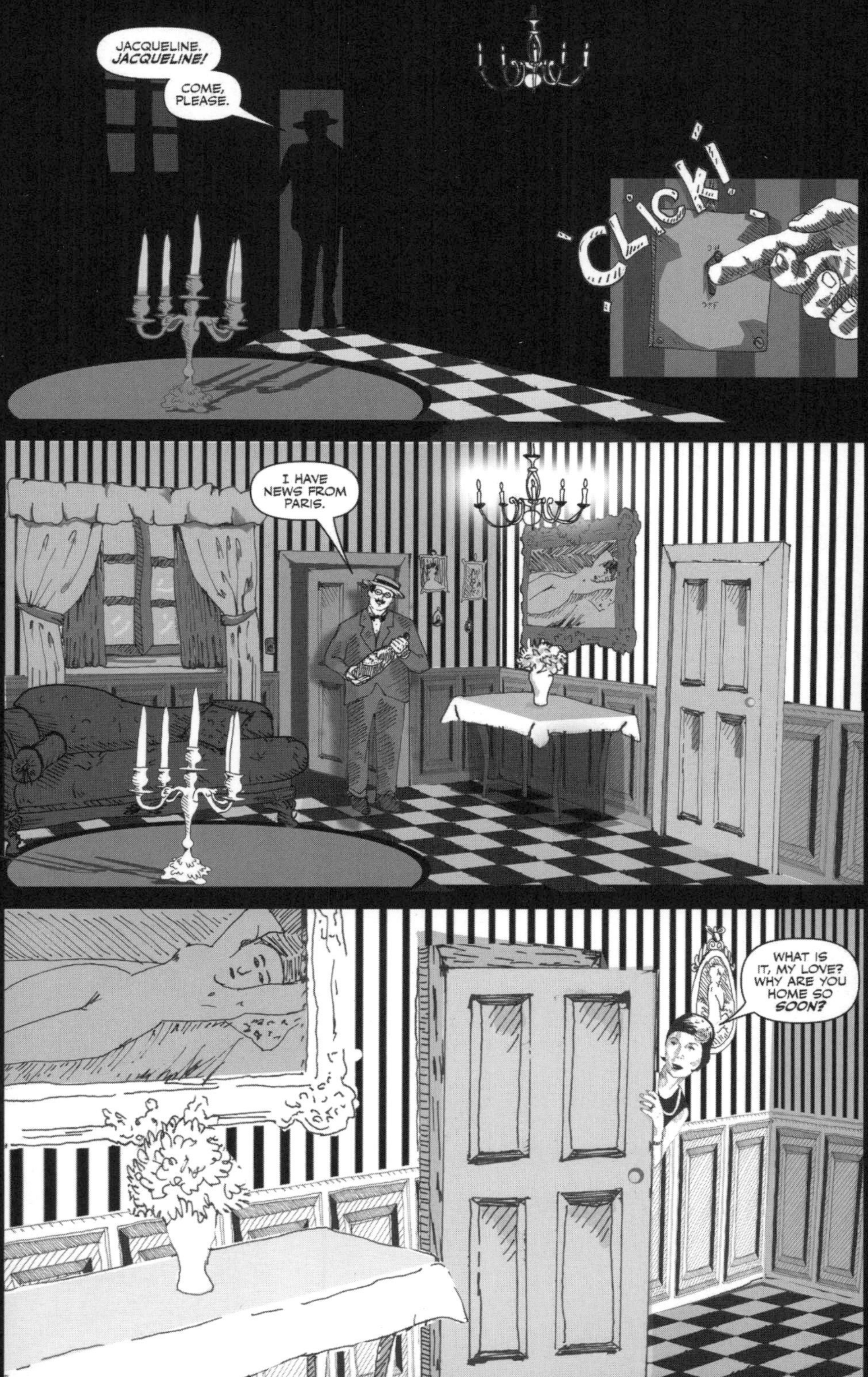
JACQUELINE. JACQUELINE!
COME, PLEASE.
CLICK!
I HAVE NEWS FROM PARIS.
WHAT IS IT, MY LOVE? WHY ARE YOU HOME SO SOON?

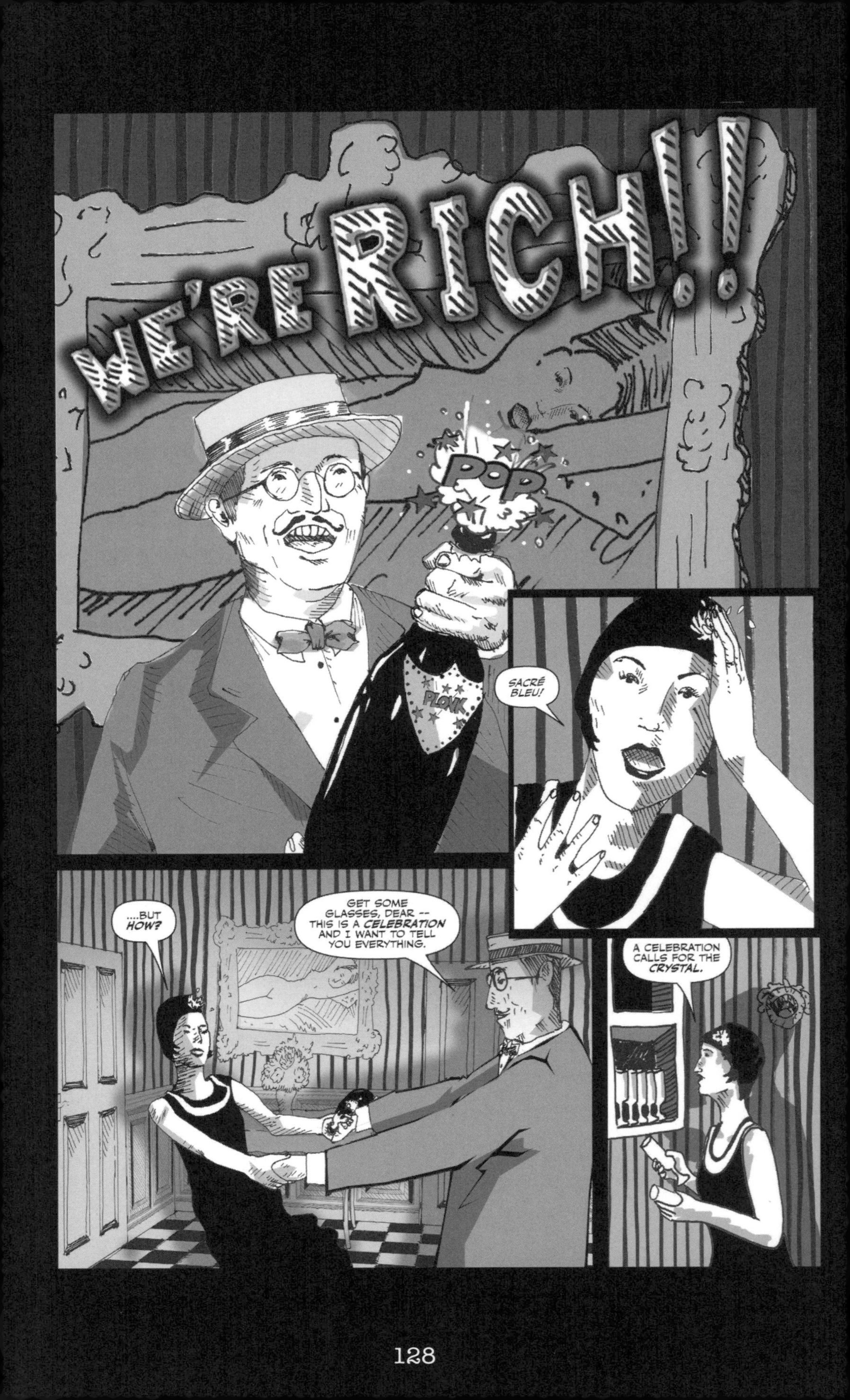
WE'RE RICH!!
POP
PLONK
SACRÉ BLEU!
....BUT HOW?
GET SOME GLASSES, DEAR -- THIS IS A *CELEBRATION* AND I WANT TO TELL YOU EVERYTHING.
A CELEBRATION CALLS FOR THE *CRYSTAL*.

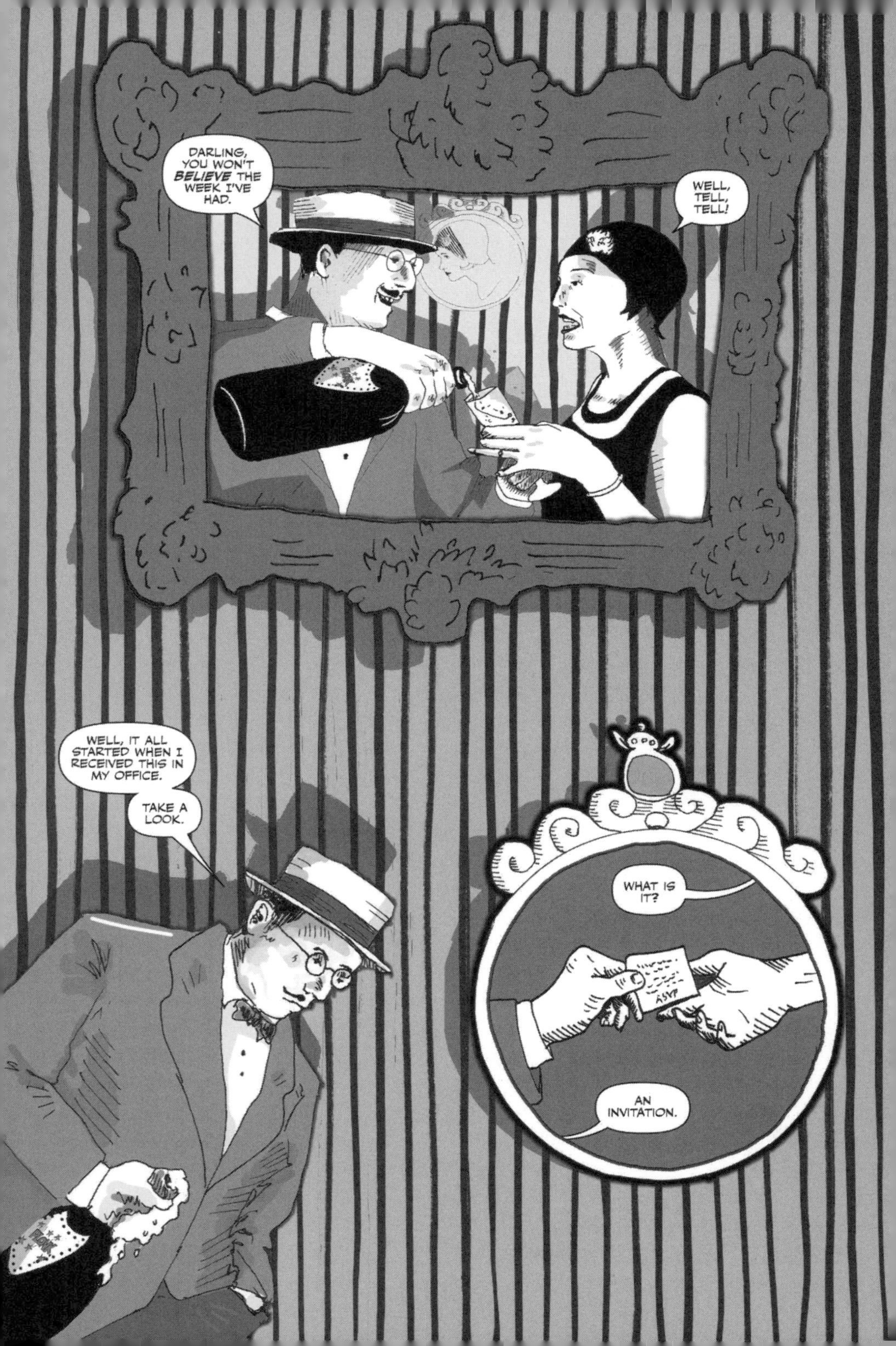
DARLING, YOU WON'T *BELIEVE* THE WEEK I'VE HAD.
WELL, TELL, TELL!
WELL, IT ALL STARTED WHEN I RECEIVED THIS IN MY OFFICE.
TAKE A LOOK.
WHAT IS IT?
AN INVITATION.

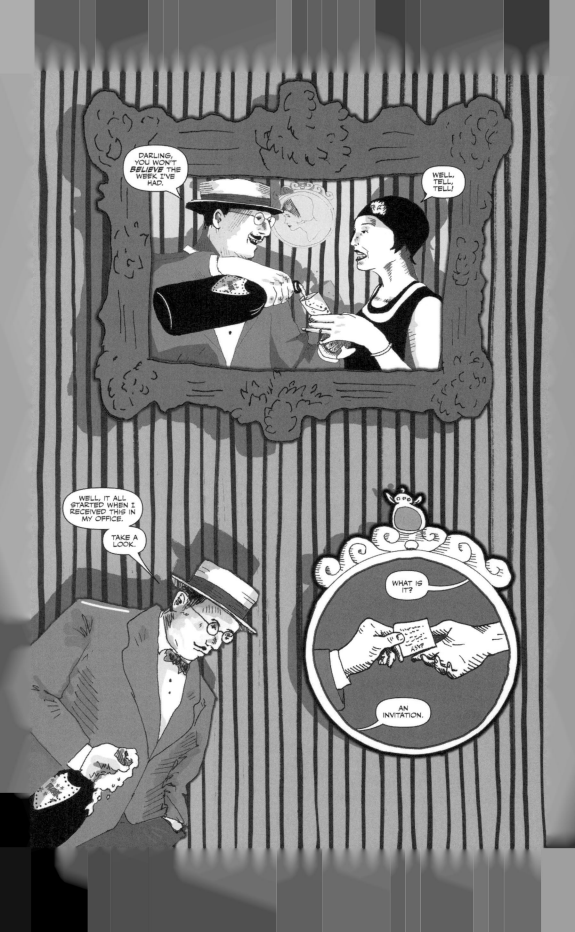

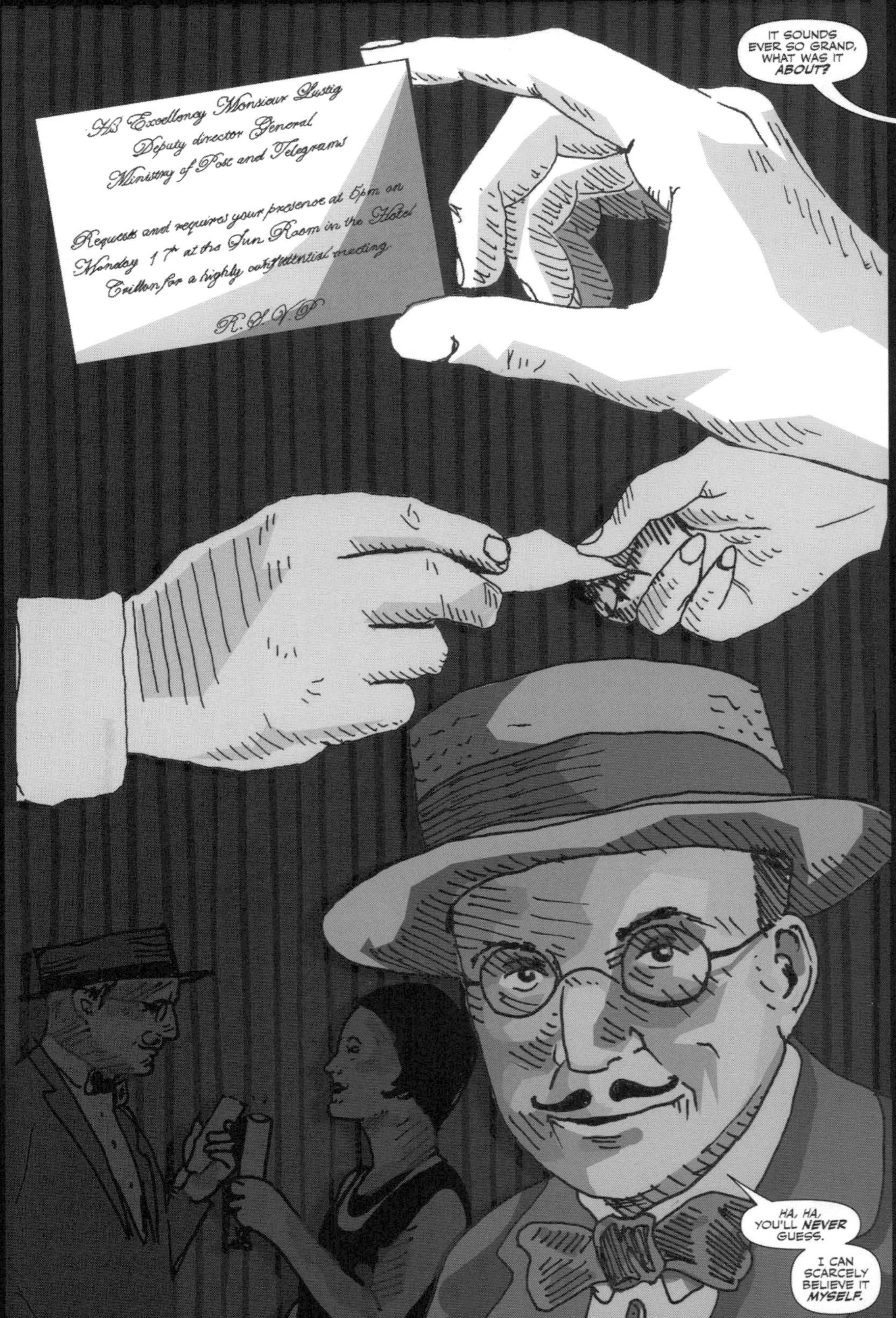
IT SOUNDS EVER SO GRAND, WHAT WAS IT *ABOUT?*
His Excellency Monsieur Lustig
Deputy director General
Ministry of Post and Telegrams
Requests and requires your presence at 5pm on
Monday 17th at the Sun Room in the Hotel
Crillon for a highly confidential meeting.
R.S.V.P
HA, HA, YOU'LL *NEVER* GUESS.
I CAN SCARCELY BELIEVE IT *MYSELF.*

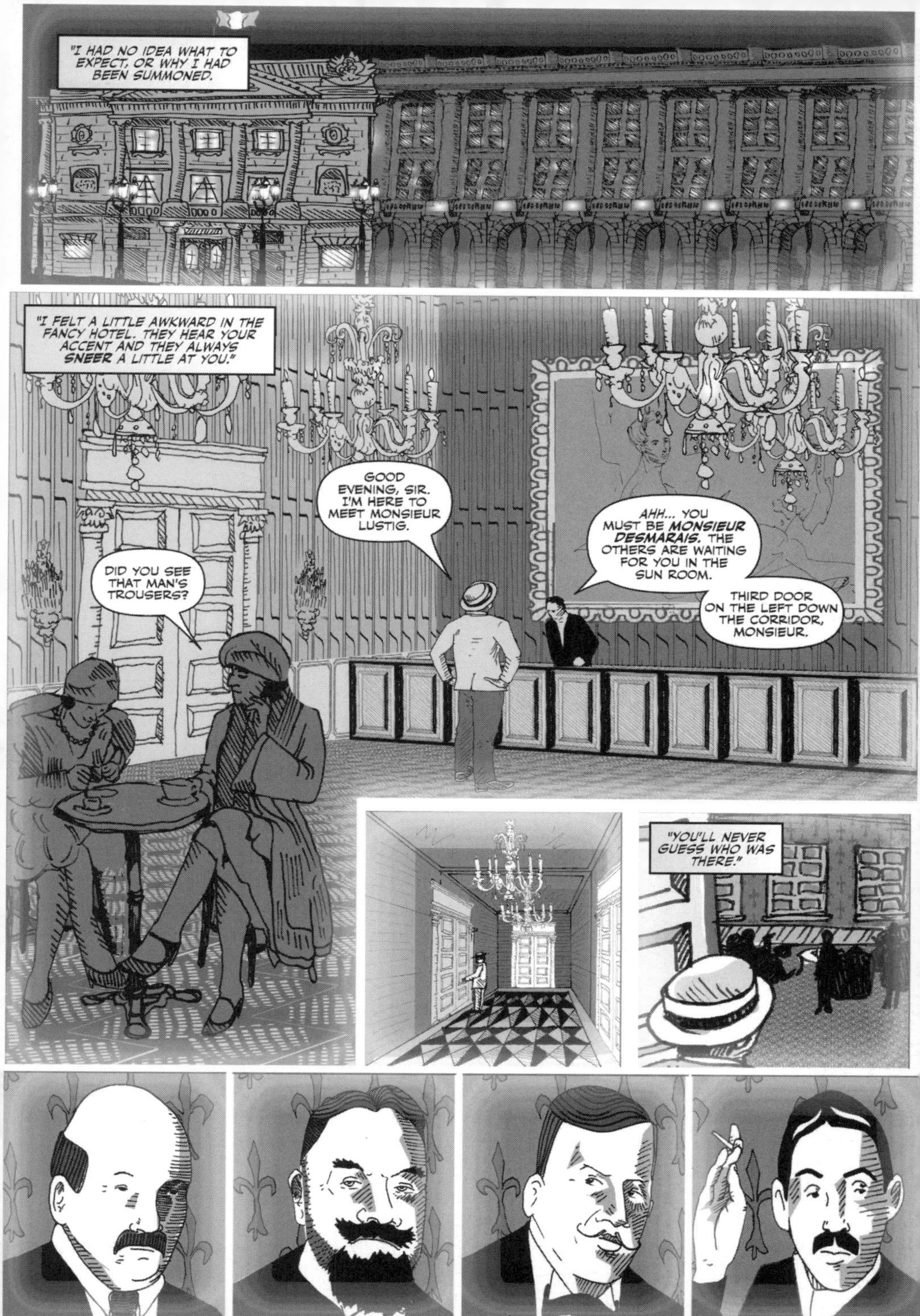
"I HAD NO IDEA WHAT TO EXPECT, OR WHY I HAD BEEN SUMMONED.
"I FELT A LITTLE AWKWARD IN THE FANCY HOTEL. THEY HEAR YOUR ACCENT AND THEY ALWAYS SNEER A LITTLE AT YOU."
GOOD EVENING, SIR. I'M HERE TO MEET MONSIEUR LUSTIG.
AHH... YOU MUST BE MONSIEUR DESMARAIS. THE OTHERS ARE WAITING FOR YOU IN THE SUN ROOM.
THIRD DOOR ON THE LEFT DOWN THE CORRIDOR, MONSIEUR.
DID YOU SEE THAT MAN'S TROUSERS?
"YOU'LL NEVER GUESS WHO WAS THERE."
Laurent D'Sejour
Francois Sacy
Olivier De Gaulle
Antoine Fitzroy

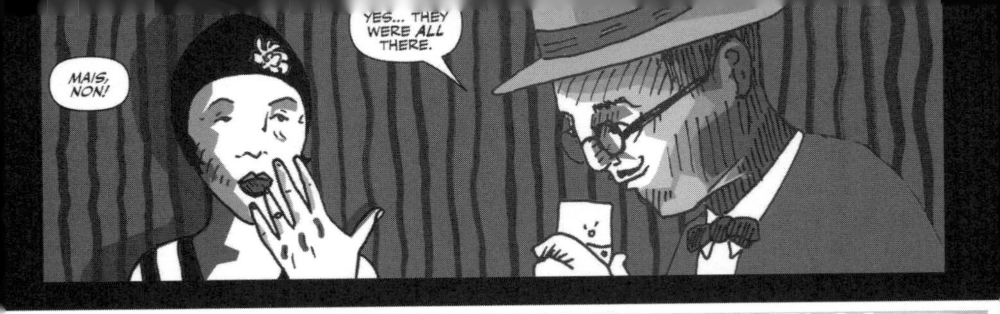
MAIS, NON!
YES... THEY WERE *ALL* THERE.

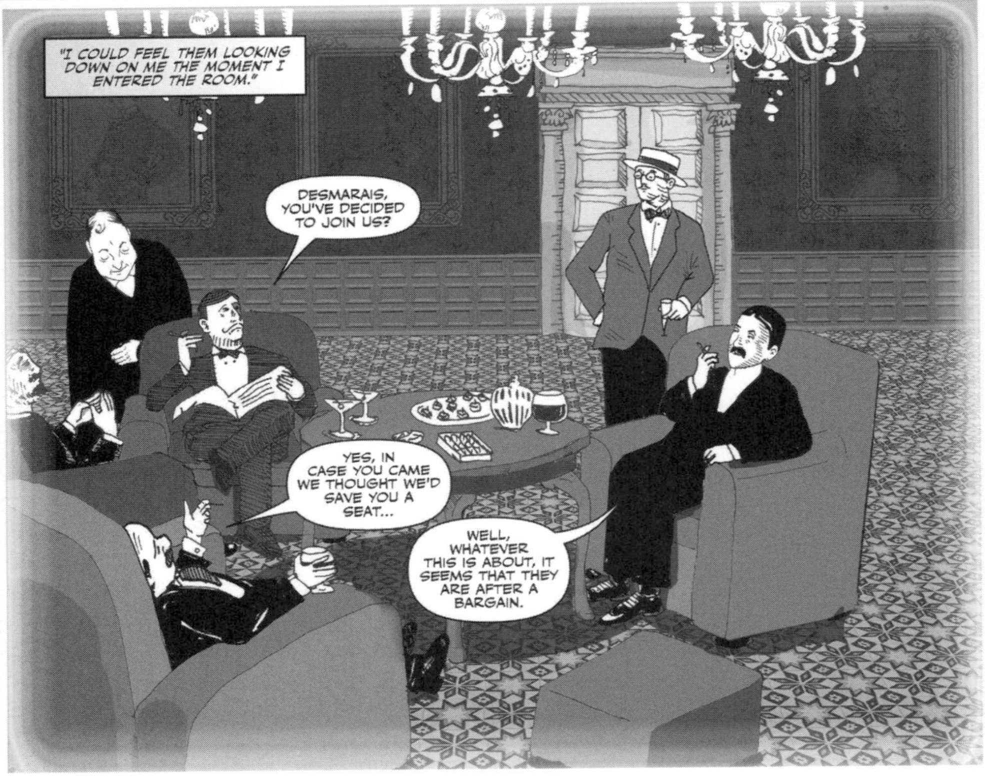
"I COULD FEEL THEM LOOKING DOWN ON ME THE MOMENT I ENTERED THE ROOM."
DESMARAIS, YOU'VE DECIDED TO JOIN US?
YES, IN CASE YOU CAME WE THOUGHT WE'D SAVE YOU A SEAT...
WELL, WHATEVER THIS IS ABOUT, IT SEEMS THAT THEY ARE AFTER A BARGAIN.

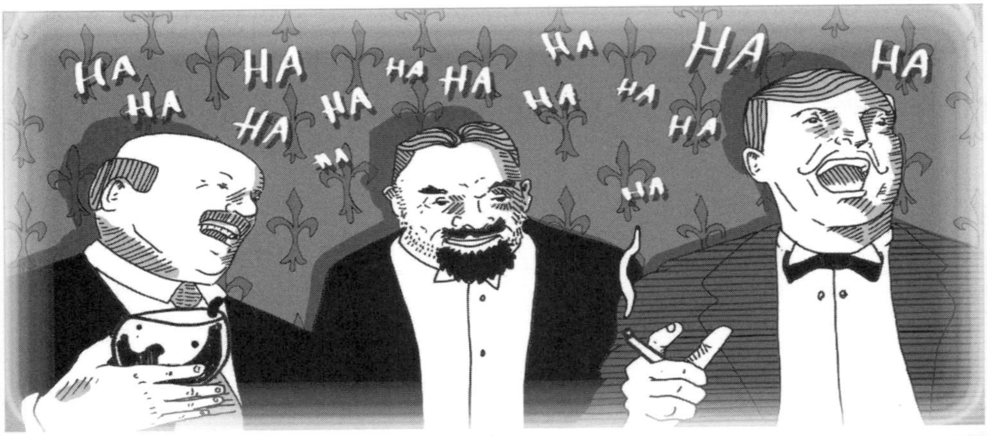
HA HA HA HA HA HA HA HA HA HA HA HA HA HA HA HA HA

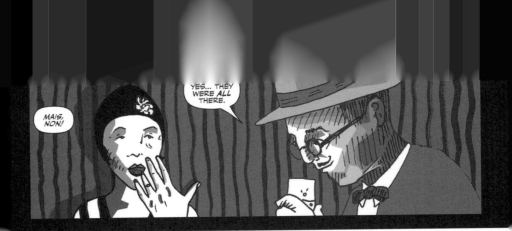

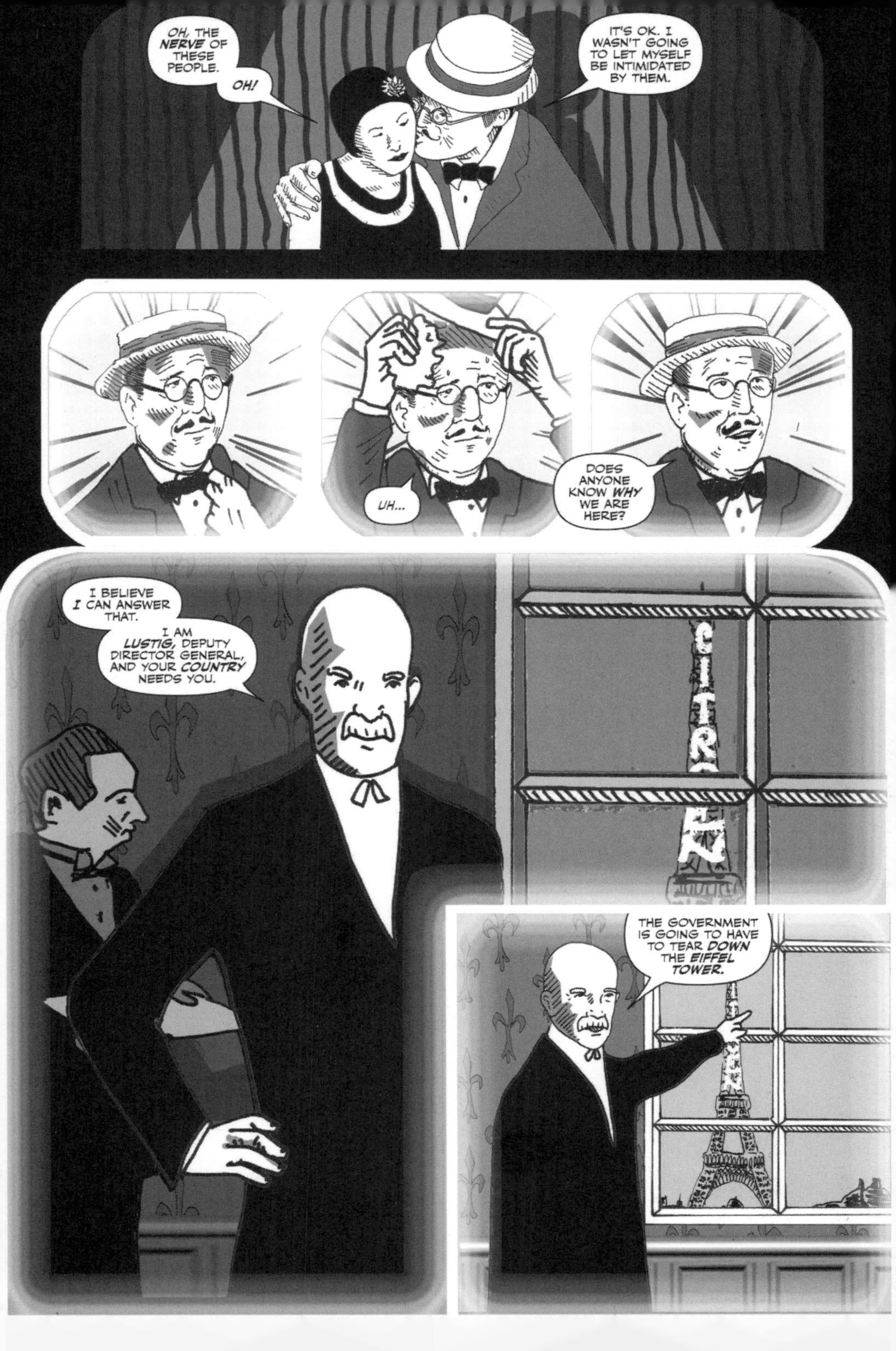
OH, THE NERVE OF THESE PEOPLE.
OH!
IT'S OK. I WASN'T GOING TO LET MYSELF BE INTIMIDATED BY THEM.
UH...
DOES ANYONE KNOW WHY WE ARE HERE?
I BELIEVE I CAN ANSWER THAT.
I AM LUSTIG, DEPUTY DIRECTOR GENERAL, AND YOUR COUNTRY NEEDS YOU.
THE GOVERNMENT IS GOING TO HAVE TO TEAR DOWN THE EIFFEL TOWER.

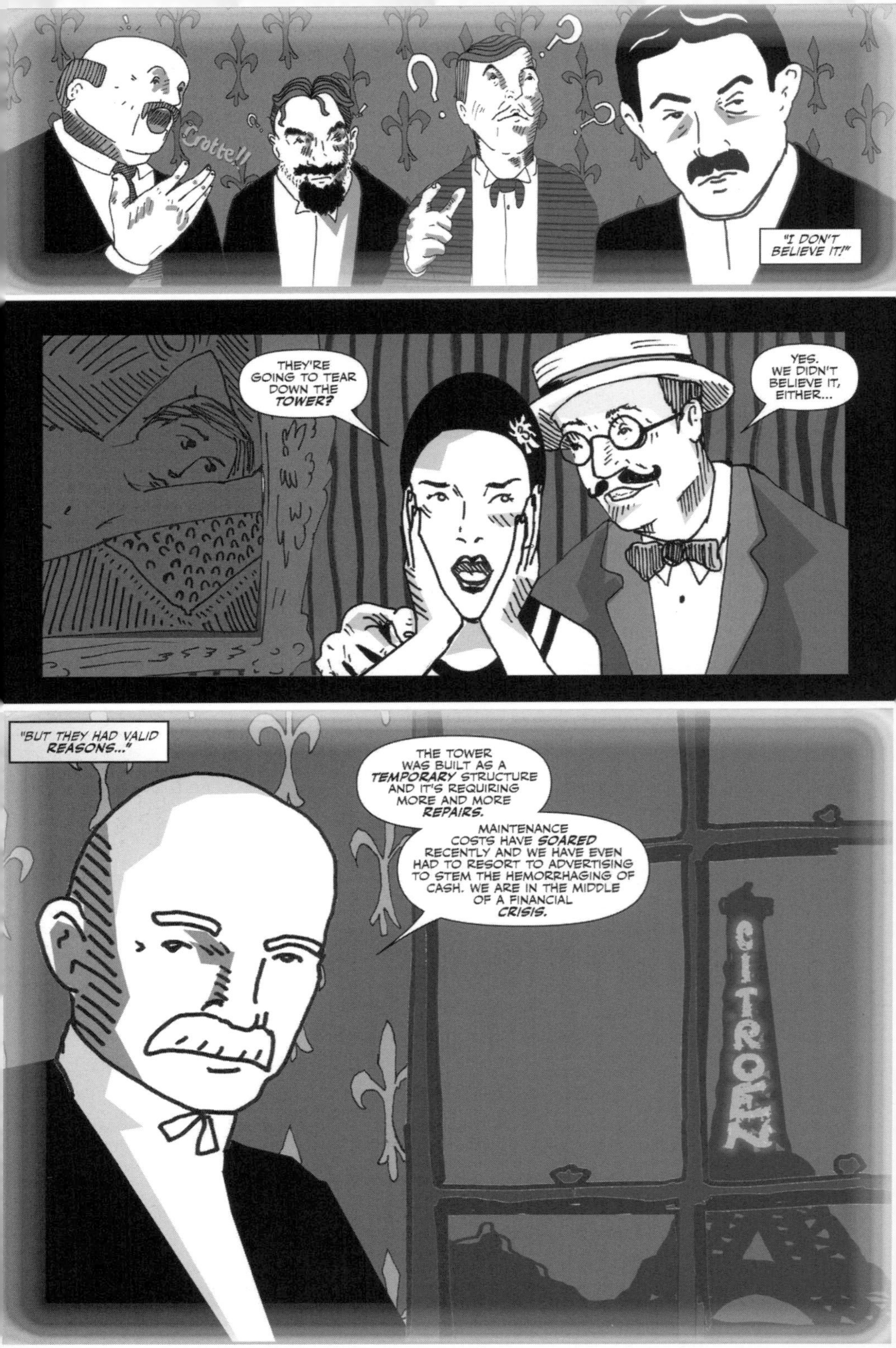
Crotte!!
"I DON'T BELIEVE IT!"
THEY'RE GOING TO TEAR DOWN THE TOWER?
YES. WE DIDN'T BELIEVE IT, EITHER...
"BUT THEY HAD VALID REASONS..."
THE TOWER WAS BUILT AS A TEMPORARY STRUCTURE AND IT'S REQUIRING MORE AND MORE REPAIRS.
MAINTENANCE COSTS HAVE SOARED RECENTLY AND WE HAVE EVEN HAD TO RESORT TO ADVERTISING TO STEM THE HEMORRHAGING OF CASH. WE ARE IN THE MIDDLE OF A FINANCIAL CRISIS.
CITROEN

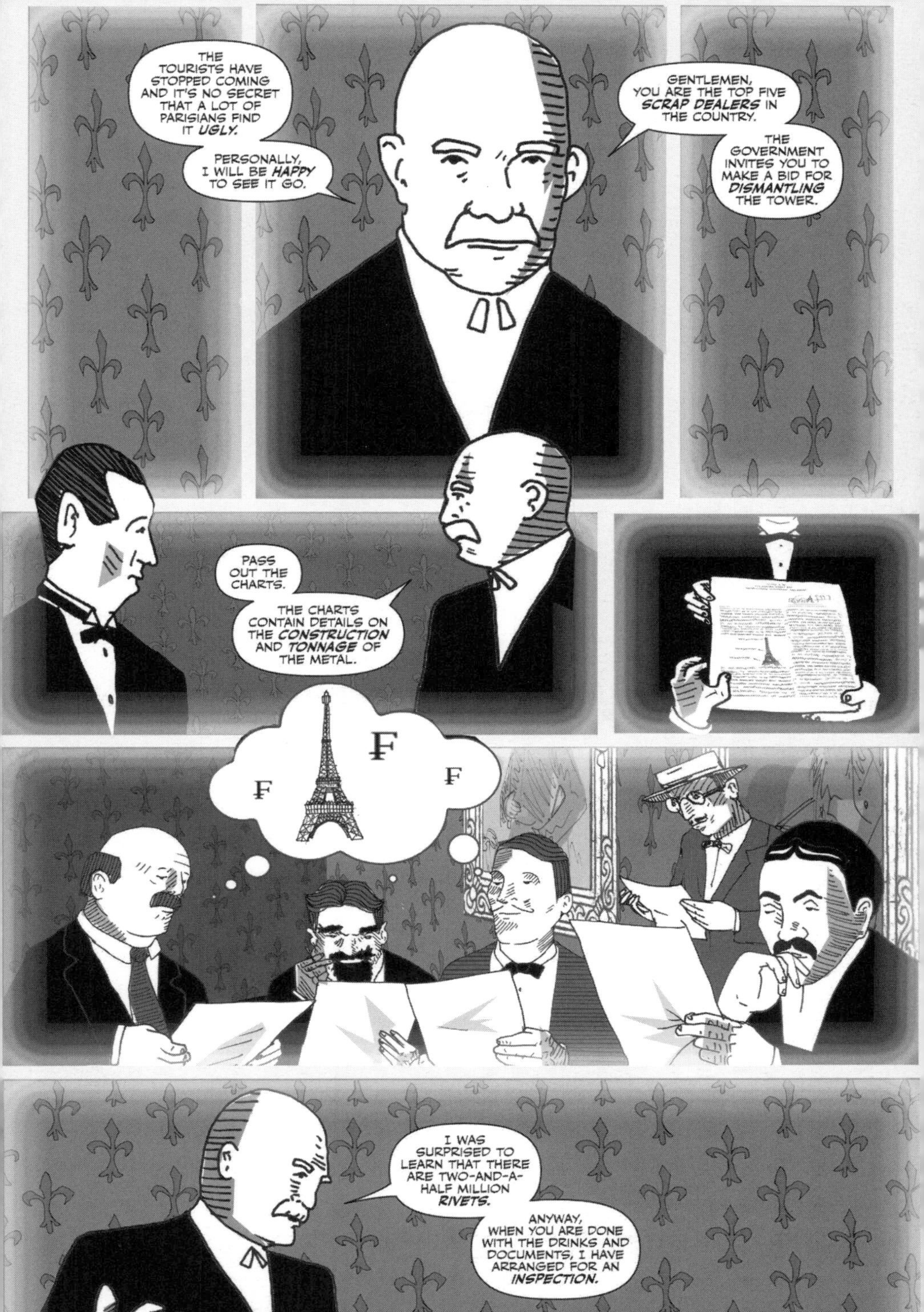
THE TOURISTS HAVE STOPPED COMING AND IT'S NO SECRET THAT A LOT OF PARISIANS FIND IT UGLY.
PERSONALLY, I WILL BE HAPPY TO SEE IT GO.
GENTLEMEN, YOU ARE THE TOP FIVE SCRAP DEALERS IN THE COUNTRY.
THE GOVERNMENT INVITES YOU TO MAKE A BID FOR DISMANTLING THE TOWER.
PASS OUT THE CHARTS.
THE CHARTS CONTAIN DETAILS ON THE CONSTRUCTION AND TONNAGE OF THE METAL.
I WAS SURPRISED TO LEARN THAT THERE ARE TWO-AND-A-HALF MILLION RIVETS.
ANYWAY, WHEN YOU ARE DONE WITH THE DRINKS AND DOCUMENTS, I HAVE ARRANGED FOR AN INSPECTION.

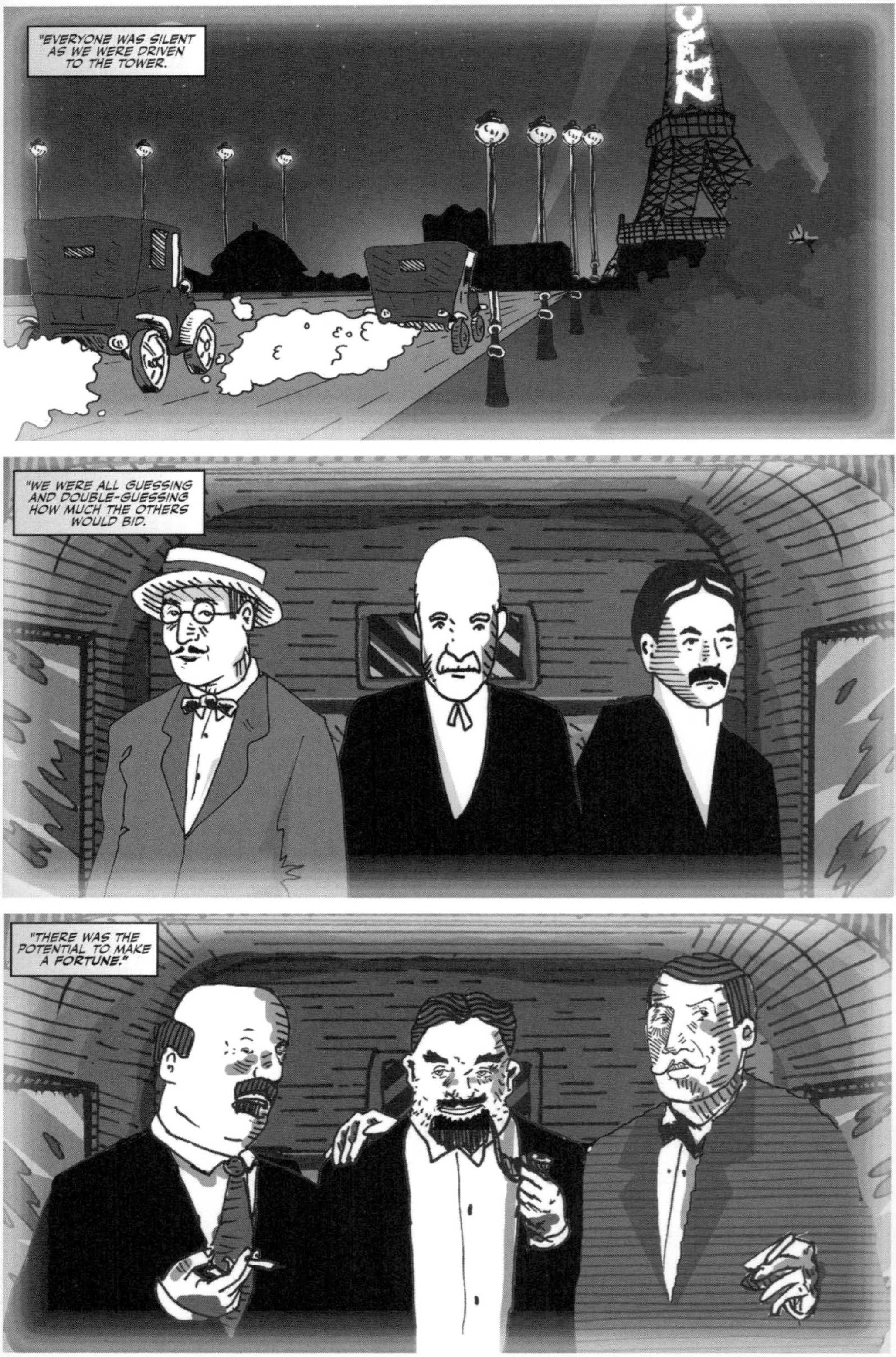
"EVERYONE WAS SILENT AS WE WERE DRIVEN TO THE TOWER.
"WE WERE ALL GUESSING AND DOUBLE-GUESSING HOW MUCH THE OTHERS WOULD BID.
"THERE WAS THE POTENTIAL TO MAKE A FORTUNE."

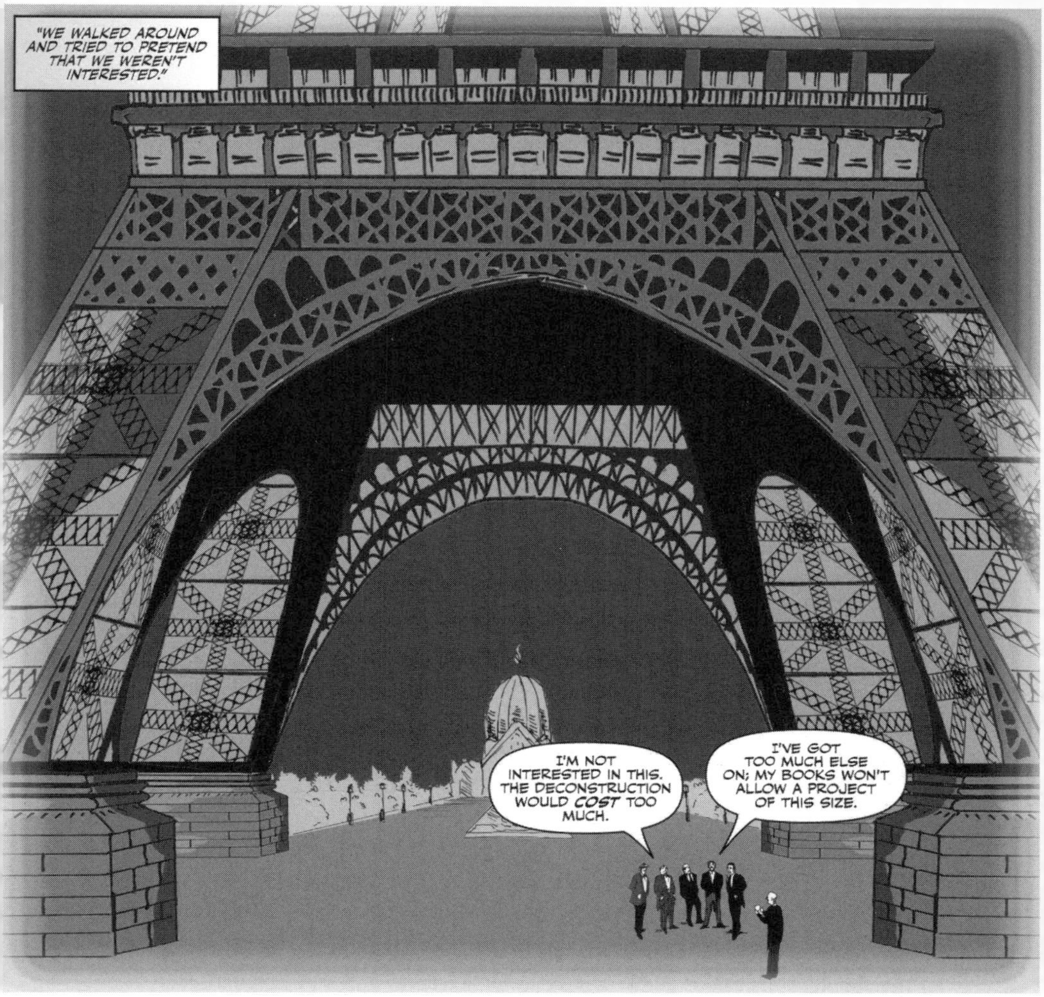
"WE WALKED AROUND AND TRIED TO PRETEND THAT WE WEREN'T INTERESTED."
I'M NOT INTERESTED IN THIS. THE DECONSTRUCTION WOULD COST TOO MUCH.
I'VE GOT TOO MUCH ELSE ON; MY BOOKS WON'T ALLOW A PROJECT OF THIS SIZE.

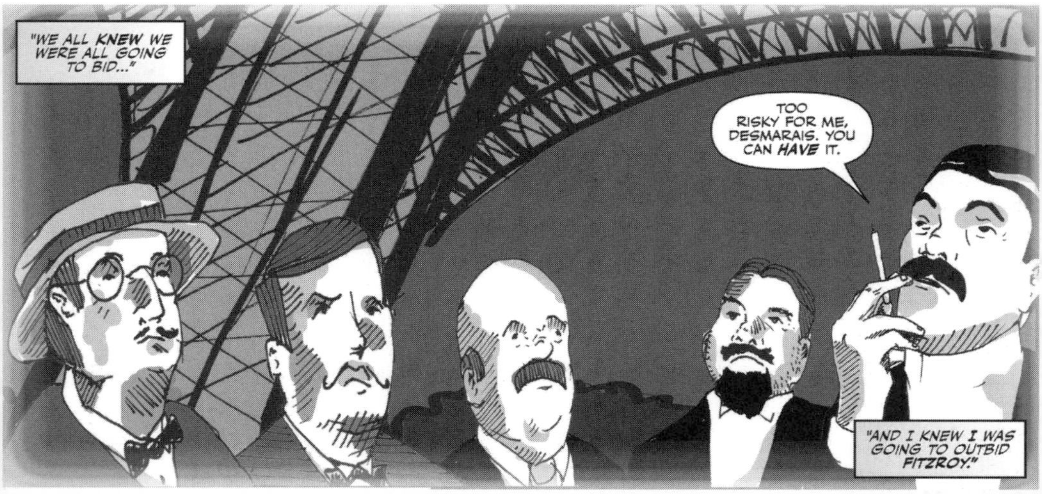
"WE ALL KNEW WE WERE ALL GOING TO BID..."
TOO RISKY FOR ME, DESMARAIS. YOU CAN HAVE IT.
"AND I KNEW I WAS GOING TO OUTBID FITZROY."

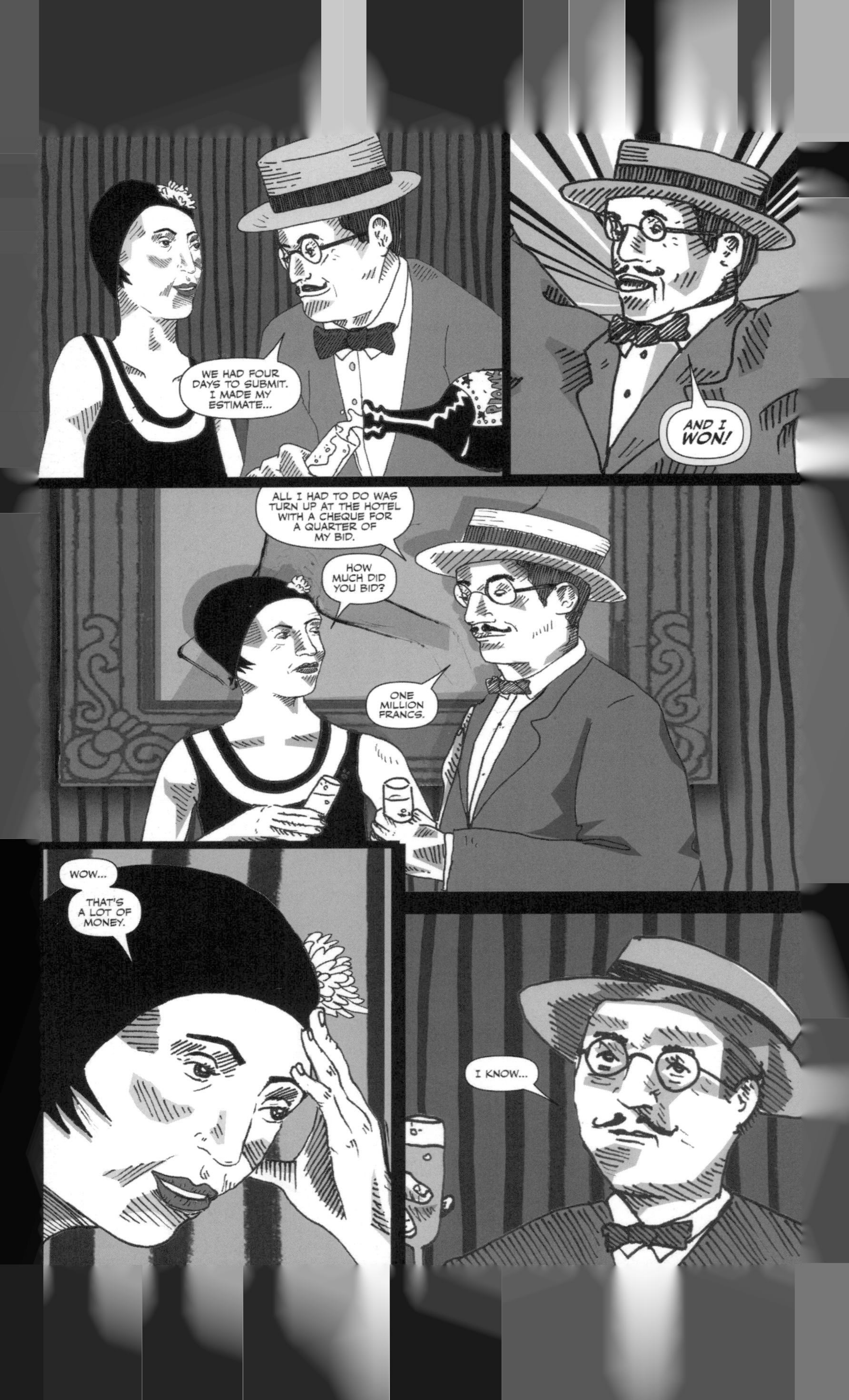
WE HAD FOUR DAYS TO SUBMIT. I MADE MY ESTIMATE...
AND I WON!
ALL I HAD TO DO WAS TURN UP AT THE HOTEL WITH A CHEQUE FOR A QUARTER OF MY BID.
HOW MUCH DID YOU BID?
ONE MILLION FRANCS.
WOW...
THAT'S A LOT OF MONEY.
I KNOW...

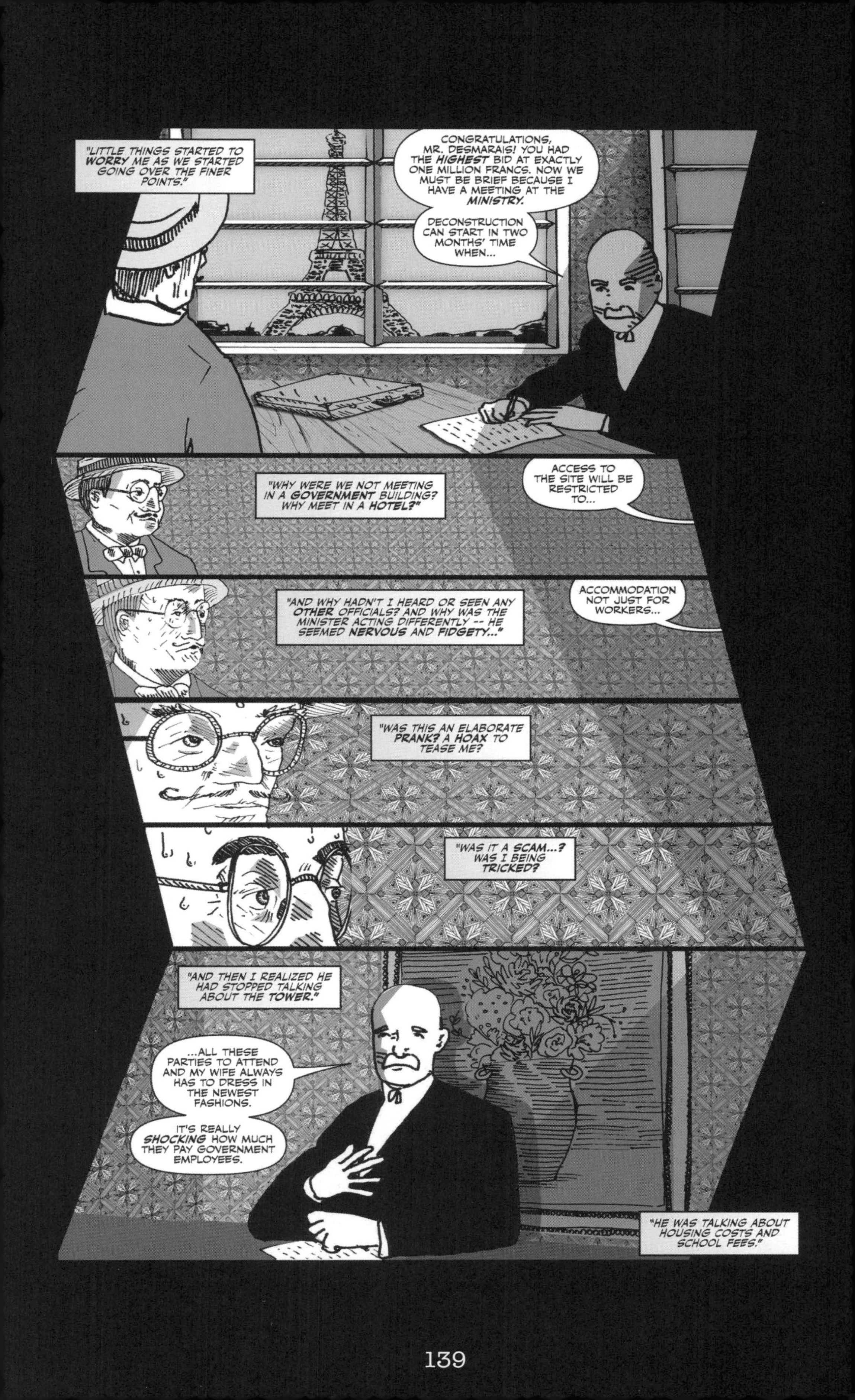
"LITTLE THINGS STARTED TO WORRY ME AS WE STARTED GOING OVER THE FINER POINTS."
CONGRATULATIONS, MR. DESMARAIS! YOU HAD THE HIGHEST BID AT EXACTLY ONE MILLION FRANCS. NOW WE MUST BE BRIEF BECAUSE I HAVE A MEETING AT THE MINISTRY.
DECONSTRUCTION CAN START IN TWO MONTHS' TIME WHEN...
"WHY WERE WE NOT MEETING IN A GOVERNMENT BUILDING? WHY MEET IN A HOTEL?"
ACCESS TO THE SITE WILL BE RESTRICTED TO...
"AND WHY HADN'T I HEARD OR SEEN ANY OTHER OFFICIALS? AND WHY WAS THE MINISTER ACTING DIFFERENTLY -- HE SEEMED NERVOUS AND FIDGETY..."
ACCOMMODATION NOT JUST FOR WORKERS...
"WAS THIS AN ELABORATE PRANK? A HOAX TO TEASE ME?
"WAS IT A SCAM...? WAS I BEING TRICKED?
"AND THEN I REALIZED HE HAD STOPPED TALKING ABOUT THE TOWER."
...ALL THESE PARTIES TO ATTEND AND MY WIFE ALWAYS HAS TO DRESS IN THE NEWEST FASHIONS.
IT'S REALLY SHOCKING HOW MUCH THEY PAY GOVERNMENT EMPLOYEES.
"HE WAS TALKING ABOUT HOUSING COSTS AND SCHOOL FEES."

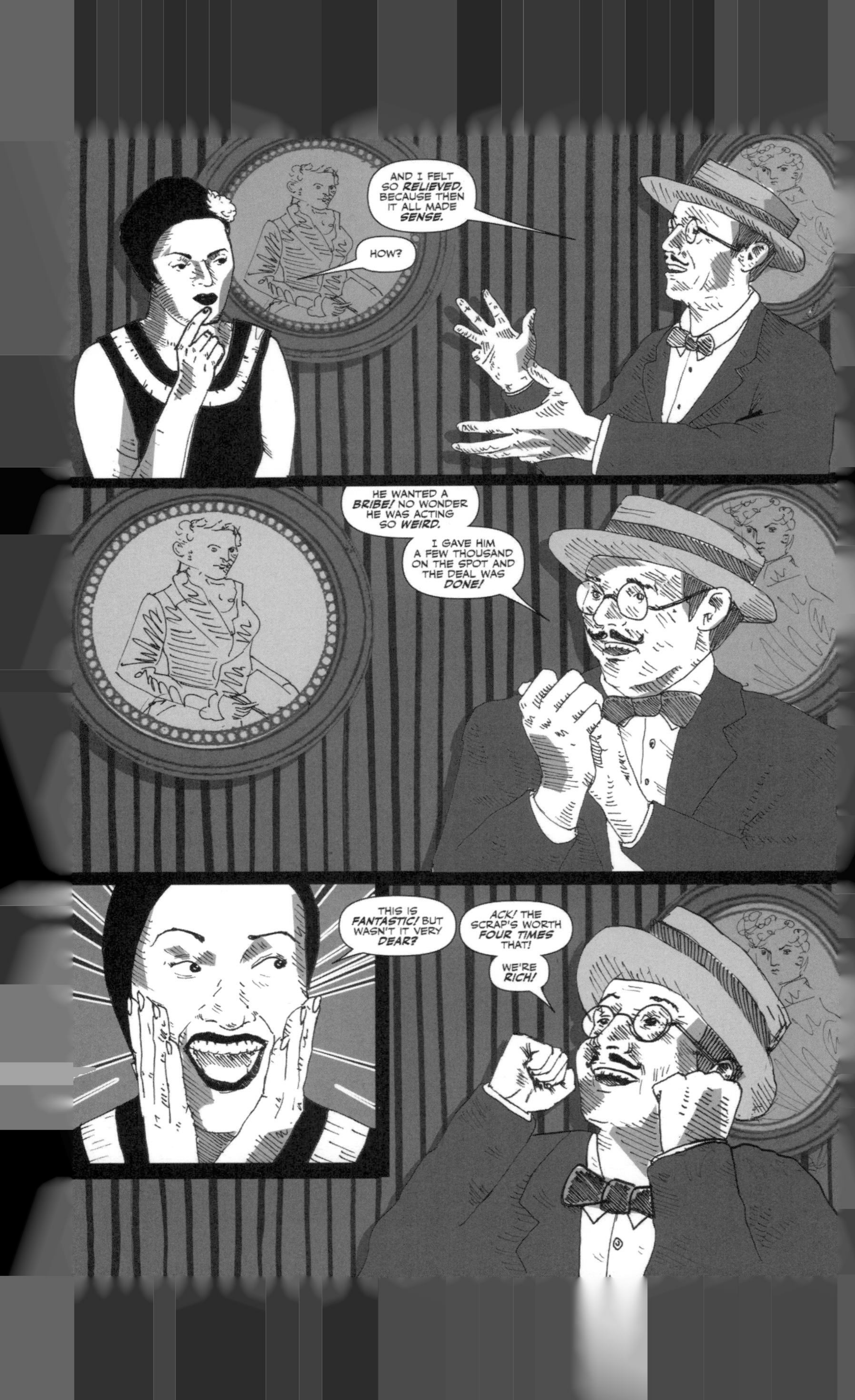
AND I FELT SO RELIEVED, BECAUSE THEN IT ALL MADE SENSE.
HOW?
HE WANTED A BRIBE! NO WONDER HE WAS ACTING SO WEIRD.
I GAVE HIM A FEW THOUSAND ON THE SPOT AND THE DEAL WAS DONE!
THIS IS FANTASTIC! BUT WASN'T IT VERY DEAR?
ACK! THE SCRAP'S WORTH FOUR TIMES THAT!
WE'RE RICH!

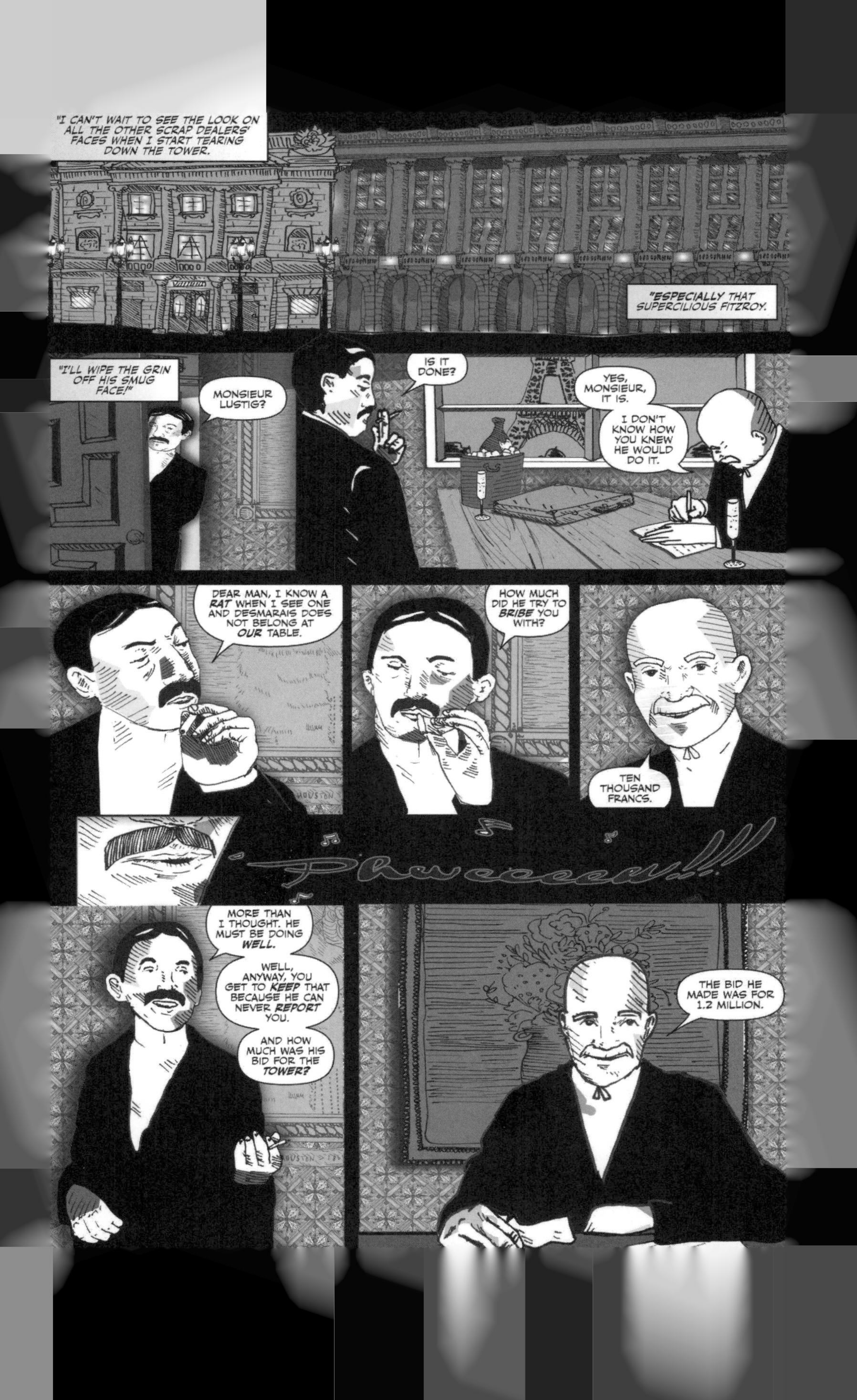
"I CAN'T WAIT TO SEE THE LOOK ON ALL THE OTHER SCRAP DEALERS' FACES WHEN I START TEARING DOWN THE TOWER.
"ESPECIALLY THAT SUPERCILIOUS FITZROY.
"I'LL WIPE THE GRIN OFF HIS SMUG FACE!"
MONSIEUR LUSTIG?
IS IT DONE?
YES, MONSIEUR, IT IS.
I DON'T KNOW HOW YOU KNEW HE WOULD DO IT.
DEAR MAN, I KNOW A RAT WHEN I SEE ONE AND DESMARAIS DOES NOT BELONG AT OUR TABLE.
HOW MUCH DID HE TRY TO BRIBE YOU WITH?
TEN THOUSAND FRANCS.
Phweeeeew!!!
MORE THAN I THOUGHT. HE MUST BE DOING WELL.
WELL, ANYWAY, YOU GET TO KEEP THAT BECAUSE HE CAN NEVER REPORT YOU.
AND HOW MUCH WAS HIS BID FOR THE TOWER?
THE BID HE MADE WAS FOR 1.2 MILLION.

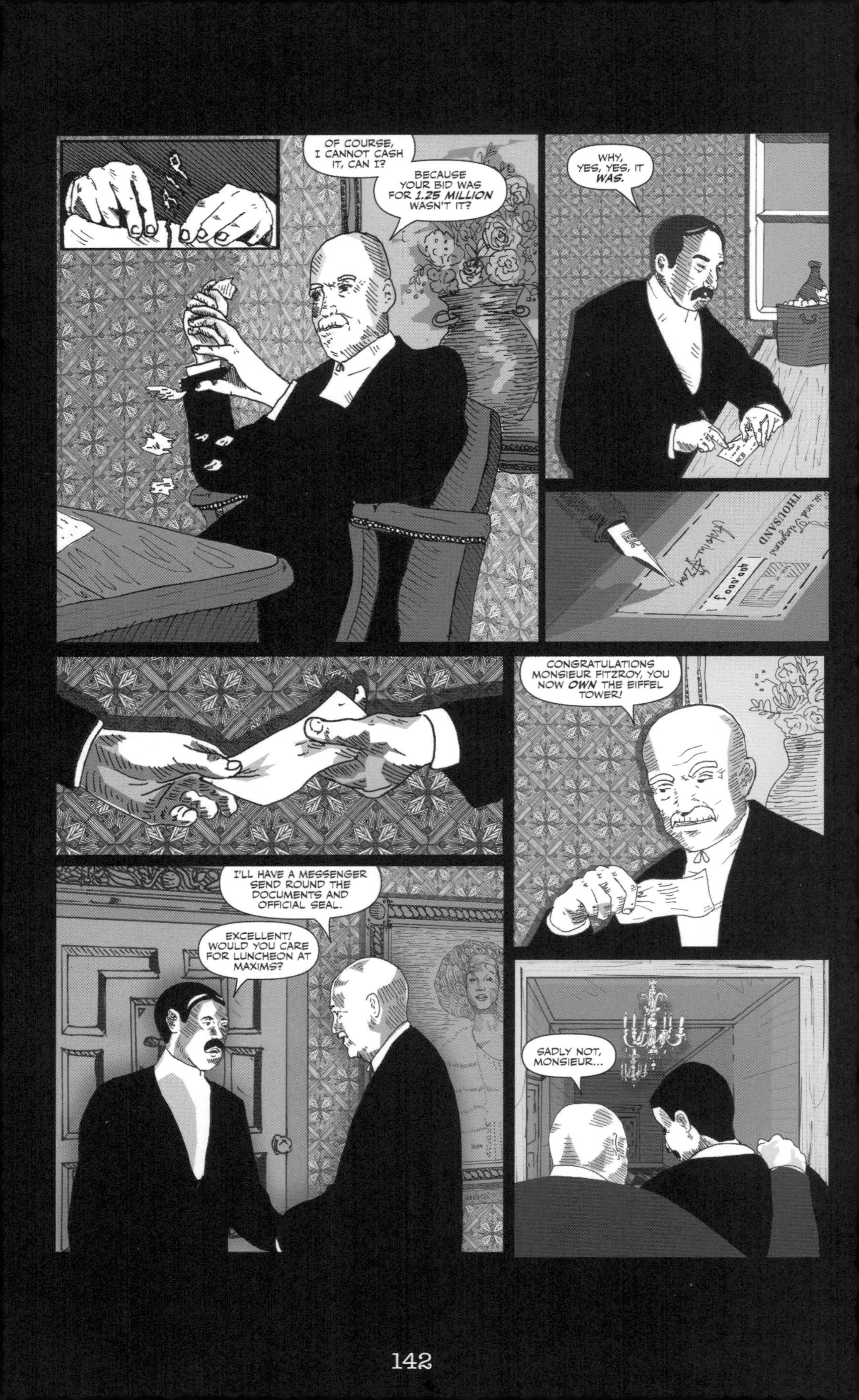

OF COURSE, I CANNOT CASH IT, CAN I?
BECAUSE YOUR BID WAS FOR 1.25 MILLION WASN'T IT?
WHY, YES, YES, IT WAS.
THOUSAND
CONGRATULATIONS MONSIEUR FITZROY, YOU NOW OWN THE EIFFEL TOWER!
I'LL HAVE A MESSENGER SEND ROUND THE DOCUMENTS AND OFFICIAL SEAL.
EXCELLENT! WOULD YOU CARE FOR LUNCHEON AT MAXIMS?
SADLY NOT, MONSIEUR...

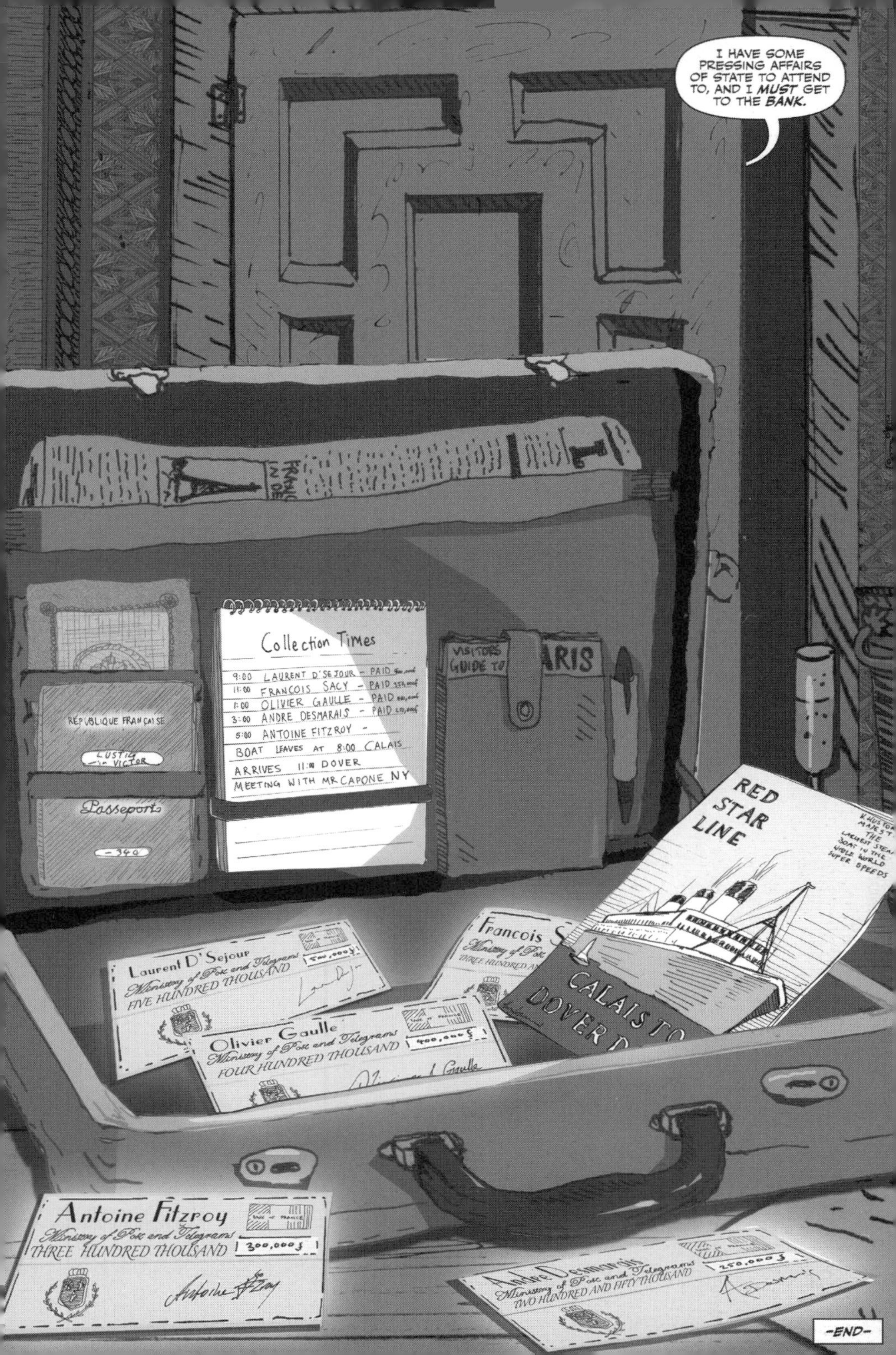

I HAVE SOME PRESSING AFFAIRS OF STATE TO ATTEND TO, AND I *MUST* GET TO THE *BANK.*
RÉPUBLIQUE FRANÇAISE
Passeports
Collection Times
9:00 LAURENT D'SEJOUR - PAID
11:00 FRANCOIS SACY - PAID
1:00 OLIVIER GAULLE - PAID
3:00 ANDRE DESMARAIS - PAID
5:00 ANTOINE FITZROY -
BOAT LEAVES AT 8:00 CALAIS
ARRIVES 11:00 DOVER
MEETING WITH MR CAPONE NY
VISITORS GUIDE TO
ARIS
RED STAR LINE
Laurent D' Sejour
Ministry of Post and Telegrams
FIVE HUNDRED THOUSAND
Olivier Gaulle
Ministry of Post and Telegrams
FOUR HUNDRED THOUSAND
400,000 $
CALAIS TO DOVER
Antoine Fitzroy
Ministry of Post and Telegrams
THREE HUNDRED THOUSAND
300,000 $
Andre Desmarais
Ministry of Post and Telegrams
TWO HUNDRED AND FIFTY THOUSAND
250,000 $
-END-

Note on the story:

Though 'The Bid' is fictional, there really was a conman called Victor Lustig who is known as the man who sold the Eiffel Tower twice. He was a genius who even had the audacity to con Al Capone out of $5,000. A set of instructions known as the "Ten Commandments for Conmen" has been attributed to him.

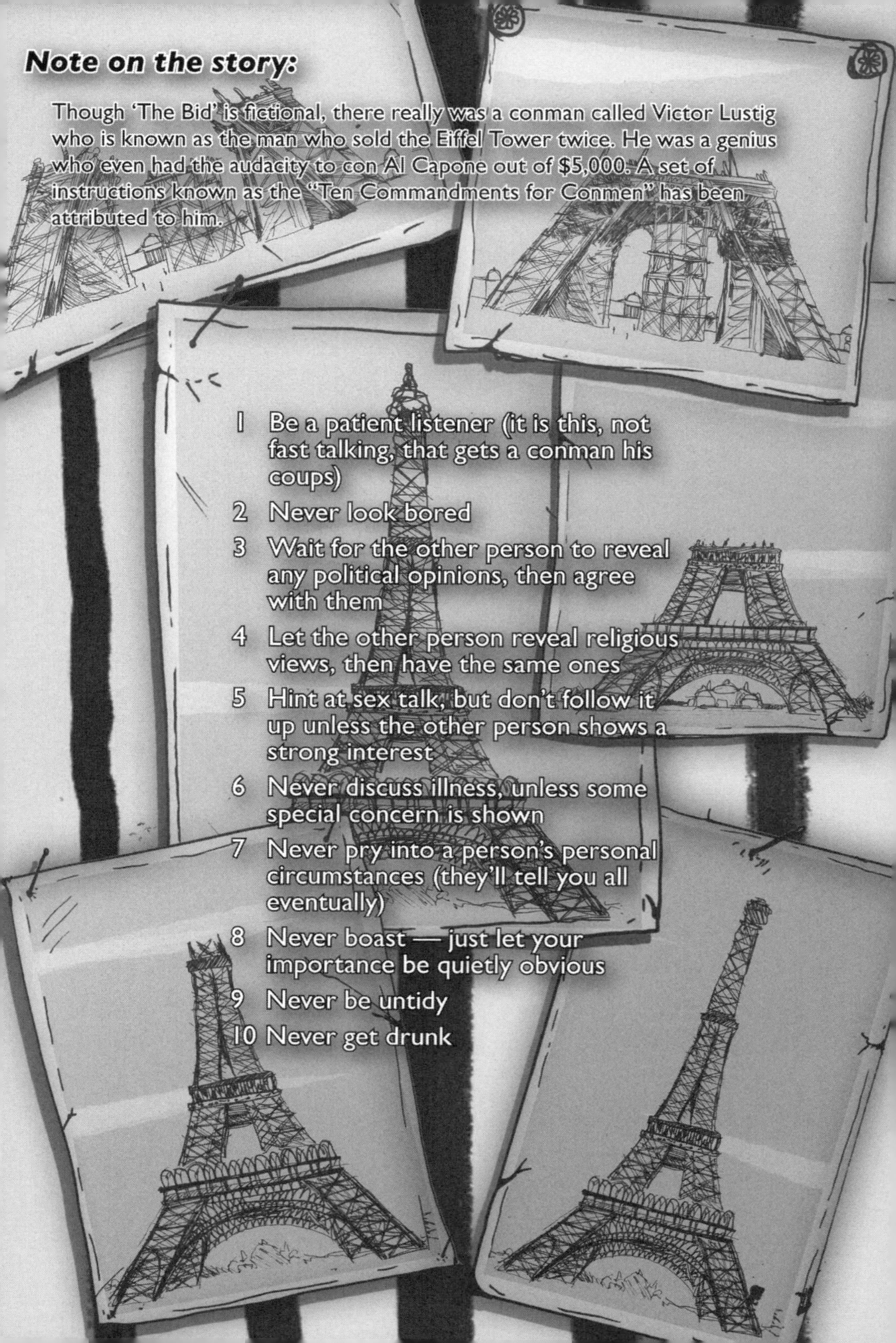

1. Be a patient listener (it is this, not fast talking, that gets a conman his coups)
2. Never look bored
3. Wait for the other person to reveal any political opinions, then agree with them
4. Let the other person reveal religious views, then have the same ones
5. Hint at sex talk, but don't follow it up unless the other person shows a strong interest
6. Never discuss illness, unless some special concern is shown
7. Never pry into a person's personal circumstances (they'll tell you all eventually)
8. Never boast — just let your importance be quietly obvious
9. Never be untidy
10. Never get drunk

Abandoned...

"Home care is a dynamic industry in the US. In 2008, 7.6m individuals received care from 17,000 providers. By 2010, 12m received care from 33,000 providers and the annual expenditure had risen to $72.2bn."

– National Association for Home Care & Hospice

Writer/Creator
Neil Gibson

Illustrator
Jake Elphick

www.tpub.co.uk

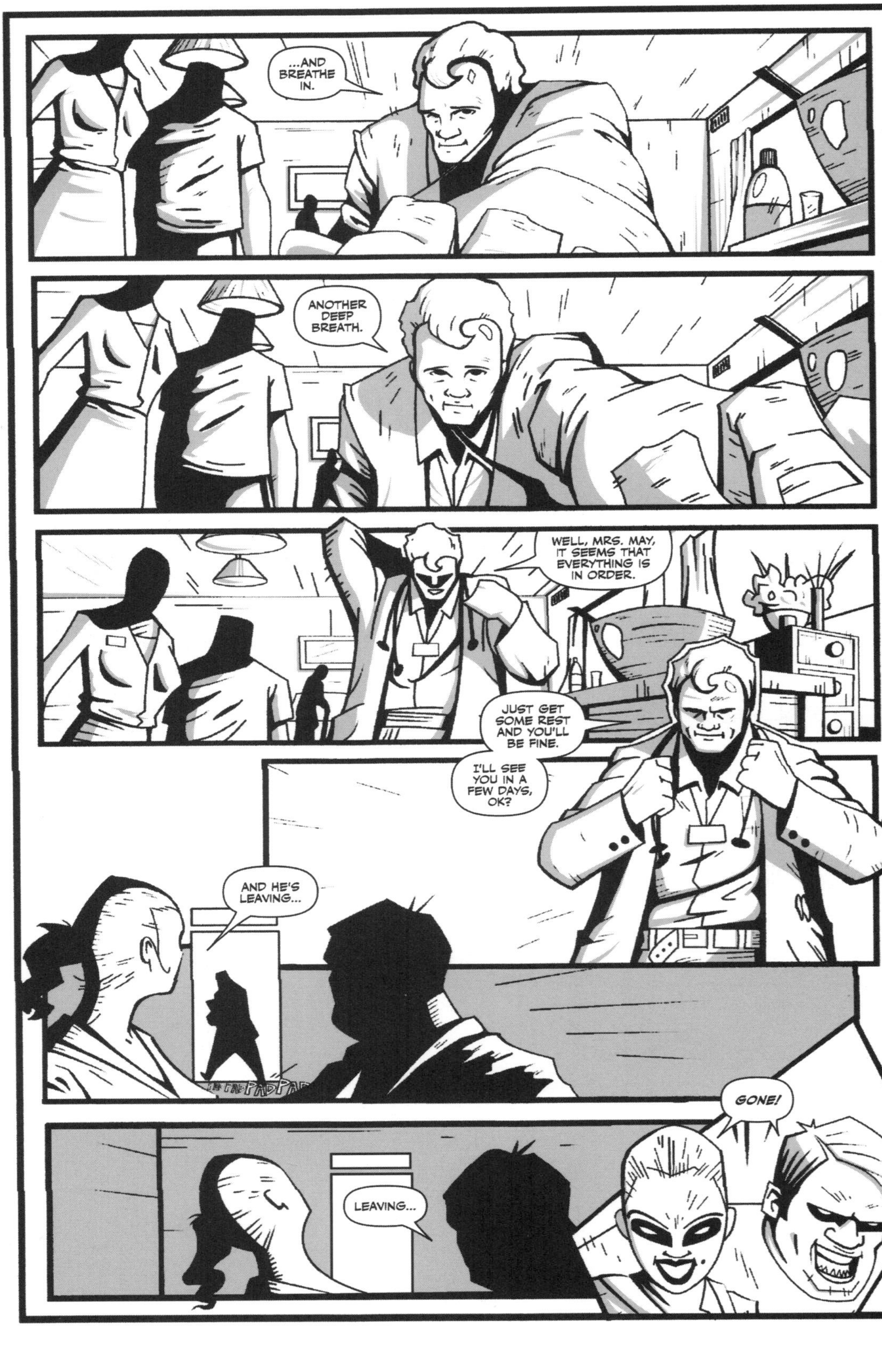
...AND BREATHE IN.
ANOTHER DEEP BREATH.
WELL, MRS. MAY, IT SEEMS THAT EVERYTHING IS IN ORDER.
JUST GET SOME REST AND YOU'LL BE FINE.
I'LL SEE YOU IN A FEW DAYS, OK?
AND HE'S LEAVING...
PAD
LEAVING...
GONE!

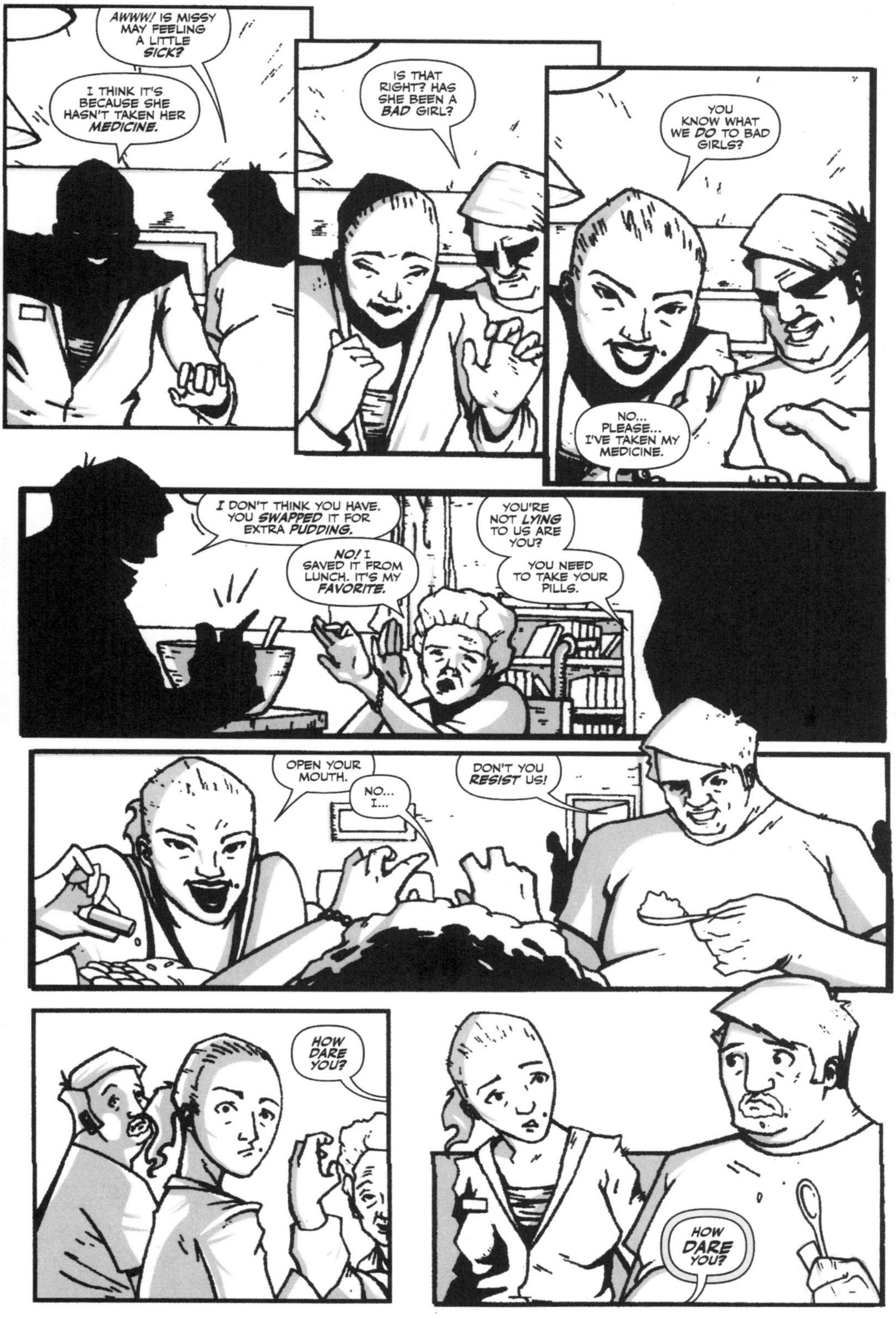
AWWW! IS MISSY MAY FEELING A LITTLE SICK?
I THINK IT'S BECAUSE SHE HASN'T TAKEN HER MEDICINE.
IS THAT RIGHT? HAS SHE BEEN A BAD GIRL?
YOU KNOW WHAT WE DO TO BAD GIRLS?
NO... PLEASE... I'VE TAKEN MY MEDICINE.
I DON'T THINK YOU HAVE. YOU SWAPPED IT FOR EXTRA PUDDING.
NO! I SAVED IT FROM LUNCH. IT'S MY FAVORITE.
YOU'RE NOT LYING TO US ARE YOU?
YOU NEED TO TAKE YOUR PILLS.
OPEN YOUR MOUTH.
NO... I...
DON'T YOU RESIST US!
HOW DARE YOU?
HOW DARE YOU?

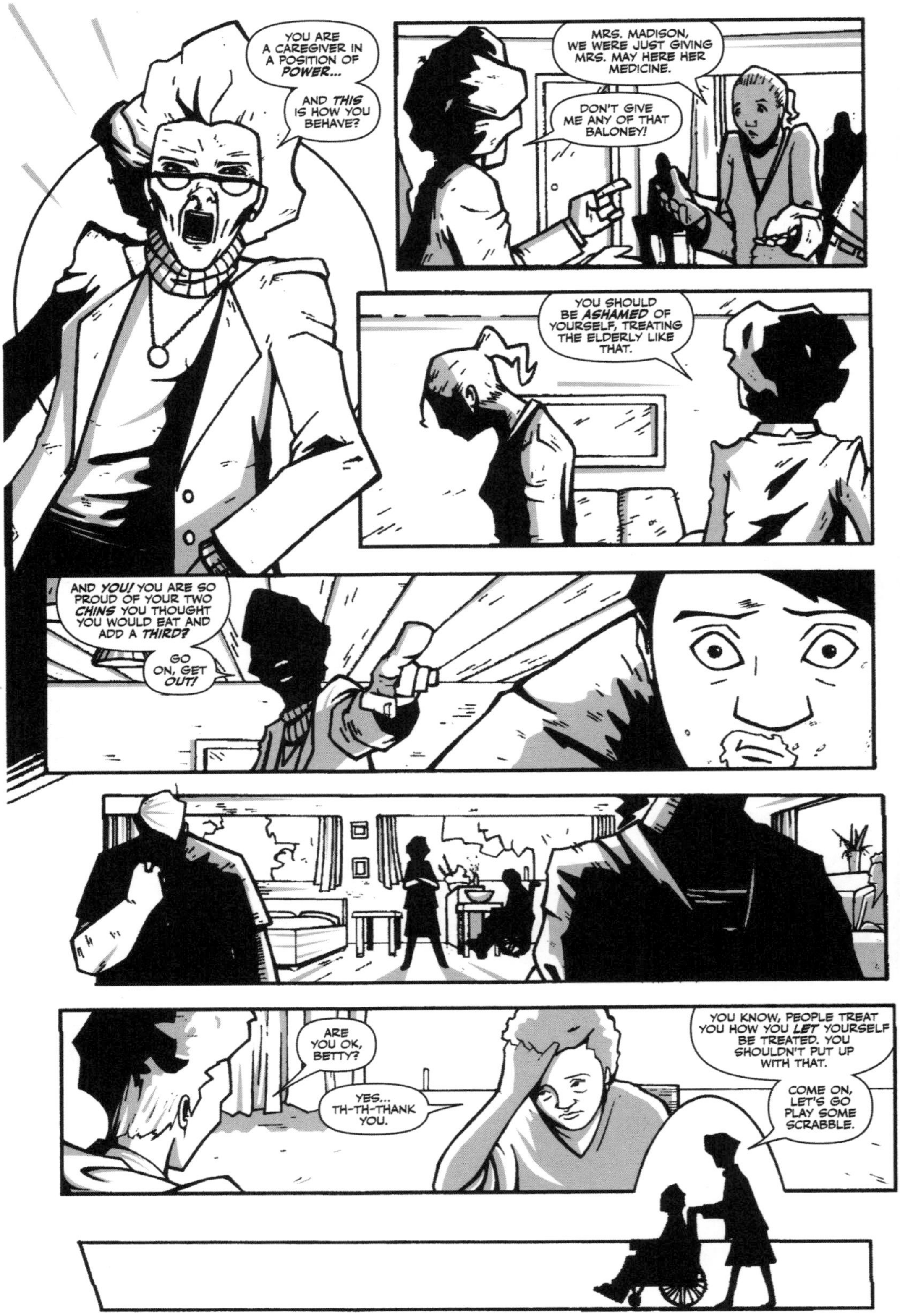

YOU ARE A CAREGIVER IN A POSITION OF POWER...
AND THIS IS HOW YOU BEHAVE?
MRS. MADISON, WE WERE JUST GIVING MRS. MAY HERE HER MEDICINE.
DON'T GIVE ME ANY OF THAT BALONEY!
YOU SHOULD BE ASHAMED OF YOURSELF, TREATING THE ELDERLY LIKE THAT.
AND YOU! YOU ARE SO PROUD OF YOUR TWO CHINS YOU THOUGHT YOU WOULD EAT AND ADD A THIRD?
GO ON, GET OUT!
ARE YOU OK, BETTY?
YES... TH-TH-THANK YOU.
YOU KNOW, PEOPLE TREAT YOU HOW YOU LET YOURSELF BE TREATED. YOU SHOULDN'T PUT UP WITH THAT.
COME ON, LET'S GO PLAY SOME SCRABBLE.

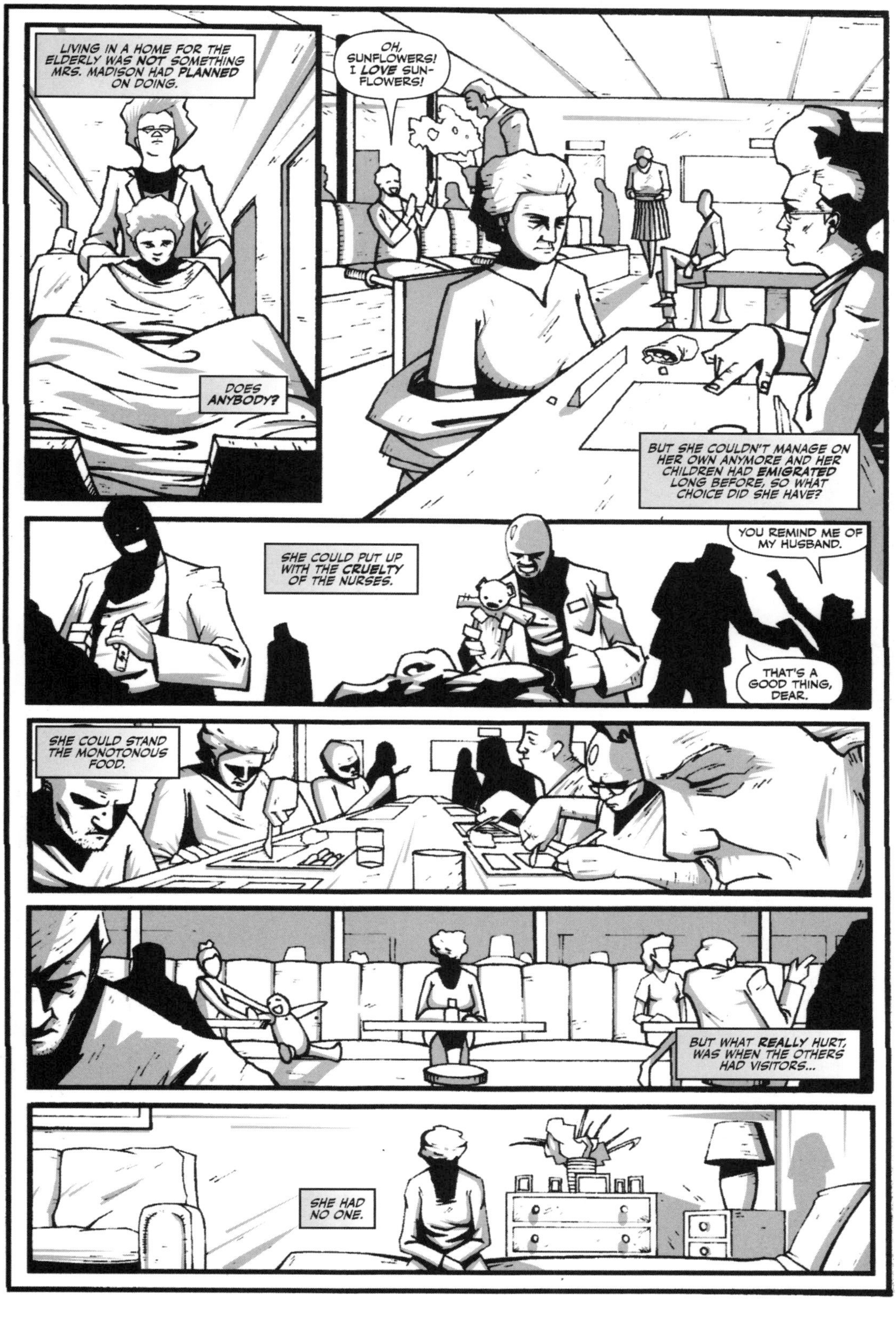
LIVING IN A HOME FOR THE ELDERLY WAS NOT SOMETHING MRS. MADISON HAD PLANNED ON DOING.
DOES ANYBODY?
OH, SUNFLOWERS! I LOVE SUN-FLOWERS!
BUT SHE COULDN'T MANAGE ON HER OWN ANYMORE AND HER CHILDREN HAD EMIGRATED LONG BEFORE, SO WHAT CHOICE DID SHE HAVE?
SHE COULD PUT UP WITH THE CRUELTY OF THE NURSES.
YOU REMIND ME OF MY HUSBAND.
THAT'S A GOOD THING, DEAR.
SHE COULD STAND THE MONOTONOUS FOOD.
BUT WHAT REALLY HURT, WAS WHEN THE OTHERS HAD VISITORS...
SHE HAD NO ONE.

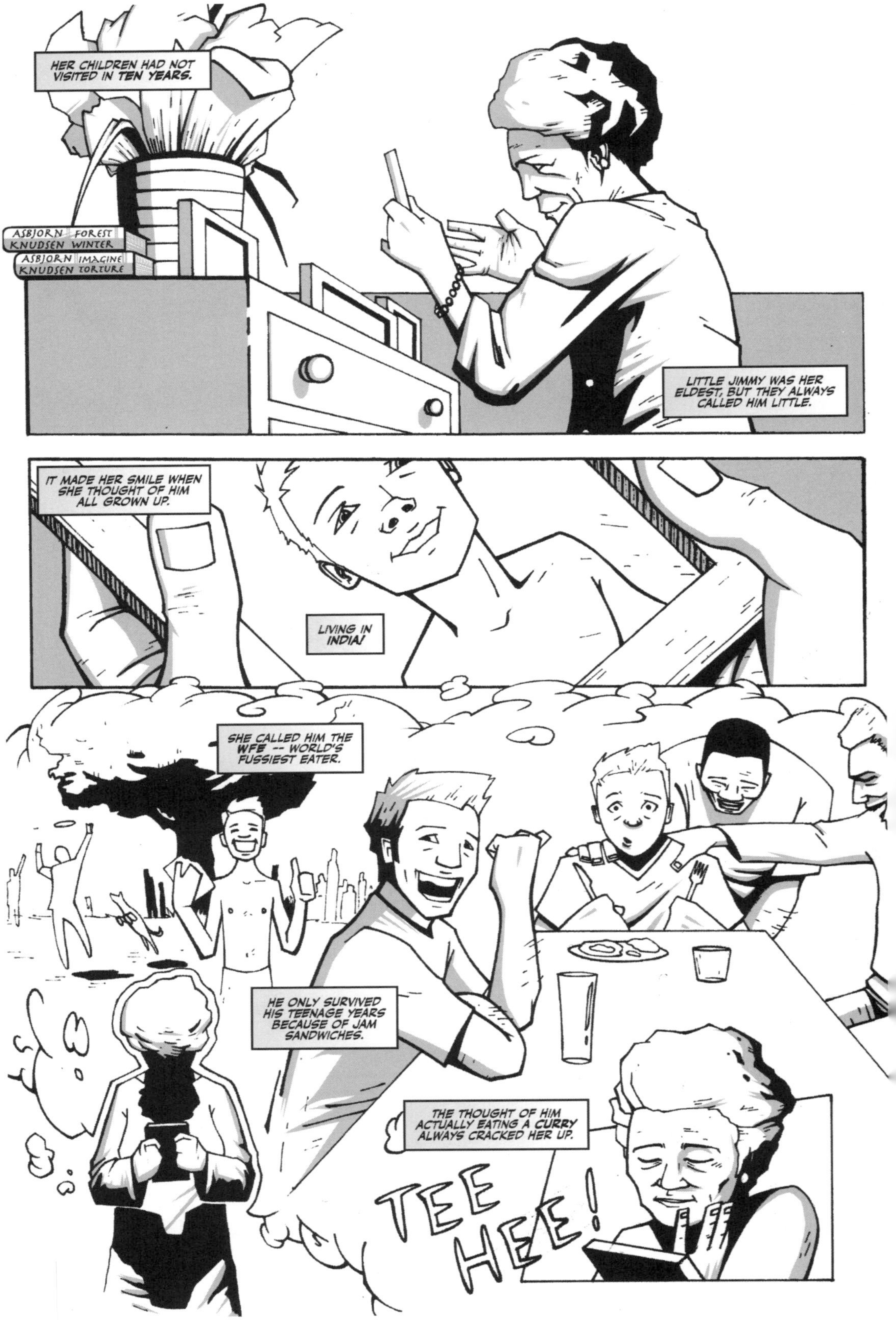
HER CHILDREN HAD NOT VISITED IN TEN YEARS.
ASBJORN KNUDSEN FOREST WINTER
ASBJORN KNUDSEN IMAGINE TORTURE
LITTLE JIMMY WAS HER ELDEST, BUT THEY ALWAYS CALLED HIM LITTLE.
IT MADE HER SMILE WHEN SHE THOUGHT OF HIM ALL GROWN UP.
LIVING IN INDIA!
SHE CALLED HIM THE WFE -- WORLD'S FUSSIEST EATER.
HE ONLY SURVIVED HIS TEENAGE YEARS BECAUSE OF JAM SANDWICHES.
THE THOUGHT OF HIM ACTUALLY EATING A CURRY ALWAYS CRACKED HER UP.
TEE HEE!

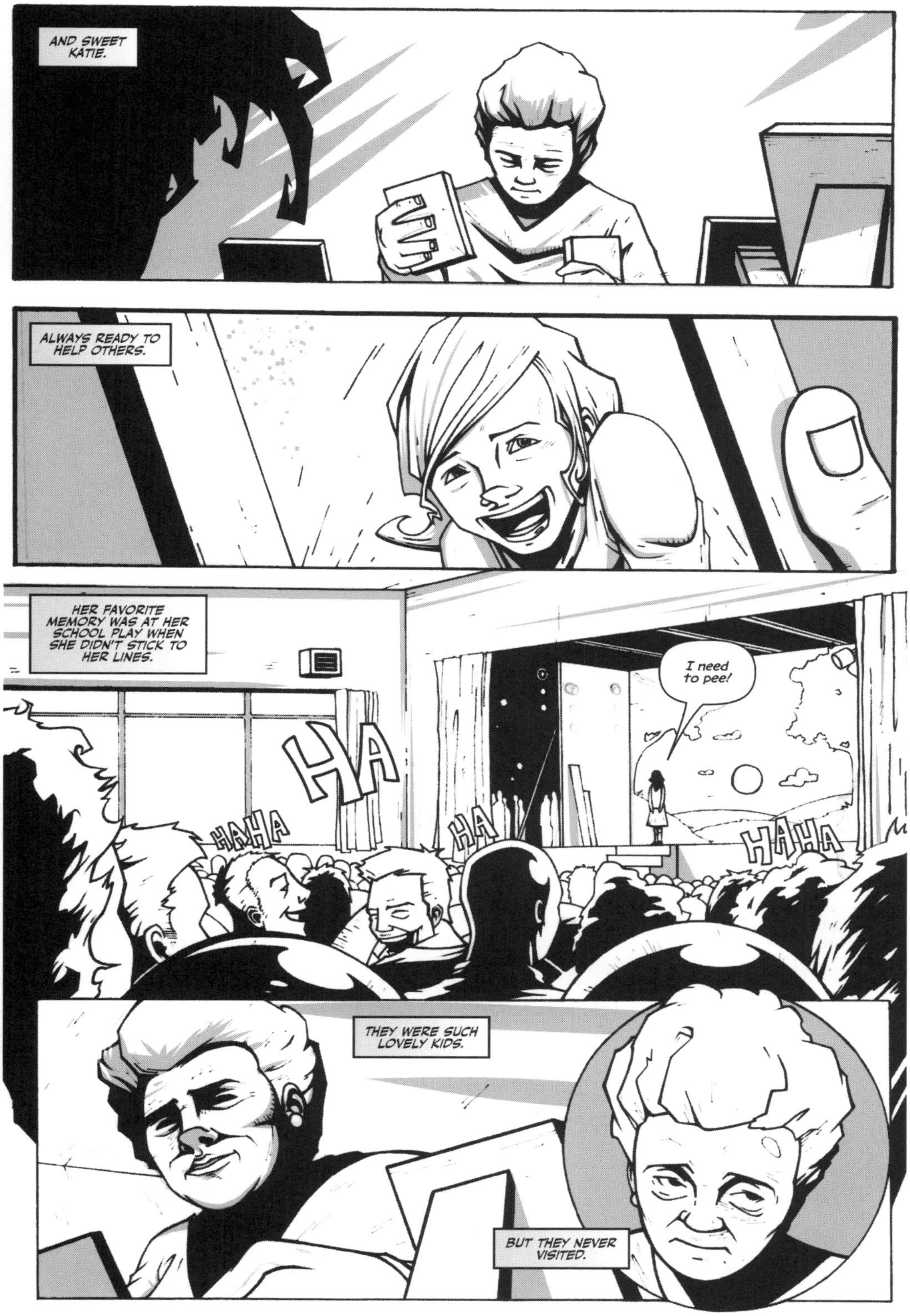
AND SWEET KATIE.
ALWAYS READY TO HELP OTHERS.
HER FAVORITE MEMORY WAS AT HER SCHOOL PLAY WHEN SHE DIDN'T STICK TO HER LINES.
I need to pee!
HA
HAHA
HA
HAHA
THEY WERE SUCH LOVELY KIDS.
BUT THEY NEVER VISITED.

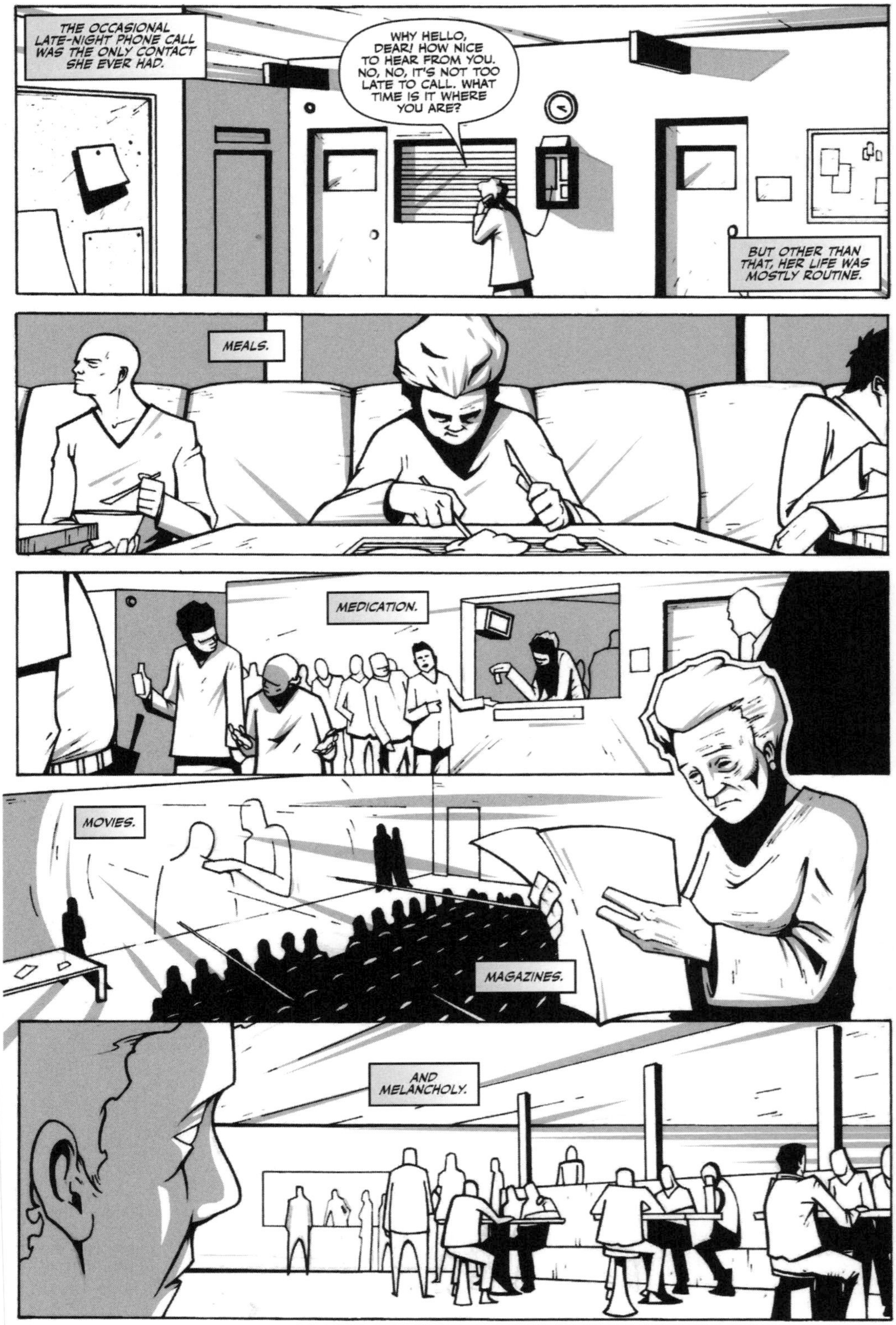
THE OCCASIONAL LATE-NIGHT PHONE CALL WAS THE ONLY CONTACT SHE EVER HAD.
WHY HELLO, DEAR! HOW NICE TO HEAR FROM YOU. NO, NO, IT'S NOT TOO LATE TO CALL. WHAT TIME IS IT WHERE YOU ARE?
BUT OTHER THAN THAT, HER LIFE WAS MOSTLY ROUTINE.
MEALS.
MEDICATION.
MOVIES.
MAGAZINES.
AND MELANCHOLY.

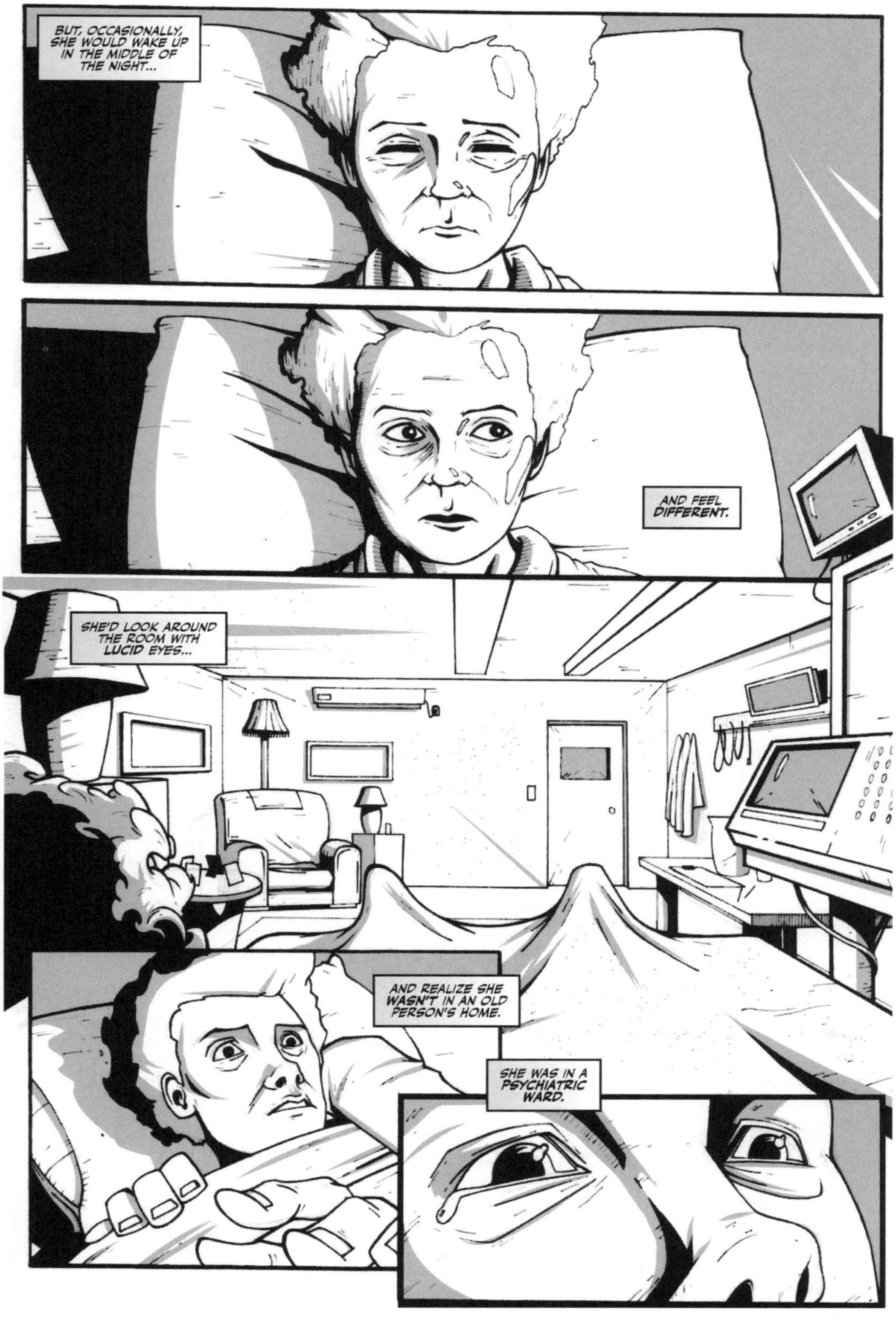
BUT, OCCASIONALLY, SHE WOULD WAKE UP IN THE MIDDLE OF THE NIGHT...
AND FEEL DIFFERENT.
SHE'D LOOK AROUND THE ROOM WITH LUCID EYES...
AND REALIZE SHE WASN'T IN AN OLD PERSON'S HOME.
SHE WAS IN A PSYCHIATRIC WARD.

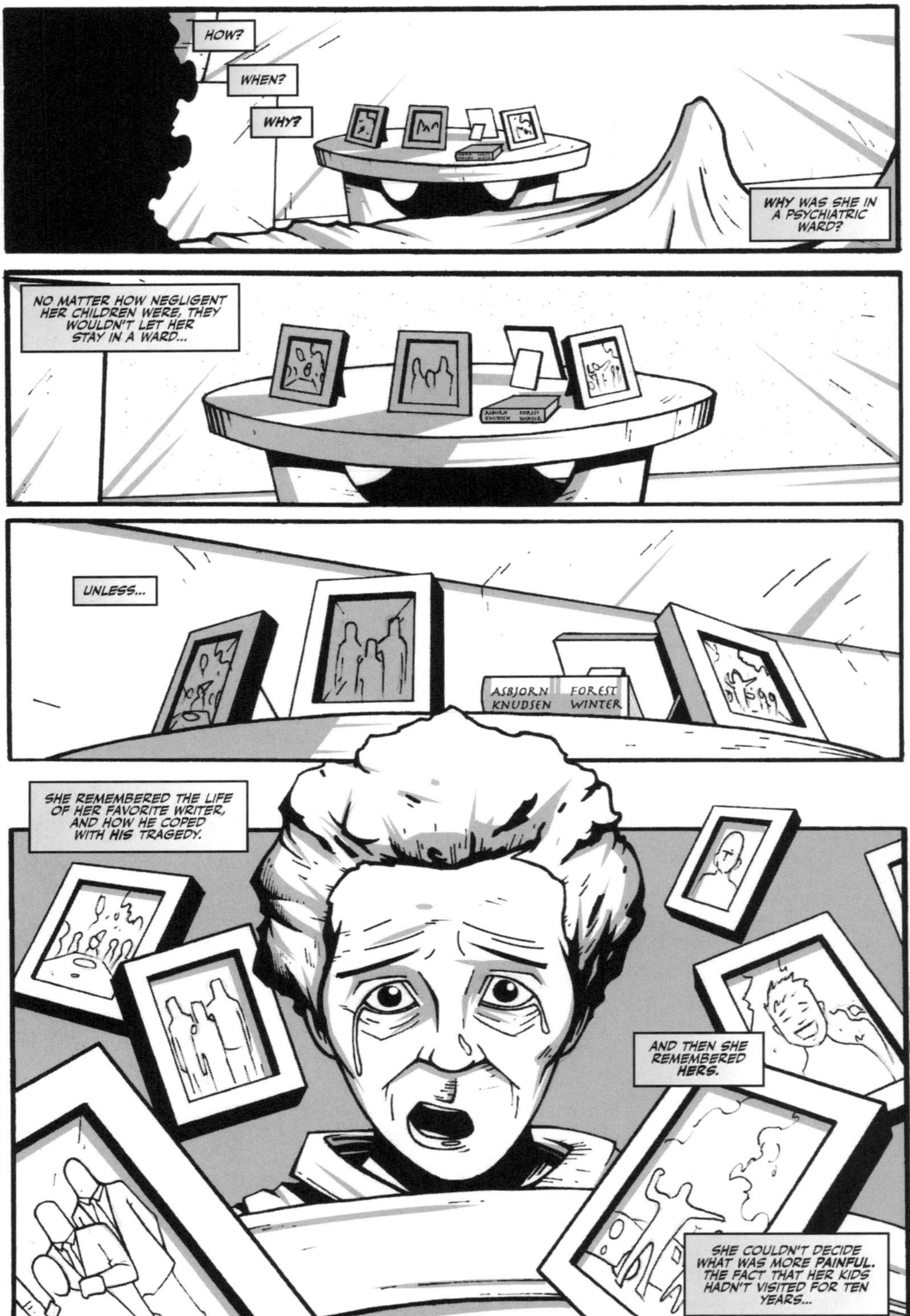
HOW?
WHEN?
WHY?
WHY WAS SHE IN A PSYCHIATRIC WARD?
NO MATTER HOW NEGLIGENT HER CHILDREN WERE, THEY WOULDN'T LET HER STAY IN A WARD...
UNLESS...
ASBJORN KNUDSEN FOREST WINTER
SHE REMEMBERED THE LIFE OF HER FAVORITE WRITER, AND HOW HE COPED WITH HIS TRAGEDY.
AND THEN SHE REMEMBERED HERS.
SHE COULDN'T DECIDE WHAT WAS MORE PAINFUL. THE FACT THAT HER KIDS HADN'T VISITED FOR TEN YEARS...

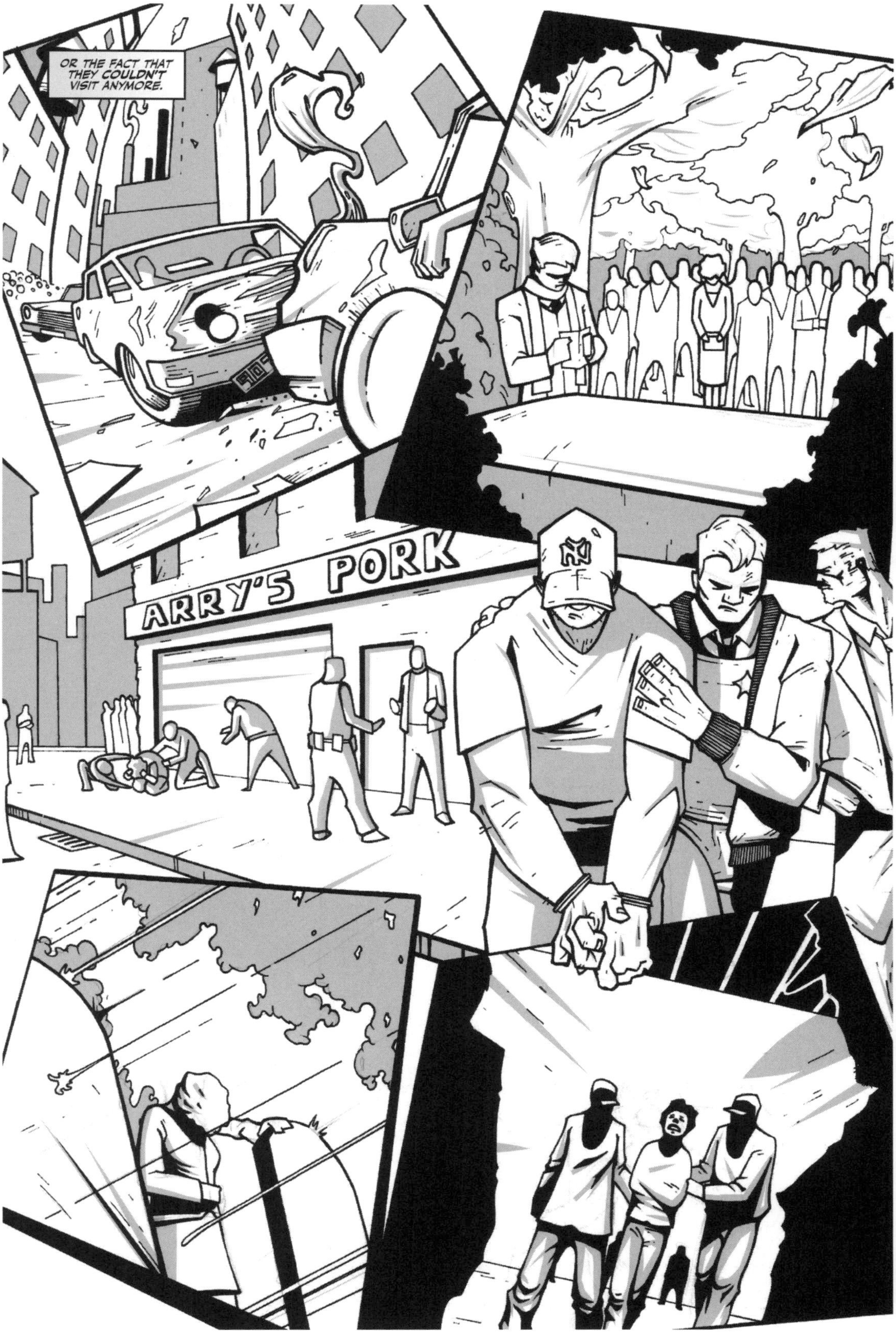
OR THE FACT THAT THEY COULDN'T VISIT ANYMORE.
ARRY'S PORK

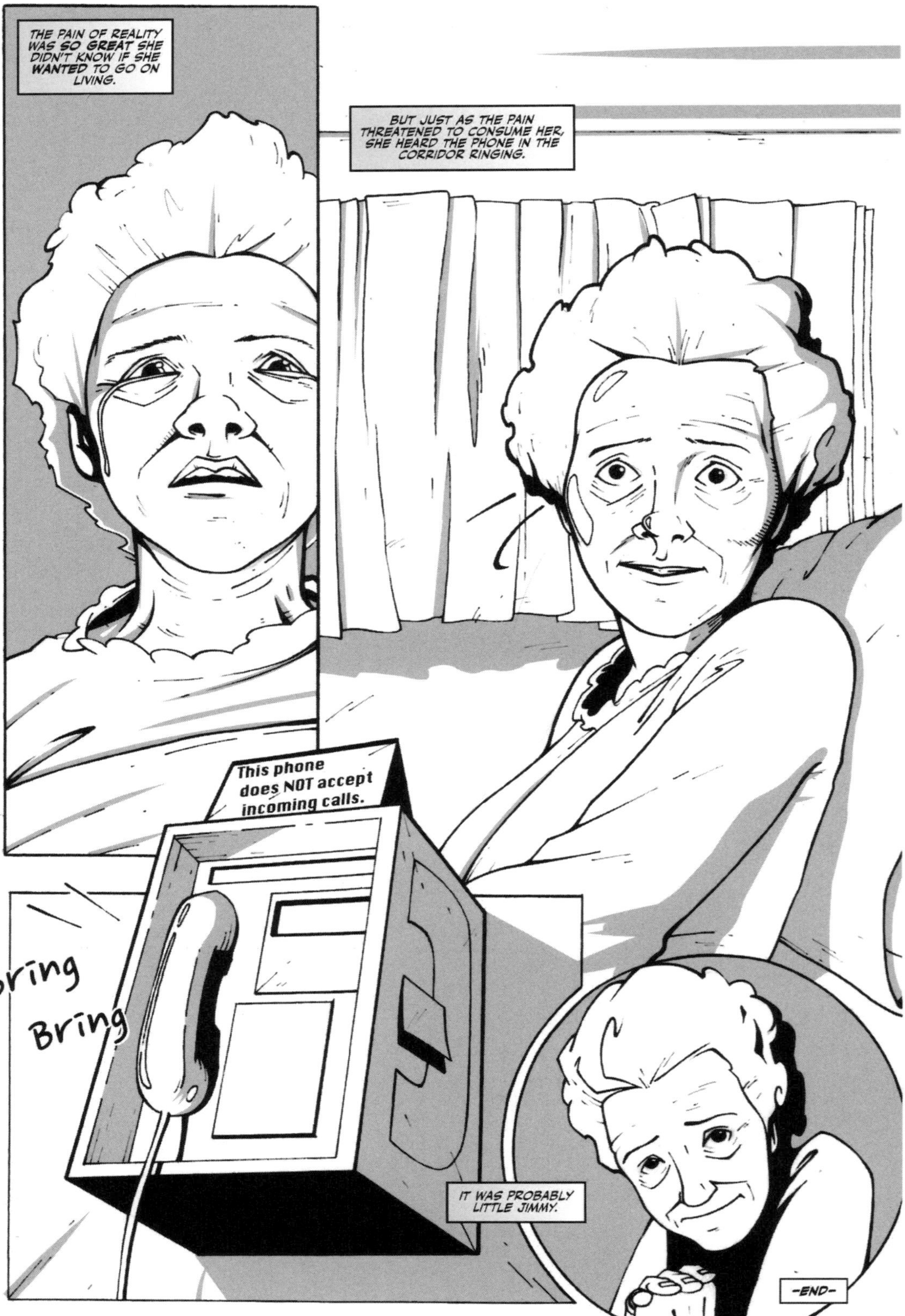
THE PAIN OF REALITY WAS SO GREAT SHE DIDN'T KNOW IF SHE WANTED TO GO ON LIVING.
BUT JUST AS THE PAIN THREATENED TO CONSUME HER, SHE HEARD THE PHONE IN THE CORRIDOR RINGING.
This phone does NOT accept incoming calls.
Bring
Bring
IT WAS PROBABLY LITTLE JIMMY.
-END-

Lifeboat...

In 1852, troopship HMS Birkenhead was wrecked near Cape Town, South Africa. Due to a shortage of serviceable lifeboats on board, the soldiers stood firm to allow the women and children to board the boats safely. Their chivalry gave rise to the 'women and children first' protocol during the procedure of abandoning ship.

Writer/Creator
Neil Gibson

Illustrator
Caspar Wijngaard

www.tpub.co.uk

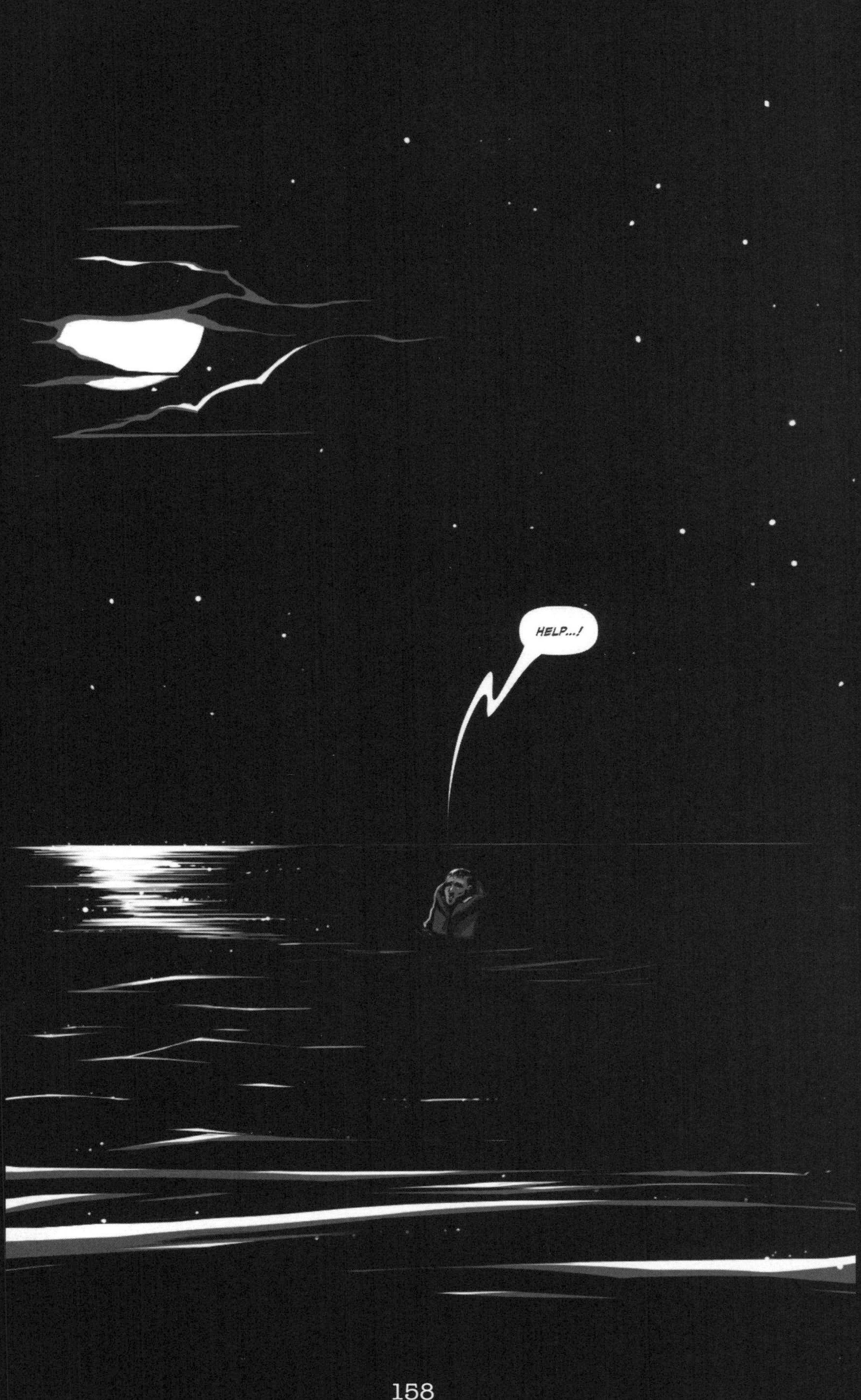
HELP...!

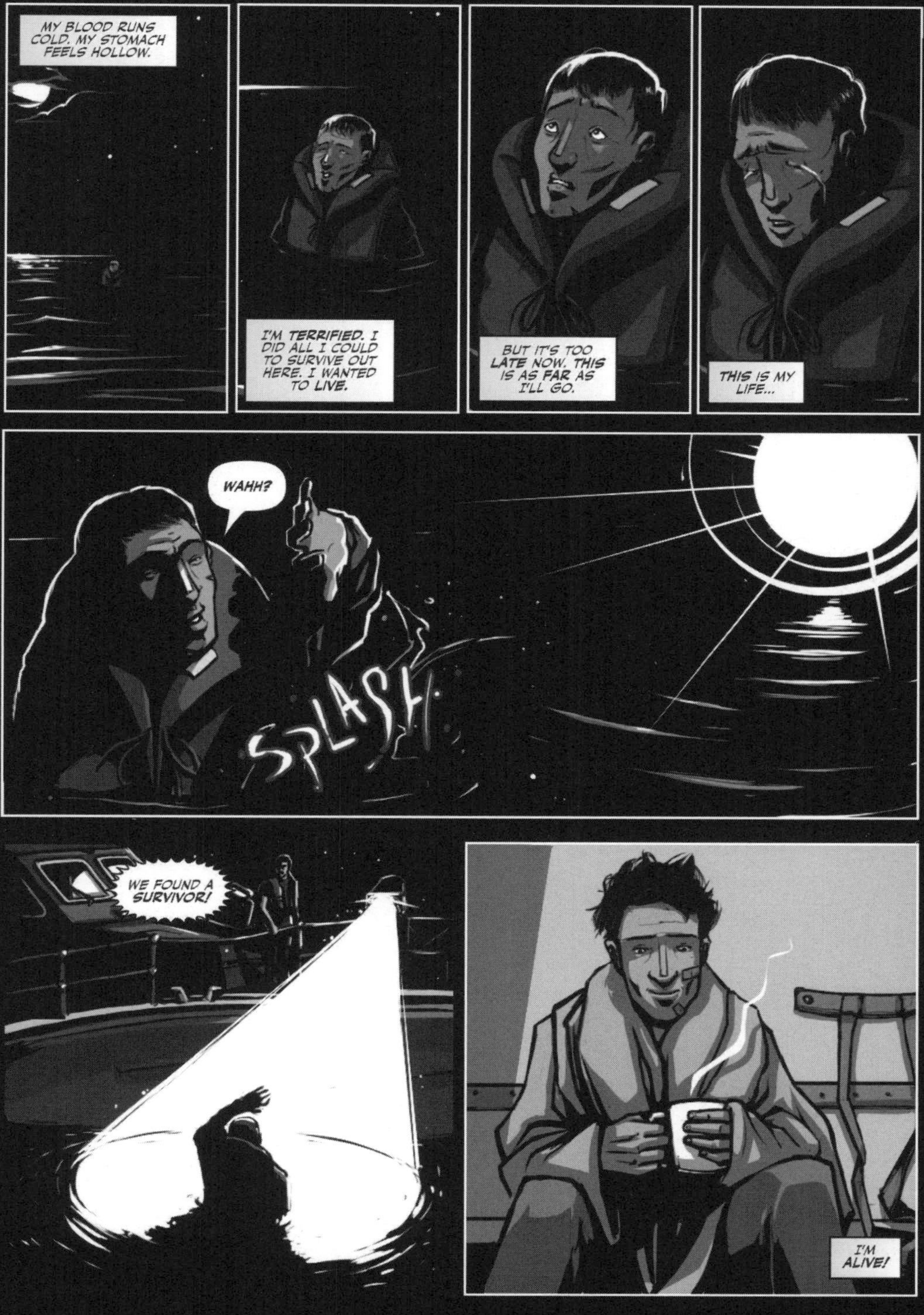
MY BLOOD RUNS COLD. MY STOMACH FEELS HOLLOW.
I'M TERRIFIED. I DID ALL I COULD TO SURVIVE OUT HERE. I WANTED TO LIVE.
BUT IT'S TOO LATE NOW. THIS IS AS FAR AS I'LL GO.
THIS IS MY LIFE...
WAHH?
SPLASH
WE FOUND A SURVIVOR!
I'M ALIVE!

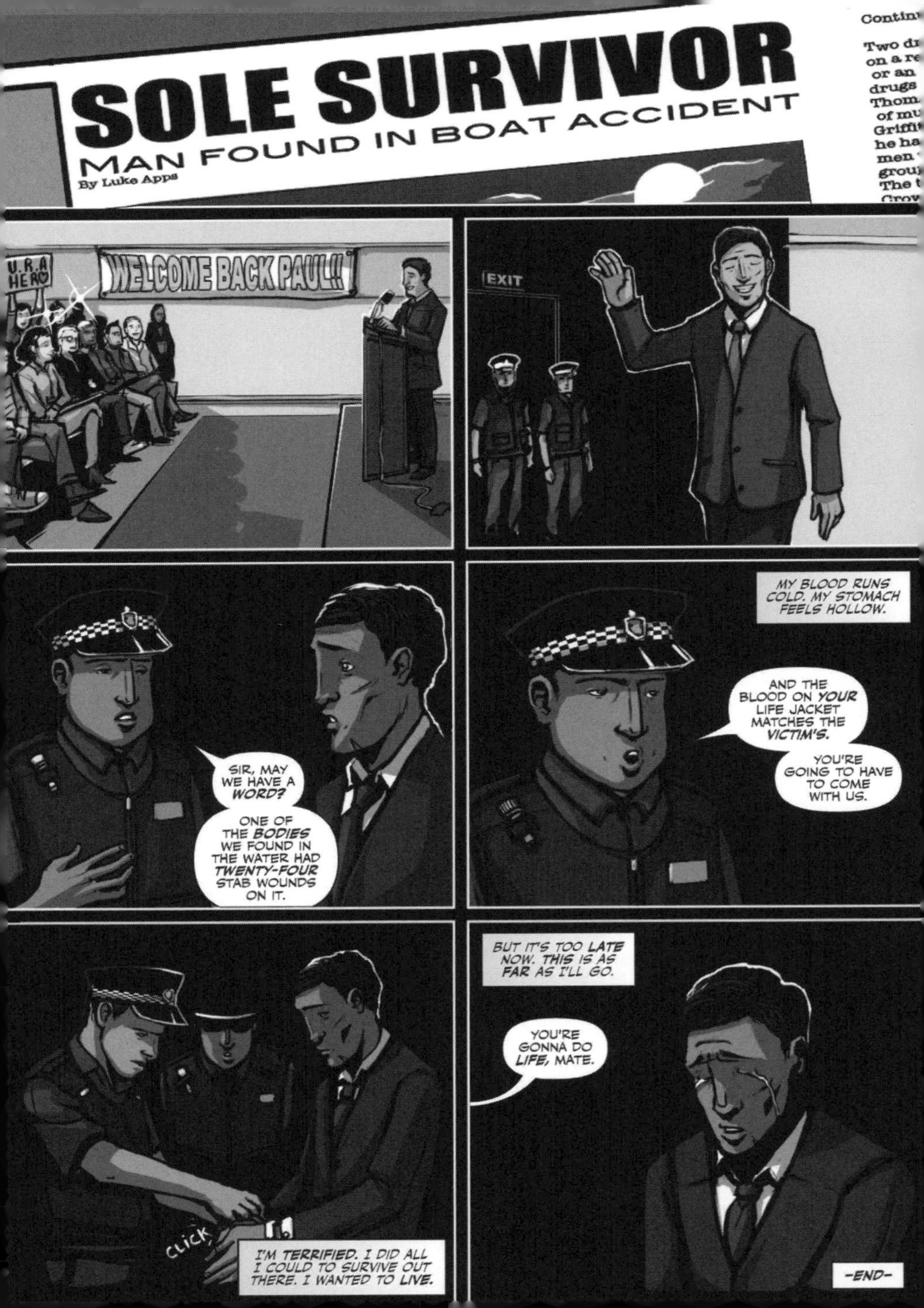
SOLE SURVIVOR
MAN FOUND IN BOAT ACCIDENT
By Luke Apps
U.R.A HERO
WELCOME BACK PAUL!!
EXIT
SIR, MAY WE HAVE A *WORD?*
ONE OF THE *BODIES* WE FOUND IN THE WATER HAD *TWENTY-FOUR* STAB WOUNDS ON IT.
MY BLOOD RUNS COLD. MY STOMACH FEELS HOLLOW.
AND THE BLOOD ON *YOUR* LIFE JACKET MATCHES THE *VICTIM'S.*
YOU'RE GOING TO HAVE TO COME WITH US.
CLICK
I'M *TERRIFIED.* I DID ALL I COULD TO SURVIVE OUT THERE. I WANTED TO *LIVE.*
BUT IT'S TOO *LATE* NOW. *THIS* IS AS *FAR* AS I'LL GO.
YOU'RE GONNA DO *LIFE,* MATE.
-END-

Peace and Quiet...

Autism is a complex neurological disorder that can lead to different forms of behavioral, communicational, social and cognitive impairment. In the past, many children with borderline autism were inappropriately diagnosed with psychosis or schizophrenia. There is still a lot of work to be done in this field and children are frequently misdiagnosed.

– Roget et al. (2006) Understanding the Notion of Borderline Autism

Writer/Creator
Neil Gibson

Illustrator
Atula Siriwardane

www.tpub.co.uk

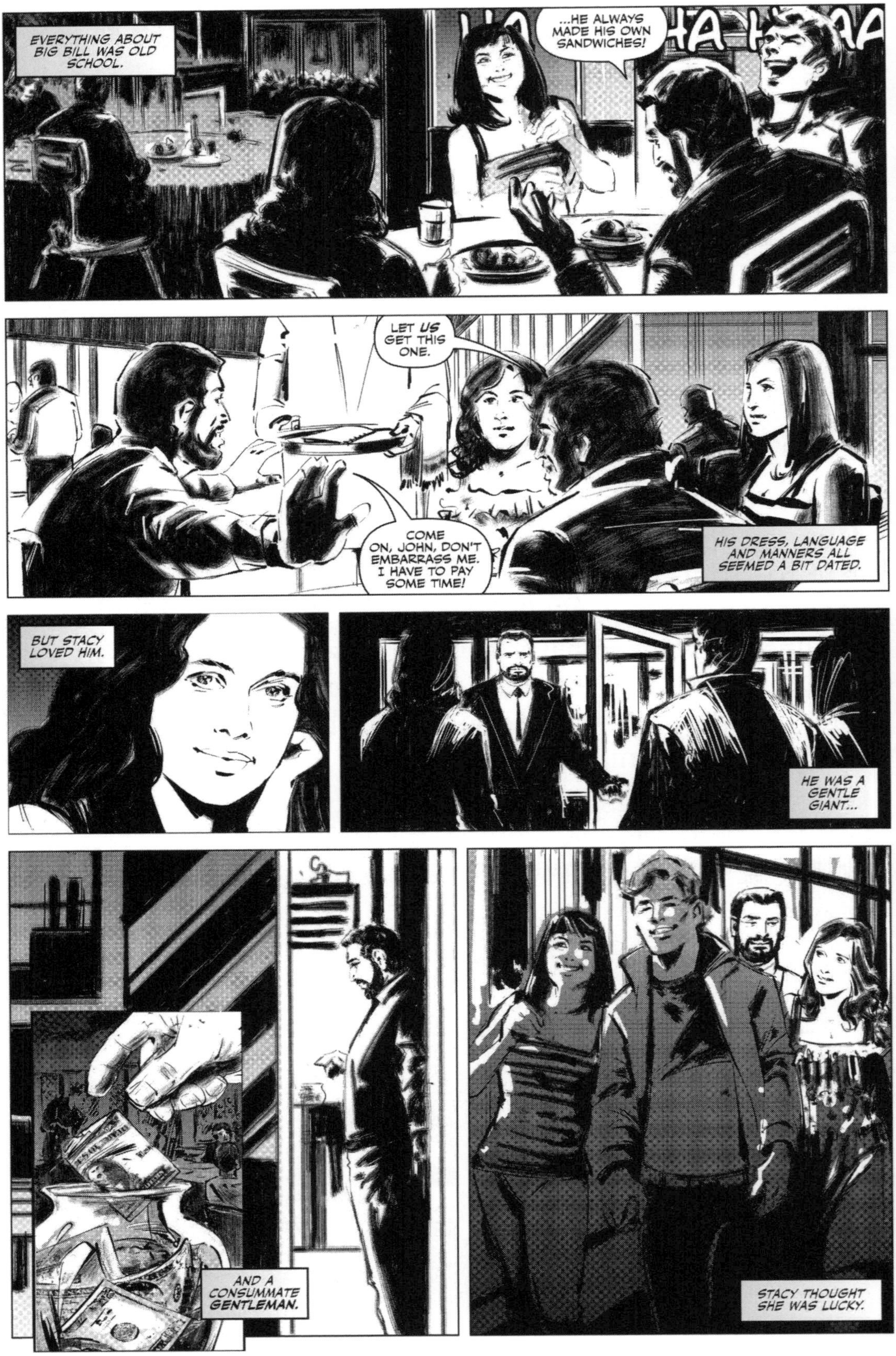

EVERYTHING ABOUT BIG BILL WAS OLD SCHOOL.
...HE ALWAYS MADE HIS OWN SANDWICHES!
LET US GET THIS ONE.
COME ON, JOHN, DON'T EMBARRASS ME. I HAVE TO PAY SOME TIME!
HIS DRESS, LANGUAGE AND MANNERS ALL SEEMED A BIT DATED.
BUT STACY LOVED HIM.
HE WAS A GENTLE GIANT...
AND A CONSUMMATE GENTLEMAN.
STACY THOUGHT SHE WAS LUCKY.

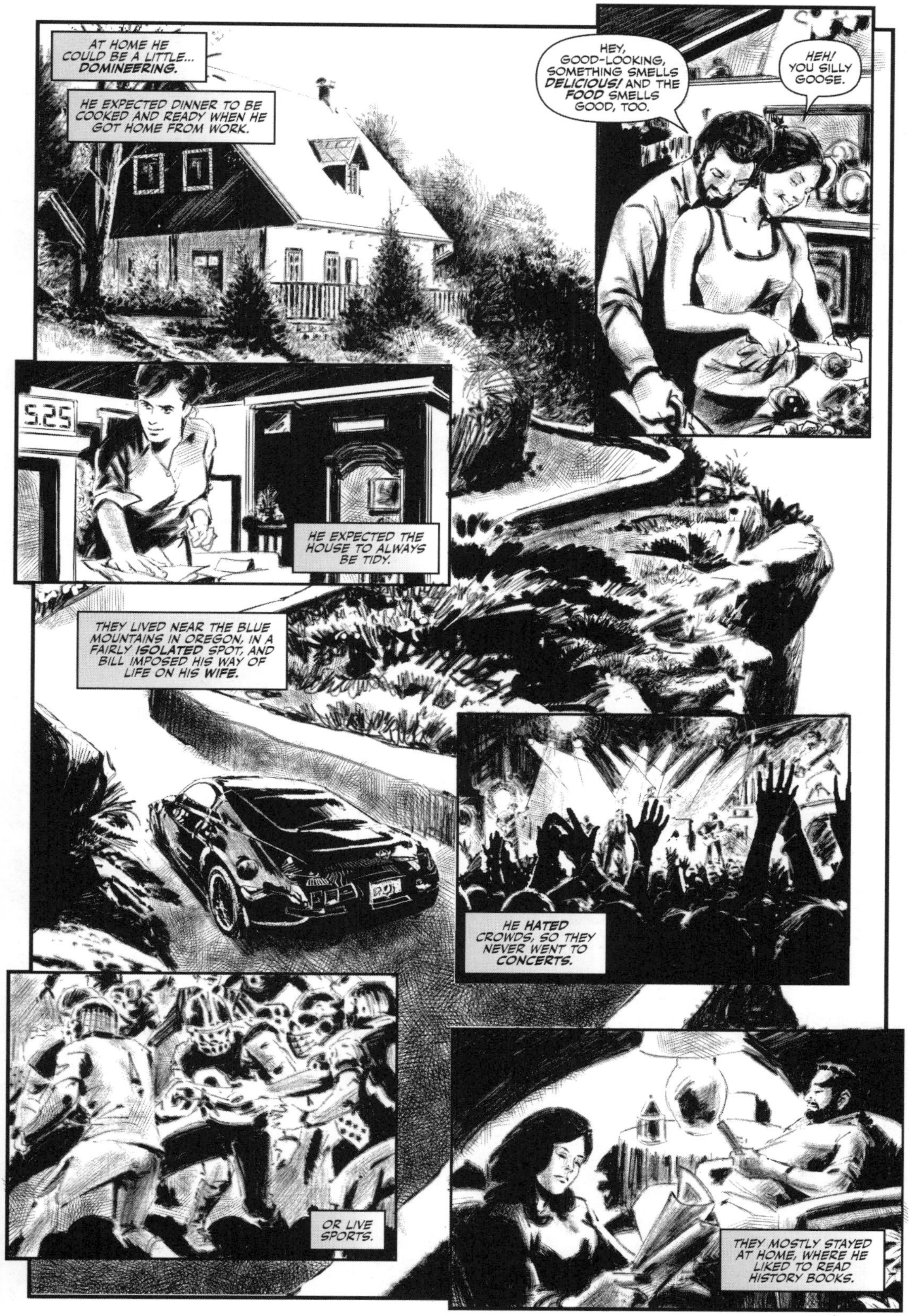
AT HOME HE COULD BE A LITTLE... DOMINEERING.
HE EXPECTED DINNER TO BE COOKED AND READY WHEN HE GOT HOME FROM WORK.
HEY, GOOD-LOOKING, SOMETHING SMELLS DELICIOUS! AND THE FOOD SMELLS GOOD, TOO.
HEH! YOU SILLY GOOSE.
5.25
HE EXPECTED THE HOUSE TO ALWAYS BE TIDY.
THEY LIVED NEAR THE BLUE MOUNTAINS IN OREGON, IN A FAIRLY ISOLATED SPOT, AND BILL IMPOSED HIS WAY OF LIFE ON HIS WIFE.
HE HATED CROWDS, SO THEY NEVER WENT TO CONCERTS.
OR LIVE SPORTS.
THEY MOSTLY STAYED AT HOME, WHERE HE LIKED TO READ HISTORY BOOKS.

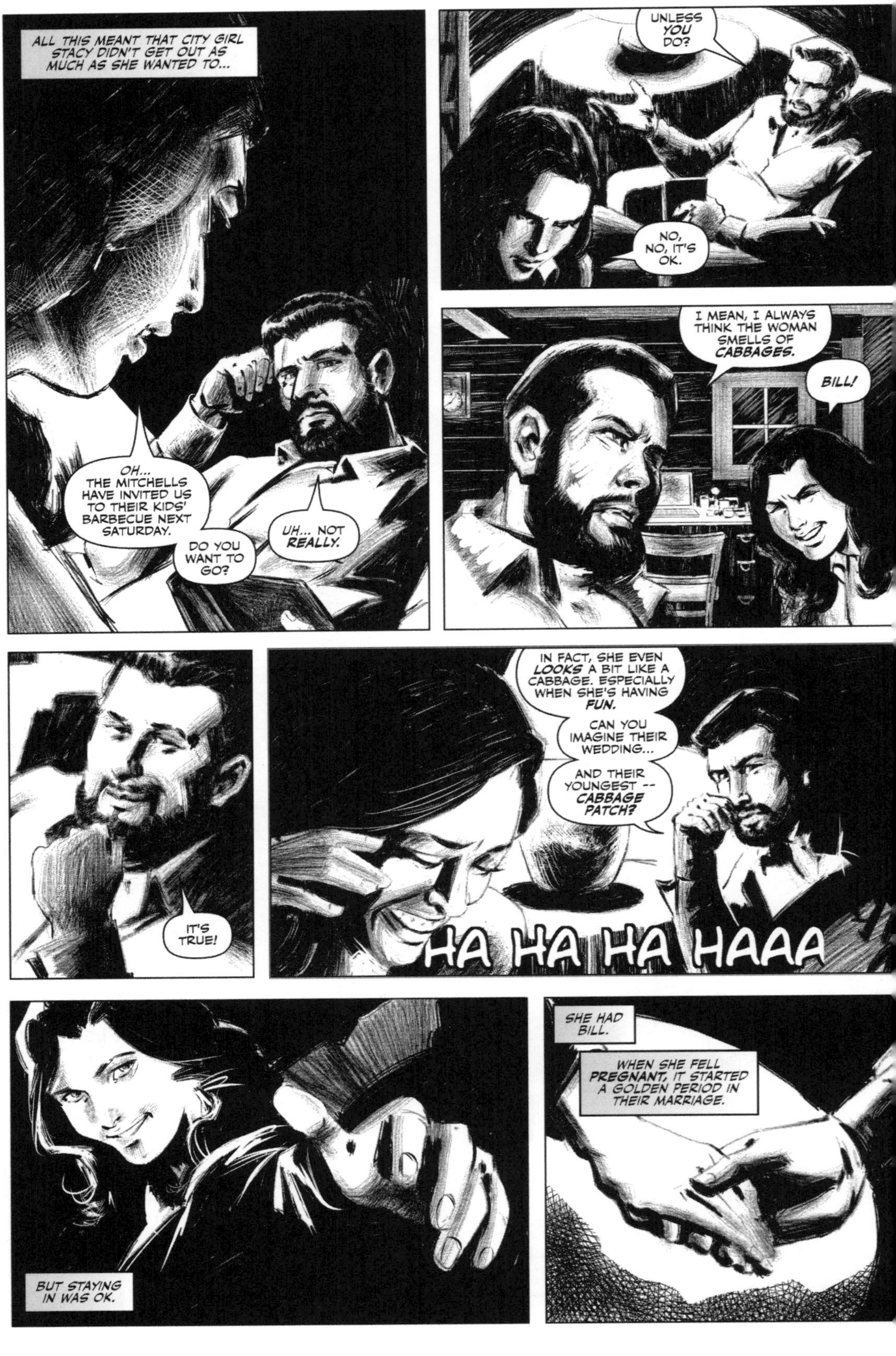

ALL THIS MEANT THAT CITY GIRL STACY DIDN'T GET OUT AS MUCH AS SHE WANTED TO...
OH... THE MITCHELLS HAVE INVITED US TO THEIR KIDS' BARBECUE NEXT SATURDAY.
DO YOU WANT TO GO?
UH... NOT REALLY.
UNLESS YOU DO?
NO, NO, IT'S OK.
I MEAN, I ALWAYS THINK THE WOMAN SMELLS OF CABBAGES.
BILL!
IT'S TRUE!
IN FACT, SHE EVEN LOOKS A BIT LIKE A CABBAGE. ESPECIALLY WHEN SHE'S HAVING FUN.
CAN YOU IMAGINE THEIR WEDDING...
AND THEIR YOUNGEST -- CABBAGE PATCH?
HA HA HA HAAA
BUT STAYING IN WAS OK.
SHE HAD BILL.
WHEN SHE FELL PREGNANT, IT STARTED A GOLDEN PERIOD IN THEIR MARRIAGE.

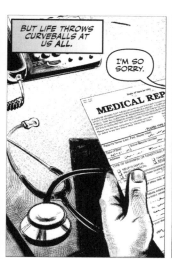

BUT LIFE THROWS CURVEBALLS AT US ALL.

I'M SO SORRY.

MEDICAL REP

I'M AFRIAD IT'S A FORM OF *AUTISM*. IT'S TOO EARLY TO TELL HOW IT WILL PLAY OUT.

BUT IT IS *UNLIKELY* THAT AMY WILL EVER EMOTIONALLY CONNECT WITH EITHER OF YOU.

IT MAY BE *YEARS* BEFORE SHE TALKS -- IF SHE DOES AT *ALL*.

THE BAD NEWS AFFECTED BILL MORE THAN STACY.

TRRIIIEENN TRRIIIEENN

THE ONLY EMOTION AMY EVER SHOWED WAS WHEN THERE WAS A LOUD *NOISE*.

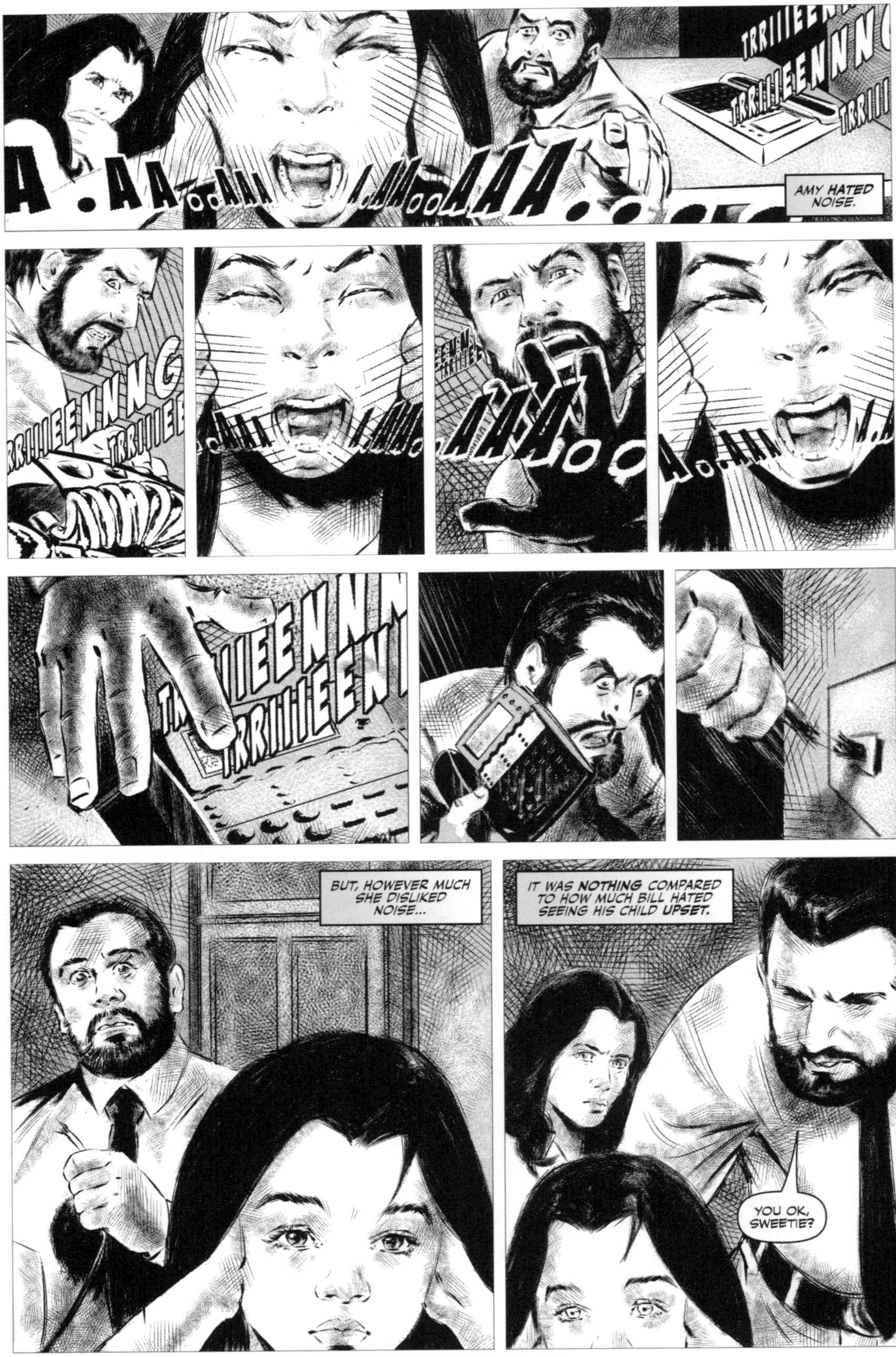
AMY HATED NOISE.
BUT, HOWEVER MUCH SHE DISLIKED NOISE...
IT WAS NOTHING COMPARED TO HOW MUCH BILL HATED SEEING HIS CHILD UPSET.
YOU OK, SWEETIE?

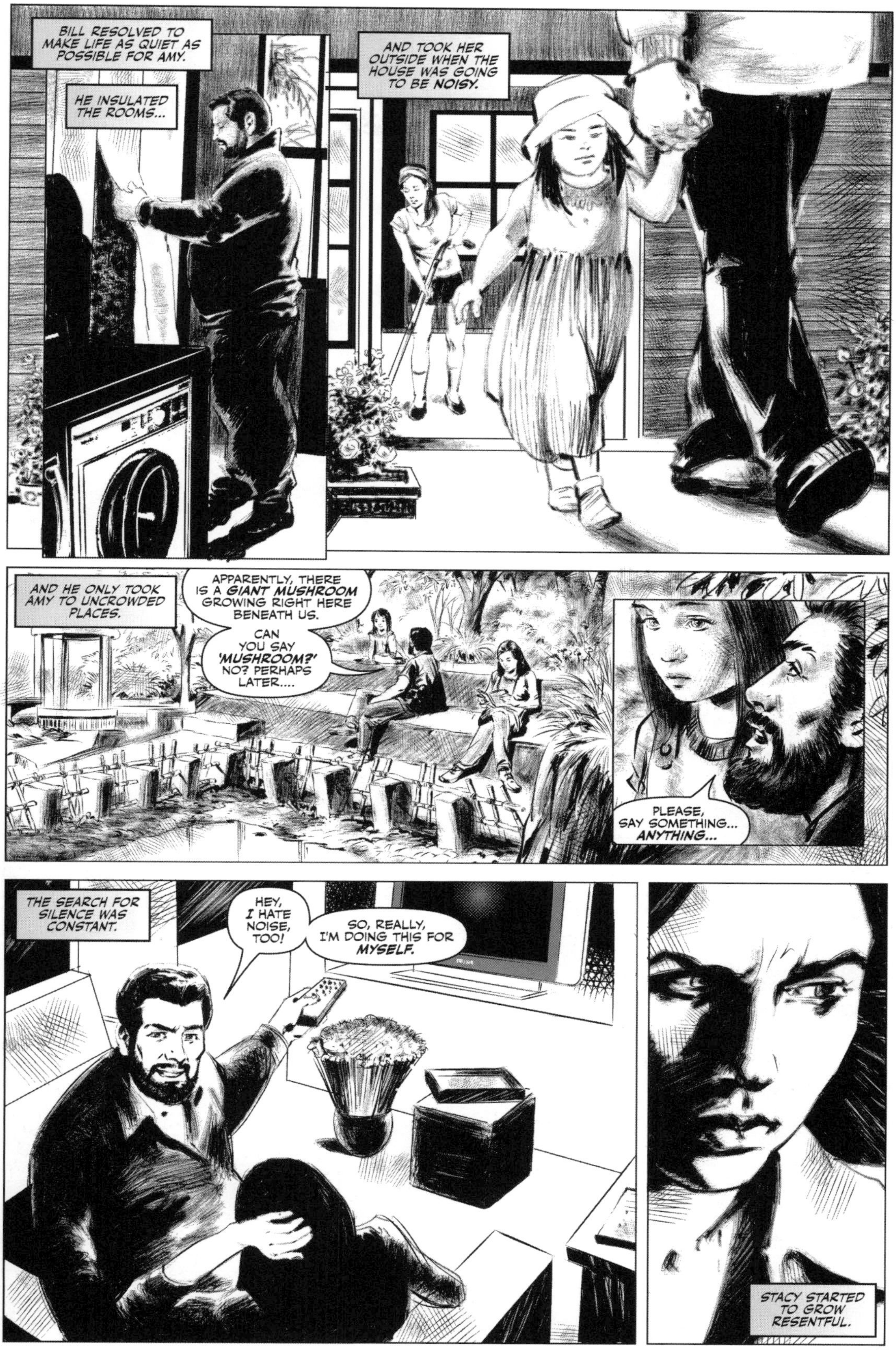
BILL RESOLVED TO MAKE LIFE AS QUIET AS POSSIBLE FOR AMY.
HE INSULATED THE ROOMS...
AND TOOK HER OUTSIDE WHEN THE HOUSE WAS GOING TO BE NOISY.
AND HE ONLY TOOK AMY TO UNCROWDED PLACES.
APPARENTLY, THERE IS A GIANT MUSHROOM GROWING RIGHT HERE BENEATH US.
CAN YOU SAY 'MUSHROOM?' NO? PERHAPS LATER....
PLEASE, SAY SOMETHING... ANYTHING...
THE SEARCH FOR SILENCE WAS CONSTANT.
HEY, I HATE NOISE, TOO!
SO, REALLY, I'M DOING THIS FOR MYSELF.
STACY STARTED TO GROW RESENTFUL.

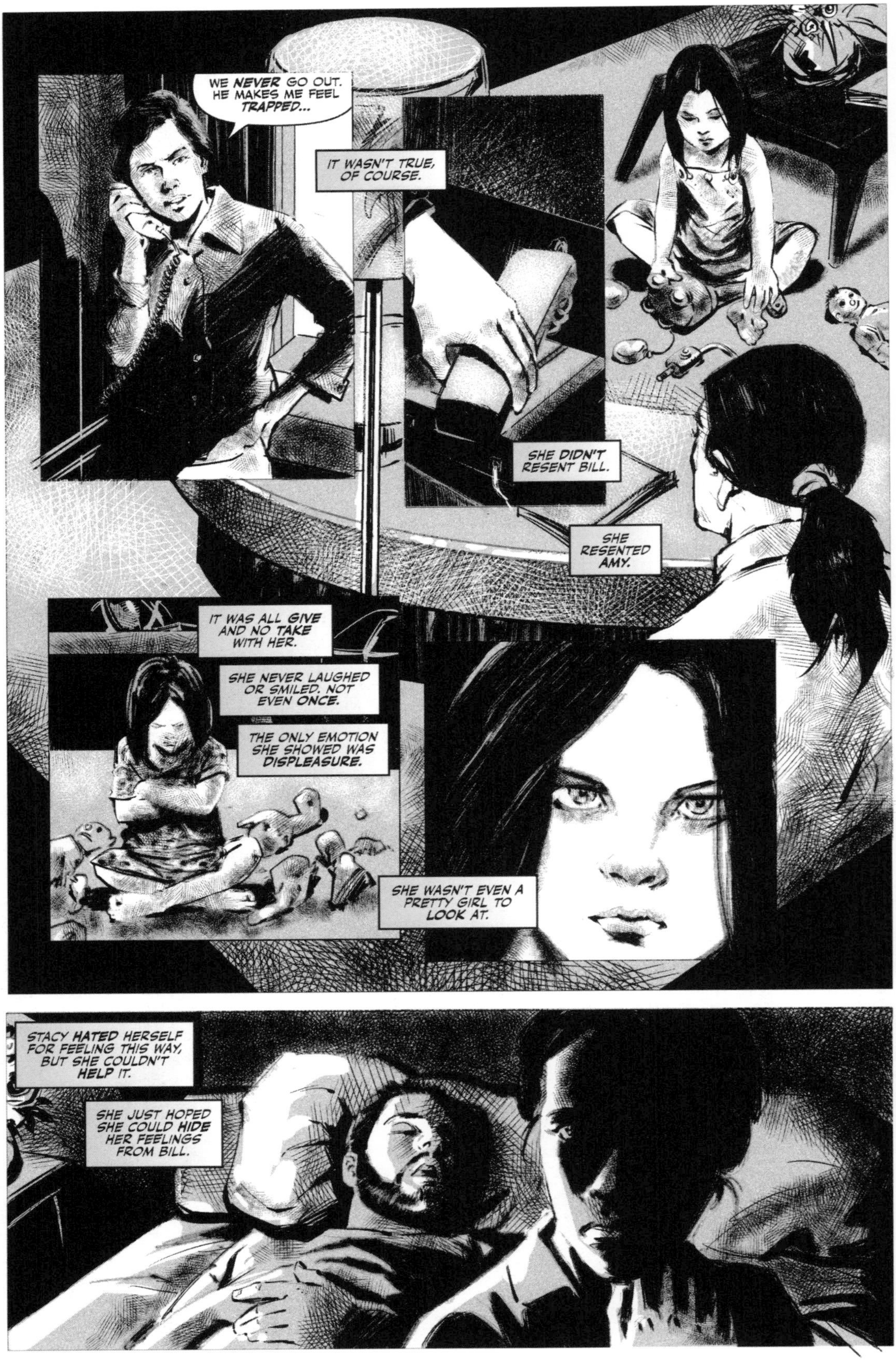
WE NEVER GO OUT. HE MAKES ME FEEL TRAPPED...
IT WASN'T TRUE, OF COURSE.
SHE DIDN'T RESENT BILL.
SHE RESENTED AMY.
IT WAS ALL GIVE AND NO TAKE WITH HER.
SHE NEVER LAUGHED OR SMILED. NOT EVEN ONCE.
THE ONLY EMOTION SHE SHOWED WAS DISPLEASURE.
SHE WASN'T EVEN A PRETTY GIRL TO LOOK AT.
STACY HATED HERSELF FOR FEELING THIS WAY, BUT SHE COULDN'T HELP IT.
SHE JUST HOPED SHE COULD HIDE HER FEELINGS FROM BILL.

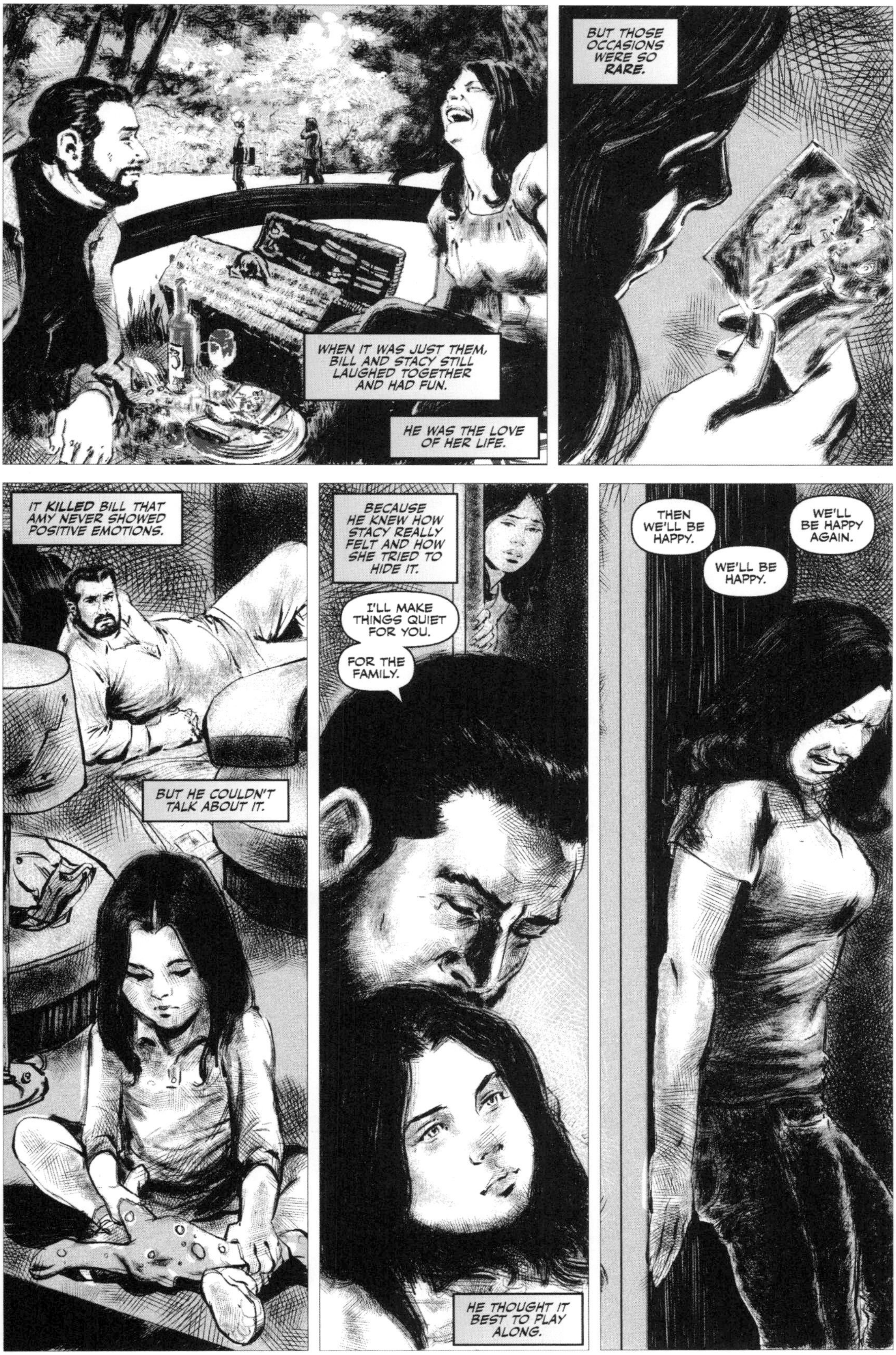
WHEN IT WAS JUST THEM, BILL AND STACY STILL LAUGHED TOGETHER AND HAD FUN.
HE WAS THE LOVE OF HER LIFE.
BUT THOSE OCCASIONS WERE SO RARE.
IT KILLED BILL THAT AMY NEVER SHOWED POSITIVE EMOTIONS.
BUT HE COULDN'T TALK ABOUT IT.
BECAUSE HE KNEW HOW STACY REALLY FELT AND HOW SHE TRIED TO HIDE IT.
I'LL MAKE THINGS QUIET FOR YOU.
FOR THE FAMILY.
HE THOUGHT IT BEST TO PLAY ALONG.
THEN WE'LL BE HAPPY.
WE'LL BE HAPPY.
WE'LL BE HAPPY AGAIN.

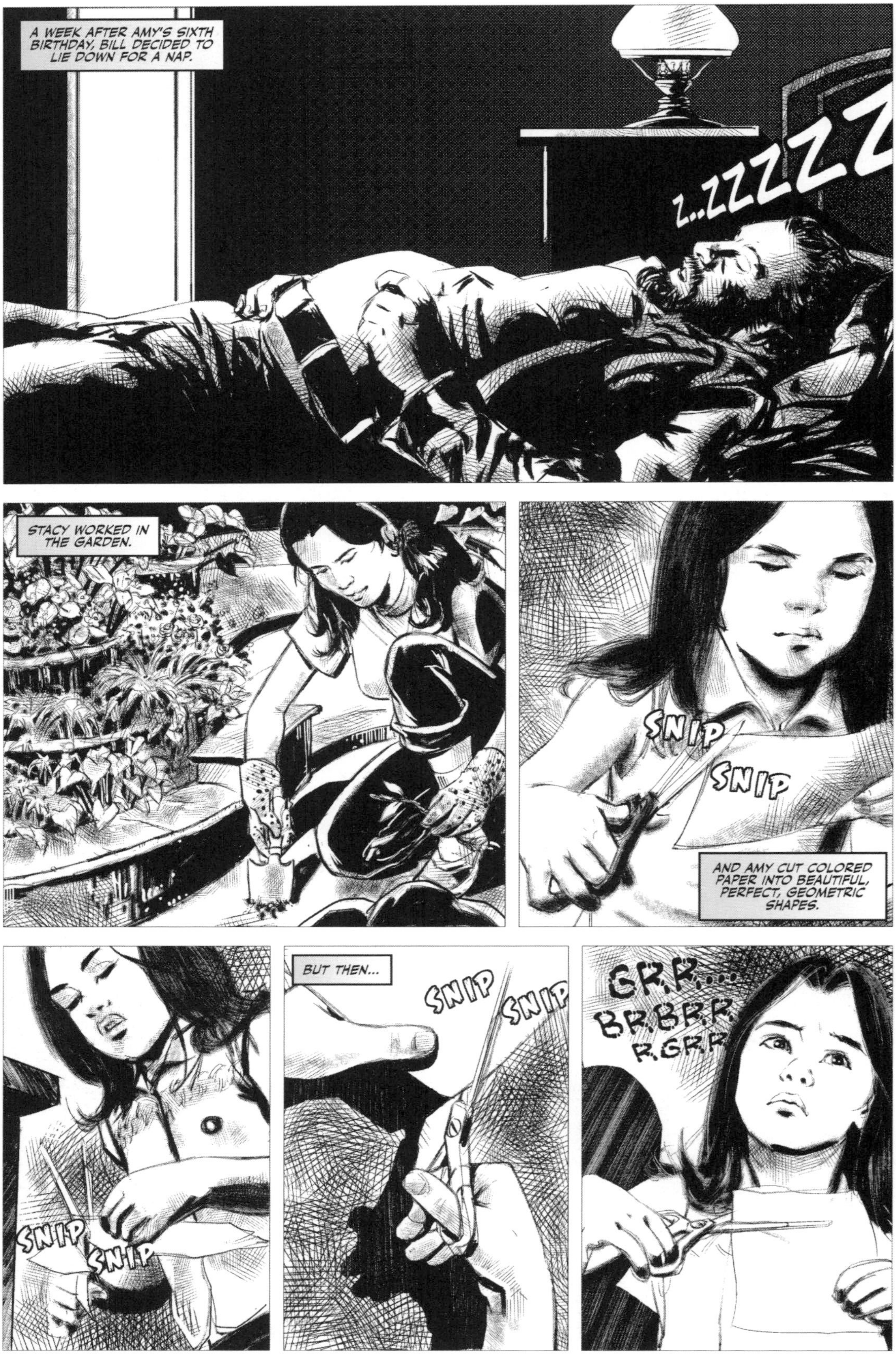
A WEEK AFTER AMY'S SIXTH BIRTHDAY, BILL DECIDED TO LIE DOWN FOR A NAP.
Z..ZZZZZZ
STACY WORKED IN THE GARDEN.
SNIP
SNIP
AND AMY CUT COLORED PAPER INTO BEAUTIFUL, PERFECT, GEOMETRIC SHAPES.
SNIP
SNIP
BUT THEN...
SNIP
SNIP
GRR...
BRBRR
RGRR

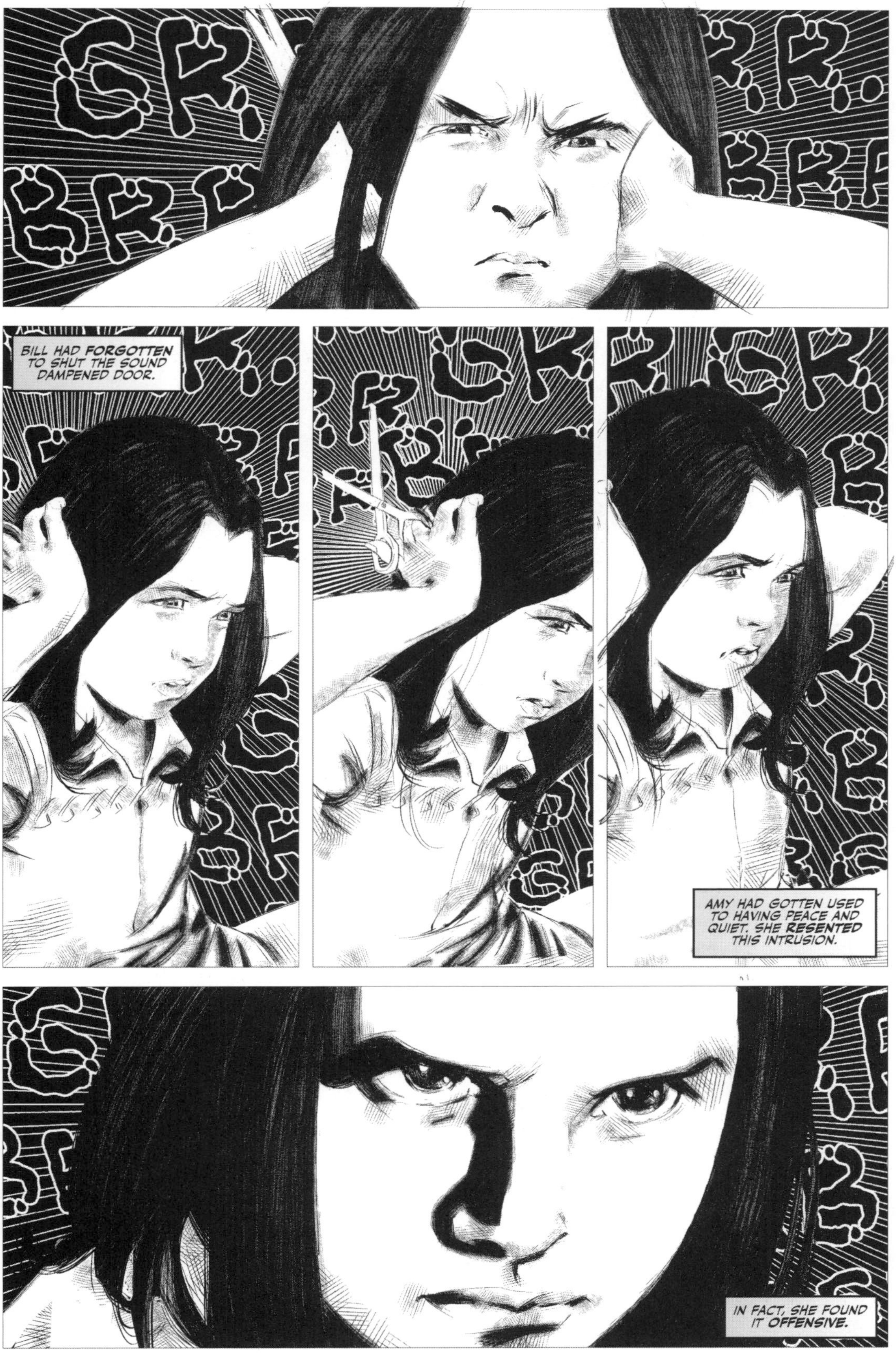
BILL HAD FORGOTTEN TO SHUT THE SOUND DAMPENED DOOR.
AMY HAD GOTTEN USED TO HAVING PEACE AND QUIET. SHE RESENTED THIS INTRUSION.
IN FACT, SHE FOUND IT OFFENSIVE.

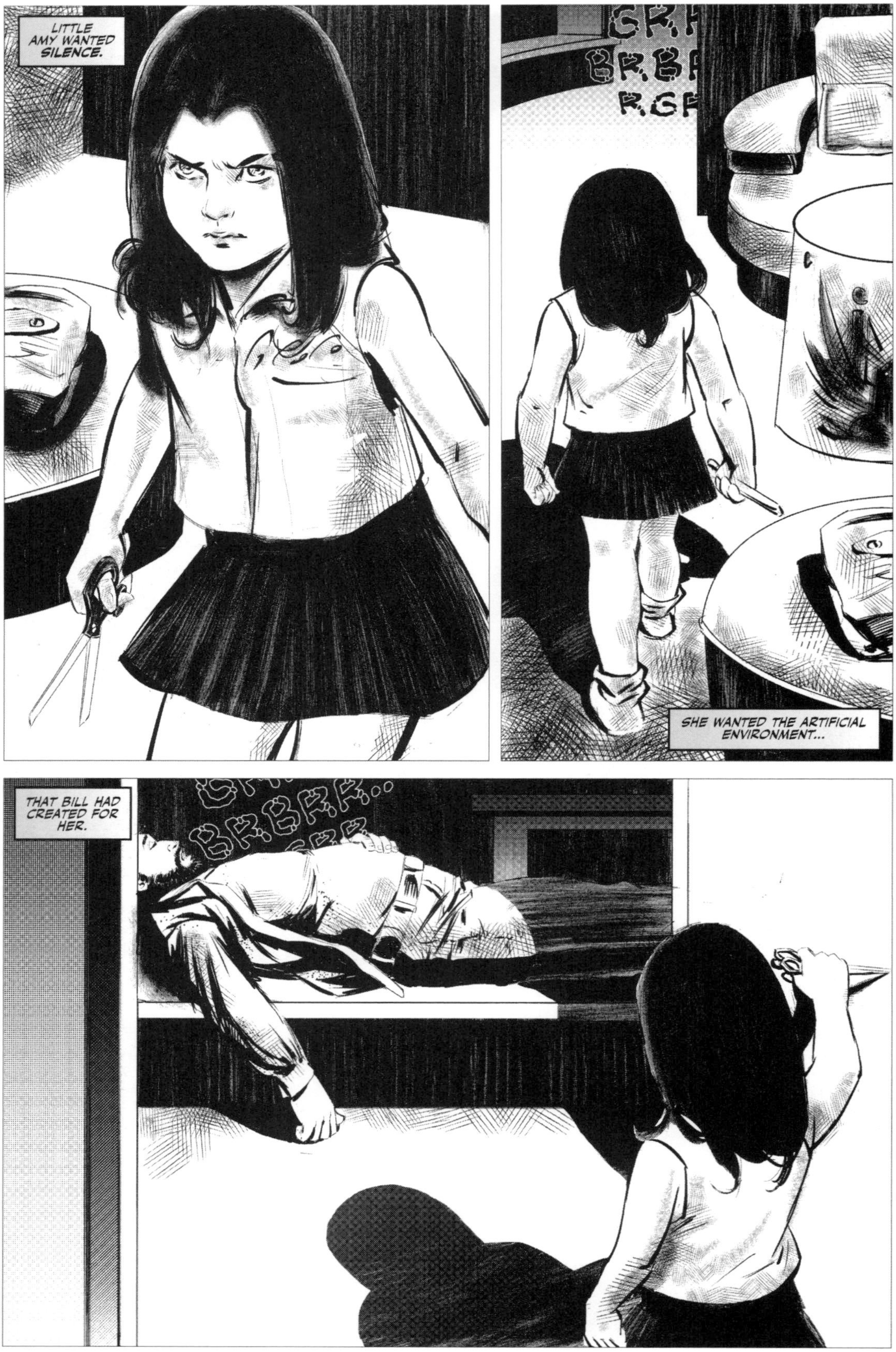
LITTLE AMY WANTED SILENCE.
SHE WANTED THE ARTIFICIAL ENVIRONMENT...
THAT BILL HAD CREATED FOR HER.

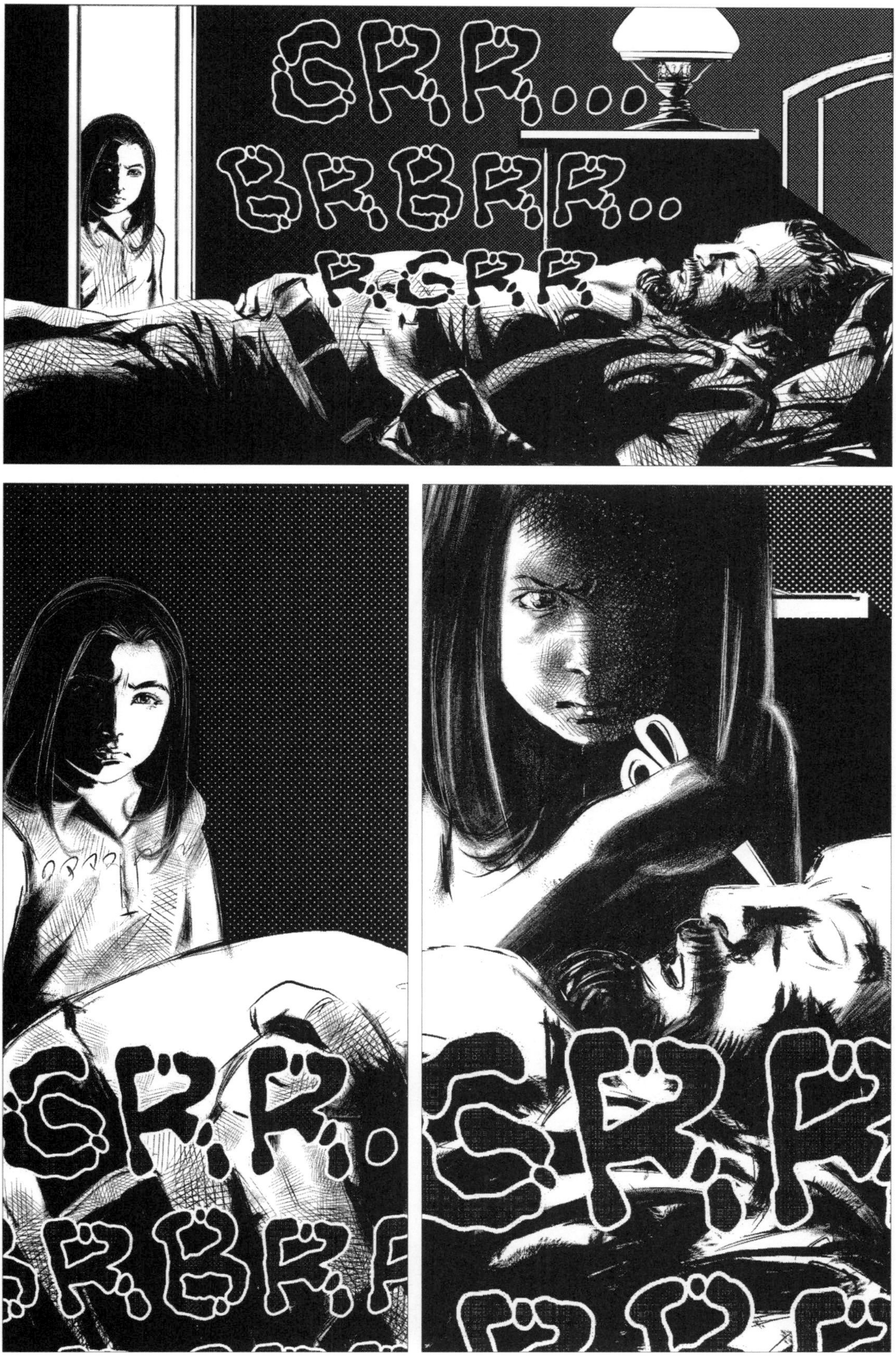
GRR...
BRBRR..
R.G.R.R
GRR.
BRBR
GRR

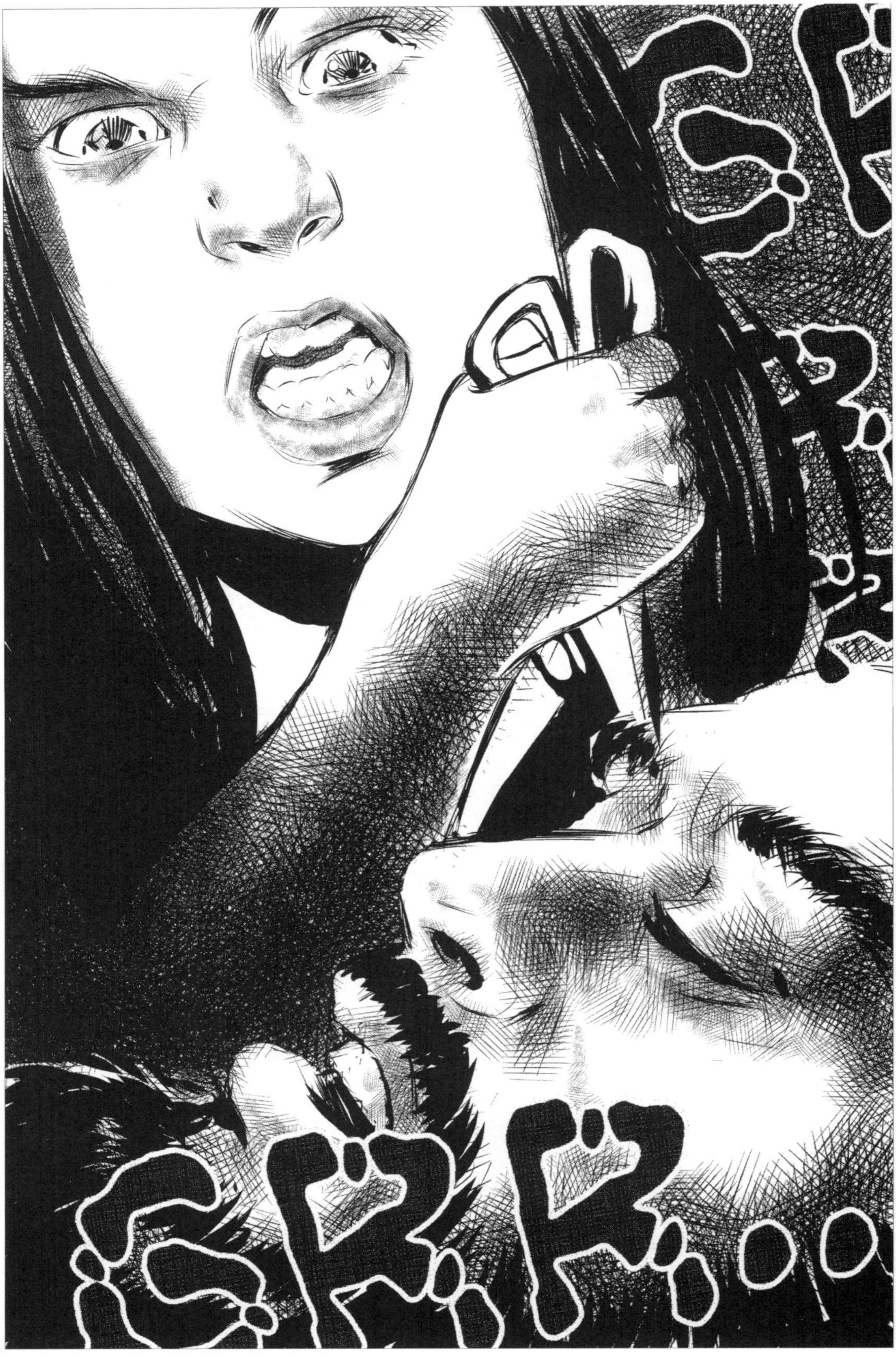
GRR...

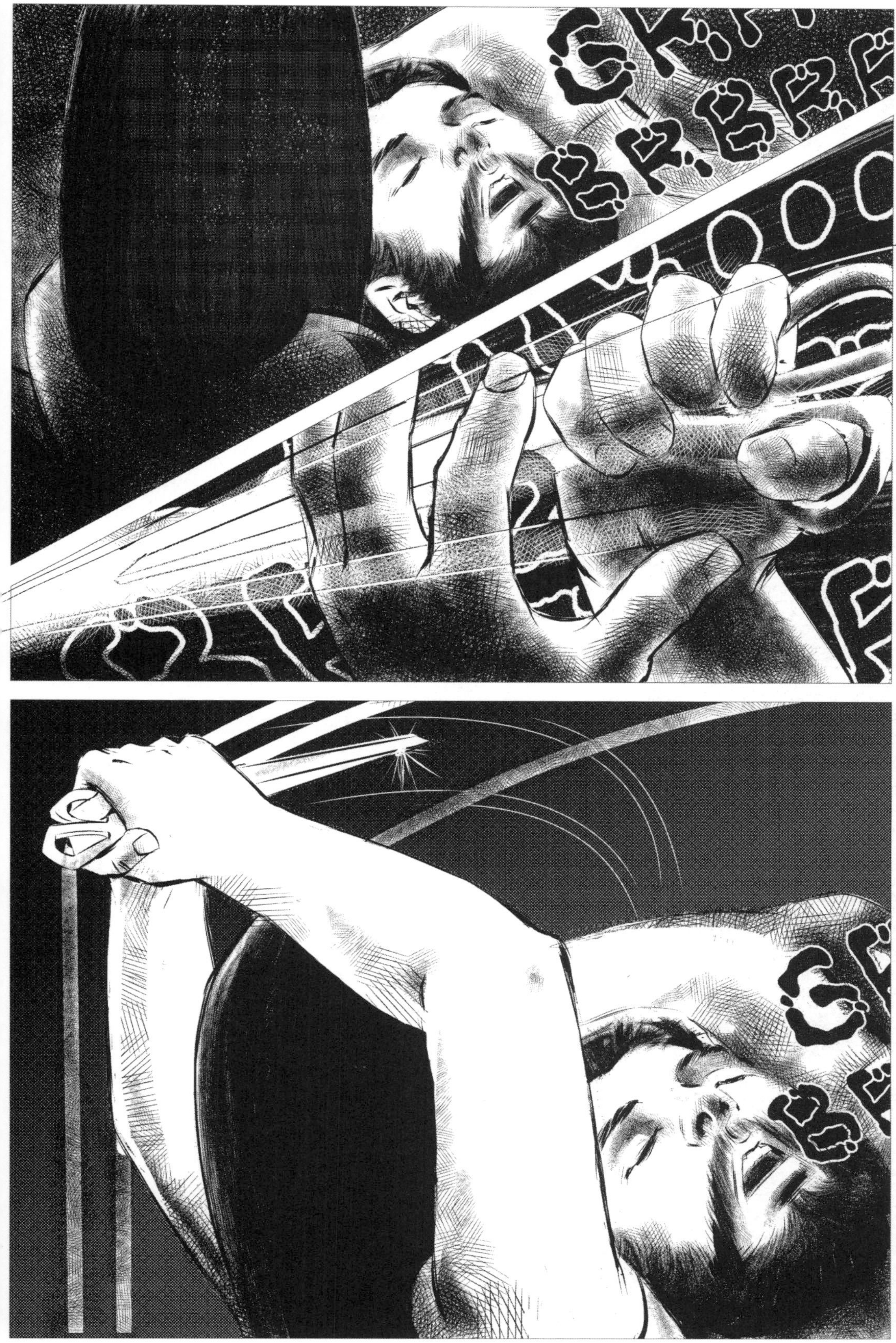

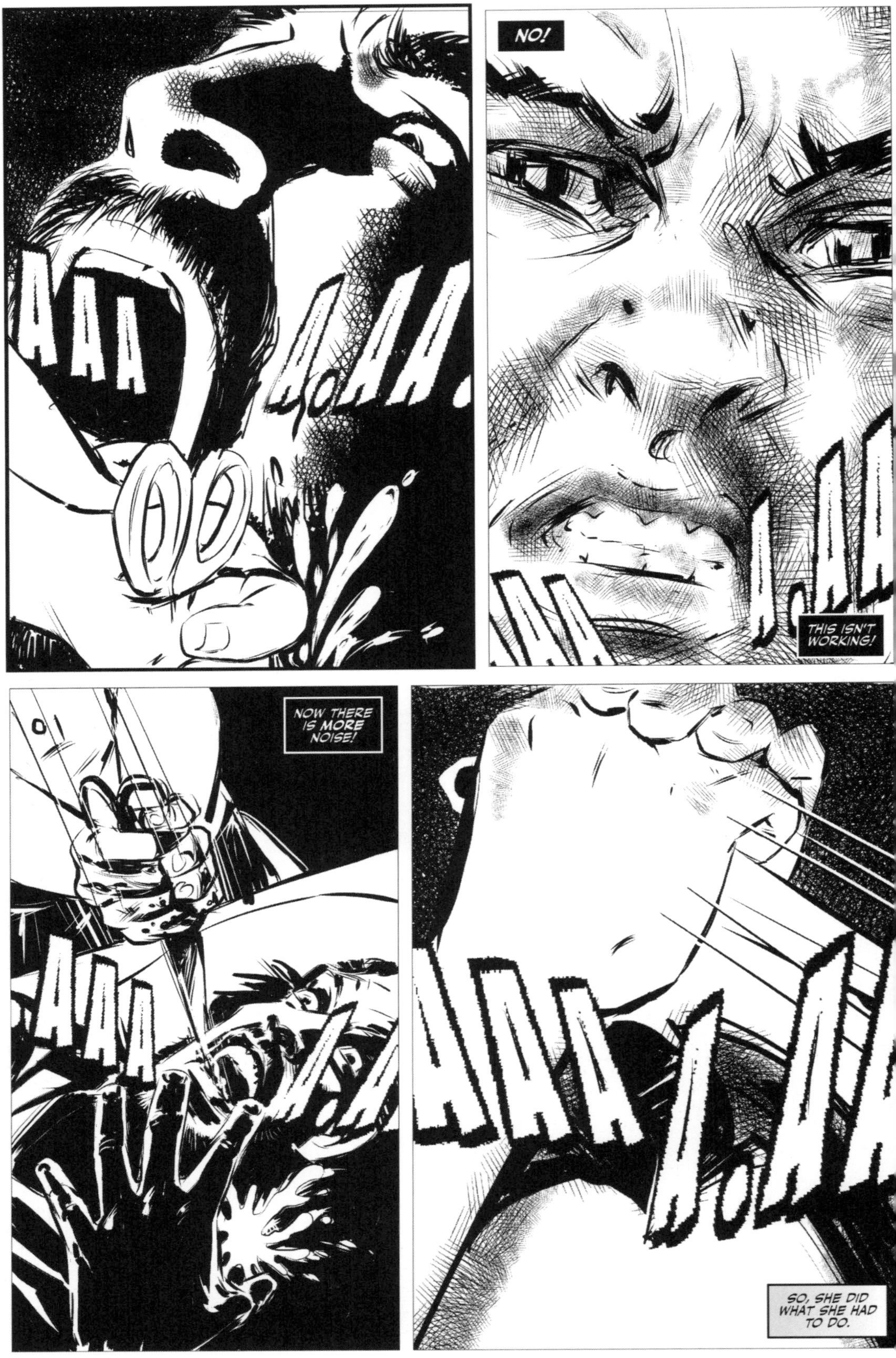
NO!
THIS ISN'T WORKING!
NOW THERE IS MORE NOISE!
SO, SHE DID WHAT SHE HAD TO DO.

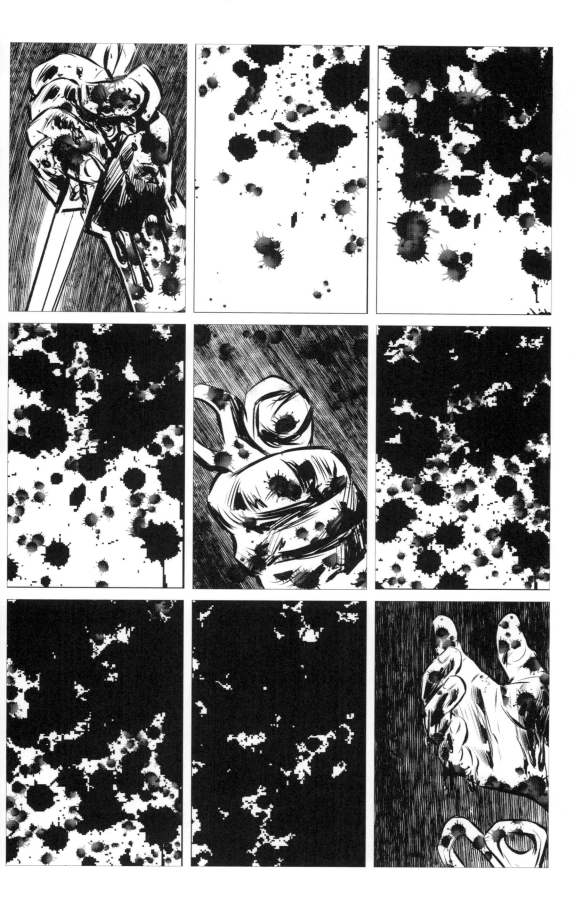

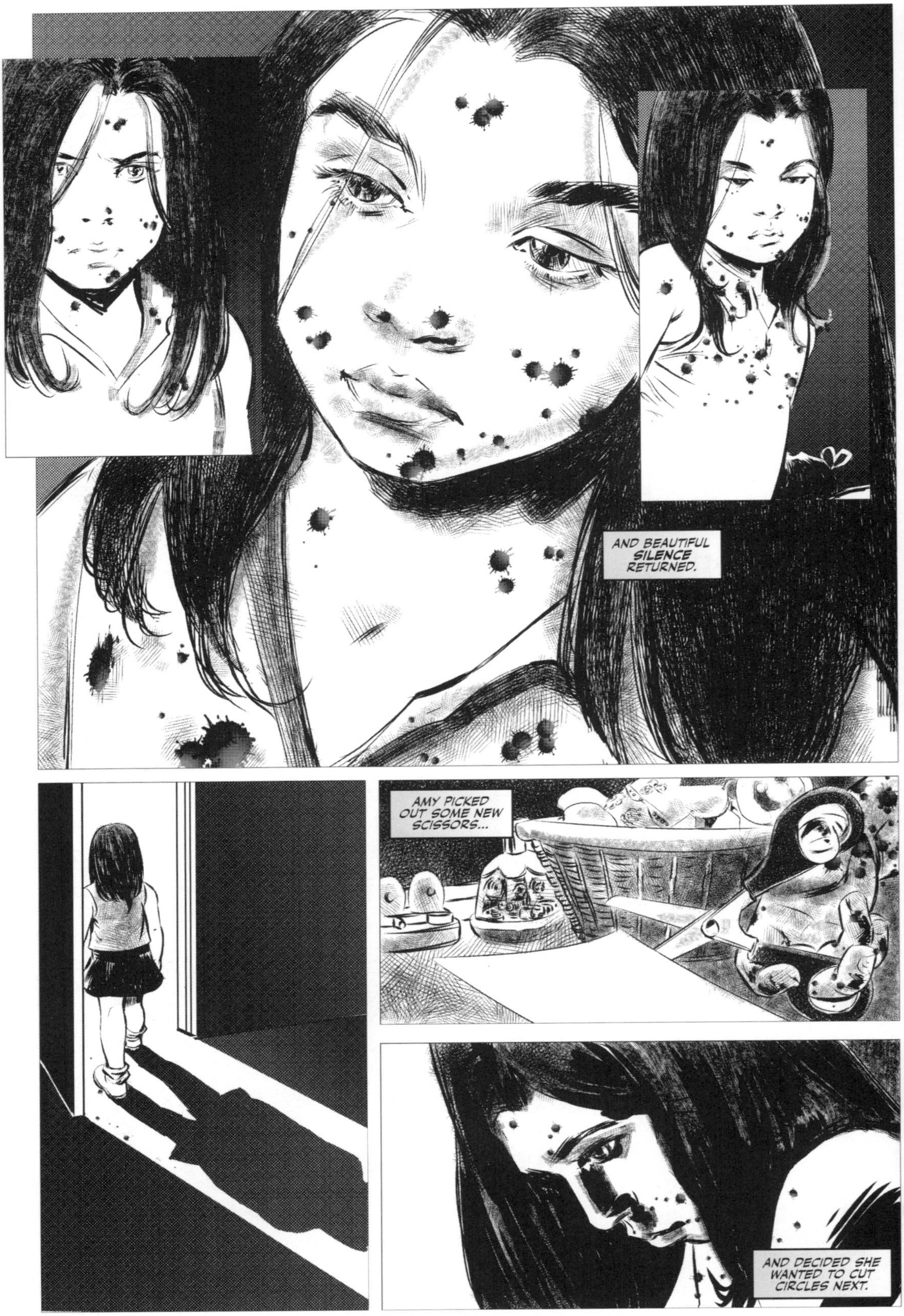
AND BEAUTIFUL SILENCE RETURNED.
AMY PICKED OUT SOME NEW SCISSORS...
AND DECIDED SHE WANTED TO CUT CIRCLES NEXT.

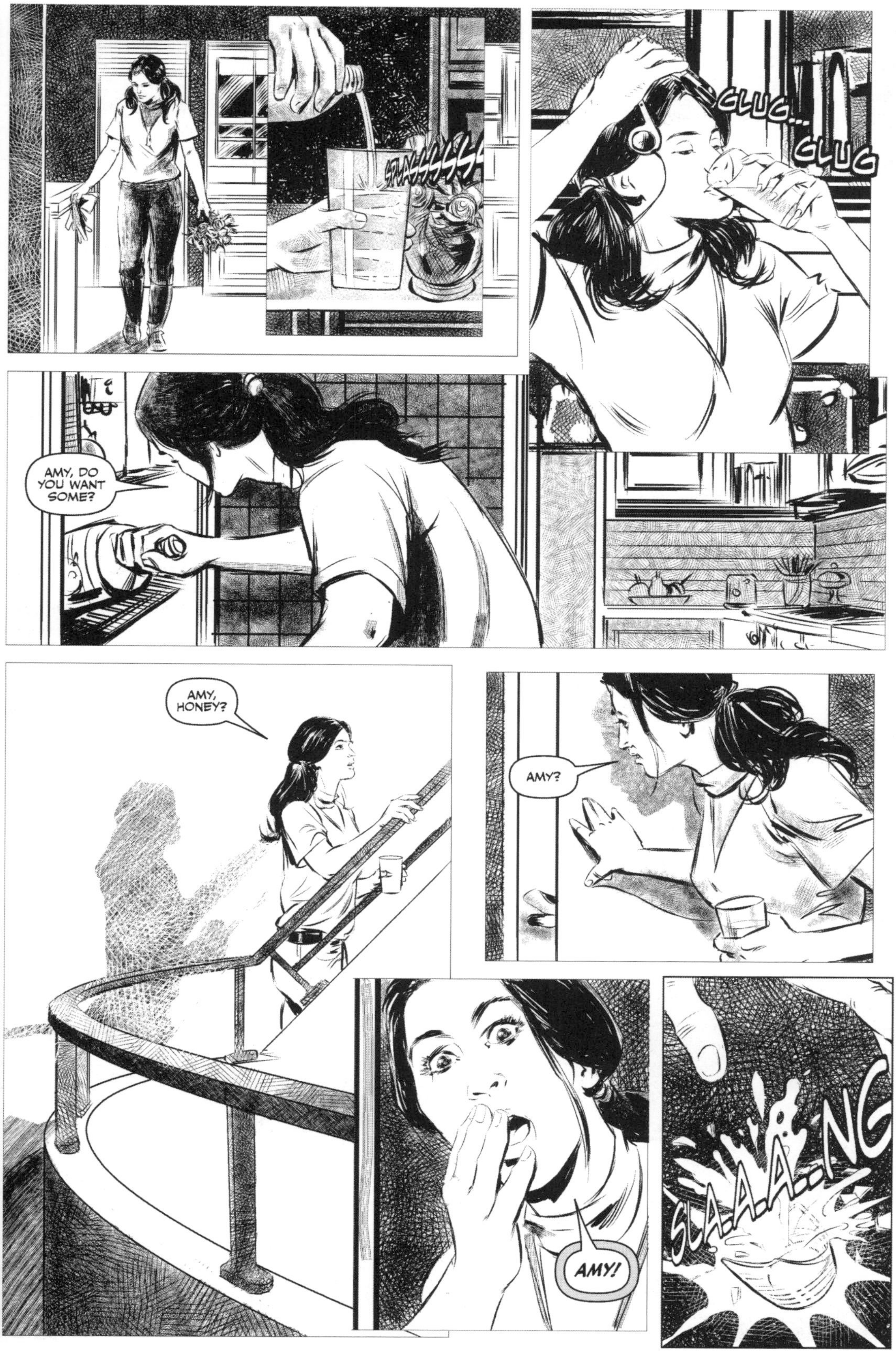
SPLASSSSSSH
GLUG...
GLUG
AMY, DO YOU WANT SOME?
AMY, HONEY?
AMY?
AMY!
SLAAA...NG

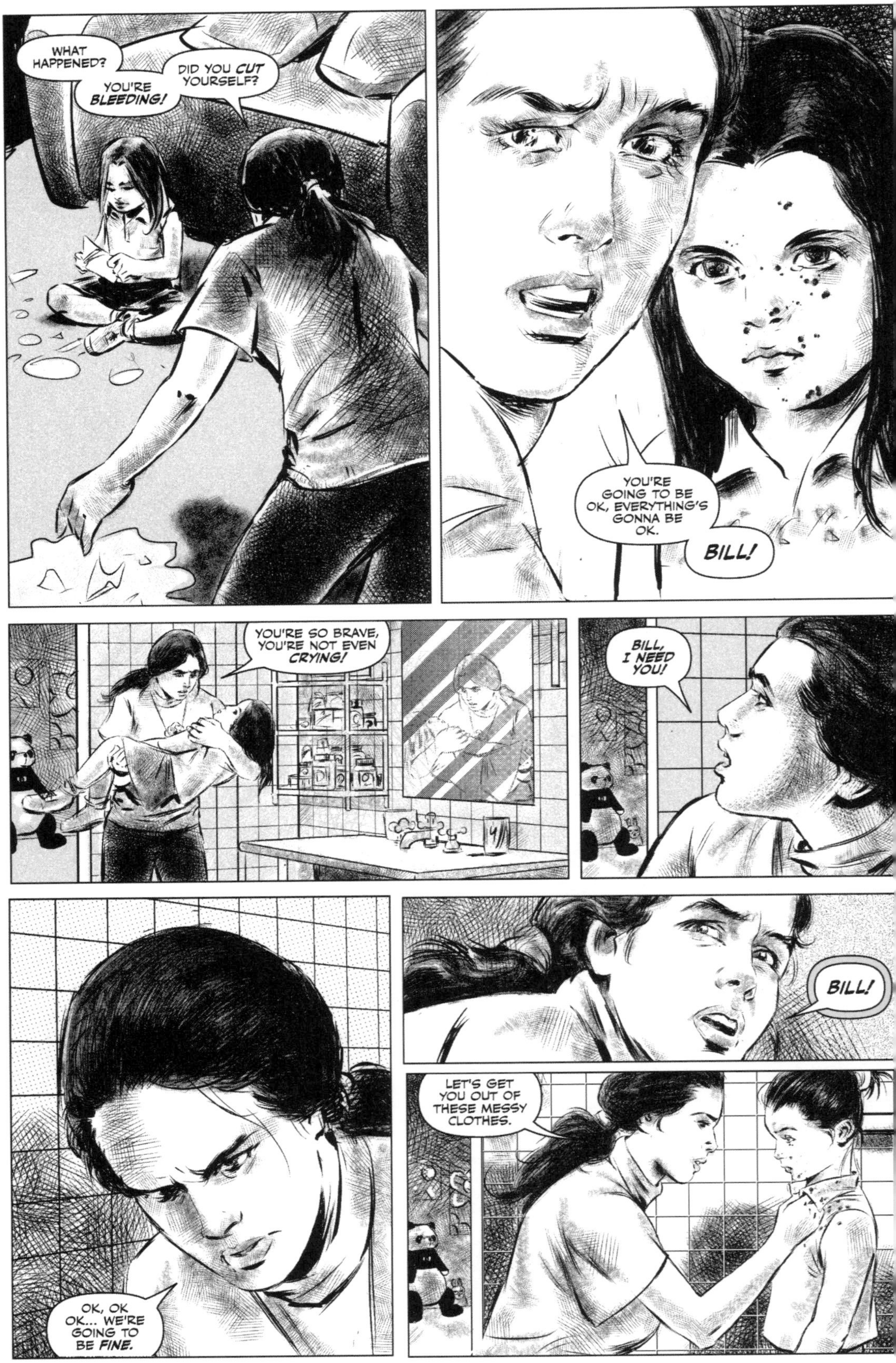
WHAT HAPPENED?
YOU'RE BLEEDING!
DID YOU CUT YOURSELF?
YOU'RE GOING TO BE OK, EVERYTHING'S GONNA BE OK.
BILL!
YOU'RE SO BRAVE, YOU'RE NOT EVEN CRYING!
BILL, I NEED YOU!
OK, OK OK... WE'RE GOING TO BE FINE.
BILL!
LET'S GET YOU OUT OF THESE MESSY CLOTHES.

WE'LL WASH YOUR CLOTHES, OK? THEY'LL BE *FINE*.

LET'S SEE WHERE YOU'RE HURT.

YOU'RE NOT BLEEDING? I DON'T SEE HOW...

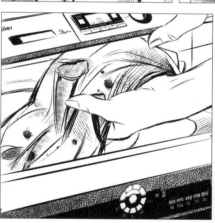

STAY HERE, OK?

BILL!

BILL?

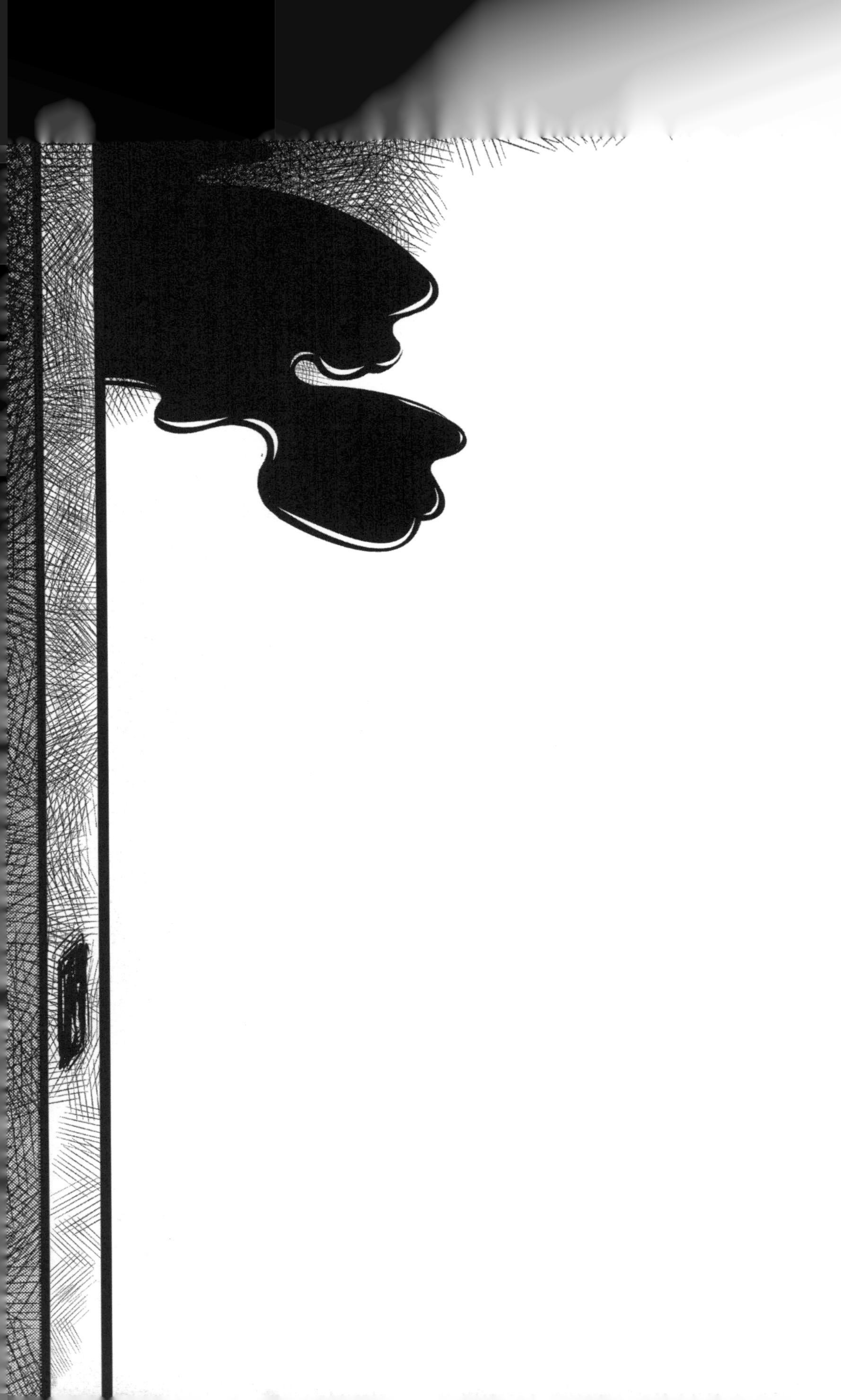

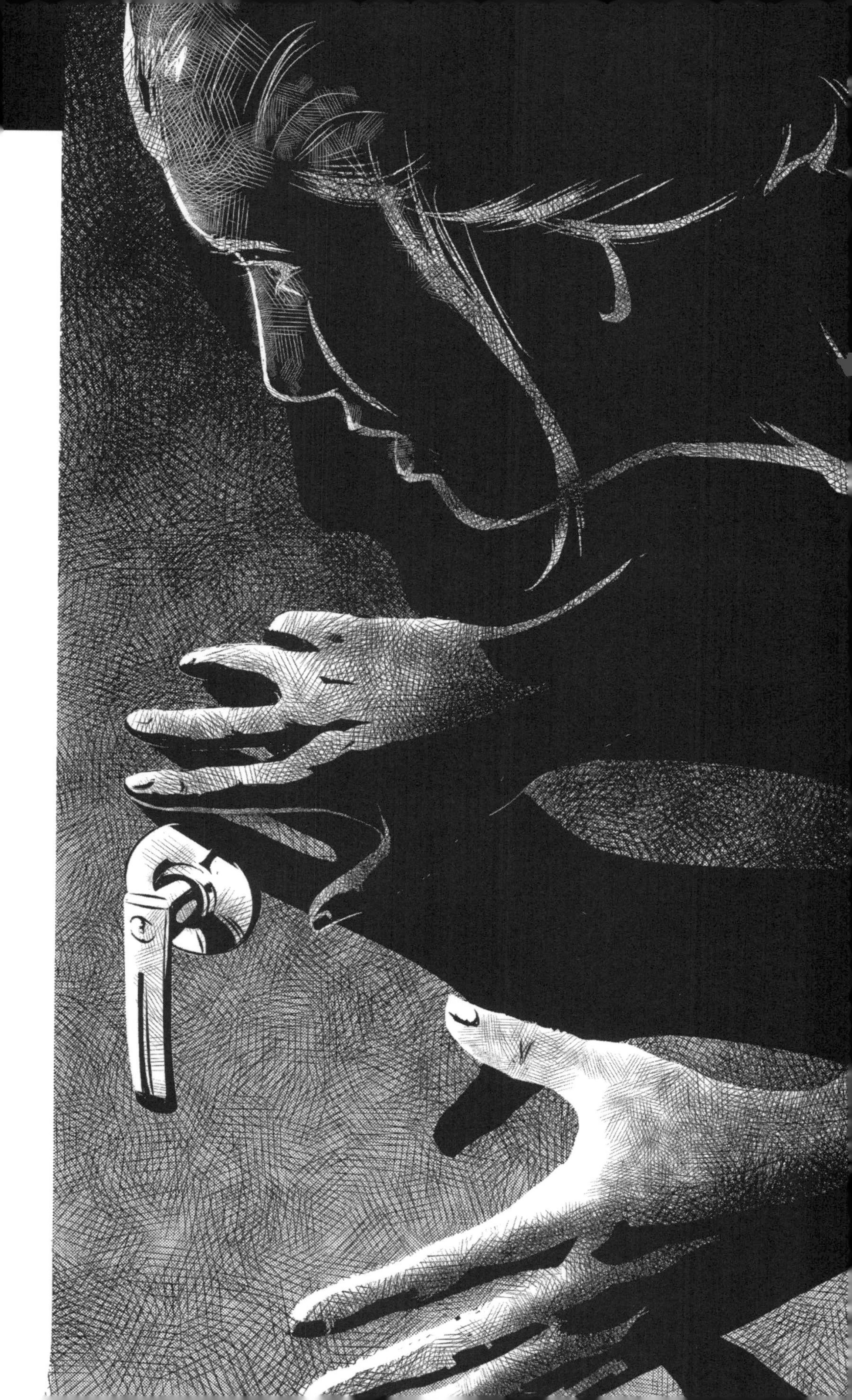

NO!

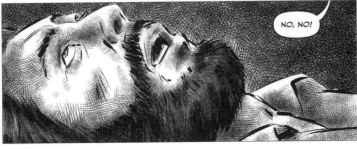

NO, NO!

Oh, please, God, *no!*

BILL? *STAY* WITH ME, BILL. YOU *CAN'T* LEAVE.

FHISSS

YOU *CAN'T* LEAVE ME ALONE.

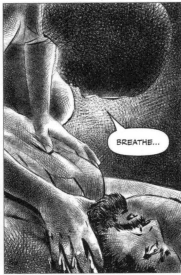

BREATHE...

HMM..M.MM..PH

BILL?
AHA!
GAH!

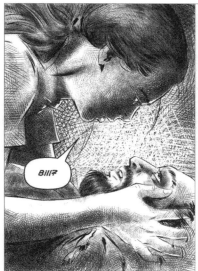

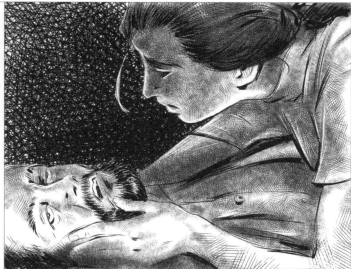

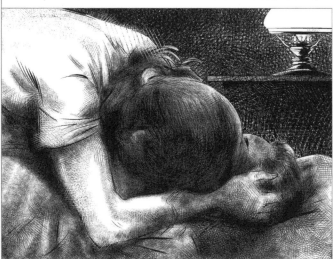

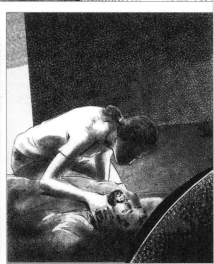

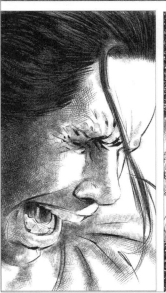

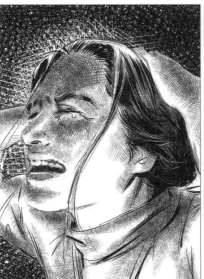

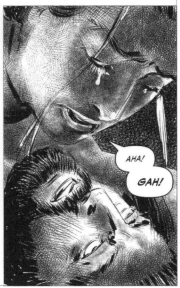

STACY ENTERED A **DAZE** THAT SHE LATER COULDN'T RECALL.

IN A **TRANCE**, SHE CALLED FOR AN AMBULANCE.

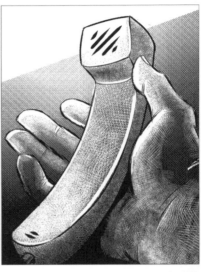

SHE DIDN'T EVEN **BLINK** WHEN THE PARAMEDICS AND POLICE ARRIVED.

MA'AM, ARE YOU OK?

MA'AM?

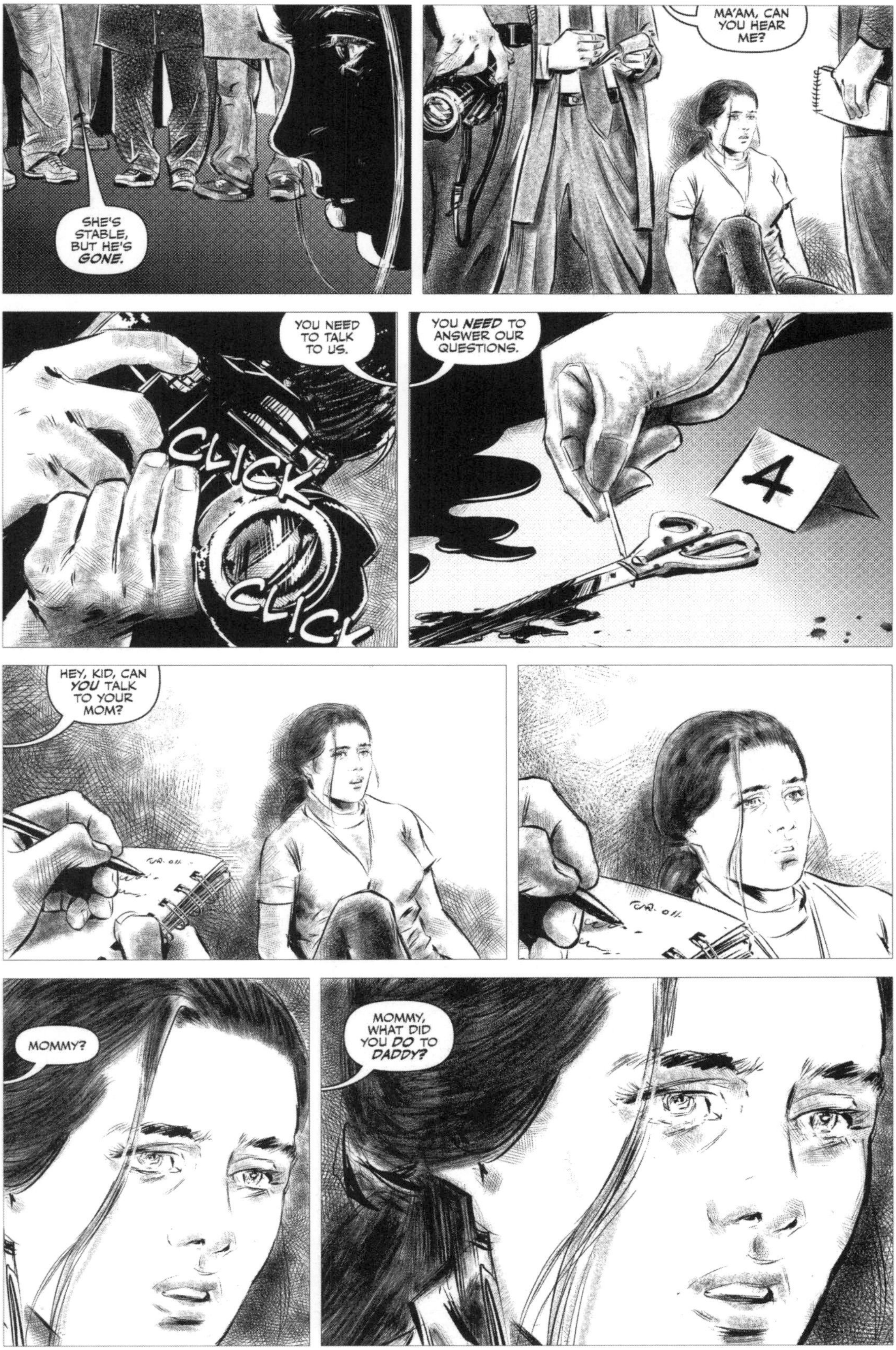
SHE'S STABLE, BUT HE'S GONE.
MA'AM, CAN YOU HEAR ME?
YOU NEED TO TALK TO US.
CLICK
CLICK
YOU NEED TO ANSWER OUR QUESTIONS.
4
HEY, KID, CAN YOU TALK TO YOUR MOM?
MOMMY?
MOMMY, WHAT DID YOU DO TO DADDY?

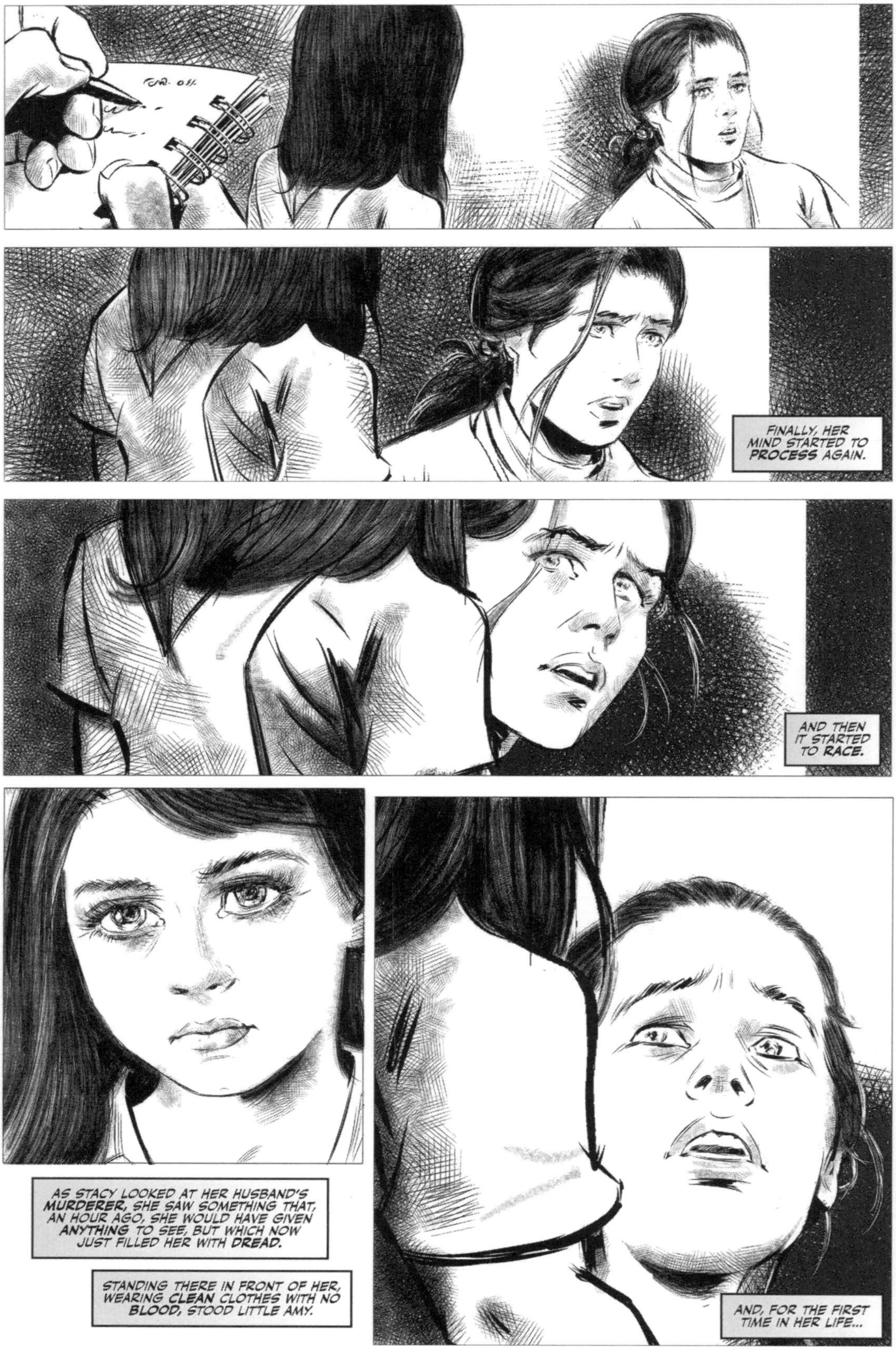
FINALLY, HER MIND STARTED TO PROCESS AGAIN.
AND THEN IT STARTED TO RACE.
AS STACY LOOKED AT HER HUSBAND'S MURDERER, SHE SAW SOMETHING THAT, AN HOUR AGO, SHE WOULD HAVE GIVEN ANYTHING TO SEE, BUT WHICH NOW JUST FILLED HER WITH DREAD.
STANDING THERE IN FRONT OF HER, WEARING CLEAN CLOTHES WITH NO BLOOD, STOOD LITTLE AMY.
AND, FOR THE FIRST TIME IN HER LIFE...

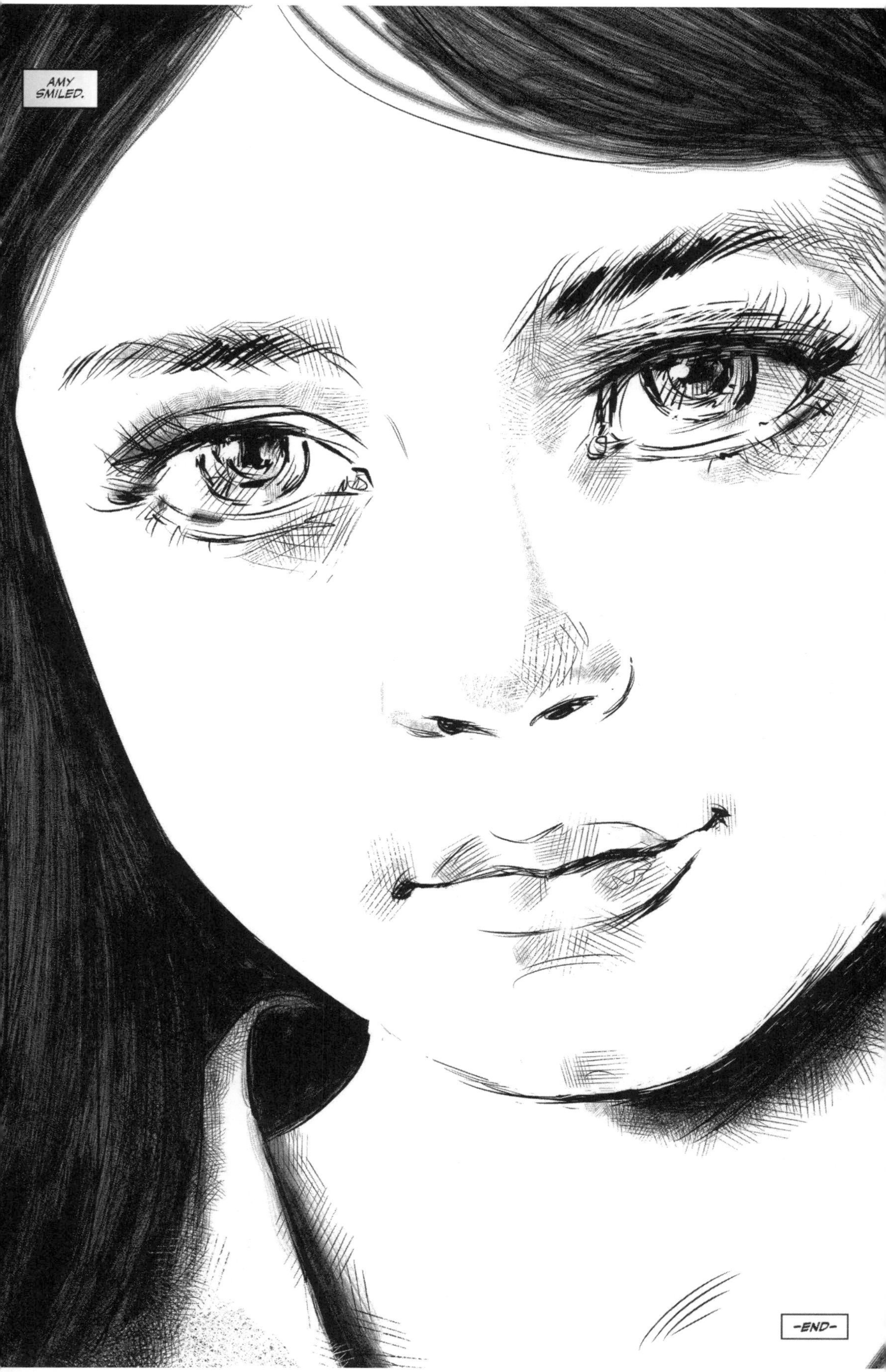
AMY SMILED.
-END-

Thanks for reading the third volume of Twisted Dark.

To see more from the TPub team, head over to our website and join our mailing list—we'll send you free comics every quarter.

By liking us on Facebook and following us on Twitter, not only will you support indie press, you'll also instantly become younger, make world peace and reduce global warming.

Also, if you haven't shared this book with all your friends and told every stranger on the street to read us, well, you're just mean.

www.tpub.co.uk
www.facebook.com/tpublications
@TPublications

Continue the journey into Neil's twisted universe...

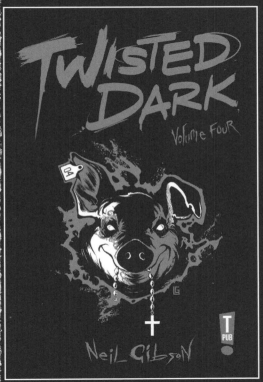

Twisted Dark Volume Four

Other Titles from T Pub

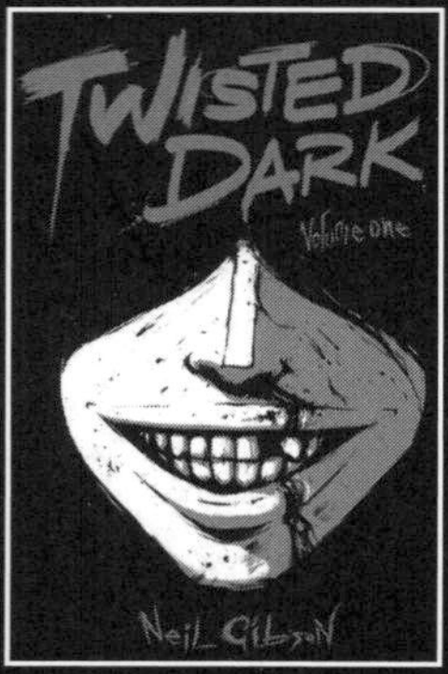
TWISTED DARK
Volume one
Neil Gibson
Volume 1

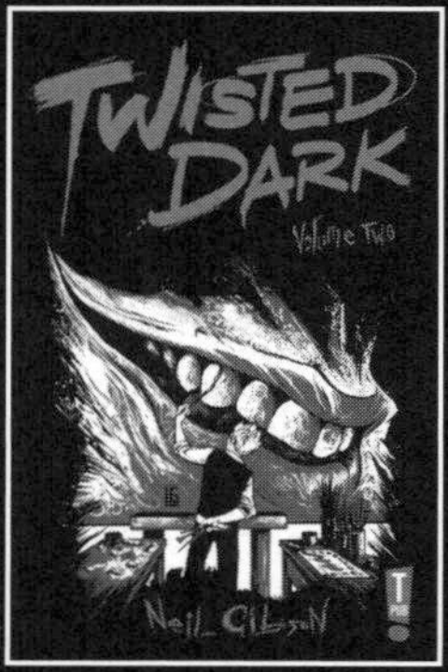
TWISTED DARK
Volume Two
Neil Gibson
Volume 2

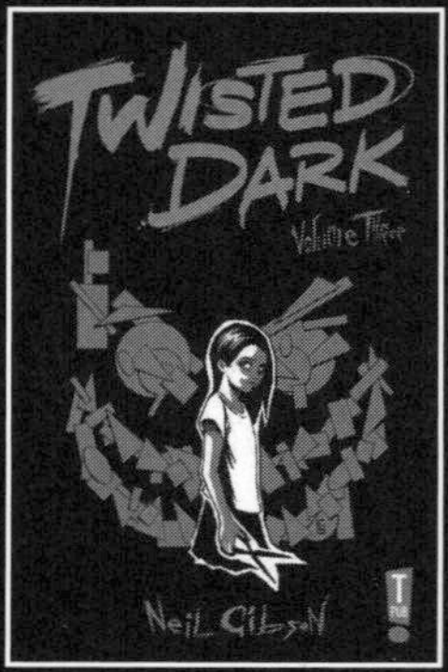
TWISTED DARK
Volume Three
Neil Gibson
Volume 3

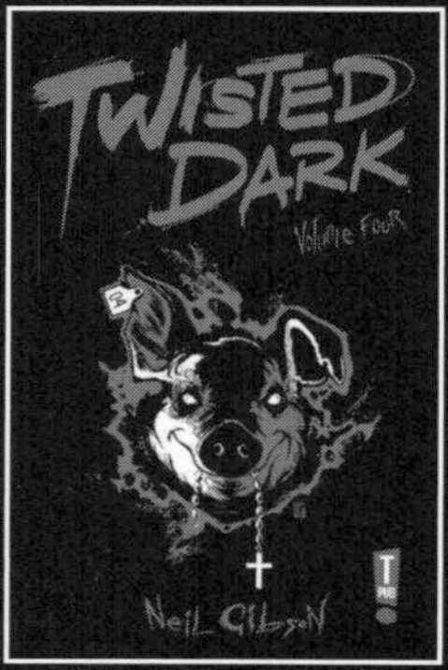
TWISTED DARK
Volume Four
Neil Gibson
Volume 4

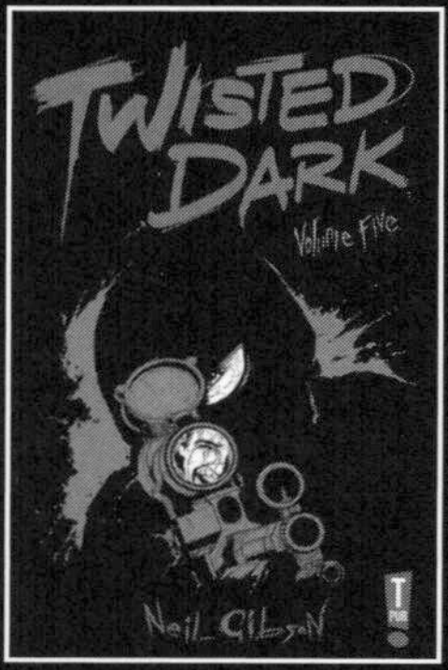
TWISTED DARK
Volume Five
Neil Gibson
Volume 5

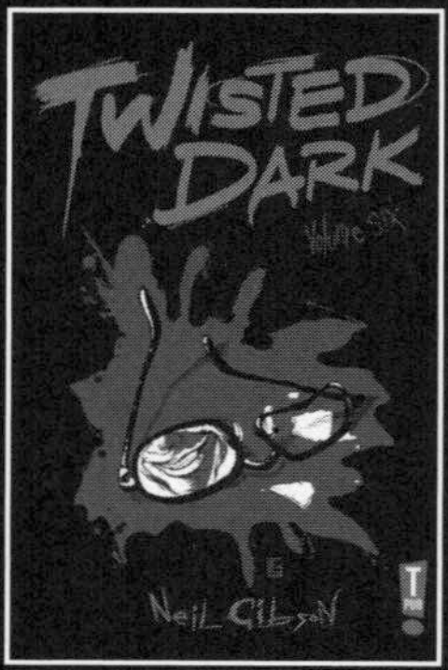
TWISTED DARK
Volume Six
Neil Gibson
Volume 6

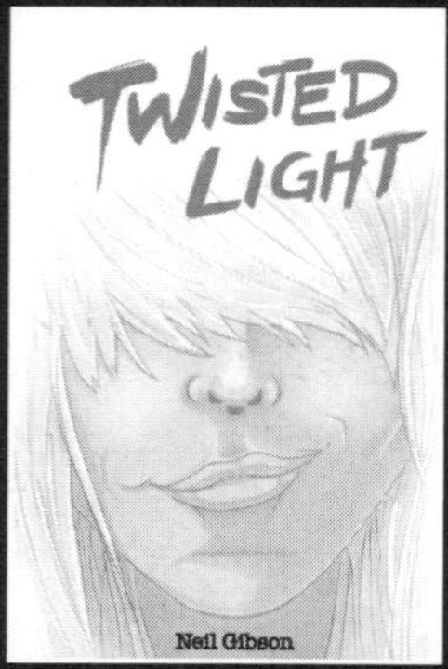
TWISTED LIGHT
Neil Gibson
Twisted Light

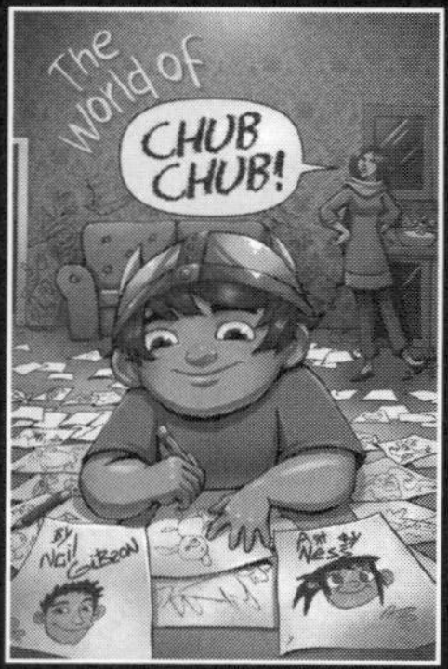
The World of
CHUB CHUB!
The World of Chub Chub

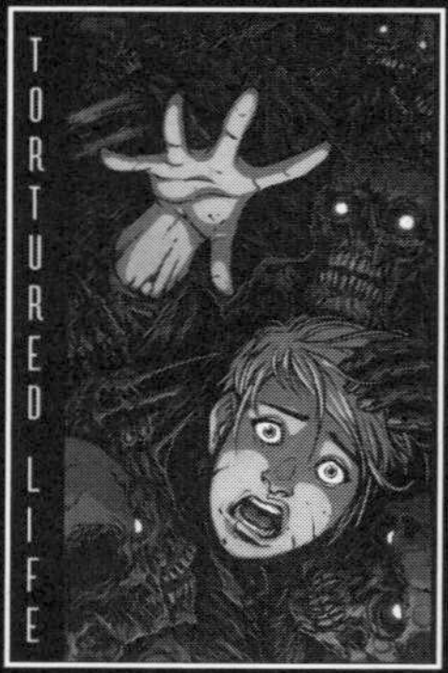
TORTURED LIFE
Tortured Life

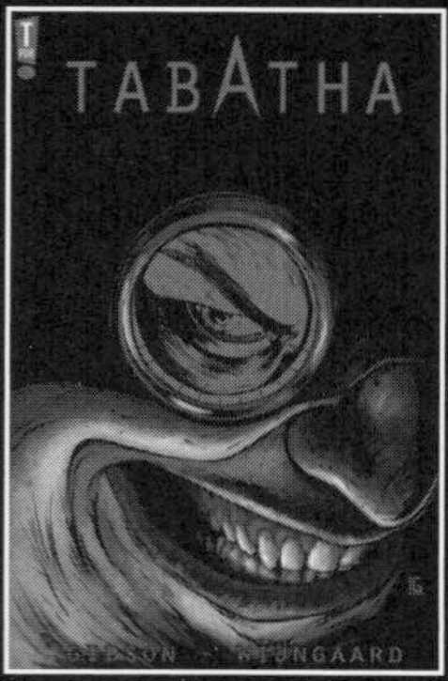
TABATHA
Tabatha

More titles coming soon...